Antisemitism in Galicia

AUSTRIAN AND HABSBURG STUDIES
General Editor: Howard Louthan, Center for Austrian Studies,
University of Minnesota

Before 1918, Austria and the Habsburg lands constituted an expansive multinational and multiethnic empire, the second largest state in Europe, and a key site for cultural and intellectual developments across the continent. At the turn of the twentieth century, the region gave birth to modern psychology, philosophy, economics, and music, and since then has played an important mediating role between Western and Eastern Europe, today participating as a critical member of the European Union. The volumes in this series address specific themes and questions around the history, culture, politics, social, and economic experiences of Austria, the Habsburg Empire, and its successor states in Central and Eastern Europe.

Recent volumes:

Volume 29
Antisemitism in Galicia: Agitation, Politics, and Violence against Jews in the Late Habsburg Monarchy
Tim Buchen

Volume 28
Revisiting Austria: Tourism, Space, and National Identity, 1945 to the Present
Gundolf Graml

Volume 27
Empty Signs, Historical Imaginaries: The Entangled Nationalization of Names and Naming in a Late Habsburg Borderland
Ágoston Berecz

Volume 26
Men under Fire: Motivation, Morale, and Masculinity among Czech Soldiers in the Great War, 1914–1918
Jiří Hutečka

Volume 25
Nationalism Revisited: Austrian Social Closure from Romanticism to the Digital Age
Christian Karner

Volume 24
Entangled Entertainers: Jews and Popular Culture in Fin-de-Siècle Vienna
Klaus Hödl

Volume 23
Comical Modernity: Popular Humour and the Transformation of Urban Space in Late Nineteenth-Century Vienna
Heidi Hakkarainen

Volume 22
Embers of Empire: Continuity and Rupture in the Habsburg Successor States after 1918
Edited by Paul Miller and Claire Morelon

Volume 21
The Art of Resistance: Cultural Protest against the Austrian Far Right in the Early Twenty-First Century
Allyson Fiddler

Volume 20
The Monumental Nation: Magyar Nationalism and Symbolic Politics in Fin-de-Siècle Hungary
Bálint Varga

For a full volume listing, please see the series page on our website: http://berghahnbooks.com/series/austrian-habsburg-studies.

ANTISEMITISM IN GALICIA
Agitation, Politics, and Violence against Jews in the Late Habsburg Monarchy

Tim Buchen

Translated from the German by Charlotte Hughes-Kreutzmüller

berghahn
NEW YORK · OXFORD
www.berghahnbooks.com

Published in 2020 by
Berghahn Books
www.berghahnbooks.com

Enblish-language edition
© 2020, 2024 Berghahn Books
First paperback edition published in 2024

German-language edition
© 2012 Metropol Verlag

Originally published in German as
Antisemitismus in Galizien: Agitation, Gewalt und Politik gegen Juden in der Habsburgermonarchie um 1900

The translation of this work was funded by Geisteswissenschaften International—Translation Funding for Work in the Humanities and Social Sciences from Germany, a joint initiative of the Fritz Thyssen Foundation, the German Federal Foreign Office, the collecting society VG WORT, and the Börsenverein des Deutschen Buchhandels (German Publishers & Booksellers Association).

Except for the quotation of short passages
for the purposes of criticism and review, no part of this book
may be reproduced in any form or by any means, electronic or
mechanical, including photocopying, recording, or any information
storage and retrieval system now known or to be invented,
without written permission of the publisher.

Library of Congress Cataloging-in-Publication Data

Names: Buchen, Tim, author. | Hughes-Kreutzmüller, Charlotte, translator.
Title: Antisemitism in Galicia: Agitation, Politics, and Violence against Jews in the Late Habsburg Monarchy / Tim Buchen; translated from the German by Charlotte Hughes-Kreutzmüller.
Description: First edition. | New York: Berghahn Books, [2020] | Series: Austrian and Habsburg Studies; volume 29 | Includes bibliographical references and index.
Identifiers: LCCN 2020017482 (print) | LCCN 2020017483 (ebook) |
    ISBN 9781789207705 (hardback) | ISBN 9781789207712 (ebook)
Subjects: LCSH: Antisemitism—Austria—History—19th century. | Antisemitism—Galicia (Poland and Ukraine)—History. | Jews—Austria—History—19th century. | Galicia (Poland and Ukraine)—Politics and government—19th century.
Classification: LCC DS135.A9 B8313 2020 (print) | LCC DS135.A9 (ebook) |
    DDC 305.892/40438609034—dc23
LC record available at https://lccn.loc.gov/2020017482
LC ebook record available at https://lccn.loc.gov/2020017483

British Library Cataloguing in Publication Data

A catalogue record for this book is available from the British Library

ISBN 978-1-78920-770-5 hardback
ISBN 978-1-80539-139-5 paperback
ISBN 978-1-80539-404-4 epub
ISBN 978-1-78920-771-2 web pdf

https://doi.org/10.3167/9781789207705

To my high school teachers who ignited my fascination for history

Contents

List of Illustrations	viii
Preface to the English Edition	x
Introduction	1
Chapter 1. Agitation	44
Chapter 2. Violence	111
Chapter 3. Politics	180
Chapter 4. Summary	258
Epilogue	277
Bibliography	280
Indexes	304

Illustrations

1.1 and 1.2. 1907 Reichsrat elections in Krakow, *Nowiny Illustrowane*, no. 31, 1907. Public domain.   64

1.3. Reichsrat deputy and priest Michał Zyguliński (Tarnów) after his vote in the 1907 Reichsrat elections, *Nowiny Illustrowane*, no. 23, 1907. Public domain.   65

1.4. Stanisław Stojałowski, *Nowiny Illustrowane*, no. 23, 1907. Public domain.   72

1.5. Populist deputies (SL) in Krakow, *Nowiny Illustrowane*, no. 34, 1907. Public domain.   76

2.1 and 2.2. Pilgrims in Kalwarya Zebrzydowska, *Nowiny Illustrowane*, no. 34, 1907. Public domain.   123

2.3. Map showing the spreading of riots and rumors from Frysztak to Lutcza. Thomas Rettig with courtesy of the David Rumsey collections.   143

2.4. K.u.k. Gendarmes in Krakow, *Nowiny Illustrowane*, no. 32, 1907. Public domain.   154

2.5. K.u.k. Dragoners at a race in Przemyśl, *Nowiny Illustrowane*, no. 34, 1907. Public domain.   166

3.1. Imperial Diet (Reichsrat) in Vienna, *Nowiny Illustrowane*, no. 28, 1907. Public domain.   182

3.2. Peasants from Tarnobrzeg accompany their recently elected deputy to the train station on his way to Vienna, *Nowiny Illustrowane*, no. 25, 1907. Public domain.   194

3.3. Farewell to the deputy at the train station in Tarnobrzeg, *Nowiny Illustrowane*, no. 25, 1907. Public domain.   195

3.4. Viennese cartoon depicting Galicia as a parasite, *Kikeriki*, 20 November 1898. Public domain.   209

3.5. The picture of Michalina Araten her father gave to the police, AGAD Min. Spraw 287. Courtesy of the Archives.   235

Preface to the English Edition

This book is a translation of the German title *Antisemitismus in Galizien: Agitation, Gewalt und Politik gegen Juden in der Habsburgermonarchie um 1900*, published with Metropol Verlag in 2012 as part of the Antisemitismus in Europa series. Thanks to a generous Geisteswissenschaften International translation funding, it was possible to present my findings and ideas on antisemitism in Galicia to a wider international audience by publishing it in English as well. I was very grateful that Berghahn Books and the former series editor Gary Cohen accepted it for inclusion in the Austrian and Habsburg Studies, a series that I have read and used intensely for both research and teaching over so many years.

Of course, the original German and the actual English version are not identical. Readers of a study in a German series on European antisemitism most likely have different expectations and knowledge than readers of a book appearing in a series on Habsburg history in English do. Therefore, the introduction on historical background and on the state of art of researching antisemitism is much shorter here. As a couple of years have passed since I finished the German version, I obviously had to include some studies that had been published on the topic since. Of course, I erased mistakes and errors that reviewers had identified, and I also engaged with their thoughts and criticisms where possible. A big thank you to all who read the book carefully and responded in journals in German, English, and Polish.

Nevertheless, as readers mostly praised the book, we decided to keep most parts as they were. Sebastian Miksch and Thomas Rettig helped me in preparing the manuscript and notes, and Charlotte Hughes-Kreutzmüller delivered a wonderful translation, which reads much better than the original. I am most grateful to the Freunde und Förderer des Zentrums für Antisemitismusforschung for their support during the translation process. I still do feel a deep and even deeper gratitude to everyone I mentioned in the previous acknowledgments. To that long list of people I would like to add the numerous colleagues and students I have had the privilege to work with in Warsaw, Bamberg, Frankfurt, Edinburgh, and Dresden since 2012.

Tim Buchen, Dresden, Spring 2020

Introduction

Nestling in the Carpathian foothills, in the Polish voivodeship named after them, lies the village Lutcza, some thirty kilometers south of the regional capital Rzeszów. The climate here is determined by the surrounding mountain peaks and plateaus, with wide temperature variations, high precipitation, and ground frost on an average of 208 days per year. "In a word that characterizes the facts fairly accurately, even if it is a bit old-fashioned":[1] winter comes early and stays long in the Carpathian foothills.

In the year 1881, when Lutcza and Rzeszów still belonged to the Kingdom of Galicia, thick snow had fallen by November that remained until early March. On 6 March 1882, the thaw exposed the previously snow-covered corpse of Franciszka Mnich, who had been missing from the village for months. Franciszka was in her mid-thirties and unmarried. She had last been seen in late November leaving the home of her aunt Salomea Stochlińska, who lived at the edge of the village in a small cluster of houses. She had gone to fetch some milk from her aunt's neighbor, a certain Moses Ritter.[2]

The Ritter family ran a farm and a *Trafik*, as tobacco stores are still called in Austria today, and enjoyed good relations with the neighbors. The villagers stored their potatoes in the Ritters' cellar, and the local farmers liked to sit and drink together in Moses's *Trafik* of an evening. Franciszka Mnich, known as Franka, was a frequent visitor to the Ritters' house. She had previously worked there as a maid. Since the spring, however, she had helped only occasionally on one or two days a week. It was said that Moses Ritter was like a father to her, and Gittla Ritter like a mother. But Moses's closest friend in the village, the locals later recalled, was Franka's cousin, Marcel Stochliński. Since he had sold his land, he earned his living doing deals at local fairs and had a reputation as a drinker. The villagers said that Marcel had learned Yiddish during his long evenings with the Ritters and their relatives and neighbors, the Felbers, and conspired with them in their secret language. They said all this later, after Franciszka had been found in a gully not far from the Ritters' home.

Her body was terribly disfigured. A medical examination showed that she had not died of natural causes. She had received a blow to the head, and her throat had been slit. Her stomach had also been cut open with a knife. The place where she was found was apparently not the scene of the murder. But two other details consternated the onlookers most, and all agreed they pointed to Franciszka's murderer. Her braids had been cut off—they were found a few yards away in the melting snow—and a child had been growing in Franciszka's belly. It would have been some four months old at the time of the attack and had been brutally cut out.

A beastly, incomprehensible murder had occurred in Lutcza, horrifying the villagers. Their mourning for Franciszka and their fear of living next door to a brutal murderer bred fantasies with which they tried to explain the inconceivable and identify the evildoer.

The imperial-and-royal gendarmerie from the district capital Stryżów arrived in Lutcza the next day to investigate the murder.³ They found the locals eager to talk. Several residents of Lutcza recounted incidents that had occurred in the last half-year that they thought might have some bearing on what had happened to Franka. Many had their own theories about why she had disappeared, though an illegitimate pregnancy would certainly have been reason enough to wish her gone. But if that was the motive, who was the father of her child? Moses Ritter was a rumored candidate. Franka's brother stated that he had never approved of his sister associating with the Ritters and had tried to deter her several times. He had even tried to persuade her to go on a pilgrimage to get away from "the Jews." Some said that Moses was oversexed; others, that he could do magic. He was said to have cursed his neighbor Mandela, who had tried to sue him, leaving him blinded. As Franka's last known movements had been to the Ritters' house, the police officers from Strzyżów started their investigations there. They noted that the cellar was very clean, perhaps indicating that traces had been removed. And they found an axe that was soiled with a dark substance, which could conceivably have been blood. During their subsequent search of the Felbers' home, they found two long knives in a black covering.

On 11 March, Moses and Gittla Ritter and Leib and Chil Felber were arrested on suspicion of murder. They all denied having anything to do with Franka's disappearance or death. Eleven days later, the police decided to question the Ritters' neighbors, the Stochlińskis. They found Marcel behaving in an extremely odd and distracted manner. Having thus roused their suspicions, he, too, was taken in. Indeed, in Strzyżów, Marcel confessed. Franka's murder had been planned by Moses Ritter, he said. Moses had "put the bun in her oven" and subsequently feared for his family's reputation. Murder seemed the last resort. He had paid Marcel fifty guilders to be his accomplice. When Franka had come to the Ritters' house on the first Sunday in Advent, Gittla had called her into the cellar to fetch some potatoes. Moses had given Marcel two shots of liquor before they went down into the cellar with the Ritters' eldest daughters, Bajla and Chaja. There, Gittla threw a blanket over Franka's head, and Marcel and the Ritter girls held on to her so that Moses could cut her throat. When Franka started to scream, Marcel ran out of the cellar. That was all he knew. The next day he received fifty guilders as promised.

On the strength of this statement, Leib and Chil Felber were released; on 4 April, Bajla and Chaja Ritter were arrested. But by this time, Marcel Stochliński had withdrawn his testimony. The police officers had literally beaten the cellar-murder story out of him on the way from Lutcza to Stryżów.

This unexpected twist did not have any impact on the investigations or the impending prosecution. Now that Moses Ritter was the prime suspect, the bizarre injuries inflicted on Franka's body seemed to point the finger directly at him. The mysterious braid-cutting and belly-slitting could be explained by the exotic religious rites that Ritter and his family allegedly practiced.

Attempting to conduct a rational investigation, the police officers sought the opinion of experts on whether cutting off braids and slitting open stomachs were traditional aspects of the Mosaic faith. Two Israelites from Strzyżów, Aron Kenner and Jakub Schutz, were consulted. They affirmed that it was common among Jews to remove the fetus from the body of a deceased mother. Cutting off the braids of dead women was also customary, they said. In preparation for the trial, due to begin in December, the public prosecutors in Strzyżów commissioned an expertise from the rabbinate in the imperial capital, Vienna.

Word of the gothic tale of Lutcza now spread far beyond the foothills of the Carpathians. In the Galician capital, Lemberg, politician and writer Teofil Merunowicz took the rumors surrounding Franciszka Mnich's death as cause to issue a warning against what he saw as the source of the menace, the screenplay for the brutal mutilations, as it were. In an address to the regional diet, he claimed that the Talmud contained secret passages that called for such rituals. Consequently, he proposed to "regulate the legal situation of the Jews," citing the much-publicized views of August Rohling, a theology professor from Prague. He also referred to the "Tiszlaeszlar affair" in Hungary, concerning the disappearance of Eszter Solymosi, which was causing a stir throughout Europe. Coverage of the events in Lutcza in the newspapers of Lemberg, Krakow, Warsaw, and Vienna not only reflected the widespread public interest in the case but also generated additional, transregional interest. As the trial thus gained importance, it was transferred from the Strzyżów district court to the regional court in Rzeszów.

During the hearings in December, the courtroom was consistently filled to bursting with curious onlookers and journalists from the aforementioned cities. The latter supplied their commissioning newspapers with reports on the trial's progress and vivid descriptions of the persons involved.

The expertise by the rabbi in Vienna contradicted the statements by Kenner and Schutz. Removing fetuses had once been permitted but only if it promised to save the life of the unborn child, the rabbi explained. However, the practice had long since been prohibited due to the possibility that the mother might not be clinically dead. Basically, Mosaic doctrine forbids any intrusion into the physical integrity of the deceased, including their hair. Moreover, it is a well-known fact that Judaism is passed on through the mother, so neither Franciszka, who was a Christian, nor her unborn child, whoever the father may have been, would have been subjected to Jewish rites.

The rumor that Franka was a victim of murder by Jews acting in obedience to their religion nevertheless persisted in the courtroom. The witness Jędrezj Noster stated that during Lent rumors had circulated in Lutcza that Franka had been murdered by Jews "for the Matza." Although this ritual-murder theory was not explicitly mentioned in the bill of indictment, it remained in the ether as an explanation for the mutilation of Franka's neck and body. The newspapers also took up the narrative thread of the bloody ritual, though none maintained it was a credible motive. Rather, journalists wove it into their vivid portrayals of the trial to convey an impression of the lives and mindsets of the people of the Carpathian foothills to their urban readerships. The interaction between the erudite judge, the uneducated villagers, the Jews in the dock, and the urban public in the courtroom resulted in highly entertaining scenes. One of the witnesses consistently began each of his answers with a confused "Huh?," eliciting laughter throughout the courtroom. Even the judge made an obvious distinction between the uneducated peasants questioned and those who, as the newspapers put it, "were fluently articulate" by addressing the former with the informal "du," like children, but the latter—principally members of the Ritter family—with the more respectful "Sie." However, to the readers of the middle-class *Czas* (Times) newspaper of Kraków, the Ritters were portrayed as somewhat alien, albeit not entirely foreign, beings who, like the rustic Christian villagers, believed in ritual murders, the evil eye, and probably ghosts and witches, too.

In an article in the December 13 issue of *Czas*, the author sketched the following images of the accused for his readers: Moses Ritter was "provincial" and had an "ordinary character" but was an eloquent speaker. His wife, Gittla, had the "typical face of a Jewish alewife," but she, too, spoke fluent Polish. One of their daughters had a stony appearance, but the other had an "engaging face" and "bright eyes."

The jury eventually found Moses and Gittla Ritter and Marcel Stochliński guilty of jointly murdering Franciszka Mnich, and they were sentenced to death by hanging. However, the Supreme Court in Vienna suspended the sentence and transferred the case to the upper regional court in Krakow. August Rohling, the theology professor mentioned above, offered his services as an expert in the new trial, but the court declined. Though convinced of the Ritters' and Stochliński's guilt, the Krakow public prosecutors dismissed the idea of religious motives. Nevertheless, the newspapers *Gazeta Warszawska* and *Gazeta Narodowa*, for which Teofil Merunowicz wrote, claimed that "religious fanaticism" was behind the murder, prompting Gittla Ritter's defense lawyer to complain that the entire Jewish religion was in the dock and under attack. The death sentence pronounced in Krakow was also suspended by the highest court. The justified doubts about the plausibility of the evidence and the quality of the forensic examinations were contested from as far afield as the German Empire. A brochure was published in Berlin, running to three editions, with the baroque title "Death in Lutcza: Documentary Description of the Murder of Franziska Mnich by the Hand of Jews and the Related Court Hearings Together with Concluding Remarks," claiming that the "mighty influence of the Jews in Austria" had resulted in the sentence being suspended twice, despite the convincing evidence against the accused.

During the third trial, which began on 17 September 1885 in Krakow, the brothers Jakub and Jan Drzewiecki spoke to the newspapers to describe why they believed that Franka had been murdered by the hand of Jews for religious purposes. Jakub was the parish priest, and Jan, the local vicar in Lutcza. Both claimed to represent the views of their congregations that the Talmud contained incitements to commit atrocities. Death sentences were pronounced on 28 September but were once again suspended by the Viennese Supreme Court, and this time orders were given for the accused to be released.

Moses and Gittla Ritter took their first steps in freedom, almost four years since Franka's body had been found, on 3 March 1886. By that time, Marcel Stochliński had died in custody. Perhaps he took the name of Franka's murderer with him to the grave. But the tale of the death in Lutcza endured, and the relations—sometimes harmonious, sometimes antagonistic—between Jews and Christians continued.

The present book will return to Moses Ritter and the other people of Lutcza thirteen years later. Although the village soon retreated into obscurity again, it is worth lingering a while and reflecting on the events that were described with such conviction. The questions that remain can serve as a window on the bygone Kingdom of Galicia and its inhabitants and as a framework for an investigation into antisemitism around 1900.

The first questions to ask are these: What kind of a place was Galicia? Where was it? How was it linked to Poland, Vienna, and Austria? Who wrote the laws governing the population's coexistence, which one local politician tried to change? What standards and rules regulated interaction between the social and religious groups, in the cities Krakow, Rzeszów, and Lemberg, and in villages like Lutcza? How was the state—embodied by figures such as the gendarmerie, judges and public prosecutors—run? Was their disrespect for the Christian villagers and greater esteem for the Jews typical? Why did they nevertheless rely solely on the testimonies of Christians?

The "Ritter affair" provoked a huge response, spanning a wide range of opinions expressed with an equally wide range of intentions. The newspapers delighted in portraying the peculiarities of village life more than in analyzing the legal aspects of the case. Neither the politician in Lemberg nor the writer in Berlin, let alone the professor in Prague or the priest in Lutcza, acknowledged the Krakow judiciary's dismissal of religious motives. But they all voiced opinions on the affair, purportedly on behalf of the Christians affected, who were not able to speak for themselves. Learned people talked for them and about them, often in mocking tones. Why did the Christian villagers, like their Jewish neighbors, have no voice of their own? Did they seek to break out of their communicative isolation? Did the sensational murder case perhaps provide an opportunity to overcome the cultural distances and differences separating the village from the city, the rural backwater from the urban center? Did the people of Lutcza, at the dawn of the twentieth century, really have no other option than to endure being patronized by the judiciary and the press? Yet despite the lack of understanding between the parties, given to speaking about each other rather than with each other, the court case marked a dialog concerning an incident in which Jews were implicated. Below, I will consider the shifts in popular perception of Jewish religious practices, of rural Christian-Jewish relations, and of national law and justice, and the political consequences those shifts had.

What impact did the commentaries from Berlin, Vienna, and Lemberg have on village life in Lutcza and the surrounding hamlets after the Ritters' release? Did the locals still gather at the Ritters' *Trafik* in the evenings, store their potatoes in the Jews' cellar, and allow their nieces to work for them as maids? How did the Ritters conduct themselves after having their religion maligned as the cause of gross atrocities? Did the accusations change the Christians' attitudes toward the Jewish neighbors they had known so long and thought they knew so well? At which point did their familiar neighbors become foreign Jews? And what role did this kind of conflict play in the campaigns of antisemitic politicians? After all, politicians respond to situations where they see a need for change, and members of parliament act on behalf of their electorate.

In more general terms, this book about antisemitism will inquire into the connections between journalism, parliamentary politics, the search for justice, and the coexistence of Christians and Jews in everyday life and in exceptional circumstances, and whether these factors were mutually influential. If it is true that the Christian population maintained close contact and neighborly relations with the local Jews while remaining isolated from and patronized by the authorities and politics, with only Catholic priests supporting their belief in medieval tales of bloodletting and magic, is it at all meaningful to speak of antisemitism in Galicia, in the sense of the modern, secular, and political phenomenon we know today?

Below, I will address these questions with respect to Galicia in the late nineteenth century and use them to develop a methodological approach to examining other similar cases in Galicia.

Background

Galicia existed as a political entity only from 1772 to 1918, yet it was more than a brief episode in history. Over the span of just a few generations, it was the scene of tremendous political, social, and economic change. The estates-based social order was dismantled, and a civil society established; its members transformed from subjects into citizens.[4] Market economy and economic competition gave them new opportunities for social advancement and material improvement, but equally carried unforeseen risks of loss and ruin. Instead of relying on their village community, guild, or paternalistic manor, they were now required to show initiative and take personal responsibility, and offered new, urban, middle- and working-class models of communitization and identification. Increasing numbers migrating within the crownland, from the villages to the cities and vice versa, whether for single seasons or for longer periods, spelled the end of rural isolation.[5] Faster communication, thanks to the railways, telegraph, and newspapers, made life more complex, multiplying both the opportunities and the challenges for the populace. Old hurdles crumbled, but new inequalities and asynchronies arose.[6] The relatively new concept of the nation motivated people to forge new bonds and dissolve old ones. The lives and thinking of these few generations of Galicians was crucially shaped by the Habsburg Monarchy.[7] It was under Habsburg rule that they experienced nothing less than the transformation of the world.[8]

This groundbreaking change is clearly reflected in the shift in the political zeitgeist from the time of the founding of the Kingdom of Galicia to the time of its dissolution. Galicia was a new state created and ruled by the Habsburg Monarchy following the partitions of Poland and Lithuania, which the absolutist empires of Prussia, Austria, and Russia had conquered and carved up between them. These partition powers regarded the Polish-Lithuanian Commonwealth, ruled by elected kings and controlled by the aristocracy, as outdated and obsolete. It was incompatible with their ideal of an enlightened state and duly consigned to history.[9]

Galicia ceased to exist with the end of World War I and the demise of those once-so-mighty empires. The former partition powers were now dinosaurs themselves. The divine right legitimizing their dynasties appeared hopelessly flimsy against the peoples' claims to governance of their nations and the historic mission of the proletariat.[10]

Invention of Galicia after the Partitions (1772–1846)

The full title of the crownland was Kingdom of Galicia and Lodomeria, and the Grand Duchy of Krakow with the Duchies of Auschwitz and Zator.[11] Galicia and Lodomeria were the Latinized names of the medieval principalities of Halych, or Galyč, and Volodymyr, which had formerly belonged to the Kievan Rus and, in the thirteenth century, the Hungarian crown.[12] However, the borders of Galicia only vaguely approximated those of the historical principalities. The name was taken as a retrospective attempt to legitimize the annexation of the new territory and as a way for Maria Theresa to assert her claim to the principalities as queen of Hungary. Joseph II, her son and co-regent, was the driving force behind Habsburg involvement in the partitions, and Galicia's first architect. But for several decades, Austrian policy on Galicia was marked by a conflict of interests: whether to integrate it into the imperial federation or to exchange it, preferably for the sorely missed region of Silesia, which Maria Theresa had lost to Frederick II of Prussia in the mid-eighteenth century.[13] Not only that, Austria constantly vacillated between disempowering and cooperating with Galicia's politically and economically dominant aristocratic elite, the *szlachta*.[14]

Experimentation in the Poorhouse

Perceiving Galicia as backward and in a state of legal and social disorder, Joseph II deemed it a suitable site for experimentation with absolutist reforms. The monarchy decided to focus on increasing the land's productivity—in other words, exploiting it for tax revenue.[15] But its economy remained weak, and—along with Galician politics—dominated by the nobility throughout its existence. Beset by a combination of fruitless imperial policy and unfortunate domestic circumstances, the crownland earned the label "poorhouse of Europe." Indeed, it was perceived in such a negative light that "Galician misery" became proverbial.[16] In this predominantly agrarian region, many craftsmen and small traders were struck by poverty as well as farmers and agricultural workers. Even at the time, the roots of the problem were seen to be overpopulation, outmoded farming methods, and a lack of opportunities for investment. Famines, epidemics, and emigration were the recurring phenomena with which Galicia came to be generally associated within the Austro-Hungarian Empire.[17]

With a more disparate historical, political, socioethnic, and economic makeup than longer-existing crownlands such as Bohemia or the so-called hereditary lands, Galicia was expected to serve primarily as a sales market and, in the case of war, a potential deployment or buffer zone for the Habsburg lands south of the Carpathian Mountains.[18] Nevertheless, the previously widely held image of Galicia as a Habsburg colony has given way to a more nuanced view in recent years.[19] The financial crisis known as "the Panic" and innovations in agriculture affecting many countries in the 1870s inevitably hit Galicia. In addition, Galicia struggled with poor harvests and imports of cheap grain from Hungary and low-cost products from the more industrially developed crownlands in the west of the empire.[20] Ultimately, then, Galicia did not benefit from the empire's customs union or economic policy.[21]

The Population of Galicia

Measures introduced to increase the crownland's productivity changed the ways in which the various social and religious groups in Galicia coexisted. For one, an official complaints procedure was introduced to negotiate disputes between peasants and landowners, which raised the peasants' self-confidence.[22] Until well into the nineteenth century, authority figures such as manor owners, foresters, gendarmes, and mayors had commonly punished adult peasants by flogging. Consequently, there was a deep-rooted fear of authority among the peasantry, as well as a newer sense of needing to fight the reactionary Galician nobility to secure the benefits offered by Austrian rule.[23]

Jews often acted as financial mediators between the landowners and the serf farmers. Prohibited from owning land, Jews had specialized in crafts, trade, and financial services since the Middle Ages, and constituted an estate of their own with peculiar rights and duties.[24] Many leased land for cultivation, obtained licenses to serve alcohol, or worked in the lending sector.[25] About 10 percent of the population in Galicia were Jews, most of whom lived in small and medium-sized towns.[26] Imperial policies designed to induce Jews to contribute more "productively" to the economy and to force those occupied in agriculture to move away from the countryside were only half-heartedly implemented in the crownland.[27]

The overwhelming majority in Galicia were Christian peasants. Most inhabitants of West Galicia, bordered by the Vistula River in the west and the north, by the San in the east, and the Carpathian Mountains in the south, spoke Polish and belonged to the Roman Catholic Church. Alongside their place of origin and residence, their religion and social status as peasants were their primary identifiers.[28] The same applied to their counterparts in the far larger region of East Galicia, bordered by the San in the west, the Carpathian Mountains in the south, Bukovina in the southeast and the Zbruch River in the east. While Catholics and Jews predominated in the towns of West Galicia, an "ethnic triangle" formed in the more pluralist environment of East Galicia.[29] The majority here consisted of Ukrainian-speaking peasant members of the Uniate Church. The heirs of the Polish-Lithuanian commonwealth, they retained their Orthodox liturgy while also recognizing the primacy of the pope.

Under the Habsburgs, the Eastern rite Uniate Christians were renamed Greek Catholics, to bring them up to a par with Roman Catholics.[30] Christians and Jews typically regarded each other as "the others."[31] The divergence between their occupations, languages, and religious beliefs informed social life and kept the two collectives separate. Yet they were financially co-reliant and shared a long tradition of living alongside and with one another. The occasional conflicts that arose between them remained embedded in the context of familiarity based on frequent local contact. This was determined by the economic functions and status associated with the respective ethnic groups within the community.[32]

The aptly titled work "Symbiosis and Ambivalence" by Rosa Lehmann, based on a historical and anthropological case study of the small Galician town of Jaśliska, paints an incisive picture of interethnic relations in Galicia.[33] Here, the term symbiosis does not connote entirely harmonious cooperation. Rather, it describes the space between the tension-laden contact, characterized by dependence and patronage, between wealthy Jews and poor peasants, whose symbiosis was rendered additionally ambivalent by cultural divergence. Focusing more closely than on a general notion of "growing antisemitism," Lehmann's work sheds light on a relationship between Jews and Christians which, though dynamic, remained generally stable beyond World War I and the interwar period. The first sections of this introduction also offer examples of the various business, neighborly, and emotional ties that linked Jews and Christians, as well as the cultural potential for otherness, such as allowed the Ritters, for instance, to so abruptly become "the Jews."[34] In the second half of the nineteenth century, major changes in Galicia's political and economic framework fundamentally altered the circumstances in which Jews and Christians interacted.

Galician Slaughter, Springtime of the Peoples and Neo-Absolutism: The End of Serfdom and the Rise of Market Economy

The year 1848 brought radical changes to Galicia and the entire Habsburg Monarchy. The first significant sign of turbulence occurred in 1846 with the outbreak of a Polish national uprising in the Free City of Krakow, auguring the "springtime of the peoples."[35] Planned by insurgent nobles—émigrés living in Paris—the uprising started under the assumption that the peasants would take part and fight the military with their scythes and picks, as they had during the Kościuszko Uprising of 1794.[36] But the peasantry associated "Polish" rule with serfdom and bondage, and feared a regression to the harder times before the Josephine reforms.[37] The internal conflict was further aggravated by the Catholic sobriety movement, whose fight against liquor and taverns polarized rural life.[38] Indeed, the sobriety movement can be regarded as an early example of a socially divisive political campaign that aroused class resentment to promote its cause. Meanwhile, the imperial authorities, then still staffed by Germans anxious to avoid deposition by the Poles, sought to harness the peasants' anger at the nobility to their own ends.[39] They offered to pay peasants to help their armed forces quash the Polish uprising and search manors for weapons.[40]

The result was a witch hunt on aristocrats and the families of estate owners, which ended in large-scale pillaging and arson. Up to a thousand people lost their lives in an orgy of violence by men, women, and children, targeting around four hundred manors. It was only after three days of violence that the military intervened in a bid to take control of the situation.[41]

The authorities' sanctioning and even rewarding of peasant violence gave rise to rumors that the emperor himself had decreed a three-day murder campaign against the nobility.[42] Bulletins were said to have circulated offering rewards for the heads, hands, or ears of insurgent landowners. For the nobility, the events of February 1846 were so traumatic that they came to be remembered as the "Galician slaughter."[43] Their shock at the peasants' brutality was compounded by the belief that government officials had incited them to act in this way. In the nobility's paternalistic view, the peasants would not have turned against them of their own volition.[44]

By the peasantry, in contrast, the "ruckus" was remembered as a sign of the power they possessed to defend the rights of their class.[45] They composed poems and songs to immortalize the events, which articulated their confidence and signalized their ability to could cause another bloodbath if their rights were ignored.[46] After the slaughter and the revolution of 1848, Austria abolished serfdom. But the memory of 1846, and concern that recently gained liberties might be revoked at any time, remained a prominent feature of peasant communication for several decades.

Following the abolishment of serfdom, the formerly dependent peasants were able to buy the land they had hitherto only tended.[47] Market economy having replaced feudal economy, peasants needed to learn to work profitably and competitively. The monarchy hoped this land "distribution" among newly emancipated peasants would bring the country's economy into line with the other crownlands. Moreover, the Galician governor Franz Stadion, Count von Warthausen, advised the young emperor Franz Joseph in this way to weaken the Polish nobility, who had once again demonstrated their seditiousness with the attempted uprising of 1846, and reward the peasants, who had proven their loyalty.[48] Yet while the reforms succeeded in cementing the Galician peasants' bond with the Habsburg Empire, they did nothing to relieve their financial plight.[49] There was simply too little land to be distributed among too many people. Meanwhile, the nobility was generously compensated for the loss of land and cheap labor they suffered and permitted to retain some of their privileges. The right to manufacture, sell, and serve alcohol, known as propination, was still conceded only to the gentry. Members of other classes needed to pay for a concession to work in this field.[50] Another bone of contention was the *Servituten*, regulations governing access to formerly communal forests and fields.[51] A special tribunal was set up to negotiate disputes over the issue but almost always ruled in favor of the landowners and against the villagers and so failed to build the peasants' confidence in the new economic order.[52] The tribunal's hearing a tremendous thirty thousand cases illustrates the huge potential for conflict that Galicia's economic reorganization generated. As the monetary economy, primarily run by Jews, gained precedence, an increasing number of Jews left the towns and sought work in the country.[53] Though still prohibited from acquiring land, they were no longer subject to restrictions on manual occupations. A conflict arose between the worlds of agriculture and finance, which was frequently perceived as a Christian-Jewish conflict.

In consequence of the upheavals of 1848, Austria introduced structural changes that altered relations between the imperial government and its provinces. Bukovina, which had been ceded to Austria from the Ottoman Empire, was formally detached from Galicia and made a separate kingdom in 1849.[54] The Free City of Krakow became a Grand Duchy, incorporated into Galicia, to diminish its importance and potential for sedition. Having lost its status as a free trade area at the intersection of three empires, Krakow's economy slumped. As a form of redress, in 1854 the government of West Galicia was relocated to Krakow, while the East Galician government was based in the provincial capital, Lemberg.[55] Although this administrative division lasted only until the introduction of the constitution in 1867, it cemented an image of Galicia as bipartite. As the empire was federalized, the possibility of formally dividing Galicia into a "Polish" western territory and a "Ruthenian" eastern territory was frequently discussed.[56]

National "Emancipation"

In 1848, the year of revolutions, the Galician Ukrainians—or Ruthenians—also rose against the paternalism of the Polish nobility to assert their rights as a nation.[57] They launched a campaign to promote the Ukrainian language, which ran in parallel to a debate on whether the Greek Catholic, Ukrainian-speaking inhabitants of Galicia were part of the Russian or the Ukrainian nation. "Russophile" and "Ukrainophile" were watchwords of the time, carrying not only cultural and national but also political connotations—of orientation toward religion and the clergy on the one hand and toward the "nation" on the other.[58] In this way, groups that had previously been excluded from political participation moved into the foreground of debate. Not least because of their sheer size, they could no longer be overlooked as a factor in political developments.

The three largest religious groups in Galicia made up the following percentages of the population: Roman Catholics around 45 percent, Greek Catholics around 42 percent, and Jews around 11 percent.[59] However, over the course of the latter nineteenth century, attributions of estate and religion became subordinate to national and linguistic identifiers.[60] Consequently, in this and other cross-class nations, peasant integration and Jewish "assimilation" occurred in tandem.[61] Conversely, each nation asserted itself by excluding the others and engaging in ongoing fights for their "vested rights."[62] After 1848, a wave of national struggles engulfed all of Central and Southeastern Europe.[63] Cities, regions, and population groups were claimed by various national movements, who symbolized their entitlement by giving them names in their own language. In the springtime of the peoples, both historic and young nations called for self-determination and for their language to replace or be added to German in education and administration.⁶⁴ This demand challenged the authority and very self-conception of the Prussian and Austrian states.

In regions with mixed-national populations where many Germans lived, such as the Sudetenland, Silesia, East Prussia, and Transylvania, the contest with the central power inevitably involved a regional conflict between the coexisting nationalities over status and influence. Galicia was characterized by a Polish-Ukrainian dualism. Neither national group fought for keeping German as the official language. They were more concerned with the relative importance of the Ukrainian or Polish language in public life. For the Austrian empire, however—an entity conceived of as a "German state"—the use of German in the administration and education of a region earmarked for civilizing by means of "German culture" was of crucial importance. The Galician Jews, whose bourgeois elites mostly identified with German culture, were caught between these regional Galician and supraregional Central European levels of conflict.

The Blurring of the "German Frontier"

Belief in having a mission to civilize central Europe with "German culture" was an integral part of German nationalism. It was one of the issues deliberated on in St. Paul's Church in Frankfurt.⁶⁵ Urban Galicians also identified with German culture and harbored fantasies of bringing it to less civilized colonies. Germans formed a diaspora nationality, living in enclaves or urban centers, in many regions of Eastern and Central Europe. Many held high-ranking positions⁶⁶ working for the Prussian or Austrian state, each of which had established systems of governance using German as the official language. A significant number of these German upper classes in Central Europe were Jewish.⁶⁷ Until well into the nineteenth century, many of them were convinced of the legitimacy of the German civilizing mission, including in the religious sphere.⁶⁸ In the second half of the nineteenth century, however, many Austrian officials and, increasingly, Jews became integrated and "assimilated" into the local non-German national communities. The children of the generation who had brought German culture to the frontier, then, were themselves Hungarians, Poles, Croats, or Czechs.⁶⁹ After decades of working in the education or administrative system of Hungary, Galicia, or Croatia, for instance, or resettling in one of the many multilingual towns in the empire, an individual's linguistic and national orientation might take a complete change in direction.

The Jewish National Dilemma in Central Europe

Within this multinational space encompassing a range of nationalisms, Jewish assimilation to the nation could never be satisfactory to all. Jews developed independent concepts of nation, which stood in competition with non-Jewish national identifiers while essentially validating the national order of the world. The Jewish dilemma arose from the diversity of Jewish designs in combination with the tendency to seek uniform categories.[70] Attempts to find them in Central Europe were bound to end in frustration not only with the categories but—by extension—with one's very understanding of the world. Central and Eastern European Jews no longer necessarily identified as German but with a range of different nations. Factors of language and parentage pointed individuals toward secular and ethnic self-definitions of Jewishness. These could potentially be ascribed and appeal to all Jews, despite the many visible variations of Jewishness, which became evident as migration from the peripheries to the capitals increased. At the same time, Jews set up their own interest groups to take an active role in international politics. Educated, middle-class Jews, some in high-ranking offices of their nation-states, worked toward helping disenfranchised orthodox Jews in Romania, Russia, and Galicia. The contrast between acculturated, successful Jews and impoverished, "foreign," and nonconformist Eastern European Jews, and the supranational assistance provided by the former to the latter, was most visible in the capital cities of the Central European empires with "Slavic-Jewish" peripheries, Berlin and Vienna.

This was where fears of the demise of German culture and foreign domination by Jews and Slavs were most frequently voiced. Here, politicians and journalists popularized anti-liberal, antisemitic notions, interweaving envy of Jewish social climbers, fears of being superseded by competition "from below," and skepticism regarding Jewish loyalty to the nation.[71] Even more than in Berlin, such ideas resonated strongly in Vienna, where Germans formed a minority within a state that was incrementally shedding its German character.[72]

The Austro-Hungarian Compromise and the December Constitution of 1867

Austria's "compromise" (German: *Ausgleich*) with Hungary and the Constitution of December 1867, designed in response to military defeats by the Sardinians and French (at Solferino in 1859) as well as the Prussians (at Königgrätz/Hradec Králové in 1866), fundamentally changed the character of the Habsburg Empire. Under the constitution, the emperor's subjects became citizens and were guaranteed equal rights regardless of religion and social background. The empire that had been held together by the Habsburg dynasty became a complex entity consisting of two equal states, dually ruled by the emperor of Austria and the king of Hungary. The kingdom of Hungary, also known as the "Lands of the Crown of Saint Stephen" and "Transleithania" due to its geographical location (from a Viennese perspective) beyond the River Leitha, was governed by a separate administration in Budapest.[73] A year later, a compromise was concluded with Croatia-Slavonia, a possession of the Crown of Saint Stephen, guaranteeing the land autonomy in judicial, administrative, and cultural affairs.[74] As well as constituting half of the empire, Hungary was a centralist Magyar nation-state.

The situation was different, however, in the western half of the empire. Cisleithania, as it was known, even came to oppose national politics. In the age of liberalism, the two German-speaking states that ruled predominantly non-German-speaking areas progressed along divergent paths. The Austro-Hungarian Compromise of 1867 benefited Hungarians, Croats, and Poles, but pitted them against Slovaks, Croats, or Ukrainians. Elections in Cisleithania in 1879 marked a shift in the balance of power away from the German nationalist Liberals and toward the Slavs and Conservatives.[75] As the German language became less attractive on the periphery, the educated Jewish middle class—hitherto an important group of German speakers—were seen not only to abandon the "German cause" but even to support its opponents, the Hungarian and Slavic nations.[76] Had they openly supported the German nation in Central Europe, they would have incurred the hostility of local nationalists. Of all groups, Jews most often embodied the entanglement of nationalities in Central Europe, which became problematic whenever a situation demanded unequivocal commitment to one nation, excluding all others. Usually, the determining factor was regarded as colloquial language. Yet after 1900, many middle-class Jews in the Habsburg Empire lived with triple identities: in terms of ethnicity and religion they were Jewish; in terms of culture, Polish, Czech, German, Hungarian, or Croatian; and in terms of political allegiance, loyal to the supranational multiethnic state.[77]

In contrast to Austria, Prussia not only persisted with its policies of Germanization and centralization after the founding of the German Empire but even intensified them around the turn of the century. Here, the German language and "German education" remained highly valued cultural assets among Jewish subjects. Yet despite the political divergence between Austria and Prussia, and the rivalry between their dynasties, subjects of both empires continued to see themselves as fulfilling a mission to bring German culture to Central Europe. After 1848, with the growing realization that there would never be a "German Central Europe," German nationalism gained an exclusive character. The more the nation was imagined as an "objective" community of ancestry rather than a subjective community based on shared ideals, the more precarious the Jewish position became in the respective national projects. Prussia was admired as a pan-German trailblazer by nationalists in Austria as well as in the German Empire. German nationalism, propagated by the rulers in Berlin to consolidate the newly founded empire, consequently served to destabilize and delegitimize Habsburg rule in Cisleithania.[78]

Before this empire was officially named Austria in 1915, it was cumbersomely called "the kingdoms and lands represented in the Imperial Diet."[79] The largest and most populous of these was Galicia.[80]

Galician "Autonomy" in the Habsburg Empire, or the Polonization of a Habsburg Kingdom

The Austro-Hungarian Compromise changed the face of the crownland Galicia and its relationship to the rest of the empire. It was preceded by a so-called minor compromise.[81] In exchange for cultural autonomy, the representatives of the Galician elites in parliament, comprising the higher clergy, major landowners, and the conservative bourgeoisie, pledged loyalty to the crown and constitution, and to support the work of the government.[82] Galicia was gradually "Polonized." Polish was made the official language of government and instruction at the universities in Lemberg and Krakow and at most schools in the land.[83] As more Poles occupied positions in administration, and Polish names became more visible in society, Polish rose in importance on a symbolic level. Middle-class Jews increasingly spoke Polish, rather than German, at home and in their social lives.[84] The Jewish reformist community in Krakow was quicker to embrace this change than the Jews in Lemberg.[85] Indeed, Krakow became something of a Polish pantheon, given to public celebrations of national heroes and landmark events. In the Galician capital Lemberg, in contrast, the different nations fought for dominance of the public sphere. The city became the theater of a Ukrainian-Polish clash of nationalities.[86]

Although the two groups were almost equal in terms of numbers, the Ukrainians were politically and culturally at a disadvantage.[87] Census suffrage and electoral fraud had cemented Polish rule in Galicia.[88] The introduction in 1906 of the universal right to vote for the Imperial Diet, and a major dispute over the choice of teaching language at Lemberg University, which culminated in the murder of Galician governor Andrzej Potocki by a Ukrainian student in 1908, shifted the Ukrainian-Polish conflict to the foreground of political debate, even straining the Habsburg Empire's relations with Russia.[89] Both the Poles and the Ukrainians regarded Galicia as their Piedmont, holding more potential for political agitation than their national enclaves in the Tsarist Empire.[90] Many nationalists chose Galicia as their center of operations, fueling fears of irredentism in Vienna and St. Petersburg. The governor's office in Lemberg, the highest level of government in the crownland, tried to allay such fears by cracking down on disloyal opposition. The governor was appointed by the emperor, even during the period of autonomy, and always from the Polish high nobility. A regional committee acted as Galicia's legislative body; the regional parliament had merely an advisory function. There was also a minister for Galician affairs in the Cisleithanian cabinet.[91] With the political turnaround in Cisleithania in 1879, when the German Liberals lost their hitherto stable majority in the Imperial Diet and the conservative Count Eduard van Taafe became prime minister, supported by a coalition of clericals and Slavs,[92] Galicians took prominent positions in government for the first time. From a Viennese perspective, Galicia was both far away and very present. On the one hand, it was geographically remote and still perceived as exotically rustic and backward;[93] but on the other, Galician members of the Imperial Diet now exerted considerable influence on Cisleithanian politics and brought political and national issues from the periphery to the center.[94] By 1897, there were Poles in key positions in the imperial cabinet: Kasimir Badeni, head of government and minister of the interior; Eduard Rittner, minister for Galicia; Leon Bilínskim, finance minister; and Agenor Goluchowski, foreign minister.[95]

A Second Boost to the Economy and the Start of "Mass Politics"

Despite Galicia having gained "autonomy," it was now more tightly enmeshed within the empire.[96] Under the constitution, Jews were citizens with equal rights, entitled to vote and stand for election and to acquire land.[97] This served to galvanize the rural economy.[98]

Jews started acquiring large estates and agricultural property, often at public auctions of foreclosure properties, and the proportion of Jewish-owned land quickly grew.[99] In 1877, the Galician diet deemed it necessary to enact a law "against dishonest actions in credit operations," which was extended to all Cisleithania in 1881.[100] While Jews entered the field of agriculture, hitherto the preserve of Christians, ever more Christians strove to earn a living in the growing trade and service sectors. This break with the traditional roles ascribed to Christians and Jews was attended and interpreted by political debate in the Imperial Diet, press, and during election campaigns.[101]

Addressing issues such as the restoration of Polish statehood or the founding of other nation-states, this debate extended beyond the borders of Galicia. Until the last third of the nineteenth century, Central Europe's political actors could only imagine accomplishing such changes by means of armed, revolutionary "liberation" from the Partition Powers. But after the failed revolt of 1863–1864, known as the January Uprising, and under the growing influence of the middle-class intelligentsia and its positivist worldview, they started to recognize the potential of "society" to author a state.[102] Intellectuals spoke of "organic work," by which they envisaged improved material and spiritual circumstances for the masses—the "people"—following reforms in education and the economy. The church started to take an active role in the social life of the villages, with abstinence campaigns and popular gatherings to appeal to the religious community. In parallel, the secular intelligentsia launched its own social improvement offensive, calling for "work for the people." For their words to make any impact, however, they needed to be followed by actions, and here again Galicia proved more dynamic than the "Vistula Land."[103]

The imperial government facilitated modern collective identification. The Imperial Diet, known in German as the *Reichsrat*, and the constitution provided a framework for society's politicization, which progressed steadily after 1867 and increased rapidly from the 1880s onward.[104] The right to freedom of opinion, which removed constraints on political journalism and generated a newspaper boom that made the press a fixture of everyday life, propelled this process.[105] But the main catalyst was the elections to the regional diets and the Reichsrat. Held on a regular basis, they motivated actors to become politically organized and form political parties according to collective markers of identification. Electoral results were interpreted as clear information on community membership.[106] But in fact, the various collectives only became reality in the process of fighting the elections.[107]

Political groups with varying social and national emphases evolved in Galicia in opposition to the long-ruling conservative forces. Here as elsewhere, the political landscape was dualist in character and dominated by conservatives and liberals. But "democracy" was the watchword unifying the opponents of the conservatives. Liberalism, in contrast, tended to be associated with foreign influences and especially German centralism within the Habsburg Monarchy.[108] The Ruthenians also had two main political camps: Conservatives, supported by the clergy and landowners, opposed to a greater extent by a down-to-earth, secular movement than bourgeois Liberals. The national and cultural conflict between Ukrainophiles and Russophiles turned into a party-political clash. Concurrently, the political frontlines shifted as the question of national or social orientation started to displace the conservative/liberal dualism. The ruling Polish Conservatives found themselves confronted by a growing Ukrainian opposition. But opposition to the conservatives was by no means exclusively national—that is, against Galicia's Polonization. Polish nationalists also criticized the elite's Austrian patriotism and alleged indifference toward the plight of the peasants and the people in general. The controversial term "Badenism" was coined—from the name of Governor Kasimir Badeni—to encapsulate the Galician elite's cooperation with the central government in Vienna.[109]

Both in the romantic and positivist traditions of nationalism, the people (Polish: *lud*) were assigned a special role in national "rebirth."[110] They formed the core and the basis of the nation. New means of communication, improved education, and the prospect of parliamentary representation thanks to extended suffrage opened a broad field of pluralist social activity in rural Galicia.

On the Kindred and the Other: Peasant Movements in Galicia

The peasant movements were the clearest reflection of the radical changes occurring in everyday village life in Galicia.[111] They manifested the end of the village communicative sphere's isolation and the dawn of modern forms of political and medial communitization based on reinterpretations of existing structures. They spawned activists, a new breed of professional politician, who set about improving the lot of the peasants after the example of populism in the Russian Empire and cooperative societies in Western Europe.[112] They gave peasants the opportunity to influence the fate of their class or local environment. The press and various societies and public assemblies joined in the discussions of peasant problems and demands, which were started by intellectuals but needed to be conducted in the language of the peasants and originate from the peasants themselves, acting as lobbyists and politicians, to make an impact.[113]

The history of the peasant movements can be regarded as a history of emancipation from serfdom, illiteracy, and the confined world of the Central European village.[114] Whether it can also be viewed as a history of national awakening is questionable.[115] Certainly, the fact should not be overlooked that one of the peasants' objectives for becoming organized was to free themselves from the "Jewish yoke" and "Jewish hands."[116] To regard the history of the peasant movements ex post as a "natural" development of the nation is to see its agitation as the expression of an "objective" conflict over resources and national ownership.[117] By this logic, the liberation of the "kindred" people had to occur at the cost of the "others." But there was no clear definition of who the "kindred" were and, conversely, who "the others" were. People could only claim to belong from the experience of social processes and subsequently transpose their claims onto real life. Communitization worked in opposition to other social groups and by updating the memory of past protests and unrest.

Peasant Revolts in Constitution-Era Galicia

In spring 1872, eleven sheriffs from central Galicia informed the governor of rumors among the peasants that the gentry (Polish: *pany*) intended to reintroduce the feudal practice of serfdom. Since the emperor, who had abolished it one generation previously, was vehemently opposed, a local manor owner had supposedly planned to assassinate him. According to another rumor, one of the "right-honorable ministers" had struck off the emperor's left ear and injured his hand during a dispute.[118] Sometimes the dispute was said to have been over the distribution of fields and forests among the peasants, which the emperor supported and the nobility rejected. In each case, a bloodthirsty tale culminated in the announcement that rebellious nobles were to be executed in Vienna and that all subjects of the empire were invited to use the train services to the capital free of charge to attend the spectacle.[119]

In 1886, there was turmoil around Easter again when the pressing *Servituten* problem of forest-and-field use was renegotiated under the peasants' threat of repeating the "ruckus" of exactly forty years previously. To make matters worse, the Easter holidays that year fell on the feast of St. Mark, when the fields were traditionally blessed.[120] But the church's Easter liturgy did not make any allowance for the blessing of fields, and the peasants feared crop failures. In this tense atmosphere, rumors arose that for a period of three days the peasants were authorized to kill anyone "wearing black."[121] This was the color worn by nobles, priests, and Jews.

Information delineating the in-group was still conveyed by traditional means of rural communication. But these were inevitably colored by the multiethnic, constitutional state's growing tendency to categorize and classify for bureaucratic purposes. Parliamentary politics also required individuals to define themselves by supposedly objective criteria and declare to which group they belonged.[122] Yet what and who constituted the nation was no more "objective" than a world divided into nations was without alternative. As life in rural Galicia became increasingly politicized, rifts emerged within groups that were presumed to share common interests—between different-class affiliates of the same nation or between same-nationality peasants who disagreed on certain issues such as the role of the church. In the 1890s, three different peasant parties—the conservative party, the Christian-social party, and the nationalist democratic party—vied for the votes of Catholic, Polish-speaking peasants. In Krakow, the Social Democratic and Christian-social proposals for organizing the workers contended for votes. These varying models of communitization only became tangible, and therefore social reality, when they clashed with others. During the election campaign in the run-up to the Reichsrat elections of 1897, organizations and newspapers in Krakow openly professed to be antisemitic and agitated against Jews, to prevent the (allegedly Jewish) Social Democrats from coming to power.

After the elections, which resulted in Galician oppositionists—some who promised anti-Jewish policies—entering the Reichsrat for the first time, there was rioting and violence against Jews in some areas around Krakow. The disturbances followed an unprecedented surge of political rivalry as the above-mentioned peasant parties campaigned for support in two constituencies. Over a period of two months, several thousand farmers and workers turned on the Jews in over four hundred local parishes. The storm went down in history as the "antisemitic excesses."[123]

The Antisemitism Years in Galicia

Modern antisemitism emerged in Galicia in a field of tension between changing economic parameters and new collective systems of meaning within the political and medial framework of a crownland of the Habsburg Monarchy. Antisemitic options arose here in competition with, and in relation to, other political designs for community. To analyze the antisemitic process, the interplay between discourse and action and the contemporary significance of the attribution "antisemitic" must be considered. Jews were not only objects in a program to stimulate the national economy. They were also the "threatening others," and articulating hostility toward Jews was a communicative technique used to mobilize voters and simplify a complex reality.[124]

Divergent opinions and perspectives divided the various spheres of the press, parliament, and rural life, as described above. In view of these, how did a broad antisemitic debate arise at all, and how was it conducted? Participation in debate is always a question of power. Gaining influence over the media discussion of Jewish integration or exclusion was analogous to obtaining power. Alternatively, control could be asserted by means of physical violence, thus impressing a personal stamp upon relations between Christians and Jews. A third source of power was the Imperial Diet, which some politicians had at their disposal after winning seats in the Reichsrat with their antisemitic election campaigns. These three paths to dominance and influencing the "Jewish question" were each subject to different conditions and show a spectrum of varying insights into collective hostility toward Jews. Yet they were also closely interlinked, and all described as "antisemitic." How then, should we conceive of antisemitism in Galicia?

What Was Antisemitism?

The main obstacle to explaining antisemitism in historical terms—what it meant in a certain space at a certain time—is the tendency toward essentialization; that is, to take the existence of antisemitism as a historical subject, so to speak, for granted. But the field must not be left to isms rather than people if historical inquiry is to be productive. Rather, it should focus on the people who spoke of antisemitism and who placed their views in relation to other speech acts, actions, or events. The questions of what people understood by antisemitism and when must be investigated, as both are an essential part of the phenomenon.[125] This phenomenon of antisemitism should not be regarded as an actor but as a social process in which actions and discourse were mutually referential and endowed each other with meaning.[126]

In this study of Galicia, the focus will be placed on the activists in the antisemitic election campaign in West Galicia and the protagonists of the riots of 1898. They were the agents of the antisemitic process: people who acted to the disadvantage of Jews, who had access to receptive publics, and who justified their actions by claiming to have a certain "knowledge" of the Jews, or who demanded political consequences. Some were parliamentarians elected expressly to implement such policy. By representing it in parliament, they legitimized and dignified their underlying "knowledge." Discourse and practice were, then, connected on many levels. Actors and speakers were mutually dependent, linked by a need to constantly refer to and reassert the connection between them. Their discourse lent legitimacy to antisemitic demands and actions. In concert, the agents of the antisemitic process tried to turn what was disallowed under the liberal constitution into social reality—namely, to deprive people of rights because of their religion.[127] Antisemitism was the name of a program designed to stretch the rules of sayability and make the formerly unsayable ideologically, scientifically, and sociopolitically acceptable in a succinct and easily communicable way.[128] In parallel, antisemitism was also used for othering and to delegitimize such efforts.[129]

Closer consideration of the interplay between journalism, politics, and social practice can shed light on the periodic increases and decreases in antisemitic speech, writing, and discrimination. The present book aims to show the extent to which (the sometimes conflictual) relations between Christians and Jews were influenced by political antisemitism and, conversely, how far conflicts and contingent events steered the construction of antisemitic meanings. To accurately reconstruct the influence and dependence of antisemitic actors on events and debates, attention will be paid not only to the opinion-making exponents of antisemitism but also to the ordinary people who embraced the antisemitic option. In addition to these, actors who resisted and opposed anti-Jewish speech and actions will also be considered. In this way, Jewish actors appear as autonomous subjects and not merely as victims.

Nationalism as a Social Process

Viewing antisemitism as a process, this inquiry follows the model of historical research into nationalism, and especially Rogers Brubaker's theses on reconstructing the process of how nations are formed and function.[130] Going beyond a history of ideas, or intellectual history, this approach also deals with the repercussions and effects of the ideas on actions.[131] It neither assumes that the nation is a stable, permanent entity nor that the idea of the nation necessarily leads to a national movement. Rather, nationalism is shown to be an ongoing exchange about the nature of national values and characteristics: about who belongs to the nation or should belong to it, to which territory it is entitled, who are its heroes, and who are its worst enemies. This public communication incorporates and processes political events as they occur. Equally, the formation of a national movement that asserts legal and territorial claims precipitates reactions by the state and/or competing nationalities, which can in turn become political events when processed and disseminated by the media.[132] The discussion of such events in the press, at mass gatherings, and by societies offers the individual the experience of belonging to a collective. From myriad interpretations and ideas of the nation, expressed in various fields of communication, a world of signs and symbols crystallizes: representations of the nation.[133] Beyond these representations, the nation does not exist. National belonging is a situational experience that must be constantly reproduced, each time differently.[134] Wars or the civilized equivalent of sporting competitions between nations create communities of fate—whether they be victorious or vanquished—cemented by emotional bonds linking people who never actually meet. Performative, meaningful acts of gathering at significant sites for public assemblies, celebrations, or commemorative events are attended by media and official commentary. This lends meaning to the actions and assures the individuals of their participation in an epoch-making event.[135] Communication and performance blend into a unit, in which the nation becomes a reality that can be experienced, narrated, and remembered.

Researchers into nationalism do not, however, focus only on its "success stories." They also consider the alternatives for collective identification—multinational empires, churches, and international political movements.[136] Historians are interested in the relationship between national belonging and regional or social identity, especially where divergent models clash.[137] They inquire not only into the integrated members of national communities, who share the fulfilling experience of belonging, but also those who become excluded from, and are made into others and perhaps even enemies of, the national community.[138] This kind of exclusion, if directed at Jews, constitutes part of modern antisemitism and is more than a by-product of nationalism.[139]

Antisemitism as a Social Process

Antisemitism can be regarded as a discrete process propelled by mutually referential speech and actions. These justify the exclusion of Jews by interpreting the coexistence of non-Jews and Jews as essentially conflictual and detrimental to the kindred, non-Jewish community, which claims a precedential right to prosperity and wellbeing.[140] Discussion of antisemitism was not purely academic and detached from reality but took place in the light of concurrent social events and developments. Antisemitic meaning-makers did not operate within a vacuum. When writing texts, devising programs, and founding societies, they always referred to specific actions by Jews, developments within Jewish communities,[141] or conflicts between Jews and non-Jews. They sought to portray isolated conflicts as evidence of a fundamental Jewish–non-Jewish antagonism, and hence emphasize the urgency of the "Jewish question."[142]

The claim that Jews and non-Jews essentially clashed was perhaps a reaction to the blurring of the once clear boundaries dividing the Christian and Jewish worlds. During the second half of the nineteenth century, these became indeterminate or even obsolete in some fields, such as urban leisure culture. Antisemitic discourse, then, drew a clear distinction that did not exist in social reality.[143]

The formative phase of modern antisemitism processed major events such as the stock market crash and economic crisis of the early 1870s, the Congress of

Berlin and the antisemitism debate, the pogroms in the Russian Empire and the Tizsaeszslar trial, the Dreyfus and Hilsner affairs, and countless minor events, such as the trial of Gittla and Moses Ritter recounted above. All these were described, discussed, and interpreted in numerous books and newspaper articles. People cited these events as grounds for acting hostile toward Jews, founding parties with anti-Jewish objectives, banning Jews from their unions and associations, and establishing "scientific" institutions to research the influence of Jews on society. The concept of "antisemitism" evolved at the interface between these various initiatives, events, and debates. Once formulated, the term allowed the wide range of related observations, opinions, and practices to be condensed into one complex. The adoption of the concept into the language of politics seemed to prove not only the existence of the "Jewish question" but also its importance. The establishment of antisemitism as a discursive fact in political communication prepared the ground for antisemitic reality to develop. One might say that belief in the reality of the concept grew as the term became established in discourse. Whenever newspapers ran articles criticizing anti-Jewish comments, violence, or discrimination, anti-Semites claimed they were proof that public opinion was manipulated by Jews, and that the press was overrun by Jews.[144]

Yet anti-Semites could not stage-manage antisemitic realities alone. They were in fact helped by the press. Scandals and media sensations invited new commentaries and explanations, some of which claimed Jews were to blame or identified them as the root cause of conflicts. By the very fact that such allegations garnered wider attention, provoked further comment, and were found to be antisemitic, the concept was reaffirmed and its agents' arrival in the world of politics ensured. They were taken seriously as anti-Semites. Actors who identified themselves—or someone or something else—as antisemitic tapped into the power to polarize, promote identification, and reduce complexity that is eagerly sought in parliamentary politics. Political debate on antisemitism negotiated more than the significance and prospects of self-confessed anti-Semites. Debate on how to define and evaluate antisemitism simultaneously negotiated the majority society's sayability and behavioral rules toward Jews.[145] When antisemitism was used for othering, actions and speech acts defined as antisemitic were rendered taboo. Anything that was not generally considered to be antisemitic, on the other hand, even if it was pejorative or critical of Jews and Judaism, was sayable even for convinced opponents of antisemitism.[146] Hence the struggle to define the attributes of antisemitism was part of the antisemitic process.

Debates on the nature of antisemitism were almost always sparked by comments or actions that had already shifted the sayability or behavioral boundaries concerning Jews. Current affairs might be interpreted in the media as proof of a general grievance with, or threat posed by, Jews.[147] These theories then influenced further developments, as protagonists referred to them to justify and rationalize statements and actions against Jews. The appearance of a hitherto unknown action or rhetoric against Jews, which social and political actors subsequently welcomed or defended, could shift the sayability rules concerning Jews and the nature of antisemitism again.[148] Public debate surrounding events with antisemitic potential fed into and perpetuated the discourse on antisemitism. At the interface between abstract discourse and tangible reality, an antisemitic option for action arose that appealed to people for various reasons.[149] It made a complex world seem easier to understand, and social problems simpler to solve. Antisemitism included people in communication processes from which they would otherwise have felt excluded.[150] Devaluing and excluding Jews helped to increase self-worth.[151] Moreover, excluding others brought material advantage, as it implied "defending" the available resources or appropriating the others' property. The others' entitlement was denied on principle or regarded as secondary to the needs of one's "own group."[152]

Antisemitism and Anti-antisemitism

Accepting antisemitism as a fact of life could even be advantageous to Jewish actors. Jewish nationalists cited antisemitism as a reason to establish a Jewish state. Jews of all nationalities could use the antisemitic label to describe incidents or a social climate, and so promote awareness of the intolerability of discriminatory practices they experienced. To acknowledge that the term "antisemitism" was deconstructed in this way is not to imply that Jews did not experience hostility or hatred. Rather, it highlights the benefits of communicating such experiences effectively—that is, normatively. The term "antisemitism" was and is an especially suitable device for purposeful communication of this kind.

This communicative process, fueled by a combination of events and their interpretation in public and political debate, is what the present book attempts to describe and place in the context of the various, shifting, milieu-specific meanings, implications, and functions of the term antisemitism. On the premise that a historical inquiry into antisemitism during a given period cannot reconstruct stable attitudes or ideologies, it focuses on tracing the anti-Jewish statements and situations that produced meaning in their specific contexts and seemed to promise an advantage for their authors. Since historical science has recourse only to the records of words and actions, but not to the thought processes behind them, statements of hostility toward Jews will not be assessed as definitive articulations of antisemitic attitudes. They merely show that their authors opted in a certain situation to speak in an antisemitic mode or to rationalize their actions in this mode. It took more than the word "antisemitism" to make conduct readable as antisemitic. The word had to be endowed with meanings and values, and these had to be popularized.

Preconditions for the Antisemitic Process

For the antisemitic process to begin, a communicative space where anti-Jewish ideas could evolve and become established needed to exist. This space was created by various political and social camps, using their affiliated newspapers and assemblies and their embeddedness in longer-established local and social communities. Their communication concerning Jews was part of a general discourse on issues such as the "Jewish question" and "knowledge" about Judaism and the Jews. Whatever was said in any given environment did not remain within the confines of a clearly demarcated community. Although such communication used peculiar semantics that were not necessarily comprehensible to all sections of society for the purpose of creating community, it simultaneously aimed to convince a broader public and participate in the world beyond the community. For this reason, milieu-specific discourse adhered to standards related to those of general politics. To be heard and not excluded from the general community of communication, it was necessary to conform to that community. Another precondition for the antisemitic process was the occurrence of events that gave cause to talk about Jews. One example was the murder of Franka Mnich, described above. Its part in the process can be schematically outlined as follows:

A young woman was murdered in a remote Galician village. Some of the villagers accused a prominent Jewish member of the local community of the murder, leading to his arrest and the start of judicial proceedings. The case became a nationwide media sensation. Within the bounds of the prevalent sayability rules, there was scope for interpreting the incident as a case of lethal Jewish rites. Indeed, "experts" were found—Jewish believers named Kenner and Schutz—who confirmed that cutting off braids and extracting fetuses were Jewish practices.[153] In this way, concrete "knowledge" was constructed ex post: on the strength of the injuries found on the victim's body, a generalizing assumption was made and subsequently disseminated. This in turn aroused further interest in the trial and the subject of the Talmud, which August Rohling stepped in to satisfy. On the political stage, Teofil Merunowicz linked the incident in Lutcza with an "expertise" by a professor from Prague and took this as grounds for demanding anti-Jewish legislation. His (and the local priest's) arguments reinforced the suspicions of the people in Lutcza that the murder must have been committed by a Jew and convinced them to testify in court that they had always been wary of dealing with Jews or had long since suspected "the Jews." The first bill of indictment enshrined the ritual-murder theory. Even in far-off Berlin, the "documentary description" of "Jewish ritual murder" added plausibility to the theory, which could be articulated in the appropriate situations.[154] The theology professor, the politician, the "Jewish experts," the files of the royal-and-imperial Habsburg judiciary, and the "violently extracted" confession delivered by the accomplice Stochliński all contributed to engendering a discursive antisemitic reality in which it was plausible that Jews slit the throats of Christians in their cellars.

Yet although this picture was popularized by the sheer frequency of its repetition in public debate, it was not unrivalled. Nobody was forced to believe it was true, let alone ensure that it remained in currency. But it seemed plausible or appealing to some people in certain situations, for which reason they postulated and circulated it.[155] Mr. Mandela enjoyed a moment in the limelight with his story of going blind. The villagers took the opportunity to besmirch the wealthy, aloof-seeming Moses Ritter by listing all the times he had attracted suspicion. Speaking the language of antisemitism was one option among several. Moses and Gittla Ritter were not imprisoned for five years because of antisemitism but because their own neighbors incriminated them. But these neighbors lent their suspicions weight by denouncing the Ritters specifically as Jews, and by borrowing from antisemitic discourse, which was kept in circulation and endorsed by actors such as Rohling, the clergymen Jakub and Jan Drzewiecki, and various supposed experts on Jewry. Their discourse consequently influenced individual conduct, including that of the court officials. Such conduct in turn facilitated Merunowicz's antisemitic politics. His demand to limit Jewish rights after the introduction of equality shifted the contemporary sayability rules. It cast doubt on the state's guarantee to respect the rights of every individual citizen, regardless of faith.

As the example of Merunowicz shows, actors not only advanced interpretations of events but used them to legitimize demands for new legislation and anti-Jewish policies. The reading of occurrences as "antisemitic events" as well as the frequent articulation of anti-Jewish policies in public debate will be regarded below as antisemitic agitation.[156]

A Process on Three Levels

This book explores the process of antisemitism in three chapters, each dealing with one level. The historical stages of each level are considered in chronological order. But since it is an inquiry into a process, they overlap and coincide, reflecting the complexity of antisemitism as it resulted from the interplay between political meaning-making and social practice.

The chapter "Agitation" describes how the Galician public interpreted events in antisemitic terms, and the negative "knowledge" of the Jews this generated.[157] It assesses the importance and functions of hostility toward Jews in peasant party mobilization and why Christian-social groupings described themselves as antisemitic.

The chapter "Violence" focuses on the "antisemitic riots" among the rural population, describing them in close detail and from the perspectives of all the groups of actors involved. It asks in what sense the riots were triggered by party-political agitation and whether they were an attempt to put thus expressed demands of economic "liberation" from the Jews into practice.

The chapter "Politics" considers the Galician politicians who were voted into the Reichsrat in 1897/98 on the strength of anti-Jewish agitation. First, it shows how they appropriated the riots and the debate surrounding antisemitism within the public arena of the Imperial Diet. The focus here is on their parliamentary work and specifically the interpellations with which they implemented their policies and included their voters in discriminatory actions against Jews. In other words, this chapter is concerned with the process by which parliamentarians utilized antisemitism as a resource for parliamentary work, along with the power of the parliamentary mandate, to assert their position on Jews and "knowledge" of Jewish practices. Second, it enquires into anti-Jewish practices that took place beyond political processes and without the label of antisemitism.

These three levels can also be regarded as phases in the antisemitic process. In the first phase, ideas about Jews were introduced into political culture. These were repeated and modified in the light of conflicts between Christians and Jews during the second phase. In the third phase, such conflicts were placed on the agenda of the Imperial Diet and thus anchored in political discourse from a high position of power.

Notes

1. Robert Musil, *The Man without Qualities*, translated by Sophie Wilkins (London, 2011), 1.
2. Maria Ćiesla, Jolanta Żyndul, and Sprawa Ritterów, "Aktualizacya legendy mordu rytualnego w Galicji końca XIX wieku," in Grażyna Borkowska and Magdalena Rudkowska (eds), *Kwestia żydowska w XIX wieku: Spory o tożsamość Polaków* (Warsaw, 2004), 439–452.
3. Gmina Strzyżów (city website), www.strzyzow.pl.
4. Civil society is understood here as a "network of human relationships and institutions beyond the direct control of the state that structure individual action and allow private persons, unconnected by personal attachments, to manage their affairs." Cit. from Joseph Bradley, *Voluntary Associations in Tsarist Russia: Science, Patriotism, and Civil Society* (Cambridge, 2009), 9.
5. Moritz Csáky, *Das Gedächtnis der Städte: Kulturelle Verflechtungen – Wien und die urbanen Milieus in Zentraleuropa* (Vienna, 2010). The term "Central Europe" is used here in keeping with his definition. Martin Pollack, *Der Kaiser von Amerika: Die große Flucht aus Galizien* (Vienna, 2010); Annemarie Steidl, "Ein ewiges Hin und Her. Kontinentale, transatlantische und lokale Migrationsrouten in der Spätphase der Habsburgmonarchie," Österreichische Zeitschrift für Geschichtswissenschaften 19 (2008): 1; Grzegorz Maria Kowalski, *Przestępstwa emigracyjne w Galicji 1897–1918: Z badań nad dziejami polskiego wychodźstwa* (Krakow, 2003).

6. Markus Schroer, "Grenzverschiebungen: Zur Neukonstruktion sozialer Räume im Globalisierungsprozess," in Carsten Würmann et al. (eds), *Welt.Raum.Körper: Transformationen und Entgrenzungen von Körper und Raum* (Bielefeld, 2007), 15–36, 20.
7. Larry Wolff reflects on the invention of Galicia and its gradual impact in his recent book, *The Idea of Galicia: History and Fantasy in Habsburg Political Culture* (Stanford, 2010).
8. Jürgen Osterhammel, *Die Verwandlung der Welt: Eine Geschichte des 19. Jahrhunderts* (Munich, 2009).
9. Michael G. Müller, *Die Teilungen Polens 1772, 1793, 1795* (Munich, 1984).
10. Manfried Rauchensteiner, *Der Tod des Doppeladlers: Österreich-Ungarn und der Erste Weltkrieg* (Graz, 1993).
11. Krakow was incorporated into Galicia in 1846 in response to revolutionary activity, having previously been a free city under the control of the three partition powers. On Galicia's borders, see Christoph Augustynowicz and Andreas Kappeler (eds), *Die galizische Grenze 1772–1867: Kommunikation oder Isolation?* (Vienna, 2006).
12. Paul R. Magocsi, "Galicia: A European Land," in idem and Christopher Hann (eds), *Galicia: A Multicultured Land* (Toronto, 2005), 3–21; Christoph Augustynowicz, *Geschichte Ostmitteleuropas: Ein Abriss* (Vienna, 2010), 67–70.
13. Hans-Christian Maner, "Zwischen 'Kompensationsobjekt,' 'Musterland' und 'Glacis': Wiener politische und militärische Vorstellungen von Galizien von 1772 bis zur Autonomieära," in idem (ed.), *Grenzregionen der Habsburgermonarchie im 18. und 19. Jahrhundert: Ihre Bedeutung und Funktion aus der Perspektive Wiens* (Münster, 2005), 103–122.
14. These two main conflicts in policy on Galicia persisted until well into the nineteenth century. Hans-Christian Maner, *Galizien: Eine Grenzregion im Kalkül der Donaumonarchie im 18. und 19. Jahrhundert* (Munich, 2007), 27–85.
15. On the Josephine reforms, see Roman Rosdolsky, *Untertan und Staat in Galizien: Die Reformen unter Maria Theresia und Joseph II*, ed. Ralph Melville (Mainz, 1992); Horst Glassl, *Das östereichische Einrichtungswerk in Galizien (1772–1790)* (Wiesbaden, 1975).
16. "Nędza Galicyjska" (Galician misery) was the title of an influential book, published in 1888, by the entrepreneur and politician Stanisław Szczepanowski.
17. Pollack, *Der Kaiser von Amerika*; Maner, *Galizien*. R. Mahler, "Jewish Emigration from Galicia," in Deborah Dash Moore, *East European Jews in Two Worlds: Studies from the YIVO Annual* (Evanston, 1990); Klaus Hödl, *Als Bettler in die Leopoldstadt: Galizische Juden auf dem Weg nach Wien* (Vienna, 1994).
18. Maner, *Galizien*.
19. A firmly postcolonial perspective is taken in the anthology by Johannes Feichtinger, Ursula Prutsch, and Moritz Csaky (eds), *Habsburg postcolonial: Machtstrukturen und kollektives Gedächtnis* (Innsbruck, 2003). See also Anna Veronika Wendland, "Imperiale, koloniale und postkoloniale Blicke auf die Peripherien des Habsburgerreiches," in Claudia Kraft and Alf Lüdtke (eds), *Kolonialgeschichten: Regionale Perspektiven auf ein globales Phänomen* (Frankfurt a. M., 2010), 215–235. Galicia's response to the oil boom in the late nineteenth century illustrated that local actors were not primarily concerned with promoting the economy but with pursuing political goals such as "autonomy" or the "development of the national community." Alison Fleig Frank, *Oil Empire: Visions of Prosperity in Austrian Galicia* (Cambridge, 2005); Klemens Kaps, "Peripherisierung der Ökonomie, Ethnisierung der Gesellschaft: Galizien zwischen äußerem und innerem Konkurrenzdruck (1856–1914)," in Doktoratskolleg (eds), *Galizien: Fragmente eines diskursiven Raums* (Innsbruck, 2009), 37–62; Slawomir Tokarski, *Ethnic Conflict and*

Economic Development: Jews in Galician Agriculture 1868–1914 (Warsaw, 2003); Michał Śliwa and Nędza Galicyjska, "Mit i rzeczywistość," in Włodzimierz Bonusiak and Józef Buszko (eds), *Galicja i jej Dziedzictwo*, vol. 1: *Historia i Polityka* (Rzeszów, 1994), 145–155.
20. Juliusz Łukasiewicz, *Kryzys agrarny na ziemiach polskich w końcu XIX wieku* (Warsaw, 1968), 220–233; Kai Struve, "Die Kapitalisierung der Landwirtschaft und die Durchsetzung der Industrialisierung als strukturbildende Faktoren in den Teilungsländern," in Michael G. Müller et al. (eds), *Polen in der europäischen Geschichte: Ein Handbuch*, vol. 3 (Stuttgart, 2019); Tomasz Kargol, "Wirtschaftliche Beziehungen zwischen Galizien und den Ländern der österreichisch-ungarischen Monarchie in der ersten Hälfte des 19. Jahrhunderts," in Augustynowicz and Kappeler, *Die galizische Grenze*, 33–50; Helena Madurowicz-Urbańska, "Die Industrie Galiziens im Rahmen der wirtschaftlichen Struktur der Donaumonarchie," *Studia Austro-Polonica* 1 (1978): 157–173; Stella Hryniuk, *Peasants with Promise: Ukrainians in South-Eastern Galicia 1880–1900* (Edmonton, 1991); Leslie Kool, *Economic Development on the Periphery: A Case Study of East Galicia* (Ann Arbor, 1994).
21. Adam Wandruszka and Peter Urbanitsch (eds), *Die Habsburgermonarchie 1848–1918*, vol. 1: *Die wirtschaftliche Entwicklung* (Vienna, 1973).
22. Christoph Freiherr Marschall von Bieberstein, *Freiheit in der Unfreiheit: Die nationale Autonomie der Polen in Galizien nach dem österreichisch-ungarischen Ausgleich von 1867; Ein konservativer Aufbruch im mitteleuropäischen Vergleich* (Wiesbaden, 1993); Rosdolsky, *Untertan und Staat*.
23. Józef Burszta, "Kultura chłopska a ruch ludowy 1895–1949," in Zygmunt Hemmerling (ed.), *Ruch ludowy w najnowszych dziejach Polski* (Warsaw, 1988), 201–237, 210.
24. Gershon David Hundert, "Jews in Poland-Lithuania in the Eighteenth Century: A Genealogy of Modernity" (Berkeley, 2004); idem (ed.), "Jews in Early Modern Poland," *Polin: Studies in Polish Jewry* 10 (1997); Saul Miller, *Life in Galician Shtetl, 1890–1907* (New York, 1980); Antony Polonsky, *The Jews in Poland and Russia*, vol. 2: *1881–1914* (Oxford, 2010); Piotr Wróbel, "The Jews of Galicia under Austrian-Polish Rule, 1869–1918," *Austrian History Yearbook* 25 (1994): 97–138. See also Heiko Haumann, *Geschichte der Ostjuden* (Munich, 1990).
25. Murray J. Rosman, *The Lord's Jews: Magnate-Jewish Relations in the Polish-Lithuanian Commonwealth during the Eighteenth Century* (Harvard, 1992); Hillel Levine, *Economic Origins of Antisemitism: Poland and Its Jews in the Early Modern Period* (New Haven, 1993).
26. Jews made up a distinctly larger percentage of the population in East Galicia (12 percent) than in West Galicia (8 percent). For information on Galician demographics, see Rudolf Mark, *Galizien unter österreichischer Herrschaft: Verwaltung-Kirche-Bevölkerung* (Marburg, 1994); Krzysztof Zamorski, *Ludność Galicji w latach 1857–1910* (Krakow, 1989). Some 90 percent of Galicians working in trade and hostelries were Jewish, and around 64 percent of those working in crafts. Cf. Jadwiga Hoff, "Stosunki wyznaniowe i struktura społeczno-zawodowa małego miasta galicyjskiego w dobie autonomii," in *Miasteczka Polskie: Z dziejów formowania się społeczności* (Kielce, 1992), 131–146, 140f. See also Józef Buzek, "Rozsiedlenie ludność Galicji według wyznania i języka," *Wiadomości statystyczne o stosunkach krajowych* 21, no. 2 (1909). On the Jewish inhabitants of the Carpathian foothills, see Andrzej Potocki, *Żydzi w Podkarpackiem* (Rzeszów, 2004).

27. For a brief survey of the emancipation of Jews in Galicia, see the following works: Małgorzata Śliż, *Galicyjscy Żydzi na drodze do równouprawienia 1848–1914* (Krakow, 2006), 15–21; Tomasz Gąsowski, *Między Galicyjscy gettem a światem: Dylematy ideowe Żydów galicyjskich na przełomie XIX i XX wieku* (Krakow, 1997), 9–29. On the situation in the Austrian empire in general, see Joseph Karniel, *Die Toleranzpolitik Kaiser Josephs II.* (Gerlingen, 1985); Kurt Schubert, "Der Einfluss des Josephinismus auf das Judentum in Österreich," *Kairos*, NF 14 (1972): 81–97; also Wolfgang Häusler, "Zwischen Wien und Czernowitz: Die Emanzipation des habsburgischen 'Ostjudentums' und der Antisemitismus," in Ralph Schattkowsky and Michael G. Müller (eds), *Identitätenwandel und nationale Mobilisierung in Regionen ethnischer Diversität: Ein regionaler Vergleich zwischen Westpreußen und Galizien am Ende des 19. und Anfang des 20. Jahrhunderts* (Marburg, 2004), 63–88. Jürgen Hensel, *Polnische Adelsnation und jüdische Vermittler, 1815–1830: Über den vergeblichen Versuch einer Judenemanzipation in einer nicht emanzipierten Gesellschaft* (Berlin, 1983), 71ff.; Teresa Andlauer, *Die jüdische Bevölkerung im Modernisierungsprozess Galiziens (1867–1914)* (Frankfurt a. M., 2001).
28. Kai Struve, *Bauern und Nation in Galizien: Über Zugehörigkeit und soziale Emanzipation im 19. Jahrhundert* (Göttingen, 2005).
29. John-Paul Himka, "Dimensions of a Triangle: Polish – Ukrainian – Jewish Relations in Austrian Galicia," *Polin: Studies in Polish Jewry* 12 (2000): 25–48: idem, "Ukrainian-Jewish Antagonism in the Galician Countryside during the Late Nineteenth Century," in Peter J. Potychnyi and Aster Howard (eds), *Ukrainian-Jewish Relations in Historical Perspective* (Edmonton, 1988), 111–158.
30. Ivan L. Rudnytsky, "The Ukrainians in Galicia under Austrian Rule," in Andrei S. Markovits and Frank E. Sysyn (eds), *Nationbuilding and the Politics of Nationalism: Essays on Austrian Galicia* (Cambridge, 1982), 23–67, 25.
31. Alexandra Binnenkade, Ekaterina Emeliantseva, and Svjatoslav Pacholkiv, *Vertraut und fremd zugleich, Jüdisch-christliche Nachbarschaften in Warschau-Lengnau-Lemberg* (Cologne, 2009), 15.
32. Heiko Haumann, "Juden in der ländlichen Gesellschaft Galiziens am Ende des 19. und zu Beginn des 20. Jahrhunderts," in Andrea Löw et al. (eds), *Deutsche – Juden – Polen: Geschichte einer wechselvollen Beziehung im 20. Jahrhundert* (Frankfurt a. M., 2004), 35–58. Philipp Ther has also underlined the long periods of peaceful coexistence in between conflicts: Philipp Ther, "War versus Peace: Interethnic Relations in Lviv during the First Half of the Twentieth Century," in John Czaplicka (ed.), *Lviv: A City in the Crosscurrents of Culture* (Cambridge, 2000), 251–284.
33. Rosa Lehmann, *Symbiosis and Ambivalence: Poles and Jews in a Small Galician Town* (New York, 2001).
34. Till van Rahden coined the term "situational ethnicity" to describe the urban bourgeois context of Jews in Breslau, which is useful for understanding Christian-Jewish coexistence in general. Cf. Till van Rahden, "Intermarriages, the 'New Woman,' and the Situational Ethnicity of Breslau Jews from the 1870s to the 1920s," *Leo Baeck Institute Year Book* 46, no. 1 (2001): 125–150; also idem, *Juden und andere Breslauer: Die Beziehungen zwischen Juden, Protestanten und Katholiken in einer deutschen Großstadt von 1860 bis 1925* (Göttingen, 2000).
35. Arnon Gill, *Die polnische Revolution von 1846: Zwischen nationalem Befreiungskampf des Landadels und antifeudaler Bauernerhebung* (Munich, 1974).

36. Inspired by the French Revolution, Tadeusz Kościuszko and his fellow campaigner Hugo Kołłątaj staged a *levée en masse*, having first improved the situation of the peasants with the "Universal" of 1793, and successfully deployed armed peasant units against the tsarist army. See Franciszek Ziejka, *Złota legenda chłopów* (Krakow, 1983).
37. Bieberstein, *Freiheit in der Unfreiheit*; Rosdolsky, *Untertan und Staat*.
38. Some Galician hostelry owners, most of whom were Jews, tried to undermine support for the abstinence campaign, which often used anti-Jewish rhetoric, by portraying it to their Catholic clientele as part of the nobility's strategy to torpedo state efforts to redistribute land. Jan Kracik, *W Galicji trzeźwiejącej, krwawej, pobożnej* (Krakow, 2008), 28–50.
39. Michal Chvojka, "Zwischen Konspiration und Revolution: Entstehung und Auswirkungen der Revolution von 1846 in Krakau und Galizien – Wahrnehmung und Aktionsradius der Habsburger Polizei," *Jahrbücher für Geschichte Osteuropas* 58 (2010): 481–507.
40. The district captain of Tarnów, Josef Breinl, was said to give especially generous rewards to supportive peasants. The uprising was known as *Rabacja* in Polish, a term originating from the German *Rabatz* (English: ruckus) or *Raub* (robbery). Cf. Andrzej Chwalba, *Historia Polski 1795–1918* (Krakow, 2001), 302.
41. Cf. Stefan Kieniewicz, *Ruch chłopski w Galicji w 1846 roku* (Wrocław, 1955), 300. The uprising and the subsequent punitive expeditions were followed by a famine attended by outbreaks of cannibalism, typhoid fever, and cholera. Robert F. Leslie, *The History of Poland since 1863* (Cambridge, 1980), 8. See also Thomas W. Simmons, "The Peasant Revolt of 1846 in Galicia," *Slavic Review* (1971): 795–817.
42. It was said that on 22 February in Tarnów Cathedral a peasant had declared, "The Emperor has decreed, our holy Father allows [us to kill the nobles]." Cited from Kracik, *W Galicji*, 48.
43. A painting by Jan Lewicki titled "The Galician Slaughter" rooted this image in the public consciousness. An interesting source on the uprising is Stefan Dembiński, *Rok 1846: Kronika dworów szlachekich zebrana na pięćdziesięcioletnią rocznicę smutnych wypadków lutego* [The year 1846. A chronicle of the noble seats, compiled to mark the fiftieth anniversary of the sad events in February] (Jasło, 1896).
44. "It is true that the peasants murdered! They murdered because they had been ordered to do so, because they had been encouraged to do so! . . . The peasants did not murder to gain revenge but to fulfil a devious plan, which is proven by the fact that all the slaughter took place at the same time within a few days, when the order was spread across the country by the servants of the system." Dembiński, *Rok 1846*, 39f.
45. A song popular among Galician peasants until World War II went "Do you remember, Sir, the year forty-six? How the peasants drove you away with sticks?" (Pamiętoś ty Panie rok śtyrdziesty szósty, Jak cię chłopy biły kijami w zapusty?). Leslie, *The History of Poland*, 8.
46. On the relationship between the nobility and peasantry in nineteenth-century Poland, see Struve, *Bauern und Nation*; also Jan Molenda, *Chłopi – naród – niepodległość: Kształtowanie się postaw narodowych i obywatelskich chłopów w Galicji i Królestwie Polskim w przedniu odrodzenia Polski* (Warsaw, 1999).
47. Struve, *Bauern und Nation*, 85ff.
48. Stefan Kieniewicz, *Pomiędzy Stadionem a Goslarem: Sprawa włościańska w Galicji 1848 r.* (Warsaw, 1980).
49. Many landowners obstructed the Habsburgs' agrarian reforms so that in some places they were implemented only very hesitantly or after long delays. Cf. Augustynowicz, *Geschichte*

Ostmitteleuropas, 68. On the myth of the good emperor, see Zbigniwe Fras, "Mit dobrego cesarza," in Wojciech Wrzesiński (ed.), *Polskie mity polityczne XIX i XX wieku* (Wrocław, 1994), 139–152; also John-Paul Himka, "Hope in the Tsar: Displaced Naïve Monarchism among the Ukrainian Peasants of the Habsburg Empire," *Russian History/Histoire Russe* 7, no. 1–2 (1980): 125–138.

50. Hillel Levine, "Gentry; Jews, and Serfs: The Rise of Polish Vodka," *Review: A Journal of the Fernand Braudel Center for the Study of Economies* 4, no. 2 (1980): 223–250.
51. On East Galicia, see Himka, *Galician Villagers*, 36–56; Jan Kozik, *Między reakcyją a rewolucją: Studia z dziejów ukraińskiego ruchu narodowego w Galicji w latach 1848–1849* (Krakow, 1975). On West Galicia, see Struve, *Bauern und Nation*, 109ff.
52. Stefan Inglot, *Historia spoleczno-gospodarcza chłopów polskich* (Warsaw, 1970), 246.
53. Himka, *Galician Villagers*, 158ff.; idem, "Ukrainian-Jewish Antagonism"; Tokarski, *Ethnic Conflict*, 69 and 102.
54. Maner, *Galizien*, 99ff. For further reading on Bukovina, see Emanuel Turczynski, *Geschichte der Bukowina in der Neuzeit: Zur Sozial- und Kulturgeschichte einer mitteleuropäisch geprägten Landschaft* (Wiesbaden, 1993).
55. Galicia's two high courts were also located in Krakow and Lemberg, as were two of the three Galician chambers of commerce; the third was in the merchant town Brody. Tomasz Kargol, *Izba Przemysłowo-Handlowa w Krakowie w latach 1850–1939* (Krakow, 2003).
56. Maner, *Galizien*, 99–105.
57. Stella Hryniuk, "Polish Lords and Ukrainian Peasants: Conflict, Deference, and Accommodation in Eastern Galicia in the Late Nineteenth Century," *Austrian History Yearbook* 24 (1993): 119–132.
58. On the various national options for Galicia's Ruthenians, see John-Paul Himka, "The Construction of Nationality in Galician Rus': Icarian Flights in Almost All Directions," in Ronald Grigor Suny and Michael D. Kennedy (eds), *Intellectuals and the Articulation of the Nation* (Ann Arbor, 1999), 109–164; Anna Veronika Wendland, *Die Russophilen in Galizien: Ukrainische Konservative zwischen Österreich und Russland 1848–1915* (Vienna, 2001); idem, "Die Rückkehr der Russophilen in die ukrainische Geschichte: Neue Aspekte der ukrainischen Nationsbildung in Galizien, 1848–1914," *Jahrbuch für die Geschichte Osteuropas* 49, no. 2 (2001): 178–199. On Ukrainian national awakening in Galicia, see Jan Kozik, *The Ukrainian National Movement in Galicia 1815–1849* (Edmonton, 1986).
59. Christopher Hann and Paul R. Magocsi, *Galicia: A Multicultured Land* (Toronto, 2005).
60. Religion is nonetheless frequently used as an identifier rather than national attributions, even when referring to nationalism's heyday, as religious affiliation is unambiguous in a way that vernacular language and nationality are not. Indeed, the imperial states based their population statistics on declarations of religion. Nationality, insofar as it is not stated in a passport or similar document, is entirely subjective. Many Roman Catholic peasants in Galicia objected to being called Poles as they did not want to be associated with the nobility, whom they saw as Polish. Similarly, Russophile supporters would have objected to being called Ukrainians. Cf. Harald Binder, *Galizien in Wien: Parteien, Wahlen, Fraktionen und Abgeordnete im Übergang zur Massenpolitik* (Vienna, 2005), 14. Certainly, a study of antisemitism in Galicia must distinguish between the categories Jewish and Christian (or non-Jewish), rather than Polish and Ukrainian, unless the latter arise in self-ascriptions.
61. Jerzy Holzer, "Zur Frage der Akkulturation der Juden in Galizien im 19. Und 20. Jahrhundert," *Jahrbücher für Geschichte Osteuropas* 37 (1989): 35–59. *Akkulturation* (En-

glish: acculturation) has today superseded the problematic term assimilation, though the latter cannot be avoided as it is ubiquitous in the sources. Cf. on Polish Jewry: Theodore R. Weeks, "Assimilation, Nationalism, Modernization, Antisemitism: Notes on Polish-Jewish Relations, 1855–1905," in Robert Blobaum (ed.), *Antisemitism and Its Opponents in Modern Poland* (Ithaca, 2005), 20–38. On the debate surrounding the concept of assimilation among German-speaking Jews, see Till van Rahden, "Treason, Fate, or Blessing? Concepts of Assimilation in the Historiography of German-Speaking Jewry since the 1950s," in Christhard Hoffmann (ed.), *Preserving the Legacy of German Jewry: A History of the Leo Baeck Institute, 1955–2005* (Tübingen, 2005), 349–373.

62. The frequency of marriages between Ukrainians and Poles shows that the boundaries between the groups became more fluid at the same time. Ihor Kosyk, "To Marry the Other: Zur Geschichte der gemischten Ehen in Galizien und Lemberg in der zweiten Hälfte des 19. Jahrhunderts," in Doktoratskolleg, *Galizien*, 99–112.

63. Pieter Judson, *Guardians of the Nation: Activists on the Language Frontiers of Imperial Austria* (Cambridge, 2006).

64. Historic nations are understood here in Herder's sense as nations with a history of independent statehood, while unhistoric nations were those that could not claim to have any statehood or aristocracy. Among the latter were Slovenians, Slovakians, Ukrainians, Belarus, Estonians, Latvians, and Finns.

65. In the debate surrounding a German constitution, East Central Europe was conceived of as the German "frontier." Cf. Gregor Thum, *Traumland Osten*. See also the introduction in Martin Schulze-Wessel, *Russlands Blick auf Preußen: Die polnische Frage in der Diplomatie und politischen Öffentlichkeit des Zarenreiches und des Sowjetstaates 1697–1947* (Stuttgart, 1995). When it came to inviting delegates to the parliament in St. Paul's Church, it became apparent that the Bohemian lands no longer wished to be regarded as "German lands." Jiří Kořalka, *František Palacký (1798–1876): der Historiker der Tschechen im österreichischen Vielvölkerstaat* (Vienna, 2007).

66. Augustynowicz, *Geschichte Ostmitteleuropas*, 101.

67. The German population in Galicia shrank considerably around 1900. In 1880, 323,612 people described themselves as German (5.4 percent); ten years later, the number had fallen to 227,158 or 3.5 percent, by 1900 to 2.9 percent, and in 1910 only 90,416 people saw themselves as German, or 1.1 percent. Cf. Franz Stefczyk, *Polen und Ruthenen in Galizien im Lichte der Bevölkerungs- und Steuerstatistik* (Lemberg, 1912), 9. This trend can probably be attributed to a growing sense among Galician Jews of belonging to the Polish nation.

68. The best-known exponents were writers such as Leopold Herzberg-Fränkel and Karl-Emil Franzos. Gabriele von Glasenapp, *Aus der Judengasse: Zur Entstehung und Ausprägung deutschsprachiger Ghettoliteratur im 19. Jahrhundert* (Tübingen, 1996).

69. Cf. Victor Karady, *Gewalterfahrung und Utopie: Juden in der europäischen Moderne* (Frankfurt a. M., 1999). The choice of language a country used in administration and education was crucially important. Beyond Austria's hereditary lands, the crownlands of the Habsburg Empire opted less and less for German. Peter Karoshi, "Patriotismus und Staatserhalt. Konstruktionen 'österreichischer Gesamtstaatsideen,'" *Newsletter Moderne: Zeitschrift des SFB Moderne*, special issue 2 (March 2003): 12–16.

70. Heiko Haumann, *"Luftmenschen" und "rebellische Töchter": Zum Wandel ostjüdischer Lebenswelten im 19. Jahrhundert* (Cologne, 2003).

71. Recurring stereotypes were the "trouser-selling lads" from the "Polish cradle," popularized by Treitschke, and the poor and sickly "Galitsians" living in the Leopoldtstadt district of

Vienna. Ulrich Wyrwa, "Genese und Entfaltung antisemitischer Motive in Heinrich von Treitschkes *Deutscher Geschichte im 19. Jahrhundert*," in Werner Bergmann and Ulrich Sieg (eds), *Antisemitische Geschichtsbilder* (Essen, 2009), 83–101; Hödl, *Als Bettler in die Leopoldstadt*.
72. Steven Beller, *Antisemitism: A Very Short Introduction* (New York, 2007).
73. Foreign policy, along with the army and navy and related finances, were the only areas controlled by imperial ministries responsible for both states. A Council of Ministers from both governments, led by the foreign minister, ruled on joint affairs. After 1878, this Council of Ministers also governed Bosnia, which did not belong either to the Transleithanian or Cisleithanian half of the empire.
74. Joachim von Puttkamer, "Ungarn," in Harald Roth (ed.), *Studienhandbuch Östliches Europa*, vol. 1: *Geschichte Ostmittel- und Südosteuropas* (Cologne, 1999), 411–430, 420.
75. Pieter Judson, *Exclusive Revolutionaries: Liberal Politics, Social Experience, and National Identity in the Austrian Empire 1848–1914* (Ann Arbor, 1996).
76. Peter Haslinger (ed.), *Die Grenze im Kopf: Beiträge zur Geschichte der Grenze in Ostmitteleuropa* (Frankfurt a. M., 1999); idem and Daniel Mollenhauer (eds), "Arbeit am nationalen Raum. Deutsche und polnische Rand- und Grenzregionen im Nationalisierungsprozess," *Comparativ* 15 (2005): 2.
77. Marsha Rozenblit, *Reconstructing a National Identity: The Jews of Habsburg Austria during World War I* (Oxford, 2001).
78. Julia Schmid, *Kampf um das Deutschtum: Radikaler Nationalismus in Österreich und dem Deutschen Reich 1890–1914* (Frankfurt a. M., 2009); Robert Kriechbaumer, "Das Trauma der unmystischen Wirklichkeit. Die Sehnsucht nach der imaginierten deutschen Heimat," in idem, *Die großen Erzählungen der Politik: Politische Kultur und Parteien in Österreich von der Jahrhundertwende bis 1945* (Cologne, 2001), 160–165.
79. Robert Musil's famous description of the Habsburg Empire as a land without a name was based on the fact that the western half of the empire did not have its own name until 1915. The imperial council met in Vienna and consisted of two chambers, a parliament and an upper house.
80. Consequently, when universal suffrage was introduced in 1905, Galicia sent the most representatives (sixty-three) to the imperial parliament. Both in view of its purported historical link with the Hungarian crown and its location beyond the Leitha, Galicia would more logically have belonged to the Hungarian half of the empire.
81. The minor compromise was concluded in 1873. Binder, *Galizien in Wien*, 39, also for further reading.
82. The pledge of allegiance, "Bei Euch Majestät stehen wir und wollen wir stehen" (By you, Your Majesty, we stand and wish to stand), became a popular saying. Cf. Stanisław Pijaj, *Między polskim patriotyzmem a habsburskim loyalizmem: Polacy wobec przemian ustrojowych monarchii habsburskiej (1866–1871)* (Krakow, 2003). Catholicism became an important legitimizing factor and a bridge between Polish-Galician conservatism and the Habsburg dynasty, as impressively demonstrated at the bicentenary celebration of the Relief of Vienna in Krakow: Harald Binder, "Kirche und nationale Festkultur in Krakau 1861 bis 1910," in Martin Schulze-Wessel (ed.), *Nationalisierung der Religion und Sakralisierung der Nation in Ostmittel-, Südost- und Osteuropa im 19. Und 20. Jahrhundert* (Stuttgart, 2006); Philip Pajakowski, "The Polish Club and Austrian Parliamentary Politics, 1873–1900," PhD diss., Indiana University, 1989; For an overview of the relevant literature, see Claudia Kraft, "Das galizische Bürgertum in der autonomen Ära (1867–1914).

Ein Literaturüberblick," in Peter Heumos (ed.), *Polen und die böhmischen Länder im 19. und 20. Jahrhundert* (Munich, 1997), 81–110.

83. Jan Fellerer, *Mehrsprachigkeit im galizischen Verwaltungswesen (1772–1914): Eine historisch-soziolinguistische Studie zum Polnischen und Ruthenischen (Ukrainischen)* (Cologne, 2005).

84. Albert Lichtblau and Michael John, "Jewries in Galicia and Bukovina, in Lemberg and Czernowitz: Two Divergent Examples of Jewish Communities in the Far East of the Austro-Hungarian Monarchy," in Sander Gilman and Milton Shain (eds), *Jewries at the Frontier: Accommodation, Identity, Conflict* (Urbana, 1999), 29–66; Heiko Haumann, "Jüdische Nation – Polnische Nation? Zur gesellschaftlichen Orientierung von Juden in Polen während des 19. Jahrhunderts," in Gabriella Gelardini (ed.), *Kontexte der Schrift*, vol. 1: *Text, Ethik, Judentum und Christentum, Gesellschaft* (Stuttgart, 2005), 442–457.

85. Hanna Kozińska-Witt, *Die Krakauer Jüdische Reformgemeinde 1864–1874* (Frankfurt a. M., 1999); Andrzej Żbikowski, Żydzi krakowscy i ich gmina 1868–1918 (Warsaw, 1994), 77–109. On the conflicts surrounding the Haskalah and use of the German language in sermons in Lemberg in the 1840s, see Michael Stanislawski, *A Murder in Lemberg: Politics, Religion, and Violence in Modern Jewish History* (Princeton, 2007).

86. On Lemberg, see Markian Prokopovych, *Habsburg Lemberg: Architecture, Public Space, and Politics in the Galician Capital, 1772–1914* (West Lafayette, IN, 2009); "Forum: A City of Many Names: Lemberg/Lwów/L'viv/L'vov – Nationalizing in an Urban Context," *Austrian History Yearbook* 34 (2003): 57–109; John Czaplicka (ed.), *Lviv: A City in the Crossroads of Culture*, Harvard Series in Ukrainian Studies (Cambridge, MA: 2000), 1 and 4. On Galicia's urban dualism (Lemberg/Krakow), see Harald Binder, "Politische Öffentlichkeit in Galizien: Lemberg und Krakau im Vergleich," in Andreas R. Hofmann (ed.), *Stadt und Öffentlichkeit in Ostmitteleuropa: 1900–1939. Beiträge zur Entstehung moderner Urbanität zwischen Berlin, Charkiv, Tallinn und Triest* (Stuttgart, 2002), 259–280. On Krakow, see Simon Hadler, "Von sprechenden Steinen. Die Mythologisierung des urbanen Raumes in Krakau," in Doktoratskolleg, *Galizien*, 159–170; Orton D. Lawrence, "The Formation of Modern Cracow (1866–1914)," *Austrian History Yearbook* 17 and 18 (1983/1984): 101–115; Larry Wolff, "Dynastic Conservatism and Poetic Violence in Fin-de-siècle Cracow: The Habsburg Matrix of Polish Modernism," *American Historical Review* 106 (June 2001): 3, 735–764; Patrice M. Dabrowski, "Cracow and Warsaw," in Emily Gunzburger Makaš and Tanja Damljanović Conley (eds), *Capital Cities in the Aftermath of Empires: Planning in Central and Southeastern Europe* (London, 2010). At the same time as being a Polish pantheon, Krakow also underwent a drastic transformation and modernization, as Nathaniel Wood has recently reconstructed in idem, *Becoming Metropolitan: Urban Selfhood and the Making of Modern Cracow* (De Kalb, 2010).

87. Markovits, "Introduction: Empire and Province," in idem and Sysyn, *Nationbuilding*, 1–22.

88. Those in power in Galicia were not so much a party as a lobby for the leading families in the land, who frequently used state institutions to block opposition. "Galician elections" became a synonym in the empire for electoral fraud. These families' representatives in government offices worked to suppress not only the Ukrainian political movements but also the Polish Peasant Parties and the Socialists. Census suffrage secured their majority in the Galician parliament, but with each stage in the extension of suffrage, in 1882, 1896, and 1906, the opposition grew stronger.

89. Alexey Miller, "Galicia after the Ausgleich: Polish-Ruthenian Conflict and the Attempts of Reconciliation," *Central European University History Department Yearbook 1993*, 135–143; Harald Binder, "Die Wahlreform von 1907 und der polnisch-ruthenische Konflikt in Ostgalizen," *Österreichische Osthefte* 40, no. 3 (1996): 293–320; Kerstin S. Jobst, "Ein politischer Mord in der Habsburgermonarchie: Das Potocki-Attentat von 1908 – Ein Kulminationspunkt der galizischen Krise?," *Österreichische Osthefte* 41 (1999): 25–45; Klaus Bachmann, *"Ein Herd der Feindschaft gegen Russland": Galizien als Krisenherd in den Beziehungen der Donaumonarchie mit Rußland (1907–1904)* (Vienna, 2001).

90. Józef Buszko, *Galicja 1859–1914, Polski Piemont?* (Warsaw, 1989); Paul Robert Magocsi, *The Roots of Ukrainian Nationalism: Galicia as Ukraine's Piedmont* (Toronto, 2002). In the German-speaking lands, a melancholy memory of Galicia and Bukovina is cultivated, based primarily on literary works such as those of Joseph Roth. Verena Dohrn, *Reise nach Galizien: Grenzlandschaften des alten Europa* (Berlin, 2000); Martin Pollack, *Galizien: Eine Reise durch die verschwundene Welt Ostgaliziens und der Bukowina* (Frankfurt a. M., 2001).

91. The lowest administrative unit was a district, of which there were seventy-four, governed by district captains. Parishes were self-governing under local chiefs or mayors (Polish: *wójt*). They formed parish councils which were led by a parish president. Urszula Jakubowska, "Galicja na progu XX wieku," in idem (ed.), *Galicyjskie spotkania* (Kalisz, 2004), 10.

92. Eduard Graf Taafe (1833–1895); this coalition was also known as the "Iron Ring." Cf. Ulrich E. Zellenberg, "Ein Konservativer über den Parteien – der 'Kaiserminister' Eduard Graf Taafe," in idem (ed.), *Konservative Profile: Ideen und Praxis in der Politik zwischen FM Radetzky, Karl Kraus und Alois Mock* (Graz, 2003), 225–243.

93. Transferal to Galicia was used as a punishment in the military, although other places had even worse reputations, such as Bosnia. Cf. Johann Christoph Allmayer-Beck, "Die bewaffnete Macht in Staat und Gesellschaft," in Adam Wandruszka and Peter Urbanitsch (eds), *Die Habsburgermonarchie 1848–1918*, vol. 5: *Die bewaffnete Macht* (Vienna, 1987), 110.

94. Maner, *Galizien*, 149–157. The Viennese public's perception of the Polish nobility controlling Galicia changed accordingly. For a wealth of material on this point, see the study by Marcin Siadkowski: *Szlachcicen: Przemian stereotypu polskiej szlachty w Wiedniu na przełomie XIX i XX wieku* (Warsaw, 2011).

95. Waldemar Łazuga, *"Rządy polskie" w Austrii: Gabinet Kazimierza hr. Badeniego 1895–1897* (Poznań, 1991); Binder, *Galizien in Wien*, 352.

96. The term "autonomy" is problematic since it de facto applied only to the Poles. Other groups in Galicia did not experience self-determination but merely a shift in predominance from German culture to Polish, and from centralist politics to nationalist politics. Cf. Harald Binder, "'Galizische Autonomie.' Ein streitbarer Begriff und seine Karriere," in Lukás Fasora (ed.), *Moravské vyrovnání z roku 1905/Der Mährische Ausgleich von 1905* (Brno, 2006).

97. The accompanying debate in the Galician diet is described in chapter 1 of the present book. See also Małgorzata Śliż, *Galicyjscy Żydzi na drodze do równouprawienia 1848–1914* (Krakow, 2006); Tomasz Gąsowski, *Między gettem a światem: Dylematy ideowe Żydów galicyjskich na przełomie XIX i XX wieku* (Krakow, 1997), 9–29.

98. Richard L. Rudolph, "The East European Peasant Household and the Beginnings of Industry: East Galicia 1786–1914," in Ivan S. Korporeckyi (ed.), *Ukrainian Economic History: Interpretative Essays* (Cambridge, 1991), 339–382.

99. The only reliable statistics available are on purchases of estate land by Jews, which rose from 0 percent in 1867 to 16 percent in 1912. Cf. Tomasz Gąsowski, "From Austeria to the Manor: Jewish Landowners in Autonomous Galicia," *Polin: Studies in Polish Jewry* 12 (1999): 120–136; Teresa Andlauer, *Die jüdische Bevölkerung im Modernisierungsprozess Galiziens (1867–1914)* (Frankfurt a. M., 2001), 135–141. On the question of rural Jewish holdings, see also Haumann, "Juden in der ländlichen Gesellschaft Galiziens," 35–58.
100. *Reichsgesetzblatt für die im Reichsrathe vertretenen Königreiche und Länder* 47 (1881): 161ff.
101. Kai Struve, "Peasant Emancipation and National Integration: Agrarian Circles, Village Reading Rooms, and Cooperatives in Galicia," in Torsten Lorenz, *Cooperatives in Ethnic Conflicts: Eastern Europe in the 19th and Early 20th Century* (Berlin, 2006), 229–249.
102. An important center was the old capital of the Polish-Lithuanian commonwealth and metropolis of the west of the Tsarist empire, Warsaw. The school of thought was therefore labeled "Warsaw positivism."
103. After the January Uprising was quashed, the Kingdom of Poland in the Vistula Land (*Privislinsky Krai*) was renamed. Theodore R. Weeks, *Nation and State in Late Imperial Russia: Nationalism and Russification on the Western Frontier, 1863–1914* (DeKalb, 1996).
104. Gary Cohen, "Nationalist Politics and the Dynamics of State and Civil Society in the Habsburg Monarchy, 1867–1914," *Central European History* 40 (2007).
105. This was, of course, preconditioned upon improvements in school education, ensuring that more people gained literacy. Andrzej Meissner (ed.), *Chłopi – Naród – Kultura*, vol. 4: *Kultura i oświata wsi* (Rzeszów, 1996); Jerzy Potoczny, "Oświata dorosłych i popularizacja wiedzy w plebejskich środowiskach Galicji doby konstytucyjnej (1867–1918)," in *Galicja i jej dzedzictwo*, vol. 10 (Rzeszów, 1998).
106. Contemporaries did not consider it paradoxical to categorize everyone in clearly defined and distinct communities within the nation even though such membership was purportedly natural and objective. In a nationalist view, the knowledge and insight that the (simple) people lacked needed to be compensated for by the elites. In the multiethnic regions of the Central European empires, competition arose between activists who tried to gain influence over people's votes by any means possible. Peter Thaler, "Fluid Identities in Central European Borderlands," *European History Quarterly* 31 (2001): 4.
107. Recently, the conflict between the activists' nationalist concept of objective exclusive national belonging and the electoral majority's indifference, in view of the prevalent multilingualism and non-nationally encoded life-worlds, has come to be regarded as an important motor of nationalist agitation, not to be equated with an expression of national patterns of perception. Cf. Judson, *Guardians of the Nation*; Tara Zahra, *Kidnapped Souls: National Indifference and the Battle for Children in the Bohemian Lands 1900–1948* (Ithaca, 2008); Jonathan Kwan, "Review Article: Nationalism and All That: Reassessing the Habsburg Monarchy and Its Legacy," *European History Quarterly* 41 (2011): 88–108.
108. The idea of democracy continued the concept of a fundamentally Polish-national, democratic mode of communitization as discussed in the lost Aristocratic Republic's "free early community" and during the European wars of liberation, supported by Polish fighters. Among Democrats, "liberalism" was perhaps viewed positively for its economic policy or support of secular government but not as a political principle in general. Cf. Binder, *Galizien in Wien*, 34ff.; Maciej Janowski, *Polish Liberal Thought before 1918* (Budapest,

2004); Zbigniew Fras, "Die liberale Strömung unter den galizischen Demokraten 1848–1882," in Hans-Georg Fleck and Ryszard Kołodzieczyk (eds), *Liberale Traditionen in Polen* (Warsaw, 1994), 143–158.

109. Kasimir Felix Badeni (1846–1909) was governor of Galicia from 1888 to 1895 before becoming minister president.

110. Dabrowski, *Commemorations and the Shaping of Modern Poland* (Bloomington, 2004); Stanisław Dąbrowski, *Chłopi, naród, kultura*, part 2: *Działność polityczna ruchu ludowego* (Rzeszów, 1996). The Ukrainian national movement inevitably focused on Christendom as Ruthenia, or Ukraine, had no aristocratic, bourgeois, or even Jewish traditions. The intelligentsia was primarily made up of members of the clergy until the mid-nineteenth century, before a secular view of the world evolved with national aspirations. Svjatoslav Pacholkiv, *Emanzipation durch Bildung: Entwicklung und gesellschaftliche Rolle der ukrainischen Intelligenz im habsburgischen Galizien, 1890–1914* (Vienna, 2002).

111. John-Paul Himka, *Galician Villagers and the Ukrainian National Movement in the Nineteenth Century* (London, 1988); Józef Buszko, "Die politischen und sozialen Bewegungen der polnischen Bauern in Galizien am Ende des 19. Und zu Beginn des 20. Jahrhunderts," in Karlheinz Mach (ed.), *Galizien um die Jahrhundertwende: Politische, soziale und kulturelle Verbindungen mit Österreich* (Vienna, 1990), 51–68.

112. Paul Robert Magocsi, "The Kachkovs'kyi Society and the National Revival in Nineteenth-Century East Galicia," *Harvard Ukrainian Studies* 15, no. 1/2 (1991): 48–75.

113. Tim Buchen, "Die Sprache der 'Christliche – Volkspartei' Westgaliziens und die Bauernunruhen von 1898," master's thesis, Humboldt University, Berlin, 2006.

114. This has been done for Polish peasants by Keely Stauter-Halsted, *The Nation in the Village: The Genesis of Peasant National Identity in Austrian Poland 1848–1914* (Ithaca, 2002); and as a comparative study of Ruthenians and Poles: Kai Struve, *Bauern und Nation in Galizien: Über Zugehörigkeit und soziale Emanzipation im 19. Jahrhundert* (Göttingen, 2005).

115. Jan Molenda claims that the national moment did not become central to the peasant movement until during World War I. Molenda, *Chłopi*. In my master's thesis, I argue against classifying the peasant movements as genuinely national movements: Buchen, "Die Sprache der 'Christliche – Volkspartei.'"

116. In 1900, 88 percent of Galicians occupied in the trade of goods were "of the Mosaic faith." Cf. Ignacy Schiper, *Dzieje handlu żydowskiego na ziemiach polskich* (Warsaw, 1937).

117. According to Klaus Bachmann, "Antisemitismus," in Andreas Lawaty and Hubert Orłowski (eds), *Deutsche und Polen: Geschichte-Kultur-Politik* (Munich, 2003), 439–450. See also Stanislav Andreski, "An Economic Interpretation of Antisemitism in Eastern Europe," *Jewish Journal of Sociology* 5 (1969): 209.

118. Alexey Miller, "Do charakterystyki wsi pouwłaszczeniowej w latach siedemdziesiątych XIX wieku. Panika galicyjska 1872 roku," *Przegląd Historyczny* 79 (1988): 103–107, 105.

119. In the Lemberg archives, however, only one peasant is on record as giving the emperor's invitation as his reason for traveling without a ticket. Miller, " Do charakterystyki," 105.

120. Cf. chapter 1. As talk of the *pany* getting revenge for the "ruckus" by reintroducing serfdom circulated, some peasants went to church armed, and many nobles sought shelter in the cities. Overall, however, the Easter holidays proceeded peacefully. Struve, *Bauern und Nation*, 112.

121. In Rzepienik-Strzyżewski, three people were arrested who had mentioned the warrant. In Zakliczyn, the military intervened to prevent the panic escalating, and gossipmongers in several places were arrested. Philip Pajakowski, "Dynamics of Galician Polish Conservatism in the Late Nineteenth Century," *Jahrbücher für Geschichte Osteuropas*, NF 43 (1995): 19–33, 25. The repercussions of such rumors and the tendency of anti-Jewish riots to fall on Christian feast days are also illustrated by the notorious case of the Warsaw Christmas unrest in 1881. These disturbances followed a panic in the Church of the Holy Cross which was allegedly precipitated by Jews and resulted in fatalities. Chief of Police Buturlin was rumored to have responded by permitting Christians to rob Jews until 6:00 p.m. on Christmas Day or, according to other rumors, for a period of seven days. As the police did nothing to prevent lootings, and sometimes even participated in them, the rumors seemed to be true. Golczewski, *Beziehungen*, 42.
122. Peter Stachel, "Ein Staat, der an einem Sprachfehler zugrunde ging: Die 'Vielsprachigkeit' des Habsburgerreiches und ihre Auswirkungen," in Johannes Feichtinger and Peter Stachel (eds), *Das Gewebe der Kultur: Kulturwissenschaftliche Analysen zur Geschichte und Identität Österreichs in der Moderne* (Innsbruck, 2001), 11-45.
123. See now Daniel Unowsky, *The Plunder: The 1898 Anti-Jewish Riots in Habsburg Galicia* (Stanford, 2018). For a detailed discussion on the literature on antisemitism and Jewish-Christian relations in Galicia, see Tim Buchen, *Antisemitismus in Galizien: Agitation, Gewalt und Politik gegen Juden in der Habsburgermonarchie um 1900* (Berlin, 2012), 48–52.
124. Joanna Michlic, *Poland's Threatening Other: The Image of the Jew from 1880 to the Present* (Lincoln, 2006). The communicative dimension of antisemitism is discussed in greater depth in the following section.
125. One could say that antisemitism was both a vocabulary of the academic language of observers and a source term used by protagonists as well as critics, who each associated it with different concepts.
126. See the outstanding study by David Nirenberg, *Communities of Violence: Persecution of Minorities in the Middle Ages* (Princeton, 1996).
127. Some studies on Germany show cases of local populations offering considerable resistance to Jewish equality in order to conserve tradition. James Harris, *The People Speak!: Anti-Semitism and Emancipation in Nineteenth Century Bavaria* (Ann Arbor, 1994); Rainer Erb and Werner Bergmann, *Die Nachtseite der Judenemanzipation: Der Widerstand gegen die Integration der Juden in Deutschland 1780–1860* (Berlin, 1989).
128. Jacob Katz, *Vom Vorurteil bis zur Vernichtung: Der Antisemitismus 1700–1933* (Munich, 1989), 9; on the concept of the rules of sayability and their connection to actions, see Willibald Steinmetz, *Das Sagbare and das Machbare: Zum Wandel politischer Handlungsspielräume: England 1780–1867* (Stuttgart, 1993).
129. Othering often worked by portraying antisemitism as German or Prussian, making it automatically a phenomenon of the others within the political commonwealth that had fought wars against Prussia. See the articles on Denmark and Poland in Christoph Wyrwa, *Einspruch und Abwehr: Die Reaktion des europäischen Judentums auf die Entstehung des Antisemitismus (1879–1914)* (Frankfurt a. M., 2010): Christoph Leiska, "'Das Geschrei des Herrn von Germanenstolz': Dänisch-jüdische Intellektuelle und der moderne Antisemitismus im deutschen Kaiserreich," 114–130; and Maciej Moszyński, "Die 'Hydra von der Spree': Die Warschauer Zeitschrift *Izraelita* und die Anfänge des modernen Antisemitismus im Deutschen Kaiserreich," 299–312.

130. I owe thanks to Daniel Unowsky for the idea of transposing the model of process-oriented nationalism research on to an analysis of antisemitism. See Rogers Brubaker, "Rethinking Nationhood: Nation as Institutionalized Form, Practical Category, Contingent Event," *Contention* 4, no. 1 (Fall 1994): 3–14; idem, "Ethnicity, Race, and Nationalism," *Annual Review of Sociology* 35 (1009): 21–42; idem, *Myths and Misconceptions in the Study of Nationalism* (Cambridge, 1998), 272–306; idem, *Nationalism Refrained: Nationhood and the National Question in the New Europe* (Cambridge, 1996).
131. It is based on sociological works on the mutability of societal structures and the connection between structure and event, also termed praxeological history. Among its most prominent exponents are William Sewell, Marshall Sahlins, and Lynn Hunt; the theoretical concepts originate from Pierre Bourdieu and Anthony Giddens. Cf. Sven Reichardt, "Praxeologische Geschichtswissenschaft. Eine Diskussionsanregung," *Sozial. Geschichte* 22, no. 3 (2007): 43–65.
132. The mutual effects of national movements in East Central Europe in the nineteenth and twentieth centuries have often been described in terms of a history of relations. See Jeremy King, *Budweisers into Czechs and Germans: A Local History of Bohemian Politics, 1848–1948* (Princeton, 2005); James E. Bjork, *Neither German nor Pole: Catholicism and National Indifference in a Central European Borderland* (Ann Arbor, 2008); Brendan J. Karch, "Nationalism on the Margins: Silesians between Germany and Poland, 1848–1945," PhD diss., Harvard, 2010; William W. Hagen, *Germans, Poles and Jews: The Nationality Conflict in the Prussian East, 1772–1914* (Chicago, 1980).
133. Representations are not only employed and illustrate precast concepts but also create meaning and "set reality" in the interplay between producer and recipient. Erika Fischer-Lichte and Doris Kolesch (eds), *Kulturen des Performativen* (Berlin, 1998).
134. The simplest way of constantly reproducing the experience of national belonging is in the context of a nation-state. Citizens of a nation-state are sent to school and perhaps the army, where its signs and symbols are continuously updated, and motivated to carry identification documents, the language and insignia of which are constant reminders of the polity to which they belong. See the pioneering studies by Eugene Weber, *Peasants into Frenchmen: The Modernization of Rural France 1880–1914* (Stanford, 1976), and Benedict Anderson, *Imagined Communities: Reflections on the Origin and Spread of Nationalism* (London, 1982).
135. Such events are commended to the collective memory by everyday public communication, or left to be forgotten by silencing, in keeping with the dictum formulated by Ernest Gellner. Cf. idem, *Nations and Nationalism* (Ithaca, 1983).
136. Scholars researching the Habsburg Monarchy / Galicia include Daniel Unowsky, *The Pomp and Politics of Patriotism: Imperial Celebrations in Habsburg Austria, 1848–1916* (West Lafayette, IN, 2005); idem and Laurence Cole (eds), *Limits of Loyalty: Imperial Symbolism, Popular Allegiances, and State Patriotism in the Late Habsburg Monarchy* (New York, 2007); Kerstin S. Jobst, *Zwischen Nationalismus und Internationalismus: Die polnische und ukrainische Sozialdemokratie in Galizien von 1890 bis 1914* (Hamburg, 1996).
137. Pieter M. Judson and Marsha Rozenblit (eds), *Constructing Nationalities in East Central Europe* (New York, 2005).
138. This applies mainly to national minorities under various systems of rule, such as, e.g., in Poland in the nineteenth century. See Michlic, *Poland's Threatening Other*; Theodore Weeks, *From Assimilation to Antisemitism: The "Jewish Question" in Poland 1859–1914*

(DeKalb, 2006); Brian Porter, *When Nationalism Began to Hate: Imagining Modern Politics in Nineteenth-Century Poland* (Oxford, 2000).

139. Klaus Holz has shown that proponents of antisemitism formulated concepts not only of excluding Jews from the nation but also of Jews torpedoing the national principle as such. See Klaus Holz, "Die antisemitische Konstruktion des Dritten und die nationale Ordnung der Welt," in Christina von Braun and Eva-Maria Ziege (eds), *Das bewegliche Vorurteil: Aspekte des Internationalen Antisemitismus* (Würzburg, 2004), 43–61.

140. I am not concerned here with comparing nationalism and antisemitism, or with analyzing the relation between the two. But I take an analogous approach to nationalism research, using the process model. Similarly, socialism, or Marxism, can be understood as a social process by which classes become historically significant subjects, making the notion of a working class become tangible reality via communication and the pursuance of practices that generate meaning. See Ulrich Wyrwa, *Branntewein und "echtes" Bier: Die Trinkkultur der Hamburger Arbeiter im 19. Jahrhundert* (Hamburg, 1990). Racism and Social Darwinism can also be conceived of as processes, by which people see their choice of mates, diet, or physical training as a service to the continuation of the race and the history of mankind as a struggle for survival between hermetic races. The various processes inevitably intersect and influence each other.

141. Or people and organizations labeled "Jewish." Albert Lindemann, *Esau's Tears: Modern Anti-Semitism and the Rise of the Jews* (Cambridge, 1997). A connection between the "rise of the Jews" and the increase in hostility toward Jews had already been asserted distinctly earlier. See the review of *Esau's Tears* by Alan Steinweis at H-Net: https://networks.h-net.org/node/2645/reviews/4124/steinweis-lindemann-esaus-tears-modern-anti-semitism-and-rise-jews, accessed 31 March 2011.

142. Rürup, *Emanzipation und Antisemitismus*.

143. Csaky, *Gedächtnis der Städte*, 261ff.

144. Daniel Vyleta, *Crime, Jews and News: Vienna 1895–1914* (New York, 2007), 48ff., 60.

145. One example is the incident described in the prolog of Merunowicz referring to an unsolved murder case as grounds to call for restrictions on Jews. Another good illustration is the Konitz case. After the Löwy family had been accused of the murder of Ernst Winter, antisemitic journalists traveled to the scene to spread this version abroad and purposefully intervene in the search for Ernst Winter's murderer. Christoph Nonn, *Eine Stadt sucht einen Mörder: Gerücht, Gewalt und Antisemitismus im Kaiserreich* (Göttingen, 2002).

146. Compared to sayability rules in Western societies today, a striking number of stereotypical notions concerning Jews were not regarded as antisemitic around 1900, which certainly would be today. See the late-nineteenth-century discussions on antisemitism described by Hermann Bahr, "Der Antisemitismus: Ein internationales Interview," (Berlin, 1893) with Wolfgang Benz, *Was ist Antisemitismus?* (Munich, 2004).

147. The high concentration of Jews in finance, academia, the arts, and professions, for example, was portrayed as one such threatening scenario. On the other hand, it was warned that the "rise" of Jews, being equal citizens, would open the floodgates to the mass immigration of "East Jews" and result in society becoming overrun by them. Combining these two trains of thought on Jews to paint a picture of the "Jewish infiltration" of capital cities was a key feature of antisemitic rhetoric, especially in the Central European capitals Budapest, Vienna, and Berlin. Cf. Beller, *Antisemitism*; Csáky, *Das Gedächtnis der Städte*, 261.

148. Research into drastic mass events such as revolutions has shown that groundbreaking actions do not always follow previously devised and formulated plans, but merely appear planned and purposeful when viewed and explained in retrospect. For a study applying this insight to radical aggression toward a group, the genocide of the Herero, see Helmut Walser Smith, *The Continuities of German History: Nation, Religion, and Race across the Long Nineteenth Century* (Cambridge, 2008), 167ff.

149. Hence, a functionalist explanation of antisemitism must take precedence over a substantialist one. Werner Bergmann, *Geschichte des Antisemitismus* (Munich, 2002), 6.

150. See Moritz Föllmer, "Gewalt und Antisemitismus," review of Nonn, Christoph: *Eine Stadt sucht einen Mörder: Gerücht, Gewalt und Antisemitismus im Kaiserreich* (Göttingen 2002) and Walser Smith, Helmut: *Die Geschichte des Schlachters: Mord und Antisemitismus in einer deutschen Kleinstadt* (Göttingen 2002), *H-Soz-u-Kult*, 8 January 2003, http://hsozkult.geschichte.hu-berlin.de/rezensionen/2003-1-010.

151. Kai Struve, "Gentry, Jews and Peasants: Jews as the 'Others' in the Formation of the Modern Polish Nation in Rural Galicia during the Second Half of the 19th Century," in Nancy M. Wingfield (ed.), *Creating the Other: Ethnic Conflict and Nationalism in Habsburg Central Europe* (New York, 2003), 103-126.

152. One example is university fraternities: Monika Natkowska, *Numerus clausus, getto ławkowe, numerus nullus, "paragraph aryjski": Antisemityzm na Uniwersytecie Warszawskim 1931–1939* (Warsaw, 1999); Norbert Kampe, *Studenten und "Judenfrage" im Deutschen Kaiserreich* (Göttingen, 1988).

153. One can only speculate what their motives were. Perhaps they were members of a Jewish reform movement who wished to discredit the Orthodox religion, or were simply seeking public attention. It is not known whether they were personally acquainted with Moses Ritter.

154. In Prussia around 1900, prominent ritual murder cases were recorded in Xanten in 1891 and Konitz/Chojnice in 1900.

155. Most examples can be found in the detailed accounts of the Konitz murder case written by Christoph Nonn and Helmut Walser Smith.

156. The diversification of the press and party-political landscape, Jewish equality, and the concept of antisemitism were three major new departures that changed society in the late nineteenth century, for which reason Christian-Jewish relations and hostility toward Jews in this period must be distinguished from that of the early modern period. Cf. Christhard Hoffmann, "Christlicher Antijudäismus und moderner Antisemitismus," in Leonore Siegele-Wenschkewitz (ed.), *Christlicher Antijudaismus und Antisemitismus: Theologische und kirchliche Programme Deutscher Christen* (Frankfurt a. M., 1994), 293–317.

157. Knowledge is understood here in a broad sociological sense as the sum of socially accepted opinions. Peter Berger and Thomas Luckmann, *Die gesellschaftliche Konstruktion der Wirklichkeit: Eine Theorie der Wissenssoziologie* (Frankfurt a. M., 1987).

Chapter 1

AGITATION

No crownland in Austria has been as relatively spared anti-Semitism as Galicia, of all places. All the baiting of the Polish press cannot turn the peaceable Galician population against the Jews.

—Joseph Samuel Bloch, 1885

The term "agitation" denotes speech or writing that addresses a public with the intention of inciting it to act.[1] It is used today, analogous to "populism," to mark out others with a dishonest, radical, and irrational style of politics. A cultural-political study of history must ignore these normative implications, and assume that politics cannot be regarded as rational, detached from emotions, or reduced to objective results.[2] Politics only become effective through the negotiation of compromises and allegiances and their transmission via verbal and nonverbal communication.[3] Even in the modern bureaucratic, constitutional state, consensus is reached through symbolic acts and rituals that the citizen must interpret and understand for law and order to prevail.[4]

These symbols trigger emotional, rather than rational, meaning-associations and appeal to the irrational and intuitive faculties. For this reason, "new" political history focuses on political communication, viewed from an ethnological perspective, in the light of speech act theory.[5]

The term agitation is useful for analyzing antisemitism as a political issue and a factor in mobilization strategies as it alludes to the connection between speech and actions. Incitement is a speech act intended to prompt further actions.[6] Where agitation succeeded, and was therefore negotiated, encounters between Jews and non-Jews took place in the context of antisemitic discourse. The repercussions of the agitation were manifested in situations where people called on others to perform actions against Jews. The range of antisemitic argumentations propagated by journalists and politicians showed various approaches of employing established agitation patterns. This is where the addressees of agitation come in. They should not be overlooked but regarded as responsible actors. Rather than merely performing what they have been agitated to do, they are to a degree convinced by the agitation. In a sense, they adopt the thrust of the agitation if it seems to their advantage. As we view antisemitism as a reciprocal process of communication, then, its analysis must include consideration of how politicians and political parties appropriated common speech acts against Jews. Agitation is a joint production in which the producers and receivers of meaning alternate roles. The first point to consider here is the communicative functions of the political speech or demand, and opinion-making by the press.

Agitation as Political Communication

Speech calling for action and change assumes a central function in political communication, which can to some extent be gauged by the results it leads to in terms of action. Actors keep it in circulation so long as they demonstrate a willingness to act.[7] Agitation can also be regarded as successful if it is not followed by any new legislation or deeds—if it finds approval among its addressees and wins new voters or readers. By demanding new legislation or policies, political communities assert their claim to participate in the body politic. Indeed, they are formed in this way—by individuals agreeing on a set of demands and ideals they wish to translate into policies. In the process, they develop a specific semantic system which embodies their community.[8] A political "home," a community, is formed in the communicative space between newspapers and organized assemblies, and in spontaneous contact between members.[9] This is where knowledge of the in-group is formed, and where its relationship to other groups and the body politic in general is defined. Elections, organized by the body politic, mark an occasion to compare and choose between the various group proposals. At no other time do members and activists speak at such length about themselves or the others or so emphatically represent their collective needs via the system of symbols established by their community.

The development of political ideas and goals is predicated on existing cultural and communicative structures. Galician actors relied on subdiscourses as connecting factors and employed traditions that were only partially compatible with party politics or parliamentary practice. Catholicism and the peasant class were long-established, potent sources of identification. But they had to be made useable under the modern conditions of representative democracy. Similarly, the peasantry had to be convinced of the legitimacy of professional politicians. Peasants were far more inclined to accept the authority of priests, many of whom, especially among the high clergy, objected to the politicization of the lower classes.

Collective political identities consisted of new and re-interpretations of existing connections and rituals. Religious life, industrial organization, and class and regional traditions and hierarchies could be both resources for and obstacles to political mobilization and meaning making. From the existing worlds of norms and symbols, in which social traditions were interwoven with religious, regional, and linguistic traditions, actors distilled their specific political profile using a semantic system that was propagated by the mass media. Areas of meaning had to be created that people could identify with and accept as their own. To rally support and win votes, the promoters of these points of common identification presented them as being neglected or threatened by established politics. Political programs by their very nature demand implementation; agitation and policy are inextricably linked.[10]

As "newcomers in the political arena,"[11] the peasant parties and the Christian-social parties that cultivated antisemitism in Galicia were especially reliant on agitation, both for promoting inner cohesion and outwardly calling for participation. Within any given community, political communication takes place in the context of a shifting discourse that is structured around central concepts. They are encapsulated by watchwords, which political actors vie to authorize and define. Discourse always involves a negotiation of power relations; a struggle for dominance in the discussion of key issues. In Galicia, as in all Central Europe, political life after 1848 was moreover characterized by multilingualism. The different languages also brought diverging mindsets into Galician politics and vocalized the broad competition for influence within the political system.[12] The other political actors' and especially the state's reactions to these new voices underscored pressing questions of community and how to form it. The new forces in Galicia, which came to take center stage, called their liberal premises into question.[13]

With respect to the first level of the antisemitic process, then, this chapter's field of inquiry encompasses the ideas and policies concerning Jews and antisemitism that emerged in Galicia after equal rights for Jews had been introduced. What reactions did the various interpretations of the idea of antisemitism and the "Jewish question" elicit, and what effect did they have on political discourse? What significance and functions did antisemitic agitation have within the various camps' political communication? To which of their calls to act against Jews did people respond? Were these addressed only to fellow community members or were they intended to reach a nationwide public? Did agitation have an impact on Galicians' sayability rules and "knowledge" of Jews to such an extent that it enabled sensational tales—such as the reports from the Rzeszów courtroom—to become established as part of Galician society's construct of ideas? To what extent did a form of agitation evolve from local Catholic and agrarian traditions to become a viable option in political discourse?

Negotiating the "Jewish Question"

> One question that has always aroused the highest interest among friend and foe; a question that has circulated all the parliaments of Europe and proven to be a touchstone of true liberalism and real civilization in all of them, in a word, the *Jewish question*, was negotiated in the Galician parliament this year. Here, too, it fortunately gained the response it has hitherto encountered in all the parliaments of *civilized* states, and which is greeted with true satisfaction by all friends of humanity and progress. . . . Despite the constitutional law [which] explicitly guarantees all citizens, regardless of faith . . . actual, full and non-curtailable equality, there were some—albeit not many—in the Galician Landtag who propounded the opinion that the aforementioned constitutional law of 21 December 1867 merely declares the equality of religions in principle, . . . while the practical implementation of said principle is the task of the Landtag. This conflict of opinions gave rise to a very lively . . . discussion about Jewish emancipation, which ended, as mentioned above, with a victory for justice and enlightenment.[14]

These lines were written by members of the Lemberg Jewish congregation in a foreword to the record of a parliamentary debate on whether to bring Galician law on Jewish rights into line with the Habsburg Monarchy's December Constitution.[15] The protocol was published—in German—by the Jewish intelligentsia of the Galician capital, shortly after the Galician Diet had passed a bill on legal equality between Jews and Christians.

On a practical level, the new legislation enabled candidates of both religions to stand for local councils, lifting the restrictions that had hitherto applied to Jews in some municipalities, including Krakow and Brody. But on an ideal level, it negotiated the entire project of Jewish equality. Its adoption by the Galician Diet sent out an important signal. It showed that Galicia did not simply implement decrees from Vienna but deliberated them independently. After intense debate, the Galician parliament had committed to the principles of "true liberalism," the spirit of which positively pervades the passage cited above. The establishment of equality seemed to mark a decisive step toward progress and civilization. At the end of this path, Galician society would be enlightened and "mature"; its members' coexistence would be regulated by a common law, and differences of opinion negotiated in considered debate. Taking a teleological view of history and trusting the real world to abide by the rule of law, it seemed as if the protracted "Jewish question" had at last been solved. The Jewish congregation's publication of the protocol of the debate was a proud demonstration that Galicia had proven its maturity and arrived in the "civilized world." By publishing it in German— the lingua franca of this "civilized and enlightened" world, the protagonists of which included many central European Jews—it sent out a signal beyond the borders of Galicia. The authors of the foreword did not deny there were voices against equality but believed them to be echoes of a bygone era that would soon fade away. However, the future was to show that they would not fall silent. On the contrary, they would grow ever louder until they eventually drowned out the liberal belief in progress. The debate surrounding the legal emancipation of Jews in Galicia provides an apt introduction, then, to the history of antisemitic agitation.

The Debate on the Emancipation of Jews in Galicia

Although the Galician Landtag did not typically exude such liberal euphoria as expressed in the above-cited foreword, it voted unambiguously liberal on the issue of equality.[16] Not only the prominent speakers—Landtag president Leon Sapieha, the speaker of the committee for the approximation of laws and dyed-in-the-wool Democrat Franciszek Smolka, and Governor Agenor Gołuchowski—but also the majority in the house showed their support for Jewish emancipation. Under the banner of progress, the Galician dignitaries voted to revoke the last remaining legal distinctions between Jews and Christians. Henceforth, the differences between the members of the two collectives would be only of a religious nature; all other differences would be resolved within civil society.

The accomplishment of legal equality marked the end of an era and the dawn of one in which the newly franchised citizens were expected to prove their willingness to conform. Both the Christian and the Jewish intelligentsia assumed the role of models to and educators of the newly emancipated majority in society—the illiterate peasants and Orthodox and Hassidic Jews trapped in their worlds of archaic religious symbols and rules. The Galician elite saw politics as a patriarchal responsibility toward the uneducated classes, who needed to be "cultivated" to achieve equality. Political representation was education by the elite for the good of the community. It was presumed that all members would ultimately recognize the necessity of "assimilation" and abandon their "old prejudices." Not even the opponents of legal equality challenged the concept of working toward a better society in the future. They, too, worked with the language of liberalism and did not overstep its boundaries of the sayable, even when arguing to restrict Jewish rights.

> In every healthy social organism, each inhabitant doubtless has the same civil rights, the same right to employment according to his abilities and merits, the same right to work and the same right to participate in autonomous spheres of activity; in a word, he has full freedom of movement in every legally sanctioned direction; as equality before the law is the essence of constitutionalism.[17]

This liberal, individualistic argument *against* equality was put forward by Franciszek Torosiewicz, manor owner and member of parliament representing landownership in Brzeżany, East Galicia. Speaking to the Landtag, he assured the house he was not intolerant of other religions before proceeding to make observations of a social and political nature that sidestepped the subject of religion. No concessions made to Jews since the Josephine Reforms and the status changes of 1848, he asserted, had resulted in Jews conforming socially or culturally to the majority society. Yet it was this process, known as civilization, Europeanization, or assimilation, by which Jews were required to sacrifice all their distinguishing traits save their religion, that was regarded as the answer to the Jewish question.[18] In Torosiewicz's view, Jews had not adapted to the social and civil organism but had remained a discrete "class" that used its peculiar religious structures to secure economic and political advantages. Jews, he argued, were not elements of progress but operated "in reaction to society."[19]

Torosiewicz regarded Jews as shirkers who evaded military service to concentrate on building trade monopolies. He opposed equality, but advocates of equality held strikingly similar views, as the response offered by Eduard Gniewosz showed:[20] "Those bad sides of the Jews are extremely familiar to all of us, and I could illustrate them further. But what does that all prove? We know that the Jews are not what they ought to be, but I ask again, what does it all prove? Really only that one would like them to become how they ought; but for that, it is necessary that they blend with our nation."

Liberals who, like Gwniewosz, supported equality presumed that Jews had hitherto been prevented from becoming citizens (and Poles) by legal restrictions, religious reservations, and discrimination. Equality would free them from the ghetto, so to speak, since they wanted nothing more urgently than to discover secular education and "European clothing." Torosiewicz, on the other hand, felt that recent pro-emancipation developments had proven this was not the case. Jews were not eager to become integrated into (national, Polish) society. They would not stop being others or representing peculiar interests just because they were conceded individual rights. As the outcome of previous measures offered no cause for optimism, he maintained, it would be better to wait for the Jews to change their attitude of distinction, regarding economics and politics as well as culture, before introducing any further steps toward equality. Torosiewicz, then, supported a policy of postponement, but was not against equality on principle.[21] Although he certainly played on Polish fears of the Jews becoming detached from society, he did not use blatant, generalizing anti-Jewish rhetoric.[22] There was no place in parliament for challenging the positive concept of progress, though elsewhere there inevitably was. Liberal criticism of Jews was typically aimed at the largest group of traditional Jews, who seemed trapped in a separate, benighted world. Liberals did not allege that assimilated middle-class Jews had too much influence. The debate about benighted Jews voiced the concerns of a "colonial" elite in the context of notions of organic work.[23] In 1868, the clear majority in the Landtag believed that ending legal discrimination would help to close the gap between Christians and Jews and voted for equality. The optimists won out over the pessimists. But it did not necessarily follow that the majority in the Christian population agreed, or that the legislation would be implemented.

Equality Denied: "No Jews in Żywiec!"

While the Galician Diet ruled to lift denominational restrictions on candidacy for local councils, citizens of the small town Żywiec (German: Saybusch) resisted the trend toward secularization by flatly denying Jews the right to residency. Although this beer-brewing town in the Beskids was an exception in Galicia, it is nonetheless worth considering more closely, especially as it was the scene of several incidents relevant to this study. The case of Żywiec shows that laws alone do not determine how life is lived, if citizens and officials do not obey them. Second, it illustrates the fact that the long tradition of Christian and Jewish coexistence could differ quite starkly from place to place, affecting how emancipation—and antisemitism—were understood locally.

Żywiec gained a town charter in 1327 and had passed through various owners by the time Constance of Austria acquired it in 1626. At the urging of Christian artisans, who felt threatened by the strong Jewish competition, she granted the town the privilege "de non tolerandis Judaeis" the same year.[24] So, while Jews were free to settle in the surrounding villages, none lived within the Żywiec town limits for several centuries.

In the late eighteenth century, when another member of the House of Habsburg, Joseph II, revised Austria's legislation on Jews, a delegation from the town went to Vienna to request confirmation of its premodern anti-Jewish privilege. The emperor agreed to extend the ban on Jews settling in Żywiec unless they were born in the town. Unsurprisingly, no Jewish woman was ever known to give birth there. To ensure this did not change, the citizens of Żywiec even voted against the construction of a railroad station. Although the conservative citizenry recognized the advantages of railroads, it also feared they might bring much harm to the town, such as pregnant Jewesses.[25] In 1878, a station was built in neighboring Zabłocie, which bordered on Żywiec's brewery grounds, to serve the Austrian imperial Nordbahn railway line. In 1884, the service was extended to connect with the Galician Transversalbahn line, de facto forming a conglomeration of Żywiec with the surrounding villages. But this did nothing to change Żywiec's intolerance of Jews. While a Jewish community became established in Zabłocie, with two synagogues and a bathhouse, there were still no Jews living in Żywiec. Any attempt by Jews to settle there was stopped by "exclusionary violence."[26] In 1871, rumors that a Jew named Arnold Lion, who worked in Żywiec, was seeking accommodation in the town for himself and his bride sparked violent disturbances.[27] Rioters attacked the couple and looted other Jews in the surrounding suburbs and threw stones at them. The Krakow military commander dispatched sixty soldiers and two officers to Żywiec, who brutally suppressed the rioting. One woman was killed in the gunfire.[28] The district captain reported that he had informed Lion of the danger of appearing in town with his bride as the townspeople objected to Jews; any other Israelites trying to settle there had been "thrown out" by force. Alerted residents would assemble and turn into a "beast prepared to do anything."[29]

In summer 1879, the district captain licensed a Jewish trader named Glesinger from Biała to open a fabric store in the town. Glesinger rented a room from a blacksmith but was prevented from opening his store there by the hostile town authorities. Glesinger then employed a Christian, Wilhelm Vignati, to give the enterprise an acceptable face. Still, the citizens of Żywiec bombarded the premises with stones. The gendarmerie drove the assailants away, but did not identify them, supposedly because it was too dark. Glesinger subsequently left Żywiec.[30]

While Żywiec doggedly continued its local anti-Jewish tradition despite legal equality between Jews and Christians, criticisms of emancipation began to be voiced elsewhere, too. One decade after its adoption by the Landtag, Galicians started to take stock of the Jewish assimilation project. Their previously optimistic view of progress was now tempered by contemporary concerns. The Jewish question returned to the public consciousness.

"Failed Assimilation": The First Phase of Antisemitic Agitation, 1879–1883

The year 1879 marks a turning point, but not because the word antisemitism arose. Although it was to both denote and define post-emancipatory hostility toward Jews, the word itself had no special significance until the 1890s; it served at most to convey the speaker's attitude to the "Berlin movement," with which it was exclusively associated for several years. The year 1879 was a watershed because it was when Teofil Merunowicz (mentioned in the introduction) published a high-profile anti-Jewish book titled *The Jews* and launched a corresponding political campaign in parliament.[31] He was Galicia's first antisemitic entrepreneur.

"Liberal Anti-Jewishness": Teofil Merunowicz

The journalist and Reichsrat member Teofil Merunowicz (1846–1919) was one of the leading proponents of antisemitism based on a liberal premise in Galicia.[32] A Polish patriot and later campaigner against the "Ukrainian element" in Galicia, but lifelong member of the Greek Catholic Church, he represented a significant tendency within Polish democratic thought. National Democrats in the kingdom of Poland rallied against the Jewish population under the banner of "progressive antisemitism," though in Galicia Merunowicz stood almost alone until the turn of the century. A long-time contributor to the *Gazeta Narodowa* (National Newspaper) and *Ekonomista Polskiego* (Polish Economist), Merunowicz's chief concern was the nation's economic development and its importance for Poland's future as an independent nation-state. The Jews, he wrote, with their strong mercantile and artisan traditions, impeded the development of the Galician and Polish economies and hence the formation of a Polish middle class, which was the basis of any nation. In an international comparison—a typical device of "organic" rhetoric informed by social Darwinism—he found that although all the countries of Europe were affected by the "Jewish question," Poland was the worst struck "patient" as it had the largest Jewish population and it was growing faster than the Christian population.

In the characteristic style of antisemitic literature of the 1870s, the book portrayed the "Jewish question" as a matter of life and death for the Christian majority society.[33] Across Europe, Jewish equality had been proven to lead to social inequality, as Jews used the dual advantage of their equal rights and their own religious institutions to retain or extend their monopolies in trade and finance. Merunowicz, too, claimed that the Jews evaded their social duty to serve in the army. As evidence, he cited sensational cases such as that of the physician Mikołaj Karmelin, who stood trial in 1870 for accepting bribes to issue exemptions on health grounds. To observers such as Merunowicz, who believed in a collective Jewish interest, the growing number of Jewish doctors was indication of a plot to systematically exempt Jews from military service. Although Merunowicz described himself as "liberal through-and-through," he could not imagine that secularly educated Jews might simply pursue the middle-class dream of personal advancement, or that Orthodox and Hassidic Jews were compelled to gain exemption from military service to obey their religious laws. Rather, in his opinion, "the Jews" used equality to maintain their parallel universe.

His controversial argument was that the Christians needed to gain equality with the Jews. While the case of the Ritter family was being heard in Rzeszów, in the Lemberg Landtag, Merunowicz proposed changing the legal status of Jews. The government should not discriminate against Jews, but it should end the discrimination of Christians.

Merunowicz believed in the anti-Jewish conspiracy theories popularized by Jakub Brafman and August Rohling concerning the might of the Kahal and the anti-Christian commandments inscribed in the Talmud. But he did not invoke a reactionary Christian utopia. He called for regulation in the name of a modern nation, governed by the rule of law. In July 1880, he petitioned for the abolition of "Jewish privileges" but failed; a renewed attempt in the Lemberg Landtag during the Ritter trial was accepted.[34] When the proposal was eventually approved by a large majority, all the customs and practices of the Jewish Community that violated Galician law became illegal. In his Landtag address of 10 October 1882, Merunowicz responded good-humoredly to the previous speaker, Goldmann, who accused Merunowicz of wanting "away with the Jews" like Georg von Schönerer,[35] by insisting he was far from it.

Indeed, in his book he had explicitly praised Jews whose "personal noble-mindedness" had a positive influence on their fellow believers, helping to raise them out of their "racial hatred of Christians" to the level of the other nations of the world.[36] The regulation he initiated was still informed by a liberalism that believed in the law and that wanted to enlighten and improve. Yet it also marked a fatefully strategic move. The Jewish members of parliament, none of whom were Orthodox followers of the Talmud but all Polish nationals, could not object to the demand that the laws of a religious community comply with the state's constitutional laws. But by extension, they thus conceded that questionable religious laws possibly existed and were observed. The implicit reference to practices such as the removal of fetuses and ritual murder, concurrently under discussion in Rzeszów, was unmistakable.[37]

Responses to the Allegations

In a bid to remedy the misrepresentation of their faith, the Jewish community in Lemberg recalled an upstanding figure of Christian national history, elected king of the Polish-Lithuanian Commonwealth Stephen Báthory. In 1576, he had decreed it punishable by death to accuse Jews of murdering Christian children. The Jewish congregation published this historical decree in the newspapers *Reforma* and *Ojczyzna* (The Fatherland) and sent copies of it to other Jewish congregations across the land for them to display outside government and church buildings. However, the information was not well received by the governor's office in Lemberg, which issued a circular instructing the district authorities to seize the dispatched copies.[38] The Krakow district captain was not alone in assuming that sections of the Christian population would see the ancient royal edict as a provocation rather than a convincing argument if Jews displayed it on church and state property. Even some of the Jewish population thought so.[39]

Legal equality did not imply that Christians would accept Jews publicly defending their interests. Jewish initiatives were regarded by many Christians as a case of the minority taking liberties. The governor no doubt intervened on this occasion chiefly to keep the peace and maintain order. But by doing so, he perpetuated the Jewish population's precarious situation. His intervention revealed the limits of legal emancipation, in which the Landtag had placed such high hopes fifteen years previously.

In a way, parliament's handling of Merunowicz's proposal seemed to reflect the picture of accord in the Lemberg Landtag that the protocol of the debate on Jewish quality had drawn. But this time, it was not the Jewish congregation that conveyed a sense of political harmony to the outside world but Merunowicz's own newspaper, *Gazeta Narodowa*.[40] Following the debate, the report said that "Jews and their opponents, progressives and conservatives, Poles and Ruthenians" had all voted in favor of the proposal.[41] That was the strongest evidence, it claimed, that the Jewish question had a very different significance in Galicia than in Germany or other countries of Austro-Hungary. Elsewhere, antisemitic agitation was conducted to prevent Jews from gaining equality and holding offices. In Galicia, the reverse was true; nobody spoke out against equality, not even Merunowicz. He was only concerned that "certain organizations of Israelite communities" should not have more rights than Christians. His proposal that Christians should be familiarized with the Talmud to realize how and where it offends the law had been vindicated. The developments leading to the emancipation debate seemed to repeat in reverse. Galicia no longer introduced measures to keep up with the progressive Western countries but set its own standards. While the Jews had been granted further rights in 1867, it had now been necessary to impose certain limitations on them. Antisemitic situations, such as the rumors concerning Franciszka Mnich's murder, were for the first time being used to political advantage and ultimately to design regulations and directives around mistrust of the Jewish religion. The Ritter affair also had an impact on another debate, considered below, which conveyed the double-edged nature of the liberal model of assimilation to Galician Jews.

"Krakow's Wagner?" Antisemitism and Jan Matejko

The affair surrounding the famous Krakow history painter Jan Matejko[42] occurred in the same context of criticisms of Jewish "non-conformity" toward the national Polish community. As rector of the Academy of Fine Arts, Matejko opened the academic year 1881 with a speech describing art as a "weapon in the hands of the nation," for which reason art could not be separated from patriotism. Subsequently, he specifically addressed his students of Jewish faith with the following words:

> And you, Hebrew students, who come to our school of fine arts, remember that art is not any kind of speculative or commercial activity, but a mission for the higher goals of the human spirit, for the love of God, which is bound to the love of one's country. Should you learn the fine arts in our artistic-academic institution merely to speculate, and feel neither gratitude nor obligation toward the country; should you, Hebrews, who have lived in our country for centuries, not feel destined to carry out more noble deeds or want to be Poles, then leave our country, go forth, to where there is no fatherland, no higher sentiments of patriotism, no higher human virtues of love for the receiving country.[43]

Matejko's speech echoed ideas expressed by Richard Wagner in his essay "Judaism in Music."[44] As well as accusing his Jewish students of having a purely material interest in art, he assigned the "Hebrews" the role of guests, who could be told to leave even after "centuries." He implied that Catholic Poles were by nature filled with idealism while Jews were driven by the pursuit of profit.

The historicist conception of Jews as guests in Poland, fixated on material gain, was also reflected in Matejko's art works, such as the painting "The Reception of the Jews in Poland" (1889), the mural "Mammon" (1883–1886), completed according to his design in the assembly hall of the Lemberg polytechnic college, and the work "The Constitution of May 3" (1891).[45] Yet Matejko did not deny on principle that Jews could be Poles or capable of great artistic and patriotic accomplishments. Indeed, he had personally supported such efforts, albeit mostly outside the Krakow art scene.

The painter Moses/Moritz/Maurycy Gottlieb (1856–1879) from Drohobycz in East Galicia had admired Matejko's work while a student at the Vienna Academy and felt inspired to become to the "Jewish people" what Matejko was to the Poles.[46] Influenced by the writings of Heinrich Graetz, Gottlieb saw an affinity between the "histories of suffering" of the Jewish and Polish peoples and sought to "serve both." In 1874, he left Vienna, against the will of his father, for the far less renowned Krakow Academy. Here, however, he was subjected to severe discrimination by his fellow students and even some of the masters. But Matejko supported him and helped him return to Vienna and finally move to Munich to complete his education.

Gottlieb received the ultimate accolade from Matejko at a banquet in Rome given in honor of Polish artists. At this occasion, one of the painters in attendance proposed a toast to Gottlieb for having brought fame to Poland and for being a model of Polish patriotism to his fellow Jews. Gottlieb later recalled how moved he had been by this encouragement from fellow "countrymen," which he had been denied in Krakow. His response, in halting Polish, prompted Matejko to embrace and kiss him.[47]

Perhaps Matejko's diatribe four years later was largely owing to the anti-Jewish climate at the academy.[48] Certainly, his words did not cause a major outrage until a few days later, when the conservative newspaper *Czas* printed the "master's" entire speech. Warsaw's *Izraelita* newspaper and the Krakow Jewish congregation responded with letters to the *Czas* protesting Matejko's blanket questioning of their place in the Polish nation.[49] It snowballed into a scandal when Matejko's assistant, Marian Gorzkowski, filed a libel suit against the lawyer Leon Eibenschütz, who had called Matejko a "scoundrel" (Polish: *łajdak*). Not content to plead a straightforward libel case, Matejko's lawyer (and Gorzkowski's brother-in-law), Jozef Mochnacki, used the court as an antisemitic stage, claiming that Eibenschütz was party to a plan "hatched in the synagogue" by Jews against the

Polish nation, of which Matejko was the "sovereign." The accusations Matejko had made against the Jews, Mochnacki argued, were based on "historical truth." Eibenschütz was condemned, although it was merely Mochnacki's word against his.[50] The liberal newspaper *Gazeta Krakowska* wrote that the trial had resembled a "formal antisemitic congress."[51]

When Mochnacki subsequently published his indictment, it was confiscated and banned as incitement against a religious group.[52] On appeal, Mochnacki justified its publication as an attempt to clarify the "vague" press coverage.[53] He seized the opportunity of standing in the dock to hold forth about the "mendacious spirit" prevalent among Jews. The mood in court was lightened by a comment from the gallery suggesting that the kettle was calling the pot black, inferring that Mochnacki was a far worse fraud, and causing general merriment.[54] As so often, the trial was also received as a source of entertainment. In the end, however, Mochnacki had the last laugh. The indictment was found not to incite readers to violence against Jews, and the ban was revoked. Furthermore, the court ruled, the facts it cited were "true and common knowledge" and as such could not manipulate the attitude of the Christian population toward the Israelites. The following lines in the court's judgment could have been written by the liberal anti-Semite Merunowicz: "Israelite individuals who devote themselves to science and labor, and act honestly, always encounter appreciation from the nation. Those Israelite individuals, however, who act dishonestly, dealing in usury, flooding the people with alcohol, or pettifogging, will experience the fury of the nation when they are ejected from society."[55]

The Polish-language press, in contrast, strongly criticized Mochnacki's ranting as inconducive to solving the "Jewish question" and called for greater restraint and discretion. While this moderate stance was typical of both the liberal and conservative urban Galician press of the 1880s, harsher opinions were voiced in the kingdom of Poland. At one end of the spectrum, the Warsaw-based *Izraelita* criticized the Jewish protest in Krakow as too cautious; at the other, Polish national anti-Jewish views were disseminated by the faction's own press organ. Marian Gorzkowski, who had filed the Matejko libel suit, reported on the trial in the Warsaw-based *Rola*, published by the declared anti-Semite Jan Jeleński, and became the newspaper's correspondent for Krakow and the Habsburg Monarchy in general. In this capacity, he covered the trial against the Ritter family and the trial in Tiszaeszlar.[56] Both Matejko's lawyer and assistant, then, promoted antisemitism by interrelating affairs which had nothing more in common than the fact that they all concerned Jews on trial. It was an approach that held occupational benefits: by focusing on Jews in court, they created popular sensations and generated news to cover. Coverage of the Ritter family trial, which was linked with the trial in Hungary, caused an upsurge in journalism on ritual murder, even in Galicia.

Genre: Science Fiction—Subject: The Talmud

As mentioned in the introduction, August Rohling was known across Cisleithania for putting forward his "expert" opinion whenever accusations of ritual murder were raised. In this way, he generated publicity for himself and reminded readers of his writings on the Talmud. Merunowicz referred to the Rohling phenomenon as well as the Ritter case when he launched his initiative in parliament. The antisemitic market, both the commercial and the political, needed events that could serve as illustrations of dubious Jewish practices. Assured of high public interest in the topic, Rohling drew on the stock of interpretations of such events to explain a wide range of murder and abduction cases, stringing together various elements of the "ritual murder script." Although he was a German professor at a college with a long-standing academic tradition, and his theories on ritual murder were lent added authority by their appearance in print, he relied on news of actual or alleged murders in the transregional press for credibility, and vice versa.

Jakob Brafman's "Kahal book" was first published in Polish in an abridged form in Lemberg in 1874, and soon followed by second and third editions. Rohling's "Talmud Jew" was also published in Polish in 1874 and reissued in parallel with the court cases in Lutcza and Tizsaezslar in 1883.[57] The first Galician book in the Talmud/Kahal genre was published in 1885, as the Ritter case was nearing a conclusion: *Judztwo*, which roughly translates as "Jew rabble."[58] The author, Edward Żukowski, wanted his book to be regarded as a scientific publication. To save the Polish people from Jewish exploitation, he claimed, they needed better knowledge of the Jews. To supply this, he started with a history of the Jewish people from Abraham to the "Jewish sects," from the Rechabites to the Frankists, and up to the Napoleonic reform and Moses Mendelsohn. His Talmud exegesis was based on familiar accusations that Jews relied on deception, profiteering, and mendacity when dealing with Christians, and so negated the idea of a civil society made up of Jews and Christians.[59]

Żukowski did not mention the central theme of the publication, ritual murder, until 150 pages into the book. But here he bluntly asserted that rabbis met at the beginning of every year to select a boy under thirteen whose blood would be used to prepare Passover matzah and treat eggs to be buried under the houses of Christians, to "mark" them and bring them bad luck.[60] Żukowski's source for these fantasies of Jewish malevolence, which he blended with Christian Eastertime traditions, was the late eighteenth-century author Gaudenty Pikulski.[61] Pikulski had written an account of a dispute between Frankists and Talmudists in Lemberg's Roman Catholic cathedral, in the course of which the Frankists had proven that the Talmud calls for Christian blood and whoever lives by it must fulfill this demand.[62]

Żukowski may have had an excellent theological and humanist education, but it did not make him a good antisemitic writer. The antiquated source to which he referred offered no explanation for why Jews were responsible for the murders of Franka Mnich and Eszter Solymosi, neither of whom were boys under thirteen. Nor was his longwinded account of the history of the Jews able to hold masses of readers spellbound.

The significance of Żukowski's book, then, lies not in the breadth of its reception or the force of its impact. It was not so widely read that it popularized any new theories. But this rather ponderous book, written for a national-minded, bourgeois Catholic readership, fulfilled a demand for readdressing the subject of ritual murder. Allegations of ritual murder had been made down the centuries and mythologized by church iconography.[63] While the middle classes in the late nineteenth century no longer related in an immediate sense to such myths, they were interested in their scientific and historical background. The phenomenon returned to bourgeois conversation, but by no means dominated it. Since the newspaper coverage of the trial in Rzeszów had highlighted the divide between the urban middle class and the "superstitious" peasants, demand arose for a work of cultural translation—from peasant folklore to the language of science.[64] Dignified by the comments of experts in criminology, medicine, and theology consulted during the ritual murder trials, these folk beliefs seemed to be more than just medieval hocus pocus. Books such as *Judztwo* promised to deliver background knowledge to, and guidance on, such issues. While there was obviously public demand for sensations and horror stories, which was satisfied by newspaper coverage of the trials as well as books of the Kahal/Talmud genre, the latter was distinguished by the bourgeois distance it maintained from rustic superstition. The activities of men like Merunowicz and Gorkowski showed that by interweaving such stories into the debate about the failed emancipation of the Jews, or their de facto privileges, the supposed findings of Talmud exegeses could be utilized to intimidate Jews.

In the mid-1880s, August Rohling was publicly discredited, and interest in the Talmud noticeably dwindled.[65] Around the turn of the century, however, it resurged following the murder of a certain Anežka Hrůzová, which led to a high-profile trial that was once again attended by explicitly anti-Jewish journalism.

Against the background of the Hrůzová murder case, the preacher of Krakow's progressive Jewish congregation swore an oath that Jews did not use any blood for religious or ritual purposes.[66] The Lemberg archivist Aleksandar Czołowski once again recalled the dispute in the cathedral, reviving the spirit of Pikulski.[67] The Lemberg rabbi Jecheskiel Caro countered with a pamphlet titled "The Frankists and the archivist of the city of Lemberg: A response to the latter's treatise on ritual murder." But unlike Joseph Bloch, Caro failed to debunk his opponent, resorting to insults instead of analyses of Czołowski's allegations concerning the Talmud. Czołowski, in turn, published a counter-pamphlet, with which he emerged as victor of the contest, according to the contemporary Jewish historian Majer Bałaban.[68]

Where antisemitic agitation and its exploitation for political purposes is concerned, it was certainly significant that by 1900, communication between the rural population, the world of politics, and antisemitic entrepreneurs was far more fluent than it had been when the affairs in Tiszaeszlar and Lutcza were negotiated in Galicia. Instead of the middle-class, conservative *Czas*, the antisemitic Catholic newspaper *Głos Narodu* (Voice of the Nation) was now the leading Krakow daily. Newspapers brought anti-Jewish interpretations of events to remote villages like Lutcza as fast as rumors spread in the opposite direction. Christian outrage at murders committed by Jews was no longer abstract and remote, refracted through several lenses, as described in the introduction. The press voiced definite opinions, with a demonstrable impact on Christian-Jewish relations, as chapter 3 will show.

Pogroms in the Tsarist Empire were another crucial factor in antisemitic agitation surrounding media events. The consequence—the emigration of Russian Jews—was felt by many countries of Europe, and especially by neighboring Galicia.

Threat of Pogroms: Of Flight and Flyers

On 15 April 1881, Christians in Elisavetgrad turned on their Jewish neighbors. The attacks and lootings marked the start of a wave of violence that lasted weeks and went down in history as "the Pogroms."[69] Many Jewish families from modern-day South and Central Ukraine responded to the violence, and the authorities' failure to curb it, by fleeing their homes for good. Heading west, the pogrom refugees traveled across Galicia, today's West Ukraine, toward the national border. Three quarters of them did not have passports and crossed the border illegally through the woodland stretching between Radzivilov (Government of Volhynia) and Brody (Galicia).[70]

For the next one and a half years, the border town Brody was transformed into an enormous refugee camp. With a population of barely 20,000, it struggled to accommodate 14,000 refugees in May and June 1881.[71] Some 20,000 of the 25,000 Jewish refugees who fled the Tsarist Empire across Austria stayed in Brody for a time.[72] Well over half of them eventually returned to Russia; some 7,000 to 9,000 emigrated to the Unites States; a mere 1,000 to 1,500 settled in other European countries, mostly France. Brody became a magnet for Russian Jews for various reasons. It was by far the largest town near the border and already a local center of trade, smuggling, and human trafficking. Although it had lost its status as a free trade area, it was prosperous by Galician standards. And it was a Jewish town; a branch of the Alliance Israelite Universelle (AIU) was established here in

1878.⁷³ When the tide of Jewish refugees hit the town, this organization set up an aid committee to help them. With the support of the AIU central office in Paris, the committee provided the uprooted families with supplies and accommodation. At the same time, it worked on a long-term solution, which it soon came to see as the United States. Some support was provided by the Federation of American Jewish Communities, which, however, insisted that only those who were fit to work should emigrate, and that they pay the travel costs themselves.⁷⁴ As many of the refugees could not afford the train journey to a seaport and the crossing to New York, the AIU raised the funds in most cases.⁷⁵

News of the transfer of funds from Paris to Galicia and the prospect of having the costly undertaking of emigration sponsored motivated ever more refugees to head for Brody, swelling the tide of immigrants. Russian newspapers reported that an aid committee had been set up there. And enterprising citizens of Brody published flyers and placed advertisements offering accommodation for rent. In this way, news of the transit town was disseminated throughout the Tsarist Empire.⁷⁶

Before long, the Austrian government was supporting Brody's role as a temporary collecting point for Russian refugees. It could not logistically prevent their illegal entry and could hardly refuse it for humanitarian reasons. But it did want to prevent Russian Jews from settling in Austria, and so avoid the cost of feeding them. It was in the interests of the Viennese Alliance to deter the refugees from traveling on to Vienna.⁷⁷ And the Galician governor's office had police patrols stationed at border crossings to prevent refugees settling in Galicia unnoticed. Wealthy refugees on their way to America were permitted to continue.⁷⁸ Any other illegal immigrants were taken to Brody. From here, they traveled on to America or back to Russia. If they fell into the hands of Russian border officials, they faced severe punishments, especially if they were evading military service.⁷⁹ Those refugees who were forced to end their journey at the Prussian border or a seaport due to lack of funds or health problems also returned to the Russian Empire via Brody.⁸⁰

Later, the authorities in Lemberg inquired of the district administrations whether any Jews had settled there and, if so, how many.⁸¹ Apart from a few isolated exceptions, the answers were all negative. The authorities had exercised special caution, not only due to concern that destitute Jews might cross the border but also that the pogroms might spread to Galicia.

Agitation "From Below"

Local authorities in Galicia had submitted occasional reports that Jews were in imminent danger of violent attack as early as March 1881. The news of disturbances in Russia and refugees' personal observations fueled the rumors and caused them to proliferate. Alarmed by the unprecedented extent of collective violence against Jews in the Tsarist Empire, the law enforcement forces in Galicia sought to nip in the bud any signs of disorder. People were arrested for merely talking about imminent raids or killings and so passing on the rumors. Agitation was conducted in Galicia not to target the newly arrived Jews, who were often destitute, but the resident Jews and their property. Galician agitators were not concerned with the rumors abounding in Russia that Jews were taking Galicia as an easy route to emigrating to the United States. There were no warnings against being "swamped" by Jews in circulation, such as characterized Western European antisemitic discourse of the time.[82] The agitators did not play on any fears of being politically or culturally overrun by Jews, but on the public's desire for material gain. In rural areas, most known Jews were tradesmen or barkeepers—the owners or administrators of valuable resources.

Agitators distributed flyers and put up notices to recruit willing accomplices and announce a time and place to meet.[83] Galicians used their knowledge of the disturbances in Russia to their own ends, as illustrated by an incident involving a guild member named Kowalski. Kowalski publicly threatened an attack on the Jews in Pilzno at Whitsun, when "the same thing [would happen] to them as in Kiev."[84] Now and then, word spread here, as in Russia, that the emperor had personally authorized the robbing of Jews.[85] This legitimization strategy built upon the narrative of the historical Galician "slaughter" (Polish: *rabacja*), during which the nobility had purportedly been outlawed.[86] Individual grounds for legally attacking Jews were also claimed. A certain Józef Głuc of Podgórze showed illiterate peasants his employment contract, claiming it was an official government permit to beat Jews.[87] The locksmith Ignacy Babiński made an interesting assertion when he called out in a barroom in Żywiec, "The Jews must be driven out; there's an elected inspector who has the right to expel all Jews."[88] In this way, he linked the contemporary "pogrom mood" with Żywiec's own brand of virulent antisemitism to fantasize that the local practice of expelling Jews was now universally applicable.

When people talked about imminent disturbances, they did not necessarily do so with violet intent. They might claim to have exclusive permission to use violence, or even just know about it, to garner some precious attention in the tavern. Many Christians aimed to blackmail or scare Jews. Some sent threatening letters to prominent representatives of the Jewish Community, reminding them of the danger they were in.[89]

Clearly, none of these antisemitic agitators needed assistance. Nonetheless, fears abounded among the native Jewish population that Russian agitators might cross the border to continue their activities in Galicia. Indeed, fear of a Russian influx was ubiquitous. Even within government offices, anxious memos were exchanged addressing the terrible consequences a growth of the "malign Jewish element" would have for the crownland. At the same time, the authorities noted with concern that the non-Jewish population was sympathetic toward the pogroms and determined to do everything in their power to prevent copycat deeds in Galicia. In an atmosphere of universally heightened watchfulness—on the part of Jews, Christians, and the authorities alike, all expecting mass violence to erupt at any time—attacks were indeed prevented or quickly stopped. Meanwhile, the fear of pogroms caused any disputes between Christians and Jews, which would previously have been contained within local limits, to generate unprecedented levels of publicity. Yet, apart from a few disturbances and physical assaults, Galicia remained generally peaceful.[90] There never was any real danger of the pogroms spreading across the Russo-Cisleithanian border. Despite this, both the pogroms and the streams of refugees and emigrants they launched left their mark on Galicia. Although Brody eventually emptied of migrants and tensions gradually eased as the anticipated attacks did not materialize, the Jewish question became a pressing issue once again. Now, however, it was no longer regarded as a purely legal question for parliament to regulate but a pan-European problem involving migration logistics, international aid organizations, and police intervention.

The tide of emigration from east to west and back affected all the countries it passed. Various groups perceived the arrival of emigrants in their hometown as a threat, or at least a nuisance. The public played a much larger role in the debate about this "new Jewish question" than it had when Jewish equality had been negotiated a decade previously. The government now listened far more carefully to the public's complaints and demands. State borders had proved permeable, and the authorities knew from experience that social upheaval not only set people and property in motion but also launched broad movements propelled by group dynamics. For the first time, the state, as a guarantor of law and order, became aware of the social dimension of the Jewish question. It found it could check and stop unrest if it had information about local relations between Jews and Christians and where the danger of unrest lurked. The Galician authorities became an important influence on Christian-Jewish coexistence.

Though dramatic, the agitation that occurred in response to the refugee movement remained limited to local contexts. No institutions drew political advantage from the events. Above-mentioned actors such as Merunowicz and Gorzkowski did not have any links with the villagers and townsfolk who sought to rob Jewish tradesmen, and were ultimately uninterested in the rural people´s concerns. Neither did they incorporate the events in Russia into their catalog of demands made of the Galician Jews. The events of 1881–1882 did not give rise to a history, or a peasant narrative, like the *rabacja* had. They did not start a tradition of peasant uprising. They did, however, pave the way to occurrences almost twenty years later in Galicia.

Jewish Responses to the Wave of Antisemitic Agitation

Galicia's Jewish population learned various lessons from the first wave of antisemitic agitation. The Jewish congregation in Lemberg, especially the "assimilatory circles," took the attacks on "benighted" Jews very much to heart. They saw the accusations, whether justified or not, as another reason to intensify their efforts to assimilate and reinforce their commitment to the Polish nation. Significantly, those first years saw the founding of Schomer Israel, an assimilatory society, and the relaunch of the Lemberg newspaper *Der Israelit* as *Izraelita*, with the name changed from German to Polish. Rural Jews were certainly more shaken by rumors about Jews being beaten and robbed than by diatribes against materialist Jewish art students. But the government and law enforcement agencies had proven willing and able to maintain order. Furthermore, the aid provided by the Alliance in Brody showed that there were organizations in the West capable of actively helping Jews in need.[91] Polish Jews demonstratively turned away from Vienna, in contrast to the majority, who allied themselves more closely to the capital. This was where the forces seeking to protect them were based—the imperial government, charitable and political organizations such as the Wiener Allianz, Josef Bloch's weekly newspaper, and the Austrian-Israelite Union.[92] Besides cause for concern, then, there was also cause for optimism in Galicia. Jewish equality had brought many advantages, such as the license to buy land. As the economy was restructured to become market-oriented, many more welcome opportunities arose for those who had hitherto had money but no land. However, Jews purchasing land and taking up agriculture was a thorn in the side of many Christians and a chief motivation behind the peasant movements and their policy of economic emancipation from the Jews. They represented a second antisemitic tendency, which no longer demanded that Jews assimilate but, on the contrary, called for separation and "liberation" and thus unequivocally rejected the liberal answer to the Jewish question.

Against Jewish Assimilation: The Second Phase of Antisemitic Agitation, 1889–1898

On an ideological level, anti-liberal tendencies in Galician politics materialized as early as the 1870s. In terms of party politics, however, they did not appear until the cusp of the 1890s, or even the middle of the decade. Around this time, the political landscape was vitalized by the founding of several new parties, by which various sociopolitical camps defined and distinguished themselves.[93] The new forces put an end to the rule of dignitaries and invited "the masses" to enter the world of national politics.[94] As parties rivaled for votes among the newly extended electorate, agitation in the public sphere substantially increased. For one, parties sought to present their policies and demands in a positive light to broad sections of the public, to make their standpoint clear and compelling. At the same time, they were at pains to portray the standpoints of their rivals in a nega-

Wybory w Krakowie: Ścisk wyborców przed lokalem »Piasek — Kleparz« w szkole im św. Wojciecha, ul. Biskupia.

Wybory w Krakowie: Kordon wojskowy przed lokalem wyborczym na placu WW. Świętych.

Figures 1.1 and 1.2. 1907 Reichsrat elections in Krakow, *Nowiny Illustrowane*, no. 31, 1907. Public domain.

tive light. Both resulted in an unprecedented quality and quantity of antisemitic agitation. For this reason, in terms of both content and time, it is apt to speak of a second wave of antisemitic agitation.

One of the new tendencies, which originated in Lemberg, can be described in generalizing terms as populism.[95] Its chief protagonists had connections with the Russian Empire and socialist circles.[96] The second was the Christian-social movement, of which Krakow was a center, and whose actors cultivated links with Rome and Vienna.[97] The Landtag elections of 1889 marked a first substantial defeat for the Galician conservatives and an upswing in populism. Consequently, a democratic, urban Polish opposition was formed in the Landtag, and a wave of new parties and newspapers was launched, which in turn initiated various Polish and Ukrainian peasant movements.

A broad, party-political, Catholic strain of agitation, virulent enough to have an impact on the cities, first materialized at the Krakow Catholics Day in 1893. This marked the start of concerted efforts by the Catholic-oriented press and

Figure 1.3. Reichsrat deputy and priest Michał Zyguliński (Tarnów) after his vote in the 1907 Reichsrat elections, *Nowiny Illustrowane*, no. 23, 1907. Public domain.

various societies and initiatives to win the lower classes for a Christian brand of socialism. But clerical politics, influenced by ultramontanism, only appealed to Roman Catholic—that is, Polish—activists.[98] Populist-democratic and Catholic-Socialist actors in West Galicia were therefore rivals for the same clientele. Despite their policies and ideologies intersecting, such parties conflicted hugely on a rhetorical, and sometimes even physical, level. The agitation climaxed during the long electoral campaign preceding the Reichsrat elections of 1897 and the by-elections of 1898, when a fifth voting class, or curia, was established, extending suffrage to all male citizens over twenty-four. In the following section, the emergence of the various political camps will be outlined in the light of antisemitic agitation, and the interdependencies that evolved between them during the electoral campaign considered.

Lemberg Populism: National, Social, and Jewish Questions

The political actors' new interest in the lower classes was not only due to the extension of suffrage. In a pan-European perspective, it can be regarded as the outcome of a long process, during which the lower classes became increasingly organized. As they did so, they articulated demands for greater participation, which in turn fostered their political communitization. Once awareness of the existence of social problems such as pauperism had been raised, political solutions for them had to be found. And in the multi-ethnic context of East Galicia, the "social question" was inextricably linked to the "peasant question" and the "Jewish" and "national" questions. Yet, although Christian farmers and Jewish traders and craftsmen were equally affected by poverty, efforts to improve the situation of all Galicia's inhabitants remained marginal.[99]

Solidarity among nationalities and religions was a far more dominant factor, which had the effect of turning the fiercely contested Galician agriculture and trade sectors into an arena of national rivalry. Modern Polish nationalism placed the peasantry at the center of its concept of the nation, seeing the peasants as guardians of an unadulterated form of Polish culture and therefore the basis for a strong future.[100] The Ukrainian nation did not have any nobility or middle class to speak of and was therefore a "people's nation" per se.[101] Jewish nationalism also rested on the lower classes as the middle-class elites aligned themselves with other national projects.[102] These three nationalities inhabited the same territory and shared the various sectors of Galicia's economy between them. But the nation was conceived of as an organism that could only thrive if it encompassed all social classes and, to an extent, functioned autonomously. So, nationalists strove for homogeneity where heterogeneity was the reality.[103]

Paradoxically, the loosening of traditional roles for Jews and Christians in the economy made a nation encompassing all economic sectors almost attainable and more remote at the same time. The increasing number of Christians taking up trade and financial services were universally supported and legitimized in their efforts. Jews entering agriculture, however, was a far more controversial change. They did so by purchasing Christian farmers' land, which was seen to occur at the expense of a Polish "national heritage."[104] Antagonism was fueled by the rise of the concept of the nation as an ethnic community on native territory, rather than the historical idea of the nation as a group aligned to one state. A driving force for basing territorial claims and national identity on ethnography rather than historiography was the Lemberg newspaper *Przegląd Społeczny* (Social Review), known for its correspondents of various nationalities.[105]

Journalism on Nations and Homelands: The Social Review, 1886–1887

Editor-in-chief of the *Przegląd Społeczny* newspaper was Bolesław Wysłouch, an émigré from the Tsarist Empire who was to become the doyen of the secular Polish peasant movement. He had spent three years in jail in Warsaw for "socialist activities," together with Bolesław Limanowski, who went on to found Polish socialism's nationalist movement and also contributed to the *Przegląd Społeczny*.[106] The newspaper's chief Ruthenian/Ukrainian representative was Ivan Franko, a socialist, who espoused the peasants' cause after initially championing the workers and strove to establish a democratic Polish-Ukrainian people's party. Wysłouch and Franko both believed that the interests of the Ukrainian and Polish peoples could harmonize and, indeed, only be satisfied in concurrence.[107]

Accordingly, they each recognized the legitimacy of the other's national claims. Their visions for their nations' futures stretched beyond Galicia and even beyond the territory of the former Polish-Lithuanian Kingdom. Their concept of national policy did not focus on restoring former territories but on creating homogenous nation-states with borders drawn according to ethnographic criteria. They did not perceive Poland as where the *szlachta* formed the upper class but where the *lud* had settled. Consequently, they laid claim to areas that had not belonged to the Polish crown even before the partitions, such as Silesia and Masuria. By the same token, Wsyłouch was prepared to renounce Polish territories east of the rivers San and Bug, where Poland had merely formed a colonizing upper class.[108] He frequently cited the fact that Polish-speaking peasants in Prussia had retained their "Polish identity" after centuries of German-language rule, while the aristocracy in Russia was already "Russified" after just a hundred years, as evidence of the "ordinary folk's" national integrity. The experiences of activists in the Tsarist Empire prompted many to go to Lemberg and left them more skeptical of Polish Jews. The "Litvaks"[109] seemed to them to be proof that Poland's Jews would disown Polish culture and the Polish nation at the next opportunity.

In the ethnically homogenous territories of the future that the *Przegląd Społeczny* envisaged, the smaller minorities would naturally assimilate. The Poles in "Ruthenia" would become Ruthenians, and the Ruthenians in Poland would become Poles. Jews, in contrast, did not predominate in any area apart from the cities, like islands on "foreign" territory, and were therefore perceived as obstacles to the Polish nation. Jews could only claim a right to exist as a nation if they emigrated and settled en bloc in Palestine. With these views, the *Przegląd Społeczny* explicitly called for an end to the assimilation project as the solution to the "Jewish question." While conceding that the relatively small number of assimilated Polish Jews could stay, it called for the majority to emigrate as they hindered the nation's development on its rightful territories.[110] The newspaper went so far as to stylize the work of the Alliance Israelite Universelle, and that of the Baron Hirsch Foundation for promoting Jewish agriculture in particular, a "Jewish conquest of Galicia,"[111] in which every Jewish entrepreneur who purchased peasants' land participated. In the light of the struggle for a national economy, barkeepers plying peasants with alcohol became the work of swindling, foreign Jews.[112] In this perspective, the Jews in Galicia were responsible for preventing the (Christian) nation from realizing its project of thriving on native territory. While Ruthenians and Poles provided mutual reassurance of a future alongside one another, on "naturally" delimited territories, "the Jews" figured as "third parties" who torpedoed the conceived unity of nation, territory, and economic life.[113]

It was less the borders of three empires, then, that frustrated the nationalists' mental maps than the presence of an impoverished minority that had been part of their worlds for centuries. This familiar minority became a problem when people started to doubt its place in the society of the future. Ukrainian nationalists already ruled out a national future with Jews, and even Polish nationalists were no longer sure that the Jews whose ancestors had immigrated to Poland long ago would ever become Poles. Populists noted that the Jewish intelligentsia aligned more with the Tsarist and German Empires and tended to adopt Russian or German as their colloquial language. As agents of Germanization and Russification, then, they seemed to be spurning Poland's centuries-old "gift" of tolerance and offer of national and cultural assimilation.[114] Indications of the reverse tendency in Galicia, where a rising number of Jews aligned with Polish rather than German culture, were overlooked.[115] Nationalists did not think in terms of crownlands and "Galician autonomy" but in terms of peoples and nations.[116]

The *Przegląd Społeczny*'s call for an end to assimilation was greeted by fierce criticisms and accusations of antisemitism, to which it responded with an article pointing out that many Jews also strove for "normal conditions for national development by forming a unified, cohesive community, residing in a separate territory."[117] The "Jewish question," it continued, could only be solved if the Galician Jews were a nation. To be a nation, they had to settle as a body in the territory to which they were historically entitled. This territory did not lie in Galicia, but in Palestine. The author of the article, Alfred Nossig, was an influential Jewish nationalist whose addition to the editorial staff added gravitas to the newspaper's transnational project of an ethnic-national order in Central Europe.[118]

Readers continued to accuse the newspaper of antisemitism and protest its calls for national policy to focus on ethnic criteria.[119] To counter the criticisms, Ivan Franko published an article titled "Semitism and antisemitism in Galicia," which discussed the feasibility of the Galician Jews' emigration to Palestine.[120] To offer a pragmatic solution, he suggested that some of the non-assimilated Jews should be able to stay in the country as legal aliens. As well as condemning assimilation and emigration, then, he was in favor of revoking equality in Galicia. Moreover, citing Teofil Merunowicz, he explicitly called for the abolition of the Kahal, which he claimed gave Jews an economic advantage. In the wake of the pogroms, socialists and populists (Russian: *narodniki*) in tsarist Ukraine had maintained that Jews constituted a harmful element.[121] The ensuing waves of migration through Galicia, when several thousand Jews emigrated overseas within a few months with the help of Western funding and logistics, had shown that mass emigration was possible. And some took it as evidence of the legendary wealth and influence of international Jewry, reaching even as far as Brody. Jews were more dominant in the rural economy of East Galicia than in the western districts, and Ukrainian Jews were not assimilated. Here, then, anti-Jewish sentiment was stronger, and Ivan Franko, as the newspaper's chief Ukrainian correspondent, formulated the harshest rhetoric against Jews.[122] Nevertheless, his comments were not exclusively Ukrainian opinions. They were printed in Polish, with reference to the prominent Polish-Galician politician Merunowicz and with the approval of Bolesław Wysłouch.

Thus, the *Przegląd Społeczny* propounded a Polish-Ukrainian populist manifesto in reaction to "Semitism." Doing so, it indirectly extended the meaning of antisemitism. As well as implying a rejection of equality and the assimilation project, it encompassed the demand for Jews to emigrate. This precipitated a sustained phase of political agitation, which was positively received by some of the electorate. The arrival of the populists and their definition of the "Jewish question" in the political arena marked the broadening of the antisemitic agenda. As well as "non-assimilated" Jews, "Jewish capitalists" at home and abroad now also became targets. Accusing them of planning to "conquer" Galicia, the populists portrayed them to the public as a threat to domestic interests.

The policies popularized by the *Przegląd Społeczny* went on to influence the leading political parties of the interwar period: the Peasant Party (PSL); the national Social Democratic Party (PPS); and the National Democracy movement (ND). The project of a Polish-Ukrainian party did not come to fruition. In 1889, an "urban diet" was held, in which Polish Democrats were able to distinguish themselves as a significant oppositional force against the conservatives. As a result, the ruling Conservatives, representing the landowning classes, suffered a bitter defeat at the subsequent Landtag elections. For the first time, starkly opposing camps emerged in parliament. The Conservatives were opposed not only by the Democrats, whose voters were mostly from the urban middle class, but also "from below," by the peasant population. Four members of the Catholic People's Club were voted in—the first peasant representatives to gain seats since the adoption of the constitution. In response to and motivated by their success, Ivan Franko and Michaljo Pavlyk founded the Ruthenian-Ukrainian Radical Party and an organ for it, titled *Narod* (The People). Not to be confused with the Ruthenian populists associated with the newspaper *Batkivsčyna* (Homeland), they thus continued the polarization and diversification of the political landscape. In the same year, Bolesław Wysłouch founded the newspaper *Przyjaciel Ludu* (The People's Friend), which was to become the platform for the People's Party.

Krakow Clericalism: Christian Socials against Liberalism and Social Democracy

Political Catholicism can also be traced back to the 1870s, a few decades before it emerged as a political movement in Galicia in the mid-1890s.[123] It evolved from clerical attempts to find Catholic answers to the country's social problems.[124] Crucial impetus was provided by the Vatican, which supported such efforts once it emerged from its self-imposed sociopolitical isolation.[125] Years of liberalism, climaxing in the founding of the Italian state, had shaken the Catholic understanding of the church's role and Catholic identity. Constitutional states asserted the right to govern areas that the church regarded as its natural prerogative. The seemingly indissoluble conflict between church and state led the Pope to declare liberalism irreconcilable with Catholicism.[126] Compulsory secular education, civil marriage, and the annulment of the guilds spelled the loss of clerical power and influence in central areas of life.[127] And in the eyes of the clergy, it caused social and moral disharmony by eroding the unity of religious doctrine and life. Concordats may have reassured the Vatican it was a supranational power with whom "consensual" arrangements had to be made, but they also placed Rome on the same footing as many other international contractual partners.

The Kulturkampf in the German empire and the abrogation of the concordat with Austria by the arch-Catholic House of Habsburg publicly destabilized the papacy's position and questioned whether the German and Austrian episcopacies and clergies would abide by the Summus Pontifex Ecclesiae Universalis in future or focus their loyalty on their respective "imperial and royal apostolic majesty." In 1870, Pope Pius IX responded to these challenges to the church's influence by publishing the dogma of papal infallibility. At the same time, there was a resurgence of ultramontanism in reaction to the increasing power of the constitutional states.¹²⁸ Pius's successor, Pope Leo XIII, then tried a new approach to reclaim the initiative for the church.¹²⁹

During Pope Leo's tenure, the church's rejection of all the unwelcome developments that "modernism" had brought gradually gave way to a sense of having to strike a different, Catholic path into the modern age. Previously, the church had frowned upon democratic contest and special-interest politics. But in 1891, Pope Leo XIII published the *rerum novarum* encyclical, calling for the establishment of Catholic societies and parties under the auspices of the clergy.¹³⁰ It was clear from the very first sentence of the encyclical that the papacy envisaged Catholic communitization in opposition to secular and materialist socialism. The Catholic Church was entering the contest of ideologies and social groupings to win back the influence it had lost in recent decades. Its basic premise was that the separation of state and church, and secular conceptions of society and politics, were unlawful intrusions on society's God-given traditions and order. It aimed to defend itself against the concerted attacks by the enemies of the church, including socialists, liberals, freemasons, capitalists, and Jews.

As Jews were internationally prominent figures in the worlds of finance, laissez-faire liberalism, and social democracy, "Jewry" seemed to the church to be the missing link between the diverse and conflicting forces it had identified as its "enemies." The last camp to become organized in Galicia, political Catholicism had to contend for participation in the community and win supporters from its established rivals. As newcomers to politics, the clergy faced the challenge of making their specific message heard over the others.¹³¹ They perceived their advance into the political arena as a campaign to defend the absolute truth. And, utilizing the church's substantial potential to mobilize, they soon brought an end to the liberal era of politics for and by the middle-class elites. With its widely ramified network of actors, along with the considerable financial means it had at its disposal, the church hierarchy put all the other political options in the shade. The lower clergy knew how their congregations' minds worked and the problems with which they struggled, and the latter accepted them as authority figures. As soon as the low-income classes gained the right to vote, then, the clergy were able to turn their knowledge and influence into political capital. The success of the Christian Social movement In Lower Austria proved the enormous potential of clerical, anti-liberal politics.¹³² In Galicia, however, political Catholicism did not first take root in the cities but in the country, among the peasants.

"Protector of the People" and "Demagogue in a Cassock": Stanisław Stojałowski (1845–1911)

In Galicia, the first person to prove that the moral authority of a priest was expedient to encouraging those who were suspicious of government and the secular authorities to take part in politics was Stanisław Stojałowski (see figure 1.4).[133] The son of a landowner from East Galicia, he had seen the poverty, shortage of land, and lack of prospects afflicting the rural Christian population while on "folk missions" during his training at the seminary in West Galicia. In the early 1870s, he spent a year in Belgium, where he was inspired by the assertive involvement in politics of the Catholic clergy, who were especially committed to helping the Christian lower classes.[134]

Figure 1.4. Stanisław Stojałowski, *Nowiny Illustrowane*, no. 23, 1907. Public domain.

On his return to Galicia, he became a central figure in the day's "village awakening." He built a large following via the newspapers he published and assemblies he held,[135] in which he encouraged the peasants to become organized in order to achieve economic autonomy. A conservative, his goal was to establish a cooperative society, and he saw modern agricultural cooperatives as a way of realizing it. The popularity of the "farming circles" he set up proved that many peasants were willing to try to improve their situations.[136] While he was certainly charismatic, his success was due in part to his strategy of linking political and patriotic events with pilgrimages and long sermons. He used these to draw a positive picture of Catholic peasants, the *lud*, and denounce their supposed antagonists, the *szlachta* and the Jews. He consequently became an enemy of Galicia's secular and intellectual elite, whom he accused of decadence and abuses of power.[137] Their counterattacks on the ultramontane priest, whom they labeled a "demagogue in a cassock," only served to reinforce his reputation as a hero in the eyes of many peasants.[138] With his frequent references to Jesus's "true teachings" and the Bible, he appeared thoroughly committed to defending the interests of the "ordinary people." His followers accepted his Manichean view of liberalism and socialism as ungodly, materialist ideologies and mortal enemies of the harmonious social order that was God's will. He styled himself a protector of the peasants, defending them against duplicity from all sides—for example, Jewish barkeepers who enticed them into drinking alcohol, took their savings, and prevented them from working, or Jewish tradesmen who paid too little for the meager yields of their backbreaking work, or Jewish moneylenders who charged extortionate rates of interest to appropriate peasant property by necessitating foreclosure sales. Jews, he preached, took power into their own hands, sometimes via straw men, by means of fraudulent electoral maneuvers, and were gradually moving from a marginalized position to dominate the Christians.[139]

Stojałowski urged his followers not to respond to these "facts" with peasant fatalism or allow themselves to be fobbed off by the idle "liberal" government. Hard work "in the sweat of their brows," he insisted, was the Catholic peasants' God-given destiny. But they could ease their burden by leading a sober life and helping to initiate and support Christian community stores and peasant banks. Farming circles, reading rooms, and libraries would, in his view, enable "the people" to emerge from "darkness." Reading rooms and the church were promoted in his newspapers as alternatives to the tavern—the hotbed of vice. He encouraged personal responsibility, discipline, and neighborhood controls in the villages, led by reliable priests. But he deemed it necessary for peasants to learn organization and gain experience on a local level before being able to represent their interests as members of parliament in Lemberg and Vienna.[140] Using Catholic and peasant idioms and symbolism, he drew an image of pious peasants with which his followers could identify. And he invited them to write to his newspapers, thus offering them a participatory device that confirmed that every individual's actions could have an impact on the world at large and that anybody could take the lead and set a good example.

Galicia had a long tradition of viewing Jews as the cause of alcoholism. The modern peasant movement took this antagonism one step further by calling for peasants to take over barkeeping, trade, and moneylending—spheres of activity that had hitherto been the domain of Jews. The establishment of peasant banks and community stores meant nothing less than the Christians' advance into fields that had hitherto been conceived of as Jewish.[141] The people of Lutcza, to take an example from the introduction, would then no longer have to buy their tobacco from Moses Ritter but could go to a newly opened "Christian" store, run by Franka's brother, perhaps, or Jędrzej Noster. With their appeals to the public, Lutcza's village priests, Jan and Jakub Drzewiecki, were typical supporters of Stojałowski's clerical movement, who saw themselves as authorities able to represent the peasants' interests and to mediate between the worlds of textual and oral communication.

The rise of monetary economy following the emancipation of the serfs and the abolition of restrictions on Jews changed the world as the peasants knew it. As estates-based society dissolved, conventional categories of profession according to ethnicity no longer applied. But they were still referred to and normatively charged in contemporary debate. Christians wanted peasants to be able to work in trade and moneylending and even run taverns, providing they only served beer and no brandy. But they wanted agriculture and landowning to remain in Christian hands, too. The increasing involvement of Jews in primary sectors of the economy was widely regarded as a violation of the law, which demanded correcting.[142]

Despite the changes in the economy, where services were gaining importance and competition was diversifying in the primary sector due to the customs union and the railways, economic processes were still regarded as a zero-sum game.[143] Whatever "the Christians" gained, the "the Jews" lost, and vice versa.[144] In an ethnocentric perspective, then, a Christian opening a village store to replace one run by a Jew was a gain, regardless of how it affected the supply of the local population. By the same token, it was regarded as a loss for the Christian community if a Jew opened a new store.[145] In this respect, the views disseminated in Stojałowski's newspapers and those of the Lemberg populists hardly differed. Both promoted education, cooperatives, and the boycott of Jewish stores and bars as the royal road to stopping the threatened "Jewish conquest" of Galicia.[146]

In view of these overlapping beliefs, several parties can be regarded as constituting the peasant movement. Their individual utopias of community forming, however, differed. To the Ukrainian radicals, the *narod* was the core of an ethnically homogenous nation alongside other nations, while to the *ludowcy* it was the *lud*. To Stojałowczyki, the *lud* was the most important estate in a Catholic, corporatist society within the community of Christian peoples.[147] The main difference between these concepts lay in their interpretation of the church's importance for the community and the clergy's role within them.[148] But what might have been a burning question for the intelligentsia hardly preoccupied the village peasants, for whom the church was simply a de facto part of everyday life, and who just wanted concrete improvements of their social and material situations. The talk of *lud* was initially nothing more than talk. But it was made a tangible reality through the performance of election campaigns and the very act of voting, marking a commitment to the political community of peasants.

One People—Three Parties: The Peasant Parties and Their Fight for Unity, 1895–1898

Prior to the Landtag election of 1895, there were two parties that claimed to represent the interests of the Polish-speaking people.[149] The first grew from the so-called Catholic People's Club, the four members of parliament whom Stojałowski's newspapers had supported. In 1892, one of his newspapers printed a "Peasant Party program," signed by the parliamentarian Stanisław Potoczek and endorsed by his brother Jan, who had become a member of the Reichsrat for the conservative Polish Club one year previously. The Potoczeks came from the area around Nowy Sącz, where the farmers were more prosperous and a farmers' lobby had existed for some time. Their peasant party union, Związek Stronnictwa Chłopskiego, declared its fundamental pillars to be "God" and "the saints," or the Roman Catholic faith and the interests of the "peasantry." Its program promised allegiance to the throne, church, and government.[150] This was the chief bone of contention between the union and Stojałowski, who was a founding member and allowed them to use his newspapers as party organs. Indeed, the union's loyalty to the official church and government not only conflicted with Stojałowski's views but also with those of the elites.[151]

As Jan Potoczek had a seat in the Reichsrat among the Conservatives and was dependent on their good will, the union—officially founded as a political society—parted company with Stojałowski, which meant losing many of his followers, too. In 1894, the Potoczeks established their own party organ, *Związek Chłopski* (Peasant Union). Their party remained a locally anchored, conservative peasant lobby that was sensitive to the recommendations of the church and the government.[152] Yet their press organ was far from moderate. *Związek Chłopski* directed the same level of hostility that Stojałowski's newspapers shared between the nobility, government, high clergy, Jews, liberals, and socialists, entirely at their immediate rivals, the secular Stronnictwo Ludowe (People's Party)[153] and the Jews.

The People's Party (SL) had emerged from the circle around Bolesław Wysłouch, also in 1895. It achieved a breakthrough at the Landtag elections when it gained nine mandates and the Lemberg journalist Jan Stapiński emerged as its clear fig-

Ludowcy w Krakowie: Wydział Rady naczelnej stronnictwa ludowców: 1. Krempa, 2. dr. Bernadzikowski, 3. Bojko, 4. Styła, 5. Olszewski, 6. Włodek, 7. dr. Bardel 8. Stapiński, 9. Bomba, 10. Bytkowski, 11. Wójcik.

Figure 1.5. Populist deputies (SL) in Krakow, *Nowiny Illustrowane*, no. 34, 1907. Public domain.

urehead.[154] Like Stojałowski, he advocated an anti-elitist agenda and was critical of the government. Indeed, the two men exchanged correspondence while Stojałowski was imprisoned in Teschen to prevent him from entering the Landtag. But they were divided on their attitudes to Catholic doctrine. Consequently, in 1896, Stojałowski decided to set up his own party, the Stronnictwo Chrześciańsko-Ludowe (Christian People's Party).[155] To prevent the Galician authorities from constantly interfering in his work, he moved his home and publishing operations away from Galicia—to Czaca in Hungary, Teschen in Silesia, and finally to Vienna. Here, he sought the support and cooperation of the Christian Socialists. He envisaged a party that was as decidedly emancipatory and anti-elitist as the People's Party, and as religious as the Peasant Union, but operated under the banner of "Christian Socialism." He, too, claimed the Catholic peasants' two most powerful identity markers for his own political party.

One year before the first Reichsrat election in 1897, in which all men over twenty-four were called upon to vote, the above three parties then rivaled for the support of the Polish-speaking peasants. The Reichsrat elections were of considerable importance as they promised to link Galicians with the capital. Vienna and the emperor were highly esteemed among the electorate, and a connection with a political sphere beyond the reach of the Conservative-dominated administration and legal system could create hitherto unprecedented possibilities for political activity. Sending a delegate to the capital to inform the emperor of the wrongs in Galicia was to many an appealing prospect.

Divided Communities: The Election Campaigns of 1897/1898

Stojałowski's points of intersection with the other two peasant parties show that they were by no means separated by insurmountable ideological rifts. On the contrary, their views on the issues that needed prioritizing and the best policies for dealing with them often overlapped. The differences between them were to a large extent construed—a product of election campaign logic—but nonetheless accentuated when scrutinizing the moral standards of their political rivals. Where they stood on the church and the Jews was regarded as evidence of how honorable they were, or not. The explicitly Catholic parties portrayed the secular People's Party as untrustworthy and unprincipled.[156]

Conversely, the secular People's Party tried to portray its two rivals as puppets of the clergy. However, this strategy failed to make any impact until Stojałowski publicly affirmed that he would desist from agitating against the governors and the episcopate in Krakow. He had been convinced to do so not by the threat of imprisonment but by his brief papal excommunication.[157]

With a major opponent—the ruling elite—rendered taboo, Stojałowski's newspapers turned to attacking the People's Party and the Jews with even greater vehemence and hinted that the two were collaborating on the party's election campaign. "Stojałowski's opponents are like Judas, a traitor, who after accepting Jesus's kiss throws himself in to the arms of the Jews."[158] By referring to the figure of Judas, the newspaper impressed a link between treachery and Judaism onto the public consciousness. When the press discredited political opponents as traitors, they illustrated their allegations with incidents that the rural electorate had personally experienced in the critical phase of the election campaign. Election meetings were held in villages to publicize party programs in the countryside. It was not uncommon for supporters of the opposing parties to mingle among the attendees at these events and deride the campaigning party's proposals and designs for community. The potential for violence at many such events, sometimes culminating in raids and stick fights, caused emotions to run high. Here, two sides came face to face, each of which claimed to represent the true and natural unity of the peasant community. Every time a section of the community chose to support one party, and therefore rejected the other, a rift cut through the village.

Mock elections were often held. During the by-elections in 1898, there were an average of two simulations per day.[159] It was not easy for a village community that traditionally sought consensus and solidarity to bear this level of tension. The polarization caused by violent election meetings was a manifestation and performance of the old order's disintegration and the loss of peasant unity and strength. Rather than regarding this as a symptom of the abstract democratic electoral system, people blamed "traitors," whom they believed to be in league with the alleged beneficiaries of peasant discord, the Jews.

Fighting for the same clientele's votes, the three expressly anti-Jewish parties accused each other of being in league with the Jews, whether by doing deals with them, by having accepted bribes from them, or by being of Jewish origin themselves.[160] The apparent credibility of such allegations was symptomatic of the collapse of the old, estates-based society and its ethnic categories. Its rhetorical separation of the Christian from the Jewish professional spheres increasingly failed to reflect reality; it was a normatively justified division that was becoming artificial.[161] If manor owners were no longer *Szlachcic* but Jews, was it not feasible that Jews were behind the democratic People's Party, or that the Peasant Union was a Jewish idea, devised to split the hitherto united *lud*? The foundations of traditional culture were additionally shaken by the peasant movement appropriating occupational fields in trade and money-lending that had hitherto been decried as foreign, harmful, and Jewish. This process was initiated by agitation and changed popular ideas of the kindred and the other. The question of whether it took on meaning on the level of action will be explored in the following chapters.

In the call to branch out, and to boycott Jewish stores and support Christian ones, the connective, communicative function of antisemitic agitation is evident. The slogan "Buy only from Christians" articulated both the populists' vision of an ethnically homogenous economic sphere and the clergy's vision of a harmonious and just Christian order. The slogan was emblazoned on all the peasant newspapers, where Christian businesses naturally advertised. Here, political agitation was closely linked with economic enterprise. An advertisement for a Christian dealer, who was of course no more honest or better value than a Jewish dealer, required justification by politics; disseminating this justification could be profitable for the individual storeowner. The notion that it benefited all members of a community if they only purchased from "their kind" was propagated by those individuals who really stood to profit from it. Boycotting the competition was presented as a step toward realizing a political vision that promised prosperity for all its members. To boycott was to act for the good of the community. This action, combined with the political debate, conveyed a sense of belonging. And there was a widespread longing for community and prosperity within the divided and impoverished peasantry, which sustained the boycott discourse.

The "others," the Jews, also changed in this context. With the appropriation and re–interpretation of branches of the economy that had hitherto been branded malign and Jewish, "Jewishness" lost its discrete place in the economic system and became a principle that could appear anywhere.[162] As Christian and Jewish spheres of activity were no longer all distinct, and Christians appealed to fellow believers to pursue "Jewish occupations," the concept of "the Jew" and

"Jewishness" became diffuse and yet a cypher for all things hostile.[163] Dealers were no longer regarded per se as dishonest, nor moneylenders as extortionate, but anyone acting unfairly was thought to be a Jew. Falsehood and duplicity were no longer considered inherent risks in any business deal but only if dealing with a "Jewish businessman." Politicians and newspapers were decried as "Jewish" if they were thought to be untruthful or acting against the interests of the people.[164]

The newspapers smelled treachery and conspiracies everywhere. Peasant party organs used nightmare scenarios of the victory of the "other" to rally their readers to the cause of the cooperative movement and the boycott and to encourage them to vote as ways to improve their situation. Agitation was a game involving promises and threats in equal parts. As the once clear allocation of Jewish and Christian rights and occupations was gone but still etched into the popular memory as tradition and norms, everything that was "sacred" to Christians seemed potentially "at the mercy" of the Jews.

If the Jews could even buy the peasants' home soil, having first plunged them into debt by fraud and usury, they would probably not stop at buying all of Galicia. Such fantasies, in the light of which the remarkable success of individual Jewish businesspeople was interpreted as the result of a concerted action by "Jewry," were disseminated not only by Ivan Franko's newspapers but also by *Związek Chłopski* and Stojałowski's publications. The Rothschilds' wealth, the Baron Hirsch Foundation's investments, and the Alliance Israelite's "universal" claim were all cited as evidence of the Jews' plot to turn Galicia into a "Jewish kingdom."[165]

Anti-Jewish rhetoric was a key component of communication within all three parties and often the lowest common denominator linking readers and editors, who were simultaneously voters and candidates. Social problems were diagnosed as the symptoms of too strong a Jewish influence, and stemming this influence—ultimately by ensuring the emigration of Jews—was prescribed as the remedy. Contemporary peasant identity, the modern "we," was constructed by means of excluding the Jews. Traditional, religious, and estates-based misgivings and prejudices were reinterpreted and harnessed for party-political purposes. The concept of Jews as the enemy was updated in the light of the altered zones of contact between Jews and Christians, which had shifted several times since the middle of the century. These changes were incorporated into allegations of Jewish arrogance and conspiracies, which the Stańczyks in their ignorance allowed to befall the peasants, in a comprehensible and self-affirming way.

Peasant movement agitation greatly advanced the antisemitic process. Jews were unequivocally identified as opponents, unless they were Zionists who agreed they should leave Europe. Political agitation not only legitimized the boycott of Jews but also demanded resolute action against Jews in everyday life. Jews were excluded from the imagined community on principle, and this community was inevitably caught in an antagonistic situation, a struggle with the Jews. To the agitators, the "Jewish question" in the age of equality was not a question of whether Jews assimilated—that is, conformed to the majority. The assimilation of the "Jewish masses" was simply not considered possible—into either the ethnically or religiously construed community. Existing parameters such as the constitutional state, equality, or even state borders were irrelevant in this context. Agitators did not even purport to work toward legislation against Jews but took a more direct route, committing their target groups to act in a specific way. They aimed to convince their clientele that they could solve the Jewish question themselves by their own everyday practice, without having to wait for the help of the state and its laws. The communicative space in which these actors circulated their messages was also a very different one from that of the first wave of antisemitic agitation. Though they did not (yet) speak from the big stages, the courts, or parliament, they spoke via channels they installed themselves—popular newspapers and rural meetings. These marked counter-public spheres that, although they were often censored, nonetheless allowed an entirely new exchange between activists and their clientele to take place, since they were assured of representing the overwhelming majority whose needs and demands would one day prevail. This agitation did not address Jews, who were allegedly damaging to an interdenominational society, but called on Christians to take resolute action against the harmful elements.

This brand of antisemitism did not appeal to Jews to assimilate or be humbler but assigned Christians a task. It did not seek agreement with the Jews but dispute. This in turn conveyed a threat to its own clientele: if they continued to support the Jews by doing business with them, thus sustaining the "ambivalent symbiosis," they acted to the detriment of their "own kind." As a result, everyday conduct toward Jews became carefully considered and awareness was raised of when and where Christian-Jewish contact occurred. Anyone operating in the context of this discourse could no longer see the Ritters just as neighbors but would always see "the Jew" in them first. From this perspective, Marcel Stochliński and Franka Mnich were a burden on the *lud* because they had a share in the Ritters' prosperity. They drew personal advantage to the detriment of their community, just like the other neighbors who gathered for a drink in the *Trafik* of an evening.

Agitation and Everyday Life: Antisemitic Practice?

Although readers and voters sympathized with the peasant parties' antagonistic interpretations of Christian-Jewish relations and their implications, they did not necessarily comply with their demand to change their behavior toward Jews in everyday life. Passing by a Jewish store to find a Christian one further away and which might be more expensive, avoiding the local tavern if it was run by a Jew, and refusing work from Jewish employers were actions that made life more difficult and created disadvantages for the individual. The purported advantage for the community arising from such practice was ultimately imagined and abstract; it only existed in the context of discourse about national vested rights. Nevertheless, the anti-Jewish boycott discourse was not unproductive. It stimulated thought about the consequences of consumer behavior and the sobriety campaign and the benefits of peasant cooperatives. In concrete situations of economic conflict, it provided a potential guideline by which to act. Following the rules of this discourse, one could generate negative publicity about any form of Jewish competition. And any kind of competition could be delegitimized as "Jewish competition." The antisemitic agitation conducted by editors, candidates, and voters therefore influenced popular ideas of Jews and was simultaneously a device used in political competition. In the peasant parties' political communication, antisemitic agitation developed, then, in both directions.

To classify a subscription to a certain newspaper or membership of a cooperative as antisemitic practice would be an inflation. Even voting for the Christian People's Party or the Peasant Party union did not necessarily imply a commitment to antisemitism. For the rural population who wanted to avoid voting Conservative, there was no alternative. All the political camps that professed to stand for change and to improve the peasants' situation were anti-Jewish. Candidates for the Social Democratic Party did not even stand in the rural West Galician constituencies for the Reichsrat elections of 1897. The party had come to an agreement with Stojałowski to leave the rural constituencies to him if he did not stand in the towns. It was a pragmatic arrangement designed to pool each party's resources where they had the best chances of success. It made no secret of the fact that the Social Democrats expected more votes from the urban population. And it showed that there was even some overlap between the Social Democrats and the Christian People's Party. Yet Stojałowski renouncing his right to campaign for votes on the streets did not mean that there was no Christian-social agitation in Krakow. This was the heartland of Polish Catholicism. Its representatives tried to revive and continue the successes of the Christian Socials in Vienna and be a force against liberalism and social democracy. In this way, they raised antisemitic agitation to new levels.

The Christian-Social Movement in the City

The following subchapter looks at anti-Jewish agitation in Catholic newspapers up to the disturbances of 1898. Like the previous section, it will not attempt a semantic analysis of anti-Jewish writing but rather describe the functions and significance of anti-Jewish agitation within political communication and consider how this propelled the antisemitic process. Aside from the religious press's usefulness or otherwise for gaining mandates, it had a major influence on the negotiation of what could be said about Jews and relations between Jews and non-Jews. The old university town of Krakow became the hub of clerical activity in Galicia. The first Galician Catholics Day in July 1893 was pervaded by the mood of new beginnings that the encyclical *rerum novarum* had engendered. Not only in Krakow, Catholics set out to establish their own friendly societies, workhouses, loan societies, and newspapers. Their goal was to apply a Catholic conception of community to all areas of society and to directly address the newly emerging professional groups and social milieus. The new Catholic organizations were intended to rival both the Social Democratic societies and the Jewish predominance in trade and industry.

Christian-Social Newspapers and Societies

In the same year as the Catholic Day, Józef Rogosz established the daily newspaper *Głos Narodu* (Voice of the Nation). By 1896, it had become the widest-selling Krakow daily under its politically active editor-in-chief Kazimierz Ehrenberg.[166] From the outset, it printed the slogan "Buy only from Christians" on the front page, which became a firm fixture of the clerical press. *Głos Narodu* struck an exceedingly militant tone toward the opponents of clericalism.

Like the peasant parties, most of the Christian-social societies were established a few years later, between the Landtag elections of 1895 and the Reichsrat election of 1897/98. In this period, over ten associations for Catholic workers were set up, each of which published its agenda in weekly or monthly newspapers.[167] The newspaper *Prawda* (Truth) was another Krakow publication, established in 1896, which was loyal to the church and addressed "the people." Funded by the Krakow bishop Jan Puzyna, it agitated fiercely against Jews.[168]

The newspaper *Pochodnia* (The Torch), the "Polish-Catholic workers' mouthpiece," was established in Lemberg in 1895. It styled itself the Catholic answer to social democracy, which it claimed was the product of Jewish manipulation. The clerical camp was the youngest political force in Galicia and sought to make its mark on existing traditions of political expression.[169] In early summer 1895 it gained an opportunity. In Żywiec again, a Galician of Jewish origin, the doctor of law Zygmunt Leser, was attacked two days after renting accommodation on Krakowska Street in the town center.[170] According to the bill of indictment, over two thousand people, some of whom had come especially from the surrounding regions, marched singing[171] to the house of the landlord, a certain Raczek. Eleven people broke into the house, smashing and stealing household items and furnishings.[172] In court, the accused cited the law of 1809 prohibiting Jews from settling in the town. The prospective lawyer Leser did not see himself as a Jew at all but as a Pole and accused the urban intelligentsia of having raised the crowd against him. The newspaper *Pochodnia* subsequently twisted his comments to portray the lawyer as a "socialist general" and the mob's carnivalesque behavior as an exemplary initiative by "Christian workers," putting a stop to the Jewish socialist's attempts to agitate. Thus, while the people on the street continued a bizarre local tradition from previous centuries, the Christian-social press tried to dress it as a political action by the working population, to serve as an example to other towns on how to deal with "Jewish socialists."

The newspaper *Grzmot* (The Thunder), established in 1896 in Lemberg as a "Catholic workers' paper," was remarkable for trying to set up an umbrella organization for Catholic associations in Galicia.[173] In November the editorial office moved to Krakow, where it was able to double its circulation.[174] Almost every one of the newspaper's articles contained the claim that social democracy was financed and infiltrated by Jews and not in fact interested in improving the workers' situation at all.[175] Its clear support of Sunday closing—less on religious grounds than to undermine the Jewish retail competition[176]—showed that it aimed to address Christian tradespeople as well as workers. The newspaper *Grzmot* ran a supplement especially for the Catholic maids among its readership, *Przyjaciel Sług* (The Maid's Friend), which illustrates the Christian Socials' efforts to provide a Catholic platform for every social group and is considered below.

The Tale of the Good Catholic Maidservant and "Jewish Women-Trafficking"

Following the tried-and-tested formula used by the peasant newspapers, the editors of the above-mentioned supplement, all of whom were priests, sought to forge a community of Catholic maids via correspondence and readers' letters, and the "Community of Saint Zyta." The supplement contained columns written by nuns, lead articles, and a popular gossip page titled "What goes on in the world?" (*Co słychać na świecie*) to offer moral guidelines and try to control the target group, which was in many respects "at risk."[177] Thrift, modest dress, diligence, and prayer were the positive reference points suggested to guarantee a contented and decent life even in the most dissolute city.[178] Jews were excluded from the Catholic system of information and controls, inhabited by priests, nuns, and "girlfriends."[179] *Przyjaciel Sług* ran purported confessionals to warn its readers against Jewish employers.[180] Containing descriptions of brutal physical punishments, sexual assault, and bad pay, they were designed to convince Catholic maids to avoid Jewish houses.

These reports portrayed Jews as the embodiment of an immoral and un-Christian lifestyle that threatened to lead Christian maids to ruin. In the worst cases, Jews abducted unsuspecting girls from the country under the pretense of finding them employment in a respectable household and sold them as prostitutes in Cairo or Buenos Aires. The trade in women, to be sold as prostitutes all over the world, was indeed especially rife in East Galicia.[181] However, not only the middlemen and the traffickers were almost exclusively Jews but also the women, whom the press referred to as "living merchandise." Young women were approached in the Galician provinces by human traffickers purporting to work for international marriage bureaus. Some women preferred the idea of earning money abroad as prostitutes to staying in Galicia in oppressive conditions with no prospects. Galicia's "white slavery" was a complex phenomenon that was discussed all over the world. While feminist and humanitarian initiatives sought to fight the causes of human trafficking, some commentators harnessed the debate on poverty for antisemitic purposes, including the *Przyjaciel Sług*.[182] According to the latter, it was Jewish traffickers who violently abducted Christian girls, or lured them with false promises, to sell them into prostitution.[183]

Portrayals such as these in *Przyjaciel Sług*, intended to demarcate the Christian world from that of the Jews and to consolidate religious ideas on morality in the minds of domestic employees, contributed to the othering and criminalization of Jews that Catholic newspapers in general conducted. Any mention of Jews and their allegedly subversive effect on society in Catholic newspapers recalled the "other," allowing journalists to address issues that were unsayable in a "respectable" Catholic context. With Jews identified as the clear causes of the dangers that lurked in the big city, a relatively straightforward solution for keeping out of harm's way could be advised. By simply avoiding contact with Jews and restricting one's movements to between the (Christian) home and the church, women would be safe from exploitation and "moral downfall." Articles to this effect were written in plain language and addressed readers directly in a familiar tone. But their paternalistic and moralizing views reflected the demands of the employers more than those of the maids.[184] Indeed, the entire Christian-social movement struggled to connect with its target public while also fulfilling its perceived obligation to promote Catholic harmony in its early years.

It had become apparent at the Catholic Day that the conservative conception of harmony and one-sided focus on "the Jews" as adversaries complicated the task of offering positive identification models to a society that was becoming more differentiated. At this occasion, the famous scholar, rector of the Jagiellonian University, and Conservative politician Count Stanisław Tarnowski had called for an "economic fight" against the Jews.[185] But at the same time, he warned against antisemitism, which he condemned as a "vulgar, mass phenomenon."[186] His comments elucidated three of the four major problems facing the Christian-social movement in Galician cities up to the Reichsrat elections of 1897—issues that become even more glaring against the background of Stojałowski's enterprises and Karl Lueger's German Christian Social Party, founded in Lower Austria the same year as the Krakow Catholic Day. This party was to become a shining example of clericalism in Central Europe in the ensuing years. Under the banner of politics for Christian tradespeople, Lueger managed to win over the lower clergy and public servants for his integrative political movement as a bulwark against the liberals and social democracy.[187] His counterparts in Krakow failed for reasons considered below.

Entanglement with the Conservative Milieu

In Galicia, the Christian-social movement's press organs, societies, and actors were supported by the bishops of Krakow and Tarnów, who saw them as means of accessing publics that conservative camps could use. It was not in their interest to have any more political rivals, so they did not back any initiatives for new parties. The bishops expected the newspapers to endorse the Christian-social candidates listed by the Conservative central election committee.

The movement was, then, too enmeshed in the establishment to distance itself from it. It could not emulate the independence of Stojałowski or Lueger to get previously disenfranchised voters involved in politics, as they had. To criticize "the system" and the government in 1880s Vienna was to condemn liberal and secular politics. The Liberal (constitutional) Party was an easy opponent as it was already in decline. In Galicia, the Conservatives represented the system, and their power, too, had become decidedly shaky since around 1889/90. Although they were not as strongly in favor of separating church and state, they advocated keeping power in the hands of the traditional elite and excluding the lower classes from political participation. In contrast to Lueger, then, who boosted his party by attacking the weakened Liberals, the Christian-social movement's attachment to the Conservatives was a millstone around its neck, impeding its mobilization of the people on the street.

Unease with "Populist" Techniques

But the Conservatives faced an even larger problem, which grew from their reluctance to speak directly to the "masses," regarding this as "sedition" that would lead to unrest and disorder. Their ideal of a "harmonious"—that is, hierarchical but cross-class—social order, in which the God-given authorities knew best how to ensure the public good, conflicted with the demand for milieu-exclusive designs for communitization. Political parties had no appeal unless they spoke directly to their target group, with knowledge of its experiences, fears, and values, in a language attuned to its educational horizons. Their claim to represent these interests gained credibility by disassociation from antagonists. Lueger and Stojałowski were political leaders who cleverly demonstrated a positive attitude to the Church and Catholicism, styled themselves pious and humble men, and showed by their dialect and sociolect that they, too, belonged to the target group, which was in fact a product of their discourse. The new voters felt vindicated by their diatribes against "them up there," attacks on middle-class affluence and intellectualness, reassurances that this had nothing to with envy but that "instinct" was akin to "decency" and "integrity," and articulations of the fear of losing social status and longing to climb out of a disadvantaged background. The much-admired Dr. Karl Lueger conveyed all this with authenticity.[188] A politician who spoke the people's language and had the wit and sharp tongue to prove he had internalized it, he was able to convince the people of his intention to represent their interests. By describing them, he proved he was familiar with them.

The Galician Conservatives did not permit the lower clergy to speak or write to the public in the popular vernacular. Their communication took a one-sided approach: the Conservatives and clergy spoke down from their elevated position, as legitimized by God, tradition, and ownership, to the "masses," whom they hoped to educate. Preachers consolidated their authority through distance—created by the sublime language of the Latin liturgy, the raised position of the altar and the pulpit, and the circumstance that they were unburdened by physical labor, the threat of unemployment, or the trials of supporting a family on a working man's pay. This clerical removal from everyday life prevented the conservatives from creating the sense of affinity with potential voters that is required to legitimize democratic politics.

Low Urban Appeal

Tarnów and Krakow became the two centers of the Christian-social movement in Galicia.[189] In both towns, Jews constituted a large section of the population—about 30 percent—a disproportionate number of which were among the occupational groups and classes that had recently benefited from the extension of suffrage: manual laborers, workers, soldiers, messenger people, clerks and sales assistants, store owners, and teachers. It was by no means natural for these urban groups to identify with expressly Catholic politics. Krakow was evolving into a regional metropolis. Newly incorporated suburbs and migration from the country caused the population to swell. Industrialization, sewerage, electricity, and technological innovations in the worlds of work and transport were changing the everyday lives and perceptions of the people of Krakow. While processing these developments, they developed an urban identity oriented toward "European progress," which had more appeal than religious or national propositions.[190] A Catholic employee who lived in a tenement and went to work by horsecar every day had more in common with his Jewish neighbor and colleague than with a Polish peasant from Lutcza.

Krakow's tabloid newspapers did not focus on Christian-Jewish conflict. Stojałowski may have done an excellent job of squaring the peasant world of experience with a Catholic identity. But the conservative-led Christian-social newspapers were not able to create a sense of urban Catholic community. Failing to pick up on any initiatives "from below," the clergy went no further than preaching to all comers. They frequently attributed specific urban phenomena such as anonymity and certain forms of criminality, which they condemned as threatening, immoral, and harmful, to the "others," the Jews. Hence, they alienated many city-dwellers, whom they were not able to offer a positive alternative with which to identify. While the people of Krakow liked to be compared with Parisians, Londoners, Berliners, or the Viennese, the editors of *Pochodnia* and *Prawda* tried to convince them to emulate the provincial town Żywiec and its anti-Jewish citizens.

"Christian" Misgivings about Antisemitism

Since Christian-social politics lacked the capacity to address different social groups due to the Catholic claim to unity, it relied on attacks on the opponents of its church-based order to mobilize support. Lay social democracy and "the Jews" were branded the main adversaries and often portrayed in the press as a hostile complex.[191] Adhering to the semantics and semiotics of the clerical newspaper editors, such commentary burgeoned into a Manichean rhetoric about the standoff between Christians and Jews. While the need to "fight the Jews" and all they stood for was essentially undoubted, the Christian commandment to love one's neighbor posed a challenge to the precept. Even Catholics recoiled at the hate felt to be pervading attacks on the "Jewish hostile complex." The antisemitic label proved problematic for the Christian newspapers. By a process of othering, antisemitism had become a synonym for hatred of Jews, and anti-Semites believed in a secular ideology. Accused of spreading hatred and promoting a secular standpoint, political Catholicism was pushed onto the defensive.

In Vienna, the Christian Socials had no qualms describing themselves as anti-Semites. The Austrian priest Josef Deckert had declared antisemitism to be not merely reconcilable with Catholicism but even a Christian duty.[192] To the people of Krakow, however, antisemitism was a German phenomenon. Here, then, political Catholicism resorted to refuting the allegation of hatred by arguing they were merely defending the church and Catholics against the Jews' hatred and attacks. "Proof" of the Jews' hatred of Christians was often sought in the Kahal and Talmud. Talk of defense was the clericals' favorite means of attack. Nonetheless, they did not want to rule out the possibility of becoming aggressive opponents of the Jews in the long term. The story of the Christian-social movement in Galicia, from its appearance on the political scene to its breakaway from the Conservatives after the Reichsrat elections of 1897, is the story of how political Catholicism appropriated antisemitism.[193]

The Antisemitic Turn and the Invention of Antisemitism

The more obvious it became that not all devout Catholics identified with clerical politics, the more radical the Christian-social press's rhetoric against the "enemies of the church" grew. Political Catholicism's anti-Jewish texts were not only harsher than ever; they were also more hermetical and self-referential than previous campaigning, which had still offered interpretations for the public's approval and tried to convince their target groups with arguments. The clericals, on the other hand, seemed to be sure of their public's support and content to utter threats and warnings. However, following the Christian Socials' victory in the Viennese municipal elections of 1895, the Galician clerical press praised the Viennese workers and urged readers to follow their example. The fact that they had voted against social democracy and the Liberals was especially remarkable as Vienna was considered a "Jewish stronghold," the home of the stock market crash and political revolution.[194] In early 1896, the papers in question ran correspondence and "original letters" from Vienna on how the real Viennese—that is, the Christians—were taking a stand against the increasing "Jewification" of the Catholic capital.

The 15 January 1896 issue of *Grzmot*, for instance, printed a letter from Vienna that highlighted the impressive "unity" of the Christian Social workers of Vienna.[195] Ten days later, it ran the news that support for the "Jewish Social Democrats" was on the wane and that workers were increasingly attending church services.[196] *Glos Narodu* reported in January 1897 that Karl Lueger had given up his law office to devote himself entirely to politics and the "Catholic people." In this daily newspaper, positive references to Lueger went hand in hand with increasingly disparaging references to Jews. By this point, coverage focused unambiguously on Jews as the source of everything pernicious. There was barely an article that did not vilify Jews and their involvement in social democracy.

In early 1897, the newspaper *Prawda* felt it necessary to explain to its readers the harsher tone it was employing against "the Jews," since antisemitism was problematic for Christians. In the fourth number of 1897, it ran the following column under the headline "An honest confession by a Jew":

> Perhaps readers are wondering why *Prawda* attacks the Jews so fiercely although our faith demands that we love our neighbors. And we obeyed this and accepted the Jews into Poland. But now they want to rule us. They want us to light their candles and make their fires and nurse their children with Christian milk, as already occurs here and there. Now and then, a Jew appears who speaks the truth about what Jews are like, for example in the Stanislau "Free Voice" [*Wolny Glos*]. This writes that Christians love their neighbors while the Jews love themselves first and then their neighbors, but only their neighbors who are fellow believers. That is why *Prawda* writes so critically of the Jews.

In view of the huge increase in vitriolic about Jews in the clerical mouthpiece *Glos Narodu*, the Kraków Jesuit Marian Morawski, professor of theology and former fellow student of Stojałowski, assumed the task of explaining Catholicism's relationship to antisemitism. Morawski was editor-in-chief of *Przegląd Powszechny* (General Review), one of the leading newspapers in the Polish clerical sector. He intended his comments to serve as a kind of catechism—as instructions for Catholics—on how to behave toward Jews and on which theoretical basis. Unlike his colleague Josef Deckert, he did not attempt to define antisemitism as Christian but invented a succinct new term, "asemitism," to denote a disallowance of Jews without the un-Christian element of hatred. Morawski published the pamphlet containing his doctrine in Krakow in 1896; it ran to several editions. It promoted asemitism as the "royal road" between the two extremes of "philo-semitism," seen as Jewish assimilation, and antisemitism, defined as "un-Christian hatred" and incitement to violence. He based his theory on theological interpretations of the history of Christian-Jewish relations. Jews, he claimed, were the product of their race under the influence of their history. When Jesus entered the world, the Jews lost their status as the chosen ones. By refusing to recognize the Messiah, Jews had always opposed the Christians and their mission. In the diaspora, the followers of the Mosaic religion had replaced the Bible with the Talmud and so turned away from God. According to Morawski's theory, then, two homogenous communities had evolved that diverged diametrically regarding morality, interests, and ideals. Judaism's "materialist contract religion" served as a negative foil for the Christian community, which Monawski, a Jesuit and an ultramontane, equated with the Catholic Church. The curtailment of papal power and the church's influence on society consequent to the Reformation and the French Revolution had been the work of Jews obeying the Talmud's call to oppose Christians. In truth, he maintained, the history of Christian-Jewish relations was a history of Jews persecuting Christians.

Referring to anti-Semites such as Gougenot des Mousseaux, Jakob Brafman, and August Rohling, Morawski advanced conspiracy theories about the Kahal and the Talmud, liberalism, and freemasons. The liberal constitutional state was responsible for the market and monetary economy, for equality among all people regardless of estate or religion, and therefore for the fact that religion was now confined to the private sphere. Linking his anti-modern narrative with Galician discourse, he accused provincial Jewish barkeepers and profiteers of robbing peasants of their moral standards and livings, and urban Jewish pornographers and female traffickers of corrupting the population's sexual morals. He saw the major threat posed by Jews as evidenced by the fact that many had become ensconced in high social positions. Christians needed to "defend themselves." Hence, asemitism was to be regarded as the Christians' defense against Jewish aggression. Jewish emancipation and assimilation were to be stopped and the

Jewish opportunities for influencing the easily manipulated Christians limited as far as possible. Morawski argued the case for a complete separation of Christians and Jews in social, economic, and working life.

Asemitism was an empty word that Catholics could utilize, and which perpetuated the notion of rampant "Semitism" as a threat to the Christian order and Christian placidity. As soon as Morawski brought the term asemitism into circulation, he surrendered control over how it was interpreted. It was subsequently used by another Galician clergyman, Mateusz Jeż, in a pamphlet that was among the most extreme anti-Jewish tracts disseminated in the period.[197] Originally published as a series of articles in *Prawda*, "Tajemnice żydowskie" (Jewish secrets) later went into mass distribution as a pamphlet, advertised in all the Christian-social papers, which recounted conspiracy theories and the ritual murder legend in simple language. Unlike Morawski, Jeż defined asemitism not as a more moderate Christian doctrine but as more radical than antisemitism: "Antisemitism means fighting the Jews, specifically as in Christian self-defense. But asemitism means more; it means doing completely without Jews, not using or needing them for anything; so, it is really saying: '*Away with the Jews.*'"[198]

In late February 1897, the Christian Socials further intensified their agitation after their attempt at endorsing an anti-Jewish Conservative failed one month before the election.[199] At a meeting on 24 February, the spokesmen representing the central election committee—that is, the Conservatives—agreed on railroad worker Feliks Gawłowicz as the candidate for the general class of electors.[200] Backed by the Catholic workers' association *Przyjaźń* (Friendship) and *Głos Narodu*, the candidate had "qualified" himself by making anti-Jewish comments. But he was forced to withdraw before the electoral list was published because Jewish members of the committee had threatened to resign in protest at his antisemitism or had already done so in response to his nomination.[201] Kazimierz Ehrenberg, who had arranged Gawłowicz's candidacy, withdrew from the election committee and henceforth refused to endorse the Conservatives in his newspaper *Głos Narodu*. Instead, he railed against their "un-Christian attitude" and openness to "Jewish interference."

As Stojałowski did not stand in Kraków, in keeping with his agreement with the Social Democrats, the clericals were missing a suitable candidate there. Rather than allow a victory for social democracy, they supported their opponent, the SL candidate Szczepan Mikołajski.[202] A defeat in the general class election by the Social Democrats, who also published their party organ *Naprzód* (Onwards) in Krakow, seemed inevitable. In this situation, the election results in Vienna were portrayed in the newspapers *Prawda* and *Głos Narodu* as a looming Armageddon. An alliance with Lueger's antisemitic party seemed the only way to avert the imminent apocalypse that a victory for the "capitalist-social-democratic-Jewish" forces would spell:

The repulsive capitalist exploitation that spurts out of the articles of the New Free Press does not conflict with the political actions of the Social Democrats, who initiated the Jewish troika of Marx—Lassalle—Engels with the goal of immediately protecting Jewish exploitation against the Aryan nations' self-defense. Because the Jews exploit the Aryans internationally, their defensive, social-democratic army is also international. . . .

Let us follow, then, the Jewish example and vocally show our delight at the victory of the Viennese people and the Lower Austrian population in general and learn from it that here, too, we can shake off the iniquitous Jewish yoke at last. It is high time, otherwise the other nations will regard us as the dogs-bodies of the Jews, who silently allow ourselves to be exploited and do not have the least power of resistance or self-preservation. That applies especially to the Galician voters, who are planning to vote for a Jew. Now that the Austrians have voted so strongly antisemitic, it should be clear that there is no point in voting for a Jew, as nobody in Vienna would listen to him. It is therefore completely pointless to vote for a Jew as he would not be able to do anything.[203]

Obviously, *Głos Narodu* had internalized Lueger's adage "I decide who is a Jew"—the Social Democratic candidate for the fifth curia in Krakow, Ignacy Daszyński, was in fact a Catholic.[204] His victory in the Krakow elections and the simultaneous success of the Social Democratic candidate Ernest Breiter in Lemberg marked far more than a mere election defeat for the Christian Socials. It spelled ignominy in the international, Manichean struggle for survival that they imagined they were fighting. In the final phase of mobilization, then, the Catholic editors threw all restraint overboard and rallied uncompromisingly to the international fight against the Jews, alongside the victorious Viennese. To gloss over any potential antagonism between Germans and Slavs, they refrained from mentioning national categories but wrote of an "Aryan" alliance. Although it was not new to address ethnicity—previously, reservations about baptized Jews had been expressed—it was nevertheless a remarkable step for a Catholic newspaper to go from contrasting Jews and Christians to using polemic about Jews and Aryans.

Along with antisemitism, then, the clerical press had adopted another secular term for their own agitation. Under the heading "antisemitic league," *Głos Narodu* commented on the Reichsrat election results as follows:

The current parliamentary election is a Jewish fight against the Christian population. Jewry has lined up its ranks everywhere to defend its supremacy over the Aryans, its hegemony, and to continue pursuing foreign work by its exploitative craft. This time Jewry has planted dynamite under the Aryan people in Austria by waving the flag of social democratic revolution. The Jew millionaire, the Jew doctor, the Jew haggler, they all fought for social democratic candidates as they hope to profit from the overthrow of society. Behind the mask of social democracy, Jewry entered combat in the civilized countries; even without a mask sometimes in poorer Galicia, with sheer cynicism. A semitic attack! The Jews beat us everywhere with their money as we are disorganized and run back and forth like sheep.

Despite the major victory for the anti-Semites in Vienna and Lower Austria, Germany's *Volksblatt* has sounded the appeal: Aryans unite! Behind this appeal lies a true concept which would benefit us greatly if we heeded it. If all Aryans united it would be a deadly blow to Jewry. Only an international fight can help against an international mob. For this, we need international tolerance and understanding, and it is precisely in this respect that we must criticize the Austrian anti-Semites. For reasons of local interest, they leaned toward the German National side and distanced themselves from the Slavic peoples. But a national league is not enough to break the Jews' supremacy. It must stand on a foundation of absolute national and social equality between host nations. Lueger's earlier program of equality between all Aryan peoples must be heeded again.[205]

In the weekly newspaper *Grzmot*, criticisms in the election context were confined entirely to the conspiratorial tendencies of the Jews.[206] Looking optimistically ahead to the next elections, the weekly also portrayed the mayor of Vienna as a shining example to its readers:

At the current elections all the Jews in Krakow and Lemberg voted as one for the enemies of our faith and our homeland. They threw down the gauntlet and struck us Christians in the face. We will rise to the challenge! Now the voice of Grzmot is but an echo of what the whole of our society feels: Vienna and Lueger will provide the templates by which we will win, like them.[207]

In preparation for the next elections, and to break away from the Conservatives, in the months after the Reichsrat elections, several parties were founded that displayed their commitment to antisemitism in their names. In the same year, the newly founded Związek Antysemitów (Association of Anti-Semites) joined forces with Ehrenberg's also newly founded Stowarzyszenie Chrześciańsko-społeczne (Christian Social Union) with its party organ *Związek Chrześziański* (Christian Association). A biweekly union journal, *Antysemita* (The Anti-Semite), with a circulation of six thousand was published in Krakow.[208] The newspaper's declared objectives were to support their "brothers'" economy, to combat the "Jewish tendencies" and to respect national needs.[209] Jews, it claimed, had abused Polish hospitality and were a hundred-headed Hydra that they had fed at their own breast.

This monothematic anti-Jewish newspaper was not financially viable and folded after a few issues.[210] Its subscribers then received *Hasło* (The Watchword) in its place. The latter newspaper sought to consolidate the Christian-social milieu by promoting cooperation between its various branches and supporting the widely popular Stanisław Stojałowski.[211] It glossed over his election arrangement with the Social Democrats and claimed that they feared Stojałowski "like the devil fears holy water." [212] Continuing the religious analogy, it maintained that the reason for the Social Democrats' anxiety was that they had turned away from their religion and joined forces with the Jews, quoting a fictional call by the Alliance Israelite Universelle to the Jews that had been circulating Galicia for some time. Adopting Stojałowski's rhetoric, *Hasło* even lumped in the mainstream secular party and its press organs with the malignant alliance of Jews and Social Democrats. Stojałowski's Christian Social People's Party had emerged the most successful peasant party at the elections, gaining six mandates.[213] He had managed to achieve a consensus since the clericals broke with the Conservatives by taking a more moderate position, canceling his arrangement with the Social Democrats and committing himself to workers' causes, especially in neighboring Silesia.[214] In March 1898, Stojałowski entered the Reichsrat following a by-election in the Łańcut district.[215]

Shortly after his election victory, Stojałowski fell out with his fellow party members and newly elected representatives Michał Danielak and Andrzej Szponder.[216] Consequently, the two renegades set up the newspaper *Obrona Ludu* (Defense of the People) and declared themselves anti-Semites.[217]

Following the elections, thirteen politicians from Galicia who had based their election campaigns on anti-Jewish agitation entered the Reichsrat. Gaining a total of seven mandates, the clerical branch of the Polish peasant movement proved the most successful.[218] It had the closest affinity to the Christian Socials' agitation and the backing of the Christian-social press.[219]

Hence, the press portrayed the two by-elections in West Galicia the next year, at each of which a Christian People's Party candidate contended with a secular People's Party candidate, as another decisive battle between the church and its enemies. This phase of the election campaign, during which agitation was brought to the villages not only via newspapers but also in a vast number of campaign meetings, contributed to the wave of violence that shook the region in early summer 1898, when the battle for votes was fought out chiefly by means of antisemitic agitation.

As the parties' antisemitic agitation was not coupled with a viable political option, it failed to convince the urban electorate. But it had a powerful impact on the rural population. Here, the developments in Vienna had started a drive toward antisemitism or its derivates, such as asemitism. On the one hand, the emergence of new watchwords was a logical corollary of a more differentiated party-political scene. They were introduced to sum up political messages and define party-political profiles. But the antisemitic turn marked a deeper incursion, beyond political opinion-making. The idea of a fundamental conflict of interests between Christians and Jews was propagated as fact by all the parties. They assured their publics that they could personally influence the outcome of this conflict by their individual attitudes and actions. By defining oneself as an anti-Semite or an a-Semite, one would be seen to be taking the consequences of the conflict seriously, whether for the economy, Christian morality, or the church's and clergy's influence on public life, and to be distancing oneself from those who were in league with the Jews or who let themselves be exploited by them.

Rallying support by vilifying and demonizing their opponents, party representatives never spoke of individual mandates—the Galician Diet was in any case largely confined to an advisory role—but of a life-and-death decision. It was no longer merely isolated intellectuals but also priests and bishops who declared battle with the Jews. The various Christian political strands, from the ethnic-nationalist populism of the People's Party via the Peasant League's and Christian People's Party's chauvinistic Catholicism to the apocalyptic clericalism of the Krakow Christian Socials, all intersected in their mobilization of voters against the Jews. They positively vied with one another to deal the heaviest blow, each attacking different aspects of "Semitism."[220] The most radical were those who saw themselves as the losers of the elections, the Christian Socials in Krakow and Lemberg and the secular People's Party. Opposition to the Jews was a defining feature of their political community.[221]

Agitation had gone far beyond complaints about the badly assimilated Jews or appeals for them to improve. It was no longer possible to speak about Jews without simultaneously speaking about non-Jews and reminding them of their duty to act against the Jews. In the context of political agitation, antisemitism had become inextricably linked with selfhood. In parallel with "the Jew" becoming a symbol in political rhetoric, and a concrete antagonist in the shape of the barkeeper or salesman, the political focus shifted to everyday conduct and the tradition of the "ambivalent symbiosis." Anyone who did not boycott Jewish stores contributed to the "Jewification" of the economy. Anyone who went to the tavern instead of to church, who did not go to the reading room, or who took employment from a Jew, if only to stoke their fires on the Sabbath, anyone who read *Onwards* rather than *The Thunder*, acted disloyally toward the imagined community.

As modern political identities were formed based on the environments the parties' aimed to represent and change at the same time, ambivalences arose. Discrepancies emerged between the reality portrayed in the newspapers and the reality of popular experience. The boundaries of the sayable had shifted in two ways. Now it was possible to be a Christian and an anti-Semite; indeed, it was necessary to be against the Jews, to "defend oneself against Jews," to avoid being the laughingstock of other nations and leaving Galicia "open to the Jews." The various anti-Jewish narrations in readers' letters and articles in the press marked out the limits of the sayable. And they were brought to the villages via election campaigns. They might also have prevailed in some churches and reading rooms, depending on the political views of the individual men in charge.

In direct conversations between residents of villages and small towns, among Christians or between Christians and Jews, these narrations were nothing more or less than a way of speaking about the relationship between Christians and Jews. As actions and discourse dovetail in connection with one another, the next chapter will explore the extent to which the antisemitic option was utilized situationally during the unrest in Galicia.

Notes

1. Brigitte Frank-Böhringer, "Angewandte Rhetorik," in Robert Ulshöfer (ed.), *Sprache und Gesellschaft*, vol. 1 (Dortmund, 1972), 158–161.
2. Johannes Paulmann, "Einleitung," in idem, *Pomp und Politik: Monarchenbegegnungen in Europa zwischen Ancien Regime und Ersten Weltkrieg* (Paderborn, 2000); Thomas Mergel, "Überlegungen zu einer Kulturgeschichte der Politik," *Geschichte und Gesellschaft* 28 (2002): 574–606.
3. Niklas Luhmann defines politics as a communicative mode with codes that aim to generate collective, binding decisions. Mergel, *Überlegungen*.
4. Historians cannot determine whether politics are rational or irrational by analysis but at most inquire into actors' use of the terms as self-attributes or the attributes of others.
5. Language is understood here as political action, in the sense of speech acts, after John Austin and John Searle. Below, I refer to findings in the following literature: Christiane Streubel, *Radikale Nationalistinnen: Agitation und Programmatik rechter Frauen in der Weimarer Republik* (Frankfurt a. M., 2010), 35f. Due to their communicative character, speech acts form the major part of political action. In cultural studies, the "representations" model is widely used to help explain how phenomena such as rule and dominion function. Cf. Jörg Baberowski, "Imperiale Herrschaft: Repräsentationen politischer Macht im späten Zarenreich," in idem, David Feest, and Christoph Gumb (eds), *Imperiale Herrschaft in der Provinz: Repräsentationen politischer Macht im späten Zarenreich* (Frankfurt, 2008), 9–16, 9.
6. Both explicit and implicit prompting is regarded here as agitation. The book by August Rohling, mentioned in the introduction, is one example. Anyone he was able to convince that Jews abducted children during Lent to take their blood would at least make sure that his child did not come in to contact with (unfamiliar) Jews (while alone, before Easter).
7. Streubel, *Radikale Nationalistinnen*, 36.
8. Struve emphasizes the active role of the peasants in breaking the isolation of the village communities, *Bauern und Nation*, 14.
9. See Alfred Schütz, *Aufbau der sozialen Welt: Eine Einleitung in die verstehende Soziologie* (Constance, 2004).
10. Christiane Streubel distinguishes between the two in the subtitle of her book (*Agitation und Programmatik . . .*) but does not define agitation more precisely.
11. Translated from Christiane Streubel's phrase "Neulinge im politischen Raum."
12. "Macht zeigt sich im Recht, zu sprechen und zu bezeichnen" (Power is demonstrated by the right to speak and to define), Mergel, *Überlegungen*, 593. See also Quentin Skinner, "Language and Political Change," in Terence Ball, James Farr, and Russell L. Hanson (eds), *Political Innovation and Conceptual Change* (Cambridge, 1989), 6–23, 13. Hartmut Rosa, "Ideengeschichte und Gesellschaftstheorie. Der Beitrag der 'Cambridge School' zur Metatheorie," *Politische Vierteljahresschrift* 35 (1994): 197–223, 200 and 209.

13. Such as the principles of confining religion to the private sphere and linking political participation with tax contributions.
14. Cf. *Die Debatten über die Judenfrage in der Session des galizischen Landtages vom J. 1868: Uebersetzt aus dem Polnischen nach den ämtlichen stenographischen Protokollen*, Herausgegeben vom Vorstande der israelit. Kultusgemeinde in Lemberg (Lemberg, 1868). [The debate on the Jewish question in the Galician Landtag session of January 1868. Translated into German from the official Polish shorthand minutes and published by the board of the Jewish Community Lemberg]. Emphasis in the original.
15. The Landtag had inconclusively debated Jewish equality, following a motion by four Jewish members of parliament, at its first session on 26 April 1861. On 28 December 1865, Agenor Gołuchowski motioned for equality; on 27 February 1866, Father Jan Guszalewicz lodged a countermotion. Stanisław Grodziski, *Sejm Krajowy Galicyjski 1861–1914* (Warsaw, 1993), 377.
16. On the Landtag in general, see Grodziski, *Sejm Krajowy Galicyjski*.
17. *Die Debatten*, 23.
18. Weeks, *Assimilation, Nationalism, Modernization*.
19. *Die Debatten*, 5.
20. Eduard Gniewosz was an imperial governor's counselor and member of parliament for the landowning party in the Sambor/Sambir constituency.
21. The speaker Cezary Haller proposed that the Jewish Community should no longer have sole authority over matters not directly concerning religion. Behind this secularizing proposal lay the widely held notion that Jews made business deals under the Kahal, which was later utilized by anti-Semites. *Die Debatten*, 20.
22. Rainer Erb and Werner Bergmann have identified anti-Jewish rhetoric as a marker of modern anti-Semitism in the age of emancipation: Erb and Bergmann, *Die Nachtseite der Judenemanzipation*, 11.
23. Weeks, *From Assimilation to Antisemitism*, 103ff.
24. "With this privilege she gives the town all rights and obligations, in particular that there be no Jews in Żywiec, but orders them to be expelled [*wyganiać*]." Stanisław Grodziski and Irena Dwornicka (eds), *Chronografia albo dziejopis Żywiecki* (Żywiec, 1987), 142.
25. The residents allegedly voted unanimously against the construction of a station.
26. Bergmann, Hoffmann, and Smith, *Exclusionary Violence*.
27. CAHJP nos. 3981 100-6074 to 100-6105, 3.
28. Ibid.
29. Ibid., 4 and no. 4188 100-6114.
30. Statement by the district captain of Żywiec of 9 August 1879, CDIAL/146/7/4188, 1–5.
31. Teofil Merunowicz, *Żydzi* (Lwów, 1879); in the same year he also published *O metodzie I celach badań nad kwestią żydowską* [On the methods and objectives of research into the Jewish question].
32. Cf. Marcin Soboń, "Merunowicz, Teofil," in Wolfgang Benz et al. (eds), *Handbuch des Antisemitismus*, vol. 2/2: *Personen* (Berlin, 2009), 550.
33. CAHJP HM 2/8290, nos. 1976, 1977.
34. In the fourth parliamentary term Merunowicz was not yet a member of the Landtag and introduced the petition via Franciszek Wohlfarth. Grodziski, *Sejm galicyjski*, 377. For the text of the proposal, see Stenograficzne Sprawozdania z Czwartej Sesyi Czwartego Peryodu Sejmu Krajowego Królestwa Galicyi i Lodomeryi wraz z Wielkiem Księstwem Krakowskiem w roku 1881, 123–24 ff.; for Merunowic's defense of it, ibid., 174–182.

35. CAHJP HM/2 9440, 153ff.
36. Merunowicz, Żydzi, 8 and 38, cited from Maciej Janowski, *Inteligencja wobec wyzwań nowoczesności: Dylematy ideowe polskiej demokracji liberalnej w Galicji 1889–1914* (Warsaw, 1996), 98.
37. Cf. Introduction.
38. On 16 November 1882, CDIAL/146/7/4188, 10; APK StT 60, 1447.
39. APK STT 60, 1451. Soboń, "Polacy wobec Żydów," 116. The district captain of Jaworów could not legally prevent the notices from being displayed but appeased his superiors in Lemberg by asserting that only the "educated classes" had read them. CDIAL/146/7/4188, 16f.
40. *Gazeta Narodowa*, 12 October 1882.
41. Ibid.
42. Matejko (1838–1893) was the leading Polish protagonist of secularization in art and history painting in the nineteenth century. In the late 1850s, he trained young painters in workshops in Munich and Vienna, among other places. His artworks were considered iconic representations of Polish history even during his lifetime. Perhaps the most famous of his paintings is *The Battle of Grunwald*, portraying the Polish army's victory over the Teutonic Order in 1410. Matejko's work continues to be enmeshed in the Polish collective memory of this event in the topography of Krakow. The academy of fine arts, of which Matejko was rector for many years, is named after him and stands on Matejko Square, on which a monument to the battle of Grunwald was erected in 1910. Karol Krawczyk, *Matejko i historia* (Warsaw, 1990); Henryk Marek Słoczynski, *Matejko* (Wrocław, 2000).
43. Cit. from Dariusz Konstantynów, "'Mistrz Nasz Matejko' i antysemici," *Kwartalnik Historii Żydów* 222, no. 2 (2007): 165. See also Żbikowski, *Żydzi krakowscy*, 280f.
44. Jens Malte Fischer, *Richard Wagners "Das Judentum in der Musik"* (Frankfurt a. M., 2000).
45. Konstantynów, "'Mistrz Nasz Matejko' i antysemici," 191ff.
46. Ezra Mendelsohn, *Painting a People: Maurycy Gottlieb and Jewish Art* (London, 2002).
47. Gottlieb was also admired for his Polish-Jewish pictorial motifs, portraying himself both as Ahasver and as a Polish nobleman. His portrait of Christ was also positively received by ethnic Polish observers, while Max Liebermann's portrayal of the young Jesus in the Temple prompted anti-Jewish attacks in Germany in 1879. Gertrud Pickhan, "Levitan – Liebermann – Gottlieb. Drei jüdische Maler in ihrem historischen Kontext," *Osteuropa* 8–10 (2008): 247–264, 252.
48. In that year, nine Jewish students were enrolled at the academy.
49. For a precise reconstruction, also of the differences between the Warsaw *Izraelita* and the Krakow Jewish Community, see Konstantynów, "'Mistrz Nasz Matejko' i antysemici," 165ff.
50. Eibenschütz was sentenced to ten days imprisonment and a fine of 150 guilders in aid of the poor. Unfortunately, the trial records have not survived.
51. In reference to an anti-Jewish congress that took place in Dresden that year, *Gazeta Krakowska i Reforma*, no. 209, 5 December 1882, 4f. Ulrich Wyrwa, *Die Internationalan Antijüdischen Kongresse von 1882 und 1883 in Dresden und Chemnitz*. On antisemitism as a European movement, see "Themenportal Europäische Geschichte" (2009), www.europa.clio-online.de/site/lang_de/ItemID_362/mid_11428/40208214/default.aspx#_ftn1, accessed 31 March 2011.
52. Józef Mochnacki, *Rozprawa w procesie karnym Jana Matejki przeciw Dr. L. E. o przestępstwo obrazi czci, przeprowadzono w c. k. Sądzie Karnym w Krakowie, dnia 2-go Grudnia 1882* (Krakow, 1883).

53. The case was heard on 10 March 1883 in Krakow.
54. According to *Izraelita* (1883), 13, 105.
55. Ibid.
56. The reception of events relating to the "ritual murder trial" in Polish-language newspapers highlights the fact that the empires formed discrete communicative spaces. While the newspapers of the "Vistula Land" covered the Bejilis affair in far greater depth than the Galician gazettes, the latter focused more on the events in Polna and Tizsaezslar. Cf. Borkowska and Rudkowska, *Kwestia żydowska*.
57. A Ukrainian translation of the Talmud was published in Lemberg in the same year: *Talmud abo nauka o zidovskoi vere* [Talmud or the teachings of the Jewish faith]; Jakob Brafman, *Żydzi i Kahały: dzieło wydane w języku rosyjskim w Wilnie w roku 1870 przez Brafmanna (żyda przechrzczonego)* [The Jews and the Kahal: Work in the Russian language in Vilnius in the year 1870 published by Brafmann (a baptized Jew)] (Lwów, 1874, 1875, and 1877); *Zgubne zasady talmudyzmu do serdecznej rozwagi Żydom I chrześcijanom wszelkiego stanu podał Professor Dr. August Rohling, spolszczył J. B.* [The pernicious principles of Talmudism for the cordial attention of Jews and Christians of all estates presented by Professor Dr. August Rohling, Polish by J. B.] (Lwów, 1874, 1876, and 1883).
58. Edward Żukowski, *Judztwo* (Krakow, 1885).
59. As in Imperial Germany, scholars and experts in Galicia debated the consequences of usury in agriculture. The Jewish economist Leopold Caro of Lemberg published a study on the subject for the Social Policy Society, in which he chiefly accused Jews of profiteering. Leopold Caro, "Lichwa na wsi w Galicji w latach 1875–1881," *Wiadomości Statystyczne o Stosunkach Krajowych* 8 (1883/1884). This study also appeared later in the series published by the Social Policy Society (Verein für Sozialpolitik) of Leipzig titled *Der Wucher: Eine socialpolitische Studie* (Leipzig, 1893). Caro also published the work *Die Judenfrage – eine ethische Frage* (Leipzig, 1892), in which he offered objective mediation between anti-Semites and Jews.
60. Żukowski, *Judztwo*, 176–187.
61. Gaudenty Pikulski, *Złosz żydowska czyli wykład talmadu i sekt żydowskich* (Lwów, 1760). On Pikulski, see Soboń, "Polacy wobec Żydów," 116; also Hillel J. Kieval, "Blood Libels and Host Desecration Accusations," in *The Yivo Encyclopedia of Jews in Eastern Europe*, https://yivoencyclopedia.org/article.aspx/Blood_Libels_and_Host_Desecration_Accusations, accessed 30 November 2019.
62. This chapter had also been published in pamphlet form the previous year: Ks. Gaudenty Pikulski, *Sąd Żydowski we lwowskim Kościele Archikatedralnym* (Lwów, 1759).
63. In Galicia, the ritual murder myth was most prominently portrayed in the frescoes of the cathedral of Sandomierz. Cf. Joanna Tokarska-Bakir, *Legendy o krwi: Antropologia Przesądu* (Warsaw, 2008).
64. In this regard, the ethnographic oeuvre of Oskar Kolberg (1814–1890) is interesting. He compiled widespread popular beliefs about "the Jews" in his eighty-volume work *Der Lud: Seine Sitten, Lebensweise, Wörter, Überlieferungen, Redewendungen, Rituale, Zaubereien, Vergügungen, Lieder, Musik und Tänze*. Taken out of context, the collected beliefs and conventions of the peasants paint a picture of a peculiar, dark world. Cf. Alina Cała, *Wizerunek Żyda w poskiej kulturze ludowej* (Warsaw, 1992); for an English version, see idem, *The Image of the Jew in Polish Folk Culture* (Jerusalem, 1995).
65. During the trial against Joseph S. Bloch in 1885, Rohling had been forced to admit that his translations of the Talmud were not his own work, resulting in his suspension from his

professorship the same year. Hannelore Noack, *Unbelehrbar?: Antijüdische Agitation mit entstellten Talmudzitaten; Antisemitische Aufwiegelung durch Verteufelung der Juden* (Paderborn, 2001), 79ff.
66. Żbikowski, *Żydzi krakowscy*, 182.
67. Aleksander Czołowski, *"Mord Rytualny": Epizod z przeszłości Lwowa* (Lwów, 1899).
68. Majer Bałaban, *Historia lwowskiej Synagogi Postępowej* (Lwów, 1937), 160.
69. On the pogroms in 1881–1882, see John D. Klier, *Russians, Jews, and the Pogroms of 1881–1882* (Cambridge, 2011); here also for further references and sources.
70. Benyamin Lukin and Olga Schraberman, "Documents on the Emigration of Russian Jews via Galicia, 1881–82, in the Central Archives for the History of the Jewish People in Jerusalem," *Gal-Ed: On the History of the Jews in Poland* 21 (2007): 101–117, 104.
71. Börries Kuzmany, "Die Stadt Brody im langen 19. Jahrhundert—Eine Misserfolgsgeschichte?," http://othes.univie.ac.at/2604/, 247–257; Björn Siegel, *Österreichisches Judentum zwischen Ost und West: Die Israelitische Allianz zu Wien 1873–1938* (Frankfurt a. M., 2010), 97–109.
72. These figures are, of course, rough estimates, see Kuzmany, "Die Stadt Brody," 256.
73. Almost three-quarters of Brody's population were Jewish.
74. Under U.S. immigration law, only healthy people were allowed entry.
75. Cf. Salomon Adler-Rudel, *Ostjuden in Deutschland 1880–1940* (Tübingen, 1959), 8.
76. For this reason, envoys wrote to the AIU urging it to stop the committee's work before even more refugees arrived in Brody in the hope of emigrating. Kuzmany, "Die Stadt Brody." See also Leo Goldenstein, *Brody und die jüdisch-russische Emigration: Nach eigener Beobachtung erzählt* (Frankfurt a. M., 1882); Moritz Friedländer, *Fünf Wochen in Brody unter jüdisch-russischen Emigranten: Ein Beitrag zur Geschichte der russischen Judenverfolgung* (Vienna, 1882).
77. The lack of solidarity shown caused one of many disputes between the AIU and the Viennese Alliance. Cf. Siegel, *Österreichisches Judentum*.
78. There are several indications in the source literature that many refugees made a sophisticated impression, even on affluent citizens of Brody.
79. Many of them made it as far as America only to be refused entry. CAHJP HM 2/9175, 72.
80. From the Prussian border they were taken to Auschwitz, from where they were transported in sealed carriages to Brody. CDIAL/146/4/3116; APK StT 60, 1504f.
81. 6/12 September 1882, CAHJP HM 2/9175.
82. Shulamit Volkov, *Germans, Jews, and Antisemites* (Cambridge, 2006), 263ff.; Sonja Weinberg, *Pogroms and Riots: German Press Responses to Anti-Jewish Violence in Germany and Russia (1881–1882)* (Frankfurt a. M., 2010).
83. In Zloczów, signs were displayed calling for a "massacre" of Jews on 1 July CDIAL/146/4/3102, 1. In Dynów, notices incited the public to riot at a local fair. The Jewish Community sent a telegram to the governor's office asking for military protection, ibid., 12. Disturbances were also suppressed in Pilzno, ibid., 50. For further reports on agitators arrested and notices seized, see CDIAL/146/4/3102.
84. CDIAL/146/3102, 68.
85. The Krakow district administration made a report to this effect on 11 June 1881, CDIAL/146/4/3102, 123f.; and in Wadowice on 18 July, CDIAL/146/4/3101, 31f.
86. Cf. Einleitung. Der k. k. Bezirkshauptmann Żywiec v. 29. Juli 1881, CDIAL/146/4/3103, 42.

87. CDIAL/146/3102, 84.
88. CDIAL/146/3103, 42.
89. Soboń, "Polacy wobec Żydów."
90. On 25 May, Christians cut off the sidelocks of Salomon Vogel of Pilzno. CDIAL/ 146/4/3102, 68. In some places, the windows of Jewish houses were smashed.
91. The pogroms are generally regarded by historians as marking a breakthrough in "Jewish policy." Klier, *Russians, Jews, and the Pogroms.*
92. Tim Buchen, "'Herkules im antisemitischen Augiasstall': Joseph Samuel Bloch und Galizien in der Reaktion auf Antisemitismus in der Habsburger Monarchie," in Fritz Bauer Institut and Ulrich Wyrwa (eds), *Einspruch und Abwehr: Die Reaktion des europäischen Judentums auf die Entstehung des Antisemitismus (1879–1914)* (Frankfurt a. M., 2010), 193–214.
93. The Jewish political landscape also gained tremendous momentum in the early nineties. See the account from the perspective of the "assimilator" Wilhelm Feldmann, *Asymilatorzy, Syoniści I Polacy: Z powodu przełomu w stosunkach żydowskich w Galicyji* [Assimilators, Zionists and Poles: In the light of the changes in Jewish circumstances] (Krakow, 1893).
94. In the years 1867 to 1889, there was not one single peasant representative in the Galician Landtag. Binder, *Galizien in Wien*, 74.
95. German-language historians rarely use the equivalent term *Populismus*. The Polish actors are mostly referred to collectively as the "peasant movement." The Ukrainian activists coidentified under the banner of *narodovci*, a term which is closer to "populists" than to *Völkisch*. However, the radicals among them broke away from 1890 on, creating an alternative populist movement. The term "populism" is used here in its original sense as a movement that claims to pursue politics in the name of an imagined people and to draw its legitimacy from its activists' identification with that people, in contrast to the professional politicians' supposed separation from those they represent. This showcasing of a direct democracy was important for the inclusion of new voters. In keeping with New Political History, this postulate should be taken seriously, and the term "populism" not used normatively, in the modern sense, as "opportunist" or "demagogic." The term "populism," moreover, highlights the contemporary predecessor of the Russian *narodničestvo*, which is lost in the term "peasant movement." On the term *Populismus* (populism) in general, see Rupert Breitling, "Populismus," in Anton Pelinka (ed.), *Populismus in Österreich* (Vienna, 1987), 26–33; Hans-Jürgen Pohle, "Was ist Populismus?," in Helmut Dubiel (ed.), *Populismus und Aufklärung* (Frankfurt a. M., 1986), 12–32; Richard Faber and Frank Unger (eds), *Populismus in Geschichte und Gegenwart* (Würzburg, 2009). On the radicals, see John-Paul Himka, *Socialism in Galicia: The Emergence of Polish Social Democracy and Ukrainian Radicalism (1860–1890)* (Cambridge, MA, 1983); Peter Brock, *Nationalism and Populism in Partitioned Poland* (London, 1973); Olga Narkiewicz, *The Green Flag: Polish Populist Politics, 1867–1970* (London, 1976).
96. Such as the founder Bolesław Wysłouch (1855–1937). See Peter Brock, "Bolesław Wysłouch: Pioneer of Polish Populism," in idem, *Nationalism and Populism*, 181–211.
97. Andrzej Kudłaszyk, *Katolicka myśl społeczno-polityczna w Galicji na przełomiw XIX i XX wieku* (Wrocław, 1980).
98. Notable exceptions were the Jesuit-influenced, clerical Ruthenian newspaper *Misjonar* (1897–1914) from Żółkiew and Przemyśl-based *Prapor* [The flag]. Binder, *Das ruthenisches Pressewesen*, 2123.

99. Famous exceptions are Stanisław Szcepanowski and Tadeusz Rutkowski, who actively reflected on how to improve Galicia's economic situation in general. See Leszek Kuberski, *Stanisław Szcepanowski 1846–1900: Przemysłowiec, polityk, publicysta* (Opole, 1997); Henryka Kramarz, "Tadeusz Rutkowski jako poseł i propagator reform gospodarczych w Galicji pod koniec XIX wieku," in Piotr Franaszek (ed.), *Celem nauki jest człowiek ... Studia z historii społecznej i gospodarczej ofiarowoanie Helene Madurowicz-Urbańskiej* (Krakow, 2000), 143–151.
100. Dabrowski, *Commemorations*.
101. Himka, *Ukrainian National Movement*.
102. Manekin, *Politics, Religion, and National Identity*; Everett, *The Rise of Jewish National Politics in Galicia*; Shanes, "Neither Germans nor Poles," 191–213.
103. Csáky, *Gedächtnis der Städte*, 69ff.
104. John-Paul Himka, "Ukrainian-Jewish Antagonism in the Galician Countryside during the Late Nineteenth Century," in Potichnyj and Aster, *Ukrainian-Jewish Relations*, 111–158; Sławomir Tokarski, *Ethnic Conflict and Economic Development: Jews in Galician Agriculture 1868–1914* (Warsaw, 2003).
105. Kai Struve "Galizische Verflechtungen: Die 'Judenfrage' in der Lemberger Zeitschrift 'Przegląd Społeczny' (1886–1887)," in Manfred Hettling, Michael G. Müller, and Guido Hausmann (eds), *Die "Judenfrage": Ein europäisches Phänomen?* (Berlin, 2013), 95–126. Wysłouch's "policy draft" can also be found in a book on peasant parties' policies: Stanisław Lato and Witold Stankiewicz (eds), *Programy stronnictw ludowych: Zbiór dokumentów* (Warsaw, 1969), 27–48.
106. Michał Śliwa, *Bolesław Limanowski: Człowiek i historia* (Krakow, 1994); Kazimiera J. Cottam, *Bolesław Limanowski (1835–1935): A Study in Socialism and Nationalism* (New York, 1978).
107. Elżbieta Hornowa, *Ukraiński obóz postępowy i jego współpraca z polską lewicą społeczną w Galicji 1876–1895* (Wrocław, 1968), 72f., 123.
108. Kai Struve, "'Chłopi z chłopami' albo 'Ziemia polska dla Polaków': Das Verhältnis des *ruch ludowy* zu Weißrussen und Ukrainern bis 1939," in Grzegorz Kotlarski and Marek Figura (eds), *Oblicza wschodu w kulturze polskiej* (Poznań, 1999), 99–122.
109. The term "Litvaks" denoted Jews from the former Grand Duchy of Lithuania. Many Jews from the Pale of Settlement moved to the kingdom of Poland, where cities were developing more dynamically than towns in the western provinces. The immigrant Jews tended to speak Russian more fluently than Polish, for which reason Polish nationalists regarded them as agents of Russification and a national threat. See Dov Levin, *The Litvaks: A Short History of the Jews in Lithuania* (Jerusalem, 2000); Weeks, *From Assimilation to Antisemitism*, 89; François Guesnet, *Polnische Juden im 19. Jahrhundert: Lebensbedingungen, Rechtsnormen und Organisation im Wandel* (Cologne, 1998), 61–64; Stephen Corrsin, "Aspects of Population Change and Acculturation in Jewish Warsaw at the End of the Nineteenth Century: The Censuses of 1882 and 1897," *Polin: Studies in Polish Jewry* 3 (1988): 122–141.
110. Wysłouch wrote of "dark masses" who would never assimilate, and even if they did, it would have a "negative [effect] on our national character." Lato and Stankiewicz, *Programy stronnictw*, 48.
111. Struve, "Galizische Verflechtungen," 13ff.
112. On the history of this accusation, see Jürgen Hensel, "Polnische Adelsnation und jüdische Vermittler 1815–1830: Über den vergeblichen Versuch einer Judenemanzipation

in einer nicht emanzipierten Gesellschaft," *Forschungen zur osteuropäischen Geschichte* 32 (1983): 7–227; Levine, *Economic Origins*; Artur Eisenbach, *The Emancipation of the Jews in Poland, 1780–1870* (Oxford, 1991); Stella Hryniuk, "The Peasant and Alcohol in East Galicia in the Late Nineteenth Century: A Note," *Journal of Ukrainian Studies* 11 (1986): 75–85.

113. Despite being mere ideas and fictions, they were a major influence on daily politics, as claims to future territories determined prospective cooperation. It was therefore important for the agitation in the newspapers and for the construction of enemy concepts, as unlikely as the distant goals might have been. On Jews as third parties in national antisemitism, see Holz, "Die antisemitische Konstruktion des Dritten."

114. Weeks, *From Assimilation to Antisemitism*.

115. Viewing the various groups of Jews in central Europe as a collective, in which various languages had lost attractivity within a few decades while others had gained, seemed to confirm their suspicion that Jews confounded the establishment of a stable national order in the world.

116. This was also the reason why the political emigrants in Lemberg from the ND movement in the Tsarist Empire were not interested in Galician and Austrian daily politics. Roman Dmowski, a resident of Galicia 1895–1905, feared that the major national questions would fade into the background. See Waldemar Potkanski, *Ruch narodowo-niepodległościowy w Galicji przed 1914 rokiem* (Warsaw, 2002), 19ff.; Grzegorz Krzywiec, *Szowinizm po polsku: Przypadek Romana Dmowskiego 1886–1905* (Warsaw, 2009).

117. *Przegląd Społeczny* 7 (1886): 54–56, 55.

118. Alfred Nossig, *Próba rozwiązania kwestji żydowskiej* (Lwów, 1887). The text was duplicated in *Przegląd Społeczny* 8: 130–143; 9: 219–232; 10: 286–293; 11: 352–363; and 12: 407–419; Struve, "Galizische Verflechtungen," 9. On Nossig, see Ezra Mendelsohn, "From Assimilation to Zionism in Lvov: The Case of Alfred Nossig," *Slavonic and East European Review* 49 (1971): 521–534. Shmuel Almog, "Alfred Nossig: A Reappraisal," Studies in Zionism 7 (1983): 1–29.

119. Vocal opponents included the socialist and former comrade of Wysłouch, Limanowski, who argued that nations cannot be defined only in terms of ethnography. In 1880, the newspaper *Ruskaja rada* ran positive reports about Stoecker and antisemitic societies; Wendland, *Russophile*, 267.

120. Iwan Franko, "Semityzm i antysemityzm w Galicji," *Przegląd Społeczny* 5 (1887): 431–444. Franko was a writer and politician, and his attitude toward Jews is unclear; a comparison of his political demands and portrayals of Jews came to an "ambivalent" conclusion. Jarosław Hrycak, "Między filosemityzmem i antisemityzmem—Iwan Franko i kwestia żydowska," in Krzystof Jasiewicz (ed.), *Świat NIEpożegnany: Żydzi na dawnych ziemiach wschodnich Rzeczypospolitej w XVIII–XX wieku / A World We Bade No Farewell: Jews in the Eastern Territories of the Polish Republic from 18th to 20th Century* (Warsaw and London, 2004), 451–480.

121. Cf. Moshe Mishkinsky, "The Attitude of the Southern-Russian Workers' Union toward the Jews (1880–1881)," *Harvard Ukrainian Studies* 6 (1982): 191–216; idem, "The Attitudes of Ukrainian Socialists to Jewish Problems in the 1870s," in Peter J. Potichnyj and Howard Aster (eds), *Ukrainian-Jewish Relations in Historical Perspective* (Edmonton, 1988), 57–68; Struve, "Galizische Verflechtungen," 18.

122. See the very similar reflections of the populist Mykhailo Drahomanov, who also came from the Tsarist Empire to Galicia. Ivan L. Rudnytsky, "Mykhailo Drahomanov and

the Problem of Ukrainian-Jewish Relations," in idem (ed.), *Essays in Modern Ukrainian History* (Edmonton, 1987), 283–297.
123. Kudłaszyk, *Katolicka myśl.*
124. On Austria, see Wolfgang Maderthaner, "Kirche und Sozialdemokratie: Aspekte des Verhältnisses von politischem Klerikalismus und sozialistischer Arbeiterschaft bis zum Jahre 1938," in Helmut Konrad (ed.), *Neuere Studien zur Arbeitergeschichte: Zum Fünfundzwanzigjährigen Bestehen des Vereins für Geschichte der Arbeiterbewegung* (Vienna, 1984).
125. David I. Kertzer, *Prisoner of the Vatican: The Pope's Secret Plot to Capture Rome from the New Italian State* (Boston, 2004); Brian Porter, "Antisemitism and the Search for a Catholic Identity," in Robert Blobaum (ed.), *Antisemitism and Its Opponents in Modern Poland* (New York, 2005), 103–123.
126. As inscribed into his "syllabus of errors," *Syllabus Errorum*, issued in 1864 with the *Quanta cura* encyclical.
127. See Christopher Clark and Wolfram Kaiser (eds), *Culture Wars: Secular-Catholic Conflict in Nineteenth-Century Europe* (Cambridge, 2003).
128. Adopted at the First Vatican Council under Pius IX on 18 July 1870. Michael Matheus and Lutz Klinkhammer (eds), *Eigenbild im Konflikt: Krisensituationen des Papsttums zwischen Gregor VII und Benedikt XV* (Darmstadt, 2009); Gisela Fleckenstein and Joachim Schmiedl (eds), *Ultramontanismus: Tendenzen der Forschung* (Paderborn, 2005).
129. In 1869, Austria dissolved the Concordat of 1885, which Pulzer claims signified a revision of the map of Europe to the "triple disadvantage of the [Catholic] Church" between 1859 and 1871. Peter Pulzer, "Die Wiederkehr des alten Hasses," in idem, Steven M. Lowenstein, Paul Mendes-Flohr, and Monika Richarz (eds), *Deutsch-Jüdische Geschichte in der Neuzeit*, vol. 3: *Umstrittene Integration 1871–1918* (Munich, 1997), 193–242, 198.
130. Oswald von Nell-Breuning and Johannes Schasching (eds), *Texte zur katholische Soziallehre: Die sozialen Rundschreiben der Päpste und andere kirchliche Dokumente* (Bornheim, 1992).
131. Almost all the parties and political camps made references to God or emphasized the compatibility of their policies with religious doctrine, as a matter of course. The major difference with political Catholicism was that the clergy fused politics with the Church and described it as the only "Christian" option.
132. Cf. John W. Boyer and Karl Lueger (1844–1910), *Christlichsoziale Politik als Beruf: Eine Biographie* (Vienna, 2010).
133. Józef Ryszard Szaflik, "Ks. St. Stojalowski – precursor ruchu ludowego, in Dąbrowski, Chłopi – Kultura – Naród," 13–26; Jerzy Myślinski, "Redaktor w sutannie i ludowy tribun: Ks. Stanisław Stojałowski," *Kwartalnik Prasy Polskiej* 30, no. 3–4 (1991): 127–132; Buchen, "Herrschaft in der Krise," also for further reading on Stojałowski.
134. In Belgium, he also met Adolf Daens, the later founder of the Christian People's Party, for which Daens entered the Belgian parliament in 1893. On Stojałowski's stay in Belgium, see Ryszard Bender, "Wokól sprawy pobytce Ks. St. S. Belgii w 1872/1873," in Stefan Wyszyński and John Paul (eds), *Z zagadnień kultury chrześciańskiej* (Lublin, 1972), 465–471.
135. The open-air gatherings continued the tradition of peasant-interest representation from the days of serfdom. Antoni Podraza, "Kształtowanie się elity wiejskiek na przykładzie Galicji na przełomie XIX i XX w.," *Zeszyty Naukowe Uniwersytetu Łodzkiego* 1 (1979): 61–68, 61f. He bought his most widely read newspapers, *Wieniec* and *Pszczółka*, in 1875 in Lemberg, and quickly raised circulation from 1000 to 1600–1800 in 1878 and

to 4500 around 1900. Cf. Krzysztof Dunin-Wąsowicz, *Czasopiśmiennictwo ludowe w Galicji* (Wrocław, 1952), 61.
136. Between 1882 and 1898, 1374 associations were founded, of which some five hundred remained active in the long term. Struve, *Bauer und Nation*, 154.
137. Anna Staudacher, "Der Bauernagitator Stanisław Stojałakowski: Priester, Journalist und Abgeordneter zum Österreichischen Reichsrat; Ein biographischer Versuch," *Römische Historiographische Mitteilungen* 25 (1983): 165–202, 166. The following accusation against S. was made by a member of the Krakow bishop Jan Puzyna's camp: "Stojałakowski's un-Christian, un-Catholic actions paved the way for a number of encounters which exploited the gloomy and poor *lud* for their own party-political or personal goals, or—so much is certain—weakened their faith, undermined their trust in clerical leadership, aroused class hatred and appealed to the lowest instincts. All that is supposedly done for the good of the *lud*, to raise its awareness and improve its current plight. This is the social and political work that Father Stojałowski encourages them to perform. A true master of sowing revolution in people's hearts and minds." Edward Komar, *Kardinał Puzyna* (Krakow, 1912), 107f.
138. Charges were brought against him a total of 212 times. Szczepanczyk, *Problematyka*, 136.
139. A reader's letter in his newspaper *Pszczółka* claimed that soon the Jews would soon bring Galicia "under the control of the Jewish kingdom." *Pszczółka* 8 (1889): 4, cited from Claudia Kraft, "Die jüdische Frage im Spiegel der Presseorgane und Parteiprogramme der galizischen Bauernbewegung im letzten Viertel des 19. Jahrhunderts." *Zeitschrift für Ostmitteleuropa-Forschung* 45 (1996): 381–409, 390.
140. In the first issue of his newspaper *Wieniec*, he told his readers to read only material that was recommended by clergymen. Until the 1880s, he advised against voting for peasant candidates as he claimed they were not yet ready for politics. He advised voting for honest "protectors" (*Opiekún*) from the intelligentsia. He first supported peasant candidacies in the run-up to the 1889 Landtag elections. *Pszczółka* 7 and 8 (1889). Indeed, priests remained the principal activists, alongside peasants, in his movement, while ever more lawyers and journalists became involved in the laicist movement.
141. Kraft, "Die jüdische Frage." The turnaround toward direct competition occurred in the 1880s in parallel with a radicalization of anti-Jewish commentary in the press. Kai Struve, "Die Juden in der Sicht der polnischen Bauernparteien vom Ende des 19. Jahrhunderts bis 1939," *Zeitschrift für Ostmitteleuropa-Forschung* 48, no. 2 (1999): 184–224; Buchen, "Die Sprache der 'Christlichen – Volkspartei.'"
142. At 1.8 percent, the proportion of Jews in Galicia's farming community remained far less than the proportion of Jews in the entire population even in 1900. The proportion of land owned by Jews, however, rose sharply. It is likely that many Jews resold their land from the late 1890s to peasants who had profited from the improved economic conditions for farmers at the time. Ignacy Schiper, *Żydzi w rolnictwie na terenie Małopolski*, vol. 2 (Warsaw, 1933), 424–431.
143. Cf. Kaps, "Peripherisierung."
144. Giving money to a Jew was portrayed as paying with "Christian sweat and blood." *Pszczółka*, no. 1, 1898.
145. One can therefore presume that the boycott movement was chiefly propelled by Christian business people, especially as boycotts would not have been possible without such businesses. The "successes" of the boycott movement in trade were consistently meager,

in contrast to the sobriety movement, which made a deep impact on a regional level. See Buchen, "Die Sprache der 'Christlichen – Volkspartei,'" 68–80, also for further reading.

146. One publication wrote that the Alliance Israelite Universelle was behind the Baron Hirsch Foundation, which in 1889 had called on its affiliates to "conquer Galicia" and "push it onward as into the promised land" since "riches" could be found there. *Pszczółka*, no. 1, 1891. Another assertion made was that the Rothschild family was so rich they could easily buy the Habsburg Monarchy. *Wieniec*, no. 24, 1898. "One will not have to wait long for Galicia to become a Jewish kingdom rather than a Polish one, as we face the prospect of losing everything, and they [the Jews] will suck the Christian people dry of every last drop of blood, and in time Siberia will probably become the land of the Polish, while Galicia will be the land of the Jews and scoundrels. *Wieniec-Pszczółka*, no. 26, 1900, cited from Kraft, "Die jüdische Frage," 404. "Brandy in the hands of Jews is the hellish weapon that kills our Polish minds and bodies." *Związek Chłopski*, no. 30, 1896, 248.

147. Buchen, "Die Sprache der 'Christlichen – Volkspartei,'" 81; James Weinstein, *The Corporate Ideal in the Liberal State: 1900–1918* (Boston, 1968). In general terms, the *Przyjaciel Ludu* spoke of a Polish-Jewish conflict, whereas *Wieniec* and *Pszczółka* saw a Christian-Jewish one.

148. In a party manifesto of 1903, the once laicist PSL stressed the "extraordinary role of the Catholic religion for the life of our nation." This is another example of nation and religion being increasingly mentioned in concert, such as by the ND after 1900, pushing intranational conflicts to the background. Stojałowski's party was incorporated into the national democracy movement in 1909.

149. Stanisław Kowalczyk, "Ruch ludowy wobec wyborów do Sejmu w Galicji w 1895 r.," *Rocznik Dzieje Ruchu Ludowego* 7 (1965): 280–318.

150. Ignacy Pawłowski, *Stronnictwa i programy polityczne w Galicji 1864-1918* (Warsaw, 1966), 53–58.

151. In a letter of 18 December 1893, the bishop of Tarnów Łobos tried to convince the peasant party union to expel Stojałowski because of his social-revolutionary agitation: "Turn away from the false teachers who talk you into this division [into *lud* and *szlachta*]. The only ones to profit from this divide are the socialists and the nihilists, who are supported by the freemasons' secret benefices as they try to sow disharmony and use us for their revolutionary goals." Cited from Józef Ryszard Szaflik (transl.: C. H.-K.), *O rząd chłopskich dusz* (Warsaw, 1976), 136.

152. Antoni Gurnicz, *O "równą miarkę" dla chłopów: Poglądy i działalność pierwszej chłopskiej organizacji w Polsce Związku Stronnictwa Chłopskiego 1893–1908* (Krakow, 1963).

153. In 1903, the party was renamed Polish People's Party, PSL.

154. Krzysztof Dunin-Wąsowicz, *Jan Stapiński-trybun ludu wiejskiego* (Warsaw, 1969).

155. Two years previously, he had founded the Christian People's Community. See Ryszard Szaflik, "Nieznana inicjatiywa polityczna ksiedza Stanislawa Stojalowskiego: Próby do powałania do życia towarzystwa chrześciansko-ludowego," *Studia historyczne* (1995): 117–132.

156. As it made no explicit commitment to Christian politics, the party was described from without as taking an "un-Christian attitude," which was declared to be synonymous with "Jewish" morality. "Where is your law?" asked the Peasant Union rhetorically, inquiring into the People's Party's tenets. "Ours is: God and fatherland." *ZCh.*, no. 7, 1894, cited from Binder (transl. by C. H.-K.), *Galizien in Wien*, 91. That secularism was tanta-

mount to willfulness was one of Stojałowski's central allegations against "liberalism." Cf. Buchen, "Die Sprache der 'Christlichen – Volkspartei,'" 60ff.
157. On the background to this occurrence, see Staudacher, *Der Bauernagitator*; also Buchen, "Herrschaft in der Krise."
158. *Wieniec Polski*, no. 18, 1898. "Stapiński geht mit den Sozialdemokraten zu den Jüdchen," *Wieniec Polski*, no. 13, 1898.
159. Soboń, "Polacy wobec Żydów"; Unowsky, "Peasant Political Mobilisation."
160. *Przyjaciel Ludu*, no. 5, 1900; In his election analysis, Stapinski called the Christian-social opponents of the secular Peasant Party a "conservative-Jewish-clerical coalition"; Kraft, "Die jüdische Frage"; Golczewski, *Rural Antisemitism*. The accusation of having Jewish origins was also directed at Ivan Franko, whose ethnic German father Jakob had the surname Frank and so the same name as the notorious Galician "Messiah." Klaus S. Davidowicz, *Zwischen Prophetie und Häresie: Jakob Franks Leben und Lehren* (Vienna, 2004).
161. However, as shown in the introduction, neighborly, consumer, and work relations were easily defined by ethnic criteria, and it was regarded as extraordinary if a landowner was Jewish.
162. Stojałowski's *Wieniec* and *Pszczółka* ran a series of articles explaining the concept of money as a means of payment and describing its uses.
163. The same applied, of course, to Jews who became leaseholders after 1848 and landowners after 1867 engaged in agriculture, which was still considered "non-Jewish" around 1900, as the memoirs of Soma Morgenstern show. Haumann, "Juden in der ländlichen Gesellschaft."
164. This strategy is described by scholars as "othering." See Kai Struve, "Gentry, Jews and Peasants: Jews as 'Others' in the Formation of the Modern Polish Nation in Rural Galicia during the Second Half of the 19th Century," in Nancy M. Wingfield (ed.), *Creating the Other: Ethnic Conflict and Nationalism in Habsburg Central Europe* (New York, 2003), 103–126; Michlic, *Poland's Threatening Other*; Binnenkade, Emeliantseva, and Pacholkiv, *Vertraut und fremd zugleich*, 13ff.
165. While the People's Party supported emigration to Palestine in its program of 1903 and took a positive view of Zionism, the Catholic parties claimed Zionism was a subterfuge or, alternatively, evidence that assimilation was not possible. The newspaper *Wieniec Polski* also perpetuated the notion articulated by Ivan Franko of a Jewish plan to take over or buy up Galicia, by citing a Jewish appeal to settle in the "promised land" (*ziemiea obiecana*), Galicia. A similarly falsified statement, preempting the technique employed by the authors of the "Protocols of the Elders of Zion," was a quote in *Związek Chłopski* by a rabbi named "Sir John Readclef," who wanted to rule the world. Retcliffe (*sic*) was the pseudonym under which Herman Goedsches published his novel *Biarritz*, one chapter of which, "Auf dem Judenkirchhof in Prag," was later incorporated into the Protocols. Kraft, "Die jüdische Frage"; Eric Stephen Bronner, *Ein Gerücht über die Juden: Die Protokolle der Weisen von Zion und der alltägliche Antisemitismus* (Berlin, 1999); Norman Cohn, *Die Protokolle der Weisen von Zion: Der Mythos der jüdischen Weltverschwörung* (Baden Baden, 1998).
166. In 1898, its circulation reached five thousand, CDIAL/146/4/4733, 80. See also Czesław Lechicki, "Pierwsze dwudziestolecie krakowskiego *Głosu Narodu*," *Studia historyczne* 12 (1969): 507–532. The establishment of *GN* marked the demise of the only other clerical and anti-Jewish newspaper that had hitherto existed in the region, *Kurjer Polski* (1889–1893), which had addressed a broad readership. Harald Binder, "Das

polnische Pressewesen," in Rumpler and Urbanitsch, *Die Habsburgermonarchie*, vol. 8: *Die politische Öffentlichkeit* (Vienna, 2006), 2037–2090, 2079. In 1902, *Głos Narodu* was outsold by *Słowo Polskie*. This formerly liberal democratic newspaper was bought by the National Democrats, who with the increase in sales proved that national views had displaced liberal democratic positions and could also absorb much of the clerical movement.

167. The statutes called for members to be "steadfast in faith" and to "defend the truth of the gospel." The Christian Social society in Biała, a subdivision of Stojałowski's Christian People's Party, used the foreign word *socyalny* instead of the native *społeczny* to underline the link with the Austrian movement. Cf. *Statut chrześć-socyaln: Związku w Białej* (Bielitz, 1896).
168. It appeared tri-monthly with a circulation of 2050 (or 1900 in 1898).
169. Michał Śliwa, *Obcy czy swoi: z dziejów poglądów na kwestię żydowską w Polsce w XIX i XX wieku* (Krakow, 1997), 53ff.
170. Unfortunately, the trial records from the court in Wadowice have not survived. For the coverage in *Pochodnia*, see no. 13 of 29 June 1895.
171. "Citizens, citizens, what have you done, you let a Jew into the town! You let him in, but we will throw him out! A Jew in the town: we won't let it pass! Hurrah, get the Jew!" (Mieszczanie, mieszczanie, coście wy zrobili, Iżeście wy żyda do miasta wpuścili! Jak wy go wpuścili tak go wyżyniemy, A żydowi w mieście być nie pozwolimy!" Hejże na żyda!).
172. They carried the bed out of the house and took a pot of cabbage, among other things.
173. It appeared tri-monthly with a circulation of between 1200 and 1000 (1989). CDIAL/146/7/4733, 80.
174. Jerzy Jarowiecki, *Prasa Lwowska w latach 1864–1918: Bibliografia* (Krakow, 2002).
175. See, e.g., "On the Jewish Payroll" [Na żydowskim żołdzie] and "Will Social Democracy Really Improve the Workers' Material Situation?" [Czy socyalna demokracya chce rzeczywiście poprawić materyalny byt robotników?] Front page of the first Krakow edition, *Grzmot*, no. 29, 15 November 1896.
176. *Grzmot*, no. 11, 1897. Stores in Galicia were permitted to open only from 3:00 p.m. to 6:00 p.m. Jewish tradespeople were under religious pressure to close their stores on the Sabbath as well, so a Sunday-closing law would have meant losing two days' business per week. See *Petition der Israelitischen Kaufmannschaft an Seine Majestät den Kaiser Franz Josef I. behufs gänzlicher Aufhebung der sonntäglichen Geschäftssperre oder dieselbe auf 6 Uhr Vorabends zu verlegen verfasst und argumentiert von Hendel Adler* (Kolomea, 1898).
177. Around 1900, Krakow had the highest density of household helpers per resident in the Habsburg Monarchy. They were mostly young women from the country who migrated to find work. It was not uncommon for sexual services to be among the unofficial job requirements of lower-class domestic helpers. Many middle-class young men gained their first premarital sexual experiences with household employees. The main occupation of most registered women who worked in prostitution was housemaid or waitress. See Lidia Zyblikiewicz, *Kobieta w Krakowie w 1880 r. Studium demograficzne* (Krakow, 1999); Michał Baczkowski, "Prostytucja w Krakowie na przełomie XIX I XX w.," *Studia historyczne* 4 (2000): 593–606; Keely Stauter-Halsted, "'A Generation of Monsters': Jews, Prostitution, and Racial Purity in the 1892 L'viv White Slavery Trial," *Austrian History Yearbook* 38 (2007): 25–34.
178. Warnings to this effect were articulated in, e.g., the fictional letter "Mother's Last Will," written to a beloved daughter, beseeching her not to bring her any shame. *PS*, no. 2, 1

February 1898; also, in the editors' responses to supposed readers' letters asking how to dress, *PS*, no. 3, 1898.
179. Employers should be recommended by priests to ensure their piety and moral integrity.
180. "Katarzyna Lazarska jumped out of a second-floor window of Isaak Goldberg's house and is now in hospital. Curiously, the same thing occurred one year ago in Nowy Sącz when a maid tried to save her innocence. One cannot help but ask why they were working for Jews at all, but often they are not aware of the fact as the agent tells them they are German households." "Co tam słychać na świecie," *PS*, no. 6, 1898.
181. Pollack, *Kaiser von Amerika*; Anna Staudacher, "Die Aktion 'Girondo': Zur Geschichte des internationalen Mädchenhandels in Österreich-Ungarn um 1885," in Heide Dienst and Edith Saurer (eds), *"Das Weib existiert nicht für sich": Geschlechterbeziehungen in der bürgerlichen Gesellschaft* (Vienna, 1990), 97–138; Stauter-Halsted, *A Generation of Monsters*.
182. Edward J. Bristow, *Prostitution and Prejudice: The Jewish Fight against White Slavery 1870–1939* (Oxford, 1982); Bertha Pappenheim, *Sisyphus: Gegen den Mädchenhandel in Galizien*, ed. Helga Heubach (Freiburg, 1992). The Krakow rabbi Osias Thon set up a society against female trafficking in the town, based on the statutes of the Catholic Women's League in Krakow and the Austrian league to combat female trafficking. AGAD Min. Wew. 191 no. 58311.1.1911.
183. At the end of the report, the author mentions the Catholic employment agency of the society Jedność (Unity), an antisemitic clerical organization. *PS*, no. 3, 1898. Many cases are known of a girl's parents or the girl herself deciding to opt for prostitution. Stauter-Halsted, *A Generation of Monsters*, 30. See also the German-language antisemitic account of the sensational trial in Lemberg, the records of which have unfortunately not survived: Alexander Berg, *Judenhyänen vor dem Strafgericht zu Lemberg* (Berlin, 1893).
184. Female domestic helpers did not have the right to vote and in a Catholic view were not meant to discuss political topics, for which reason the newspapers did not have any political content.
185. Witold Chotkowski (ed.), *Księga pamiątkowa wiecu katolickiego w Krakowie odbytego w dniach 4, 5 i 6 lipca 1893 r.* (Krakow, 1893), 163f.
186. Soboń, "Polacy wobec Żydów."
187. John W. Boyer, *Karl Lueger (1844–1910): Christlichsoziale Politik als Beruf; Eine Biographie* (Vienna, 2010).
188. Johann Dvořak, *Politik und die Kultur der Moderne in der späten Habsburger-Monarchie* (Innsbruck, 1997); Albert Lichtblau, "'A Hetz muaß sein!' Der Wiener und seine Fremden," in Susanna Fuhrherr, Peter Eppel, Rainer Hubert, and Eva-Maria Orosz (eds.), *Wir: Zur Geschichte und Gegenwart der Zuwanderer nach Wien; Sonderausstellung des Historischen Museums der Stadt Wien* (Vienna, 1996), 145–150; Isaak Hellwig, *Der konfessionelle Antisemitismus in Österreich* (Vienna, 1972).
189. Another significant force, in Przemyśl, was the *Echo przemyskie*, funded by Bishop Józef Pelszar (1842–1924). *EP* attacked the freemasons and sought links with the secular and Church actors of the Christian-social movement. Cf. J. S. Korczyński (J. S. Pelczar), *Masoneria: Jej początki, organizacja, ceremoniał, zasady i działanie* (Krzeszowice, 2006).
190. Nathaniel Wood, *Becoming Metropolitan: Urban Selfhood and the Making of Modern Cracow* (DeKalb, 2010).
191. A rash of pamphlets also contributed to this agitation, warning Christians that socialists and Jews were planning to lead the Catholics away from their faith. See, e.g., Father Józef Dziedzic, in Śliwa, *Obcy czy swoi*, 56ff.

192. Josef Deckert, *Darf ein Katholik Antisemit sein?* (Vienna, 1892). Two years previously, antisemitism had been declared a sin. Julius Lang, *Der Antisemitismus vom katholischen Standpunkte als Sünde verurtheilt* (Vienna, 1890). See also Olaf Blaschke, "Wie wird aus einem guten Katholiken ein guter Judenfeind? Zwölf Ursachen des katholischen Antisemitismus auf dem Prüfstand," in idem (ed.), *Katholischer Antisemitismus im 19. Jahrhundert: Ursachen und Traditionen im internationalen Vergleich* (Zurich, 2000), 77–110.
193. For a more in-depth inquiry, see Tim Buchen, "'Learning from Vienna Means Learning to Win': The Cracovian Christian Socials and the 'Antisemitic Turn' of 1896," *Quest: Issues in Contemporary Jewish History* 3 (2012), http://www.quest-cdecjournal.it/focus.php?id=302.
194. In the book *Asemityzm*, Vienna is described as an "uncaptured fortress of Semitism." Marian Morawski, *Asemityzm: Kwestia żydowska wobec chrześcijańskiej etyki* (Krakow, 1896).
195. *Grzmot*, no. 2, 15 January 1896.
196. *Grzmot*, no. 2, 1896.
197. In 1897, the pamphlet was published under the title "On the Jews" but appeared in later editions titled "Jewish Secrets." Jeż, who published his first writing in 1857, used the pseudonym Miłkowski. *Gazeta Narodowa*, no. 181, 1882.
198. Mateusz Jeż, *Tajemnice żydowskie* (Krakow, 1898), 78. Stress as in the original.
199. On 1 January 1897, *Głos Narodu* ran a lead article containing the recommendations of the "national Catholics." This was a framework program based on anti-Jewish, predominantly economic arguments that did not endorse any specific party but was intended as a catalog of criteria for recommended candidates. *Głos Narodu*, no. 1, 1 January 1897.
200. Binder, *Galizien in Wien*, 211.
201. Ibid.
202. On 11 March, *Głos Narodu* printed voting recommendations for the fifth curia in the left column, elucidated the importance of the elections in the middle column, and reported on the election successes of the Christian Socials in Vienna and Lower Austria under the headline "Victory for the antisemites!" in the right-hand column. *Głos Narodu*, no. 57, 1897.
203. *Głos Narodu*, 13 March 1897, 2. An article in *GN* of 17 March, under the heading "Let us awake!" reiterated the exemplary character of the Christian voters in Austria: "Let us awake! Today the municipalities of Lower Austria are voting. You do not need to be a political prophet to predict the result. The peasants will give the same clear signal against Jewish exploitation and Jewish predominance as the general-class Viennese voters. The nation here senses its honor, defends its interests and is consistent. Galicia is not a place where they lead the people a merry dance while the entire civilized world looks on and laughs, where Christian voters kiss the feet of Jewish candidates."
204. While Polish social democracy had many Jewish supporters, a Jewish social democratic party was not founded until the early twentieth century. Jobst, *Zwischen Nationalismus und Internationalismus*.
205. *Głos Narodu*, 20 March 1897.
206. *Grzmot*, 25 March 1897.
207. On 1 June 1897, *Prawda* also asserted a special bond between Lueger and Krakow with a report on the second mayor "Dr. Karl Lueger" staying in Krakow at Whitsun, during which he visited its national monuments and the salt works at Wieliczka.

208. The first issue of 5 June 1897 bore the slogan "Newspaper for all," while the following numbers added the subtitle "Organ of the Christian Social Community."
209. The close connection between Christian businesses' boycott agitation and marketing strategies became especially clear in *Antysemita*, which drew readers' attention on the very first page to the advertisements for "Christian firms" on the last page. "Christians! Take a close look at the firms in the Christian company guide [*przewodnik firm Chreściańskich*] advertising on the last page!"
210. It was discontinued in October after seventeen issues. Majchrowski, *Antysemita*.
211. *Hasło*, special edition of 29 January 1898. Ehrenberg later also tried to win Stojałowski's support for *Głos Narodu*. The latter, however, refused to relocate his newspapers to Krakow. *Hasło* tried to present cooperation with Stojałowski as an alliance of equally strong movements which brought together the rural and urban working populations. *Hasło*, no. 5, 1898, 3.
212. *Hasło*, no. 5, 1898, 5f.
213. Michał Danielak (editor) for Kraków; Jan Zabuda for Biała, Auschwitz, and Żywiec; Andrzej Szponder (priest) for Wadowice, Kalwaria, and Zator; Tomasz Szajer (farmer) for Rzeszów, Strzyzów, etc.; Tobert Cena (farmer) for Jaroslau; Jan Kubik (farmer) for district 503; and Jan Potoczek (farmer) for Nowy Sącz.
214. The elections, therefore, marked the birth of "Christian democracy" in Krakow: Czesław Lechicki, "Chrześcijańska Demokracja w Krakowie 1897–1937," *Studia historyczne* 4 (1974): 585–608.
215. The previous representative of the Polish Conservatives in the Reichsrat, landowner Ferdinand Hompesch, had died in October 1897. Binder, *Galizien in Wien*, 679.
216. Furthermore, Tomasz Szajer and Antoni Zabuda left the party. See the letter by Zabuda on his resignation in *Przyjaciel Ludu* 5 (28 January 1900); Jósef Buszko, *Polacy w parlamencie Wiedeńskim 1848–1918* (Warsaw, 1996), 221.
217. With a print run of five thousand, the newspaper initially had a very high circulation. The following year, however, it dropped to two thousand. CDIAL/146/7/4733, 80. Danielak and Szponder also tried to cause a rift between the Christian Social Association (*stowarzysznie chrześciańsko-spoleczne*) and Stojałowski's party. See the police report on a meeting between Stojałowski, Szponder, Danielak, and Grzegorz Smolski concerning a replacement editor-in-chief, 87. *Obrona Ludu* 73 (1900), "Organizacja naszego stronnictwa," 1–2; no. 14, 1899, ibid; "Dobry chrześcijanin i Polak musi być antysemitą [A good Christian and Pole must be an anti-Semite]," *Obrona Ludu* 6 (1899): 1–3.
218. The peasant league representative Jan Potoczek had previously been a member of the Reichsrat and re-joined the Polish Club, while the other representatives of the peasant parties, the radicals and the Social Democrats, opposed the Polish club.
219. Prior to the first Reichsrat elections based on universal (male) suffrage in 1907, it spawned Zentrum [Center], a mainstream clerical party that aimed to appeal to both urban and rural Catholic voters.
220. The Peasant Party used "semitism" not only to denote the "Jewish element" but also those forces that did not work against Jews. *Przyjaciel Ludu*, no. 13, 1899, 202.
221. By February 1899 at the latest, the *Przyjaciel Ludu* used the word antisemitism to define its own program. It is likely that usage began earlier, but there is no evidence available as many omissions were caused by the period of unrest and state of emergency. Cf. Kraft, "Die jüdische Frage," 395.

Chapter 2

VIOLENCE

The mobilization and politicization of the crownland, which climaxed in the election campaigns of the years 1897 and 1898, was followed by a summer of "antisemitic riots."[1] Assuming that an antisemitic process had taken place, how were the agitation and violence linked? To what extent was agitation used to provoke violence against Jews? Was violence committed with the political intention of ousting Jews from the economy and the consumer world? Was this policy in effect implemented by peasant actions rather than via political channels? Were there any coincidental motives behind the acts of violence that did not stem from the political parties' antisemitic agitation?

The relationship between words and deeds in an era of antisemitic agitation is explored here on the premise that physical violence is readable. It has an inherent grammar and semantics which can be deciphered and so open a door to the mindscapes of those who have left no textual documents.[2] Reading violence in this way can compensate for a scarcity of source material, such as exists on semi-literate peasants. With an anthropologically and sociologically trained eye for pogrom and violence research, historians can in a sense translate acts of violence into texts.

Violence as Communication

Unlike research into the causes of violence, the historical study of violence focuses on the act of violence itself. This is regarded as a dynamic, interactive process influenced by all those involved—perpetrators, victims, witnesses, and other third parties. Those confronted with violence react to it according to their individual personalities, situational possibilities, and cultural backgrounds. Their reactions are in turn interpreted by their opponents.³ Due to the dynamism and processual nature of violence, it always has an open ending. The parties involved can never be certain of the course it takes or how it ends, but have certain expectations nonetheless. This is because violence does not breach the conventions of coexistence but is an integral part of everyday experience, albeit occurring more frequently in some contexts than others.⁴ Where untrammeled violence is rare, the participants have an inherent awareness of the framework within, and rules by which, it takes place.⁵ Notions of the likely form and extent of violence arise from conflict settlement against the background of a common experience-horizon, shared by perpetrators and victims alike. In Galicia, these rules evolved from the coexistence of Christians and Jews within the common order of a society divided into estates.⁶ Translating their social order—determined largely by structures of distribution—into a symbolic order, the individual actors and groups of actors found their positions in the social world.⁷ These interactively deduced positions can also be regarded as roles, which is why collective violence is sometimes referred to as a theater.⁸

The common tradition of violent conflict settlement is akin to a drama, with a script by which participants are unconsciously guided in the moment of violence. It assigns them roles, makes them perpetrators or victims, and prescribes how they should behave. Although these roles are not compulsory, they offer a reassuring framework to regulate the conflict. If a party acts according to them and elicits the expected reaction, they feel understood and their evaluation of the nature and gravity of the conflict is confirmed. When participants actualize the script in conformance with expectations, they not only reaffirm group hierarchies but also their concept of society in general. They demonstrate conflict settlement based on agreement. Conduct by an individual or a group that deviates from the script asserts a claim to change the status quo. If the new conduct is accepted, this claim is recognized.

Collective violence is, then, a reflection of social reality.⁹ During Galicia's existence, the "old order" became defunct and society was rearranged under the new conditions of a constitutional, multiethnic state with a market-based economy, democracy, and mass media, and an emerging awareness of an ethnic-nationalist order among its members. As established distribution structures crumbled, tried-and-tested positions became unreliable. With the transformation of old and emergence of new opportunities for identification, such as nationalism, socialism, and populism, once-held certainties of collective belonging and their hierarchies became obsolete. The constitutional state formulated new conditions for coexistence, installing a bureaucracy and "officials" to ensure that the rules were translated into social reality. A new consensus had to be reached on the basic categories shaping society. Antisemitic discourse provided new possibilities for talking about the coexistence of Jews and Christians, which in turn gave rise to new options for action. Violence had been part of such negotiations since time immemorial. The monarchy and the nobility had always embodied biased powers in the negotiation process. Every act, every speech and every instance of side-taking slightly changed the rules by which people structured their everyday lives. But if they transgressed them, they were punished.[10]

Power and Violence

Violence has a communicative function, which is apparent even if it is only threatened and not actually executed. For a threat to be effective, it must be credible. No ruling power is tenable unless it communicates the possibility of violence. The modern state, which claims a monopoly on the use of violence, does not have to employ violence for its citizens to follow the rules. They do so because they believe in the state's potential to make use of its monopoly on violence to enforce the rules. Power arises from this perpetuation and regulation of the violence prerogative.[11]

The Habsburg Monarchy regarded itself as a modern state in the above sense.[12] Its representatives, clad in the uniforms of police, soldiers, and local sheriffs, intervened in conflicts between individuals and groups.[13] They, too, influenced the process of violence and created or quashed options for action.[14] By cracking down on violence among certain sections of the population, they could issue warnings and demonstrate the power of the state. On several occasions, attacks on Jews spilled over into conflicts between Christians and representatives of the state. Then, government authority was renegotiated and the state was called upon to prove that it could assert its claim to a monopoly on violence, anytime and anywhere. If its subjects, who became citizens in 1867, did not perceive this, they would not accept and trust in the state order.

Galician Jews closely observed the state's trustworthiness. It was of existential importance to them to know whether the state's promise of equal rights implied it would condemn and prevent discrimination against Jews as a group. Did the state provide Jews with options for action in situations of violence? Could Jews, as citizens, avert discrimination by the Christian majority? Were they able to resist violence with the help of the state and by asserting their rights and so run the risk of entering new territory in relations with Christians? Or was it wiser to assume the role of the acquiescent victim and endure the rituals of the Christian majority, to be spared aggression in the future? In other words, was it better to continue the ambivalent symbiosis—that is, accept the inequality between Jews and Christians? Or did the history of Christian-Jewish conflict settlement no longer offer any pointers for orientation, because antisemitic agitation and the political peasant movement had ended the tradition shared by Christians and Jews? Reading acts of violence against Jews in the light of the conflict-settlement script outlined above reveals much about relations between Christians and Jews.

Which expectations of the others' behavior were not met? What significance did this have for the positions of Jews, Poles, and peasants in Galician society?[15]

This chapter aims to decipher the messages sent by acts of violence, whether targeting people or objects. These physically conveyed messages should not be confused with the perpetrators' own justifications and rationalizations, or their interpretation by victims or third parties. Ex post interpretations are examined in the next chapter. To understand them, all verbal articulations made during the process of violence must be taken into consideration, including slogans and rumors. They create the requisite conditions for collective violence and are embedded in it. To properly assess their function, they must be viewed in the general context of the dynamics of violence.[16] Rumors in this context serve to mobilize potential perpetrators by offering prospects of material gain or imminent threat to which they are intended to respond. Rumors also indicate the target of the violence: mostly an ethnic group or representatives of an antagonistic system. They serve to propel individuals across the threshold from words to action and synchronize the perpetrators. Advised on the appropriate time to set out, individuals gather and become a perpetrator group. If the group reaches a critical mass, it can absorb the individual and convey a sense of anonymity and so develop its own dynamic, prompting members to do things they would never do alone.[17] To reconstruct the dynamics of violence, densely detailed descriptions of pertinent situations containing evidence of participant interaction and rumor communication must be analyzed. In this way, insights can be gained into both the organizing structures that provided orientation to the actors and their personal interpretations of the events, which in some cases altered those structures.[18] Rumors and violence are interrelated. Each endows the other with meaning. Therefore, they must be considered in concert, analogously to discourse and action.

Rumors and Violence: Rumors Create Community

All the rumors concerning the disturbances in Galicia asserted the mobilized peasants' authority. The motif of a warrant to inflict violence was widespread across Europe, occurring as a form of protest when dynastic regimes and parliamentary politics clashed. Communicatively mediated, it was a vehicle for collective hopes and helped speakers legitimize their actions.[19] Rumors could be inscribed with both memories of better times in the past and hopes for improvement in the future. In the case of the Galician peasantry, such visions were informed by uncertainty and fears about the fragility of newly gained freedoms, and dissatisfaction with the state's handling of rights to formerly communal forests and fields.[20] In 1846, Galician peasants directed their anger at the feudal lords; in 1872, at the nobility.[21] In 1886, they rallied against the Jews who had recently risen to become their competitors, as well as the clergy, and in 1898 they opposed the Jews alone. The exclusion of these nonpeasant groups from the peasants' narrative illustrates the rumor's potential for building community among speakers who share a positive marker of identification—in this case, the peasant class. To properly evaluate the function and significance of these mobilizing and community-building rumors, and to exploit their potential as sources, we must be clear about the pragmatic nature of rumors.

Rumors against Rulers

Rumors are always spoken against the background of other representations of reality, such as government reports and newspaper coverage. They are circulated when people do not believe the official news because they do not trust the people or institutions that deliver them.[22] In authoritarian systems that aim to control all written and spoken communications, rumors are a corrective instrument at society's disposal. In freer communities, rumors can be used to sidestep taboos. Rumors can then verge on, or give rise to, conspiracy theories if they portray the sayability rules imposed by a certain group as distorting or concealing the truth. Orality and literacy are key factors in the spread of rumors, coloring incidents such as oral pronouncements of written authorizations. Written texts are indeed always read and interpreted according to the norms and standards of the given cultural system. Oral communication is effective precisely when it appropriates and reinterprets existing information.[23]

The Re-emerging Rumor

German scholarship uses the concept of the "re-emerging rumor" (*Tauchgerücht*) to refer to a spoken motif of supposed truth that surfaces at various intervals in different places.[24] Likening the spread of rumors to an epidemic, the intervals between its re-emergence are sometimes referred to as latent periods.[25] In both perspectives, rumors are seen as a historical subject and the object of historical research at the same time. While this sheds light on the collective memories of communicative communities, it can obscure the individual actors and their influence on the respective speech situations, allowing the—supposedly objective—talk to unfold its intended purpose once again. Paradoxically, rumors have a dual character. They are both medium and news, messenger and message in one. Speakers of rumors claim to communicate facts rather than their own individual perception, experiences, or opinion. Yet these facts are only established by the act of speaking. Speakers of rumors purport to pass something on that has already been told. Indeed, this claim proves to be true in every narrative situation as, at the time of speaking, the speaker narrates the incident.[26] The rumor makes itself the subject of the narration, as it were. Its self-referential mode displaces the individual speech act and its speaker from the center of the communication.[27] When starting or passing on a rumor, the speaker falls out of focus as an individual; he or she retreats behind the rumor.[28] To use rumors as sources, the context of the speech act must be recalled and the individual and motives behind the rumor brought to light.

"Antisemitism is a rumor about the Jews"[29]

When a community of speakers spread rumors about Jews, they practiced hostility toward Jews. They excluded Jews by talking about them as the "others." By propagating knowledge about Jews, the community created a backdrop against which individuals continued to spread rumors in the hope of gaining material or symbolic advantage.

Rumors are social constructs, formed from discrete speech situations, each referring to the "meta-rumor" in which they participate. In this field of tension between the concrete situation of narrating and the store of knowledge required to understand and believe the rumor (and which thereby consolidates it as knowledge), the spoken words gain meaning and become a historical event.[30]

It is worth reflecting on the connection between the one-off, situational telling of rumors and the texts advancing supposed truths that function as established knowledge. The examples of 1872 and 1886 constitute only a fraction of the wide range of variants. In each one, the speaker emphasized different aspects and details, made different causal links, and drew different conclusions as he or she pursued individual goals in diverging contexts.[31]

The historian can only encounter these rumors in sources. The texts containing them are isolated snapshots of what was once a broad fabric of interwoven rumors.[32] Both firm frameworks and unrelated extemporization are alien to the rumor, which is distinguished by immediate actuality and "wild, disordered talking" in multiple entanglements with the reality that surrounds it. Reconstructing rumors and their impact is therefore complicated but fruitful, and indeed essential, for exploring the world of the Galician peasant. In view of their complexity and interconnection with reality, rumors cannot be regarded as an expression of "primitive culture," limited to retelling stories about the nobility, the emperor, and Jews. In this chapter, Galician peasants will be treated as thinking actors. They not only received rumors and reproduced them in the process of retelling, but also shaped them.[33] Despite Adorno's famous definition, antisemitism research has hardly touched on the concept of rumors.[34] Inquiring into the ways people operated with "rumors about Jews," and their reasons for doing so, provides insight into the social dimension of hostility toward Jews and how this related to the semantics and agitation employed by antisemitic politics and journalism.

The Dynamics of the 1898 Peasant Unrest

It was shortly before Easter when Stanisław Wysocki died. A Christian conservative politician, he had been elected to the Reichsrat the previous year by the general class of electors of constituency 507 in central Galicia. Before the dust had settled after 1897's troubled elections, then, another by-election campaign was launched (after Stojałowski's election in the fall).[35] The familiar narrative of treason, with its Jewish connotations, was used again to discredit opponents, this time in conjunction with the Lenten liturgy and popular pre-Paschal traditions. A climate was created in which people readily believed that Wysocki's death was linked to a Jewish conspiracy. Once again, various rumors were blended and updated with new argumentation, naming new enemies and victims. Patterns of organization and justification that had emerged during previous phases of peasant unrest were repeated in the election campaign context. Where previously issues such as serfdom and the *Servituten* question had sparked conflict, it was now mass political mobilization that raised tensions during the traditionally volatile Easter period.

Violent Prelude: The Easter Troubles in Wieliczka

On 11 March, a rumor started in Wieliczka that Jews were planning an attack on the politician and local parish priest Andrzej Szponder.[36] A recently elected Reichsrat member for the Christian People's Party and active campaigner in the coming by-election, Szponder was the very personification of Galician society's intermeshing of religion and politics. Young people were especially outraged by the suggestion of an assassination attempt and gathered in front of the church that evening. Two gendarmes ordered them to disperse, assuring them the rumors were unfounded. Half an hour later, some of them were found smashing the windows of Jewish houses in the side streets around the market square. The gendarmes broke up the crowd, which then moved on to the station to wait for Szponder's arrival. When he finally alit from the 9:00 p.m. train from Kraków, the district captain asked him to say a few words to calm the crowd in the station hall.[37]

In church two days later (according to a district administration report), Szponder preached that people should not smash Jews' windows or hit Jews with sticks. In his "treatment of the Jewish question" during the sermon, however, he had warned Christians to avoid Jews and their taverns.[38] It was hard to tell where his sermons ended and his political agitation began. After the above-mentioned Mass, there was more stone-throwing, not only at houses but also at the local synagogue. Eighteen individuals were arrested,[39] including a Jewish manual worker who had injured attackers while trying to protect his house, and the apprentice shoemaker Zawadzki. The latter had started the rumor about the Jewish plot after he had seen a couple of Jews "creeping around" Szponder's house. Noting that Zawadzki had tried to enter a Protestant monastery, the public prosecutors found he suffered from "religious delusions."[40] But the fact that his rumor had been believed and had incited attacks showed that suspicions were rife and that Christians seriously feared an attack on "their" representative.

From Wieliczka to Kalwarya; or, Between Easter and Whitsun—the Dynamics of Two Rumors

Although the rumor of a plot to kill Szponder had proved unfounded and had even been discounted by Szponder himself, the unrest it fomented spread to the surrounding villages.[41] In Dobczyce, Jews leaving their Friday prayers were threatened by some "lads" they did not know, who said they would "sort them out so that none of them stayed." They were also physically attacked and their property destroyed.[42] This occurred after the daily newspaper *Głos Narodu* had supported the rumors by writing that the Jews were the root cause of the attacks because of their plot against the preacher-politician.[43]

Publications continued to fuel the widespread suspicions of a Jewish conspiracy in the ensuing weeks. The pamphlet *Jewish Secrets* was circulated more widely than ever across Galicia and was allegedly even used in Catholic school instruction.[44] Andrzej Szponder vigorously promoted it in Wieliczka. The rampant rumors that Jews were about to "get their comeuppance"[45] alarmed the authorities as well as the Jewish communities. The governor's office banned the pamphlet following the incidents in Wieliczka.[46]

Gossip about the incidents in Wieliczka and their alleged causes brought the "Jewish question" back into the focus of debate.[47] Any publication on Jewish plots and Jews in general, from sensationalist newspapers to scare-mongering pamphlets, were eagerly received and scrutinized for indications of the truth behind the unconfirmed rumors. All manner of phenomena was interpreted as signs of impending violence. The talk was quickly passed on, gathering momentum with each exchange among and between Christians and Jews as they went about their entangled daily lives.

The rumor of an imminent "reckoning with the Jews"—which could not be dismissed as false as it concerned an indefinite point in the future—mentioned neither a reason for, nor the agents of, the threatened violence. But it was received with a gloating sense of anticipation by some, and trepidation by others, which kept it alive until an occasion arose, such as a celebration or other major gathering, to provide a real context for violence.[48]

Hence, it is likely that the gossip concerning a crackdown on Jews sprang partly from popular hopes for one. Many people welcomed the prospect of a "reckoning" with the Jews. They read in pamphlets and heard at election meetings the supposed arguments in favor of such a crackdown. Cause and effect merged into one. One could read *Jewish Secrets* and conclude that Jews should be punished, or one could rationalize a desire to punish the Jews by referring to the pseudoscientific findings on the Jewish character that had been published.

Rumors of Violence: The Parable of the Prodigal Son and Tragedy in the House of Habsburg

From the widespread anticipation of a crackdown on the Jews, a second rumor soon emerged which configured the past and the future. It reworked the rumor about a planned attack on Andrzej Szponder with a familiar narrative that had appeared in 1886 and in variations many other times before and since: a Jewish plot to murder the emperor.[49] This time it was said that the plot had been exposed and the emperor had granted the public permission to beat and rob Jews as a punishment, albeit for a limited period only. The emperor evidently still held an important place in the peasants' mindscapes.[50] Since the abolition of unpaid labor, they had come to perceive him as their liberator and a guarantor of order. His murder might have put their rights at risk. The rumor that he had granted special permission to attack Jews, then, presumably reflected the peasants' wishes as well as their fears.

In this instance, the conflict with the Jews was not negotiated in national categories.[51] It was regarded as a conflict between the peasant masses and the nobility, Jews, and clergy. It echoed the preceding wave of rumors that had concerned a conflict between the nobility and the emperor. Indeed, the trigger in 1872—the claim that someone had cut off the emperor's ear—now reappeared in a slightly modified form in Pielgrzymka near Żmigród. It was said that "the Jews" had commissioned a barber to cut the emperor's throat while shaving him. But when the barber came face to face with the stern but gracious emperor, he collapsed in tears and confessed.[52]

Other members of the dynasty played different roles in the public consciousness. One variation of the rumor in circulation was that Emperor Franz Joseph had initially granted permission to beat the Jews for one month, but his wife, Empress Elisabeth, had appealed to him to be merciful, persuading him to reduce the period to two weeks.[53] Elisabeth appeared here as the maternal figure—a feminine, empathetic corrective to the just but strict head of the Habsburg family of nations—in keeping with the image of the imperial couple that the court sought to portray.[54]

The imperial-patriotic element of the rumors of violence is, then, undisputed.[55] Similarly, the pogroms in Tsarist Russia had been fueled by rumors that the Tsar had granted permission to beat the Jews. Here, it was said, the punishment intended by the Tsar had been stopped by the peasant-hostile, hidebound class of officials.[56] Where charismatic systems of rule were in place, the apologist view often prevailed of a benevolent ruler surrounded by inept or malicious henchmen. The rumors in Russia illustrated the myth, promoted by the Tsar himself, that his down-to-earth autocracy clashed with an "un-Russian bureaucracy."[57]

The rumors circulating in Galicia in 1898 show that imperial Habsburg rule had become as absorbed into the contemporary peasant identity as national and religious discourses.[58] Even Archduke Rudolf, the emperor's only son, who had died nine years previously, still lingered in the minds of the Habsburgs' subjects. In summer 1898, the story of his mysterious death in the Mayerling hunting lodge was recalled and woven into popular gossip.[59] Some said that Rudolf had not died but gone into hiding to escape a Jewish attack. In a story that verged on a conspiracy theory, they claimed he had recently returned to court and ordered the Jews to be collectively punished for what some of them had done. According to another version, Franz Joseph had bestowed the "gift" of permission to beat the Jews on the Christian population to celebrate the return of his son.[60]

From the parable of the prodigal son to the tragedies in the House of Habsburg, Galician peasants had a rich store of narratives to draw on for an imagined warrant to attack Jews. The stories about the tsar and the emperor can be regarded as isolated occurrences or as building blocks (or memes) of rumors, circulated for the purpose of organizing collective violence. Certainly, it is striking how persistently they use the motive of a limited-term privilege granted by the highest authority.

In another instance in summer 1898, a woman in Sambor claimed that the pope had granted Christians permission to beat Jews because they had planned to murder a priest.[61] Like the emperor and the tsar, the pope was thought to be above all reproach and to possess such ultimate authority. And if the act of beating Jews was explicitly approved by these authorities as a penalty for treason, participating in it was a patriotic act, or a Christian duty. By claiming to have the pope's permission, Christians could sidestep the church's ban on violence against Jews, of which they were repeatedly reminded in church and in writings on Christian antisemitism. In this exceptional case, the woman in Sambor claimed, the severity of the crime had justified the punishment and the papal consent to assault Jews.

The Habsburgs, meanwhile, were a conspicuous presence across the empire for another reason in 1898: it was the year of Franz Joseph's golden jubilee. Although none of the sources directly correlate this with the disturbances, there can be no doubt that, in view of the celebrations and the abundance of patriotic postcards and pamphlets, Franz Joseph was a far more tangible part of the Galicians' everyday lives than usual.[62] The imperial celebrations contrasted with the turmoil in France in the wake of the Dreyfuss affair, moreover, in which Jews had committed high treason.[63]

The second recurring theme in the rumors was the idea of the limited period. Semantically, this element built on the sanction idea to lend the story greater credibility. On a functional level, it added dynamism, urging people to act before the period was over and synchronizing those who were already mobilized by the alleged threat to their revered ruler.[64] The rumor was spread as an item of news, told with the intention of motivating as many peasants as possible to lay their hands on Jews and their property. It was also a collective act of self-empowerment. It assured the collective's members of their values and the ascriptions and attributions that defined their world and the world of the others. The rumor-tellers were on the side of the benevolent emperor with his family and loyal subjects. They punished the unscrupulous Jews, on the other side, who had tried to topple the established order by killing the emperor.[65] By recalling older rumors, they shared knowledge of the nobility, clergy, and the unjust *Servituten* regulations governing field and forest usage, which contributed to mobilizing the peasants.

But the rumors were not merely fantasies circulated within a secluded community. The peasantry was not a hermetic group; external parties inevitably participated in their communication. Their stories could only be convincing, moreover, if linked to more realistic contexts beyond their own wishes and imaginings. Rumors were often conveyed briefly in oral contexts as news. Many speakers added authority to the fleeting influence of word-of-mouth communication by referring to a written, sometimes official, source, or to a certain functionary. This also lent their stories greater credibility. According to one version, the parliamentarian Tomasz Szajer had brought the news straight from Vienna; in another, it had been Stanisław Stojałowski.[66] Evidently, these politicians were known to be anti-Jewish. Although both explicitly opposed violence toward Jews, as their fellow party member Szponder preached in church, they failed to demarcate the thin line between boycott and physical assault. The peasant parties and the Christian-social press had encouraged and hence legitimized certain fundamentally anti-Jewish actions.

In the minds of many Galicians, the parliamentarians were their link with Vienna. Indeed, the elected representatives liked to be regarded as envoys of the peasants, conveying their concerns to the emperor by interpellations in parliament.[67] The rumors now portrayed them performing the inverse task—bringing news from the emperor to the peasants. As they were well-known, respected figures with anti-Jewish opinions, the news was both credible and welcome. And by weaving them into their story, the rumor-tellers could shift responsibility for asserting it was permitted to "beat the Jews" away from themselves and on to the politicians.

In another version of the permission rumor, a "fine gentleman on a bicycle" had read out a warrant. There was also talk of official notices, proclamations, and even permit cards. While each embellishment served to make the story more credible, it placed the onus on the individual narrator to provide objective proof.

Hence, people created their own social realities in which assaulting Jews was legitimate. Below, two incidents will be recounted which illustrate how this reality was generated, and in which situations the tale of imperial authorization seemed truthful. They both occurred in the small town of Kalwarya Zebrzydowska, where there were anti-Jewish riots on 25 and 26 May. That weekend before Whitsun, during which two rioters were shot, marked the start of a wave of violence which convulsed the crownland all summer.

Official Permit Cards in Kalwarya

In May 1898, a sales representative for a company named Baumann visited the Christian storeowner Leo Kakol to promote a new product for removing ink stains. The salesman left Kakol a batch of leaflets advertising the new product, "Statim," which Kakol duly distributed among his customers. This sparked a rumor that Kakol was issuing the eagerly awaited permit cards for assaulting Jews, and consequently a minor run on his store. Sources show that three young men asked for extra leaflets, and an apprentice named Johann Wojas tried to obtain one even after Kakol was reported to have run out.

What led the residents of Kalwarya to believe that a leaflet advertising stain remover was in truth a permit to assault Jews? Crucially, many of them were waiting for such a permit card without having any idea of how it might appear. In theory, any written document that a stranger brought to town could be associated with the imperial warrant. Coincidentally, moreover, Jews were colloquially known as "ink spots" in Polish.[68] If one was so inclined, the leaflet could be interpreted as promoting an agent to remove all ("ink-like") Jews.[69]

The advertisement would certainly not have convinced any skeptics of the truthfulness of the rumors. But in conjunction with the widespread anticipation of such permit cards, and the popular inclination toward conspiracy thinking, which left scope for a message being conveyed in a slightly cryptic way, the leaflets could be overwhelmingly convincing.

Signposts to Violence

Kalwarya Zebrzydowska was a place of pilgrimage (see figures 2.1 and 2.2). Its religious significance was such that it was known as the Polish Jerusalem. Local dignitaries had earmarked it for celebrations marking the centenary of the birth of Adam Mickiewicz shortly before Whitsun.[70] They hoped that the public festival in honor of the national poet would swell the patriotic spirit of the *lud*, the people. But the rumors about an imperial warrant to assault Jews were also circulating in Kalwarya. To many locals, the festival preparations seemed to cor-

Na Kalwaryi: Pątnicy, zebrani pod kościołem

Figures 2.1 and 2.2. Pilgrims in Kalwarya Zebrzydowska, *Nowiny Illustrowane*, no. 34, 1907. Public domain.

roborate the rumors. They read them as a sure sign that the time had come for "the strike." A railroad worker named Franz Namer was told by his maid, Maria Wróbel, that "the peasants are going to beat up the Jews" and that the district captain had already given his approval. According to her version, the pope had granted permission to attack the Jews because Jews had beaten a clergyman to death in Sułkowice. That, she claimed, was the real reason why people had been invited to Kalwarya.[71] Indeed, for much of the population, a dead poet was not a valid reason for a public celebration. The majority was illiterate and therefore not interested in Mickiewicz's work.[72]

The notices that the festival committee had displayed in the area were received with excitement, then, not because they invited the public to join in a tribute to the "Slavic bard" but because they were believed to be the anticipated public warrants to assault the Jews.[73] Scanning them perfunctorily, people noted just the place and the date, and the color of the paper they were printed on. It was blood red, which illiterate peasants interpreted as a sign of imminent violence. It was said that the notices were authorized by "his Majesty" and colored red to indicate that Jewish blood was to be shed.[74] It was with expectations such as these that hundreds of peasants from the surrounding villages came to the festively decorated town on Whitsun weekend.

Fear and Expectations: Preparations for the Centenary Celebrations in Kalwarya

The rumors were, as mentioned above, a ubiquitous talking point and by no means confined to a select group. It was inevitable, then, that the Jews of West Galicia also heard about the threat of imminent attacks. To prevent it coming to this, some understandably concerned Jewish residents of Kalwarya reported the rumors to the local police chief prior to the festival. The police consequently questioned a community leader from the surrounding area to find out how far the rumors had spread. They were told the rumors were untrue, and that the commotion was merely excitement about the forthcoming festival. Other Jewish citizens turned to the district captain in Wadowice for help. In a verbal statement made after the riots, he told the public prosecutor that some Jews had come to see him on the morning of 25 May, "asking for protection because a rumor was circulating that they were to be subjected to murder and looting." The same day, he received a report from the municipal authority in Kalwarya, "the content of which confirmed the Jews' verbal allegation." He immediately sent a trainee named Szajnowksi from the governor's office to Kalwarya "with the corresponding instructions" and ordered that eight police officers (instead of the planned four) were deployed to maintain law and order. Interestingly, while he emphasized his resolve in his report to Sułkowski, the imperial-and-royal prosecutor, he showed greater concern not to appear to have acquiesced to the Jews in his communication with the governor's office, which was not supervised by the authorities in Vienna.

In his report to the governor's office in Lemberg, the district captain stated that a Jewish delegation from Kalwarya had come to him as early as 20 May, because Jews had been collectively threatened with beatings and robbery on 25 May. As he was visiting the Galician capital Lemberg at the time, he could not deal with them. So, they made another, last-minute attempt in the morning of 25 May. It was a "delegation of four of the most influential Jews," who reported that rumors were circulating that people intended to kill Jews and rob them "to a fantastic extent." Still, the district captain did not take this as cause to act: "As I am familiar with the Jews' anxious nature and tendency to tell national-tinged fairytales, I did not believe them. Especially as I had not heard the slightest mention of impending unrest, never mind any active preparations to this end."[75] However, as news of the unrest reached him over the course of the day, from the Kalwarya local police chief among other sources, he sent his assistant to order reinforcements in the form of two police officers from Wadowice and two from Andrychów.[76]

His account of the instructions he gave as district captain tallied in the two reports. But the accounts nevertheless differed, in keeping with the local authorities' tendency to change their tone regarding Jews according to the addressee. When dealing in German with authorities under the Ministries of Justice and the Interior in Vienna, they refrained from making any critical comments about Jews and always conveyed the impression of swiftly taking the necessary steps to maintain public safety and order. When communicating with internal actors in their native Polish, however, they not only admitted that their scope for action was limited but also echoed the widespread disapproval of Jews who turned to the authorities for protection. The reason for the local officials sending divergent signals to Lemberg and Vienna will emerge in the course of events. And the district captain in Wadowice will reappear in a far more inglorious role. At this point, however, the delegation of Jews, who were not merely repeating rumors they had overheard but reporting a threatening incident, eventually had their request heard. Reinforcements were deployed in Kalwarya.

From Kalwarya to Frysztak; or, Between Whitsun and Corpus Christi—Deadly Disturbances in "Polish Jerusalem" (25–26 May 1898)

The first attacks occurred in the evening of 25 May. As the procession of some three hundred people and a brass band paraded through the town, festooned and illuminated in commemoration of Adam Mickiewicz, a total of fifty-nine windows were smashed in Jewish homes. The incident illustrated the parallel existence of divergent interpretations of the occasion, arising from the public's reception of the red notices. Although the parade toward Zebrzydowice had been officially organized in honor of the national poet, some participants interpreted it as a ritual hoax, and the playing of the brass band as a mock serenade to intimidate the Jews, to which end the participants also—as a matter of course—smashed the Jew's windows.[77]

The next day started peacefully with a Mass and the unveiling of a commemorative plaque in honor of the poet. But in the evening, there were even more graver disturbances than on the previous day. A crowd of about a thousand people marched through the town chanting "Hurrah countrymen, get the Jews!"[78] The windows of every Jewish house were smashed; one house was even looted. The law enforcement unit, consisting of eight gendarmes, two policemen, and thirty firefighters, steered the crowd out of town and toward the monastery on the hill (the "Calvary" of the place name).[79] Following orders from the district authority, they apprehended anyone who resisted or threw stones on the way, and made eleven arrests. The crowd responded angrily to the crackdown, which crushed their hopes of an attack on the Jews. One person in the crowd is said to have shouted, "Why did they write to us to come to the revolution in Kalwarya?."[80] A peasant named Felix Kluska collapsed on the ground, allegedly because an officer had struck him in the back with a rifle butt. This prompted a certain Heinrich Filako, a law graduate and "scribe for the Kalwarya district court," to call out, "The gendarmes have killed a countryman, . . . those rascals, Jewish devotees, they defend the Jews because they gave them brandy worth 20 kreutzers on the house." As he was arrested, he shouted, "Attack, save me, the gendarme is taking me away!"

The misinformation about the death of a peasant and drunken gendarmes inflamed the crowd, who started throwing stones at the officers. A gendarme named Kraus sustained a rib injury and reacted by firing at the crowd. Michał Balik of Strzyżów was killed instantly. Two other people were seriously wounded; one of them died later of his injuries.

The Rumor's Transformation

The gendarmes had frustrated the visiting peasants' hopes and expectations of looting Jewish houses[81] by what seemed to the peasants a completely arbitrary show of force. In the peasants' view, the police had interfered in a legitimate action to punish the Jews. The situation had escalated further when shouts were heard that a peasant had been killed. As well as the court scribe Heinrich Filako, a Franciscan friar named Otto also agitated the crowd by claiming that the officers had been plied with liquor by the Jews and that the head of the unit, Jan Wilk, was himself a Jew.⁸² Furthermore, he asserted that the gendarmes had disobeyed orders not to shoot.

While the violence was escalating far beyond a dispute between Christians and Jews and into one between peasants and law enforcement agents, the warrant rumors gained a new twist. The gendarmes were said to have been paid by the Jews or bribed with alcohol to protect them.⁸³ Thus the anti-Jewish narrative persisted despite the intervention of all the local authorities—clearly disproving the theory of state approval. The episode illustrates the rumors' potential to generate counterproposals to the official standpoint. The gendarmes had forfeited the peasants' trust by shooting at countryfolk to defend Jews. Therefore, the crowd did not believe the gendarmes' assertion that there was no authorization to attack Jews. The notion took root—supported by the news that Jewish "delegations" had been to see the district captain and the local gendarmerie—that the officers were working for the Jews. Following the events in Kalwarya, then, popular narratives consigned the gendarmerie and the military to the "other" side, along with the Jews and in opposition to the peasants and the emperor. In the ensuing weeks, the peasants observed the military's actions in the Christian-Jewish conflict very closely. They noted where reinforcements were brought in and where they were withdrawn, as it had become clear that the armed forces would respond to any assault on the Jews or their property. It was a different experience than in 1846, when for a few days nobody had prevented the peasants from going on the rampage against the manorial gentry.

Written Rumors: The Aftermath of Kalwarya

Newspapers picked up on the word-of-mouth rumors surrounding Kalwarya and fed them into an emotionally charged discourse, rousing public opinion. The clerical daily *Prawda* wrote, "On the day of the Mickiewicz celebrations Christian blood was shed to protect the Jews."⁸⁴ The leading Krakow daily *Głos Narodu* printed a letter from Father Andrzej Szponder in Wieliczka, accusing the authorities of abusing their power during the riots and of subservience to the Jews.⁸⁵ But those who approved of assaulting Jews could find affirmation even in less biased reports. They could read any news item in the light of their personal store of knowledge and regard the sheer authority of the written word as evidence of a warrant. One example of peasants creating their own truth *after* the riots in Kalwarya was an incident following an article in *Kurier Lwowski*. The 19 June issue had merely reported assaults and the widespread belief in an imperial warrant to commit them. But at a gathering in Zagórz, a certain Michał Sęk claimed that the newspaper had written that it was permitted to beat the Jews that day and on the 19th of every following month. He called on those present to fetch the newspaper and read out the report so that everyone could hear the official announcement. Later, others demanded the newspaper too, as it could apparently be used as a kind of permit card.[86]

The Spread of Violence

As the continuing rumors were compounded by newspaper coverage of recent riots, and emotionally charged commentaries whipped up public opinion, unrest grew and caused further outbursts of violence in Jewish taverns in Myślenice and Podgórze counties.[87]

Taverns were the most frequent scene of disturbances, which almost always occurred on market days or holidays. In fact, the trouble often started in taverns. This was where Christian peasants and Jews most often met, since most barkeepers were Jewish. And alcohol consumed in large quantities, of course, acts as a catalyst for violence. Drunken guests would become aggravated when called upon to pay their bill or if refused more liquor. They would then proceed to threaten the barkeeper, steal things from the bar, upturn tables, knock over chairs, and smash glasses and bottles.[88] The statistics on the frequency of disturbances in the worst-affected districts illustrate the extent of the violence: Attacks on Jews were reported in 44 percent of the local communities in Jasło county, in 49 percent in Nowy Sącz, in 45 percent in Strzyżów, and in 36 percent in Frysztak. By 14 February 1899, 964 perpetrators had been convicted with an average sentence of one month's imprisonment.[89] Official communication pointed out that the number of arrests fell "far behind" the actual number of participants in the violence.

The riots gained a dynamic that was as much influenced by the reactions of the Jewish victims as by those of the authorities seeking to suppress them. The scope for action and patterns of conduct of these actors differed greatly from region to region.

Jewish Reactions: Individual Scope for Action

It was not the case that entire localities turned, united, on their Jewish neighbors. Cooperation between Jews and Christians, which in an hour of need could prove invaluable, varied by degrees. Some Jewish barkeepers, for instance, asked their Christian neighbors to defend their taverns or tend their bars for them. For a certain fee, then, Jewish taverns could be temporarily turned into Christian establishments.[90]

Another strategy used by Jewish storeowners was to hide with their valuables in the houses of Christian neighbors. In some cases, they paid to do so, but in others the arrangement was purely neighborly. Other Jews tried to pay protection money directly to the "malefactors" to avert robberies. In one case, the marauding peasants were not satisfied with the guilder offered and took some soap, weights for scales, cheese, and leather soles as well, but left the store's stocks untouched.[91] Sometimes the targeted Jews responded aggressively or threatened violence. A Jewish barkeeper in Osielec was thrown to the floor while trying to fend off looters. He managed to crawl into the back room where he kept a pistol, which he then directed at his assailants, injuring two of them. He was subsequently convicted.[92] In another case, two Jews were sentenced following an attack, one of them to three days' detention because he had "intentionally and with malice aforethought" thrown stones at a group of rioters. A Jewish butcher was even sentenced to one month in prison for threatening a rioter with his butcher's knife.[93]

Some barkeepers responded to the threat of attacks by trying to shift the focus of hostility away from themselves. A case in Jawornik is documented in which a barkeeper named Emanuel Heitlinger engaged in agitation himself by deflecting his guests' aggression onto the nobility and authorities. He was said to have interrupted a conversation between four peasants about the disturbances with the following words: "It starts with the Jews, but it ends with the *pany*. People shouldn't beat up the Jews, they should beat up the *pany*: all those officials in court, lawyers, notaries, who impose such high taxes." He then went on to list all the taxes they had to pay. In court he was found to have unduly sown "mistrust toward the upper class," which could lead to "unrest in the current circumstances," and sentenced to one month's detention with one "day of fasting" per week.[94]

This case demonstrates the continuing impact of the events of 1846 fifty-two years later. Then, barkeepers had successfully diverted the hostility roused by the sobriety movement away from themselves and onto the authorities. Officials feared nothing more than the people's aggression turning toward the state and the nobility. The Jawornik barkeeper's strategy backfired on him, but the episode illustrates the close daily contact between the potential perpetrators of violence and their victims. Barkeepers and their customers sat together and discussed the peasants' plight, and who was responsible for it, in the tavern.

Targeted Jews often tried to flee, especially if a gang of robbers approached with whom they were not connected by any kind of relationship. As the riots went on for several weeks, interactions could not be entirely evaded. Relying on the protection of the state always remained an important, though double-edged, option.

Punishment over Profit? Cacophonies in June 1898

A recurring feature of the disturbances was the use of cacophony outside Jewish houses, often accompanied by stick-banging and stone-throwing. While the latter acts could indicate the start of lootings, as shown below, cacophonies were made to satisfy a desire to mete out symbolic punishment. The rumors of assassination attempts fueled a group dynamic that mobilized the peasant collective to perform such actions—to intimidate and humiliate their victims. Cacophonies were frequent following the events in Kalwarya. Peasants discussed the fact that their countrymen had died to protect Jews with pronounced indignation. The Christian community felt the Jews' "employment" of a third party—the military—to protect them deserved punishment. When Christians accused Jews of showing impertinence and arrogance by their response to the arrest of troublemakers, they were essentially complaining that the Jews were violating the traditional rules of coexistence.

In general terms, a desire to give the Jews "something to think about" pervaded the land in summer 1898. The time had come, it was widely felt, for the much-discussed "reckoning." The slow process of change that had been launched by the introduction of equality and mechanisms of market economy had caused a "constitutional conflict."[95] The status of Jews and Christians had been made pliant, and Christians' imagined superiority had been challenged. The situation in 1898 echoed the *Servituten* dispute in previous decades. True, life for the peasantry was generally much improved by the 1890s, with major disputes such as those over forest-and-field use and frequent foreclosures having been settled. But this exceedingly tradition-conscious class still struggled with fundamental changes that challenged its very concept of self and were too far-reaching to be internalized within one generation. Political representation played an important role in facilitating the peasant collective's self-affirmation. Yet although the peasant parties sought to improve conditions by adapting traditional ways to a "modern," rational economic system and establishing independent channels of distribution, they could not erase the memory of bygone importance and the identity and assurance found in productive work and cultivating one's own land.

To the peasants, Jews who claimed what was not historically theirs were the adversary. Peasants presumed that property and wealth that had not been gained by production but by trade—in some cases, in peasant land—had been unjustly acquired at their expense. And every time they dissociated themselves from the Jews, they implied an assignment of guilt; they held Jews responsible for their plight. In the critical phase of the election campaigns, politicians not only trumpeted such allegations but also accused Jews of preventing the peasant parties from achieving their rightful electoral success.

All it took, then, was the bloodshed after the first disturbances to accelerate the Christian tendency to incriminate the Jews—to demand retribution for the Jews' allegedly provocative behavior and the way they had "got off lightly." In the eyes of the Christian community, the authorities had acted with wrongful bias by arresting and firing at peasants while leaving Jews unchallenged. Although peasants compared information on the casualties inflicted by the military, they did not hold the armed forces responsible for the outbreak of the conflict. Those were two different issues in their eyes. The conflict between (Christian) peasants and Jews was one thing; the state getting involved was another. The peasants were genuinely indignant that the armed forces had so obviously prioritized the Jews, causing the drama to fatally escalate and fail as a lesson to the Jews. They overlooked the fact that all citizens, regardless of faith, had been equal before the law for a whole generation, and still conceived of society in terms of rigid classes and the Christian order. They resorted to the traditional catalog of measures at the disposal of their class to punish the Jews—by making cacophonies and throwing stones—for calling in the military.

During the unrest in Galicia, Jews and Christians renegotiated their status in relation to each other and their relations to the state. Every encounter in the riot context could be charged with symbolic meaning and become a Christian attempt to gain the upper hand over, or at least an equal footing with, the Jews. In one incident near Nowy Sącz, a peasant stopped the coach of a Jewish man named Samuel Körbel and tried to get in. Körbel repelled two of the peasant's attempts by force, but the latter was determined and shouted, "If you ride, I'll ride with you, but if I walk, you have to walk too."[96]

Almost all forms of disturbance in the summer of 1898 were sparked by a desire to punish and intimidate Jews for allegedly inappropriate behavior and to warn them of worse consequences to come. But these were never the sole or unambiguously primary motives. An idealized picture of the disturbances as a lower-class protest at the break-up of the moral economy is, then, inapposite.[97] The often-employed strategy of making a cacophony, referred to disarmingly as *Katzenmusik* (cat music) in German, could take on dramatic dimensions and have grave consequences. This was evidenced in the area around Żywiec, where Jewish equality was never achieved in practice.

Exclusionary Violence: Cacophony in Koszarowa

Every night from 11 to 21 June, a crowd of up to two hundred people gathered to make an infernal noise outside any Jewish houses in the parish of Koszarowa.[98] The local mayor had tried to intervene but had been driven away by rioters who threatened "the Jews' mayor" and then turned their dreadful "serenade" on him.[99] During the nightly sieges, windows were smashed and some peasants broke into a Jewish family's house, bringing a goat. They threatened to tie up the inhabitants and shake salt over them to induce the goat to lick them.[100] Later, as the terrorized Jews were able to name some three hundred perpetrators to the Wadowice public prosecutor, the attackers' sadism was brought to justice. The public prosecutor Sułkowski also condemned the negligence of the local authorities, who by treating such acts of terrorism as harmless de facto tolerated them, and so allowed the perpetrators to continue believing that the state approved of their actions. Cooperation between the public and the local authorities on anti-Jewish actions was a peculiarity of the area, previously manifested in the unauthorized, anti-constitutional ban on Jewish residents and purge of "Jewish social democrats."[101] It was no surprise, then, that the police drove perpetrators away rather than making any arrests, allowing the rioters to continue their troublemaking elsewhere. Though conceding that there was severe understaffing in the province, limiting the authorities' scope for ensuring public safety, Sułkowski criticized the law enforcement officers' actions as participation in the ritual chase. When they appeared on the scene, they added a new dynamic to the drama, sustaining it, and ultimately becoming victims of the perpetrators' antics themselves, as they always remained one step behind.

Despite their carnivalesque character, these nightly goings-on were by no means harmless, nor in any way fun for those affected. A cacophony made in Targanice, in front of the house of a certain Samuel Feiner, was especially ominous. It started at eleven o'clock at night on 10 June and continued until 16 June. Sułkowski reconstructed the incident as follows:

> They shouted, howled, banged on wooden boards and drummed on crates and various other wooden and iron objects they had brought for the purpose, and so caused an infernal noise that could be heard far and wide. While they made this cacophony, they threatened the Israelite [and] forced him to give them tobacco and cigars.
> . . . Their actions filled the Feiner family with fear and anxiety, especially as they were accosted like this for several nights and Feiner's wife was in her confinement. The troublemakers did not desist even when Feiner pointed out the above situation to them and implored them to leave off the excessive noisemaking out of consideration for his poor bed-ridden wife. To elude further attacks, Feiner was compelled to leave Targanice completely. He moved to another town.[102]

Sułkowski's account sheds light on both the festival aspect of the cacophony and Samuel Feiner's expectation that his neighbors would stop harassing him if they knew his wife and their newborn baby were affected. But the unrest caused—previously ambivalent—relations between neighbors to turn hostile. Having found that even appealing to the troublemakers' human kindness was to no avail, Feiner decided to leave the neighborhood. Similarly, a certain Moses Schöngut from neighboring Jastrzębia was compelled to move away from his Christian neighbors and sold his house.[103]

The nightmare did not end until an investigating judge appeared in Jeleśnia and ordered the arrest of seventeen troublemakers. But on 17 July, they were surprisingly acquitted. Assessing the consequences of this decision, Sułkowski wrote, "Because the detainees were acquitted, they continued their activities, believing the court to see nothing punishable in them."[104] The district captain of Krosno agreed that the decision to release 102 troublemakers, arrested for rioting, appeared to confirm the rumors that assaulting Jews was legal.[105] Yet it was not common for officials to reflect on the impact of policing in this way. Having hundreds of prisoners to be accommodated and provided for all at once simply confronted them with considerable logistical problems. It was more expedient for the military to intervene vigorously to prevent acts of violence in conflict situations. To do so, however, they needed to be on the scene prior to the outbreak of disturbances. They were assisted in this regard by the Jewish communities who asked for protection. The Jewish population, then, influenced the course of events by their actions, alarming the authorities or attempting to pacify mobs. But, especially in East Galicia, Jews also defended themselves by striking back.

Violence between Equals? An Overview of the Unrest in East Galicia

Attacks on Jews also spilled over into East Galicia. Here, too, rumors played a crucial role in mobilizing local populations. Agitators talked about the riots in West Galicia which, they warned, would soon spread to the eastern part of the province. But the small towns of East Galicia had a peculiar ethnic and social composition that gave the disturbances there a different character. Violence had already erupted between Christian and Jewish workers one year previously in Schodnica.[106] It was one of the new towns that had sprung up during the oil boom, to which young men flocked, seeking to earn money for their families in the country. Ethnic conflicts were a typical symptom of life in these industrial centers.[107]

New towns like Schodnica, Borysław, and Drohobyc, where Jews, Poles, and Ukrainians rubbed shoulders, soon grew beyond their limited infrastructures and sanitary facilities. Workers of one ethnicity tended to hold the same position in works' hierarchies as they were generally educated to the same level. While many Jews were pit owners and employed family members as supervisors or foremen, it was principally Ukrainians who performed the dangerous—often deadly—work underground. Disputes over pay or conditions frequently turned violent.[108] Then, the conflicting groups of workers met as equals. Rather than performing dramas of humiliation and submission following the conventional script, they confronted each other in fistfights and direct bids for revenge. Certain rules applied here, too. But they did not involve adhering to a specific role assigned to one's collective. Society here had no distinct majority or minority; it was a dynamic ethnic triangle in a constant state of flux.

The differences in social composition were found not only in East Galicia's new oil-producing towns; the East Galician countryside also differed from the west of the land. It had a dominant Ukrainian population, who surrounded the Polish-Jewish towns, so to speak. In the towns of East Galicia, Jews often made up the majority. Consequently, the urban (Polish) Christian minority was not only separated geographically from the rural (Ukrainian) Christian population but also by denomination and language. Coexistence between Christians and Jews was different here than in West Galicia.

During the troubled summer of 1898, there were major incidents in Tłuste, Bursztyn, Borszczów, and Przesmyśl. However, the violence in the latter fortress town can hardly be described as antisemitic: it involved attacks on Jewish bread-sellers by gangs that included Jewish residents. In Tłuste and Bursztyn, Jewish tradesmen were attacked and beaten up, mainly by Roman Catholic migrant workers. These groups of up to five hundred men, who worked during the summer on the railroad between Czortków and Zaleszczyki, often argued with the local Jewish merchants, who were entirely unfamiliar to them, over the price of food and accommodation. In Tłuste, an argument escalated when some of the local Jews physically attacked a migrant worker. Workers then started smashing windows and beating up Jews in the town. The local Jews subsequently sought revenge by attacking several workers. Eventually, the military intervened to reestablish order, arresting six workers and two Jews.

Similarly, in Bursztyn, two Catholic workers were beaten up by a group of Jews after an argument in a butcher's shop. Subsequently, a crowd of several hundred Christians of both denominations gathered to go on the rampage, demolishing Jewish houses, seriously injuring the rabbi, and physically abusing a Jewish woman.[109] The workers were temporarily in the area to carry out river regulation work.[110]

While most of the migrant workers who attacked Jews in East Galicia were "Masurian"—that is, Roman Catholic—the occasional belligerent gang consisted chiefly of Ukrainians.[111] Nonetheless, the riots of 1898 were predominantly the work of Polish-speaking peasants and workers. They had heard and read about the events in West Galicia and tried to orchestrate similar lootings in the east in a bid to likewise profit at the expense of the Jews.

Newspapers and Trains: Conveying the Rumors to Eastern Galicia

News of the disturbances in Kalwarya had traveled up to the River San, which marked the boundary between West and East Galicia. The public prosecutor in Zagórza in Sanok district attributed the increase in communication to the newspapers and trains. Zagórza, he explained, was a rail junction where the "latest news" was relayed "live" and in minute detail by train travelers and railroad staff to the credulous and "less intelligent people in the villages." Rather than eliciting horror, these reports of atrocities had encouraged copycat deeds. Stojałowski had prepared the ground, sowing hatred with his demand for liberation from the Israelites, whom he accused of yoking and exploiting the Christian population. The news arriving by train and the unguarded press coverage "of the entire tale of a warrant from the highest authority" had reinforced this attitude. The final straw was provided by the *Kurier Luwowski* of 19 June, which was used as evidence of the truth of the rumors, as well as a permit card, as described above. At one point during the disturbances, someone had shouted that even a hundred gendarmes could not prevent what was "destined to happen."[112]

While some Ukrainians also utilized newspaper coverage of the rumors as proof of their accuracy, many seem to have simply understood it as such. An article had appeared in the Ukrainian-language newspaper *Slovo Ruskie* (Ruthenian Voice) on the disturbances, prompting readers in the small town Czarna to spread the news of an imperial warrant.[113] In a bar in Zagórza, three men, named Ivan Sulima, Lesio Hoschyluk, and Lesio Fedyschym, cited the same article as grounds to avoid paying their bill. Despite their threats of violence, the barkeeper called the police. On their arrival, Hoschyluk asked why they should act as usual if the papers said it was permitted to rob Jews, while Fedyschym maintained he had not believed the newspaper reports at first.[114] Near Kolomea, the daughter of the local teacher, Tomas Jarusiewicz, claimed she had found a "sealed letter" outside the schoolhouse containing a "call to the Christian people" to "drive away the Jews."[115]

In Sambor, too, Ukrainians spoke about the riots and the rumors. Sometimes their talk gained an anti-Polish thrust. The son of a certain Lesio Dutko claimed that the "young emperor had asked the old emperor to allow the robbing of the *pany* and the Jews, but the old emperor had refused." The young emperor to whom he referred was probably Archduke Rudolf, who had been especially popular among Ukrainian peasants.[116]

Tradespeople in East Galicia were more likely to respond violently to attackers and even be the first to strike if insulted. They were dealing with complete strangers—Polish-speaking migrant workers with whom they had had no contact in the past and would most likely not have any in the future. These men, employed to build railroads and regulate rivers, spent their summers far away from their homes and families in surroundings to which they had no connection. For months in succession, their lives consisted of hard manual labor, from which they sought release in alcohol. This constellation resulted in a high potential for aggression, which was not channeled into collective ritual acts such as making cacophonies. In this situation, Jews who were threatened with violence often responded with violence.

This first phase of unrest ended in tragedy on Corpus Christi in the small town of Frysztak. After this bloody encounter between violent rioters and gendarmes, the governor's office changed its strategy for dealing with violence and consequently the entire character of the disturbances.

The "Galician Blood-Feast": Corpus Christi in Frysztak

Frysztak was a small market town in the parish of Jasło where a market was held on Corpus Christi Thursday. A dispute in a Jewish tavern spilled out on to the market square and some Jewish-owned stalls were overturned. When the gendarmes appeared on the scene with a few military reinforcements, they came face to face with a large, angry crowd. A peasant injured a gendarme with a scythe. The officers fired fourteen shots in response. Eleven people were killed, including some elderly bystanders. The fact that the gendarmes were so distinctly outnumbered yet equipped with far superior weapons resulted in disaster. They fired at the crowd, apparently without orders, because they had felt threatened themselves.[117]

The tragic events in Frysztak gave rise to many more rumors and malicious gossip. It was claimed, for instance, that lead shot was found in the body of one of the victims, implying that he was not killed by a gendarme's carbine but by a civilian shotgun.[118] People sent death threats to Winiarski, the local police chief, and demanded that the district administration explain why so many Christians had been killed but no Jews.[119] There was even speculation that Winiarski and his family were congenitally violent, which was brought up in antisemitic interpellations in the Reichsrat.[120] Again there were rumors about drunken gendarmes who had been bribed by Jews with alcohol and money. There was also talk that the Alliance Israelite made relief payments to Jewish victims.[121] The death of innocent people who had not even been involved in the disturbances was cited as verification of the general blamelessness of the Christian population. As in Kalwarya, the rumors sidestepped the actual cause of the bloodshed to point the finger at Jewish tradespeople—the initial victims—and the gendarmes as perpetrator collectives.

The Riots from the Perpetrator Perspective

As the above reflections on the rumors circulating between Easter and Whitsun have shown, it cannot be claimed that the perpetrators were misled by false information. People deliberately linked the rumors they heard with information from other contexts to *make* them more credible when they passed them on. They tried to convince each other it was legitimate to attack Jews. No doubt some individuals were convinced that a warrant existed. But it would be wrong to say that "the people" had been duped by manipulative politicians. The rumors were composed of elements from the collective store of peasant knowledge. How and why the peasants used the warrant as a motive for violence will be described below with reference to statements made under interrogation and an indictment by the Rzeszów public prosecutors shortly after the tragedy in Frysztak.[122] One of the many raids in summer 1898 can be reconstructed by comparing these accounts. They concern various offences committed in Lutcza and the surrounding area by eighty-three men and women. The focus, then, will return to Christian-Jewish relations in the small town near Strzyżów that was the main theater in the introduction.

"On Saturday we'll get the Jews":
Statement by Eyewitness Mikołaj Chciuk

Mikołaj Chciuk was a 28-year-old father of two who earned his living as an agricultural worker in his home town Lutcza. Under interrogation, Chciuk described how all week, people "everywhere" had been saying it was permitted to assault Jews and destroy their property. On Friday, 17 June, he had met Stanisław Marczak, who had told him that the windows of Jewish houses had been smashed in Strzyżów, the county town. As the attackers had not been stopped, they assumed it was permitted. On 18 June, Chciuk continued, he had met Franciszek Świnicki, who had urged him to beat up Jews and destroy their property that evening. At the end of their conversation, Świnicki had warned him, "Don't argue and all go together, after all, it is allowed."[123]

In the evening, Chciuk had set off for a meeting held by Stojałowski in the neighboring village Domaradz. On the way, he met two pairs of brothers from Domaradz, Józef and Jan Bara and Antoni and Tomasz Koszarski, who told him the meeting had been postponed to the following day as Stojałowski had had to go to Golcowa. So, they decided to go to the tavern on the outskirts of Lutzca. Some other peasants had already gathered there, but whether out of general reluctance or because they felt they were too few—Chciuk did not say—they did not start any trouble. One of them suggested going into the village. As they proceeded, they were joined by more peasants and collected still others from their houses. Franciszek Świnicki now also reappeared. The men encouraged each other to "beat up the Jews," firing themselves up with their talk. A certain Jan Krupski said he had been to Łęki and seen how the Jews there had been robbed of everything and had all their windows smashed, and that it was all allowed.[124] Another participant mentioned notices on stables and barns that declared it was permitted to beat and rob Jews for three days but not to kill or pillage them.[125]

Meanwhile, the growing gang had arrived at the tavern run by Salomon Diamand, where two hundred people were said to have gathered. The barmaid Feiga Diamand went out and asked the crowd, "What do you want people, is this a hold-up?"[126]

This act, if it occurred as described, is indicative of the familiarity between peasants and Jewish barkeepers in rural Galician society.[127] Despite the negative stereotyping and frequent cursing, tavern staff enjoyed a certain degree of authority; they knew their clientele and how to deal with them.[128] But Feiga Diamand's spirited appearance did not discourage the two hundred peasants outside the tavern. On the contrary, Jan Krupski stepped out from the crowd and called, "Hey, lads, where are you?" In this way, he fired the starting gun for the peasants, who proceeded to bang the windows with sticks and throw stones until nearly all the windowpanes were smashed. It is significant, however, that the peasants had initially hesitated to damage Jewish property. They were not overcome by a violent frenzy; individuals were always needed to animate the group to make the next move.

When all the windows had been smashed, someone called out to go inside. Again, Chciuk identified Franciszek Świnicki as the ringleader, saying he had struck open the counter, containing money, tobacco, and glasses, with an ax. He then shouted, "If they'll hang me for one leg, they might as well hang me for two: if we're going to do a raid, let's do a proper one!" His words show that the premise of authorization alternated between wishful and useful thinking but was by no means taken as certain. The perpetrators still reckoned with the possibility of punishment. While a whole group entered the tavern, only a few followed Świnicki's call to go down into the cellar. They cracked open the vodka barrel and stole bottles; Chciuk admitted taking one and a half liters of vodka for himself.

It was important to the "malefactors" that they committed their deeds under the cover of darkness. Whenever Feiga tried to illuminate the tavern by lighting candles, Antoni Koszarski or one of the other raiding peasants blew them out. Chciuk claimed this was the reason he was not able to name any other accomplices. The barmaid's constant attempts to literally throw some light on the events, repeatedly thwarted by an adversary blowing out the candles, resembles a game. It illustrates the ritual, prank-like character of the attack, despite the acts of vandalism and robbery committed. Nobody was assaulted—just candles blown out! The barmaid was left unharmed to continue her futile attempts to light the candles. Perhaps it was a sense of shame that made the peasants reluctant to be seen causing damage,[129] or a form of cowardice, contrasting with the ax blows and swagger. In any case, all participants adhered to a conventional system of reference, regulating their interaction. Feiga maintained her brave stand even after the hail of stones on her house, seeming not to fear a physical attack. But she knew that lighting candles would disturb the unwelcome guests.

Once the alcohol had been seized and the furnishings demolished, the vandals left the tavern and set off for the next one, belonging to Iznak Steinmetz, known as Itzig. On the way, the now reduced group rallied round with calls of "Beat them! Beat them!" Mikołaj Chciuk claimed not to have entered Itzig's tavern but stayed outside to drink the looted vodka with several others. Next, they went to the store belonging to Moses Ritter, who had previously been incriminated by his Christian neighbors and spent four years in jail in the 1880s.[130] On this occasion, he was the victim of peasant crime. While they stole tobacco from his store, Ritter hid in his attic to avoid being physically attacked by the drunken mob. Apparently, Jewish males were less certain of being spared by the rampaging peasants.

Mikołaj Chciuk bought a looted packet of tobacco from Jan Krupski. After the group had raided three taverns, they robbed the deserted houses of a shoemaker and the sons of Hersch Felber, Ritters' neighbors. Some women were seen carrying sacks full of stolen grain. Świnicki was always at the forefront, wielding his ax.

Evidently, Chciuk and some of the others were only interested in obtaining alcohol and tobacco. Once a few taverns had been raided, then, some members of the group started to lose interest. It became harder to maintain the momentum that held the group together, which was essential for conducting raids. Indeed, it had taken a while to gather. The group had still been too small on its way from Domaradz to Lutzca and lacked commanding ringleaders such as Gostyła, Krupski, and Świnicki, whose words were heeded. These figures had joined together outside the Diamands' tavern and motivated a critical mass with their rallying cries so that in the end a majority took part in the attack—whether by throwing stones, raiding the premises and stealing goods, or buying loot from the thieves outside.

The perpetrators stood not only to profit from the raids; they also faced penalties in court. Chciuk therefore played down his involvement under interrogation and protected friends by claiming not to have recognized the others involved. Conversely, he linked some individuals, such as the Krupski brothers and Franciszek Świnicki, to several offences. Thus, he took the opportunity to incriminate the formidable ringleaders, who sought to maintain their community of violence not only by promising material gains and assuring the others it was permitted, but also by threatening the reluctant with violence. They had blackmailed Chciuk and threatened to beat anyone who refused to join in the raids on the estates of Chaskel Wallach and Israel Wichner, known as Śrul. A certain Wojciech Bara, whom Chciuk had purportedly advised not to go along, insulted him while simultaneously trying to motivate him by portraying the military as a key antagonist. Clearly, the warrant rumor was only one of many. Bara allegedly said, "What of it, you son of a bitch, come too! If you don't do it today you won't do it at all, because tomorrow the military will be on to you."[131] Chciuk then went along but did not participate in any further lootings. He named a few other individuals whom he allegedly saw carrying sacks of loot from Chaskel Wallach's farm and reported hearing a loud bang, perhaps from an explosion. According to his account, Mateusz Urban announced the end of the lootings with a blast on his trumpet.[132]

"Everyone had to become part of this whole thing that broke over the victims like a storm": The Rzeszów Indictment

Chciuk's statements tallied to a large extent with the public prosecutors' findings.[133] The latter questioned over a hundred people: as well as the fourteen Jews who were robbed or harassed on 18 and 19 June, they interrogated the eighty-two people accused of offences and the mayor Jan Nowakowski. Among the accused, there were seventy men and twelve women. Their average age was thirty-one; the youngest was fourteen, and the eldest, fifty-five. They were not all uncouth adolescents, then, but mostly married men—and women—with children.[134] Most were from Lutcza; fifteen came from Domaradz, and two from other parishes.[135] It is possible that more people from the surrounding area had been involved but could not be called to account, as the witnesses could identify only the locals familiar to them. The prosecutors estimated that some one to two hundred persons had been involved.

All the accused were manual laborers, apart from one—a farrier named Piotr Bober—and all were employed as either day laborers or agricultural workers. Remarkably, two of the accused, Mateusz Urban of Domaradz and Jędrzej Łukaszek of Lutcza, also worked as local community policemen. The public prosecutors listed fourteen crimes committed by groups of varying sizes and gave the context of unrest in Galicia and the specific relations between Christians and Jews in Lutcza as grounds. Their indictment started by echoing the official line that the "hitherto unknown perpetrators" of the "antisemitic disturbances" had pursued "secret objectives." It then went on to interpret the violence according to the Christian peasantry's collective motives: it was an attempt on their part to "crush" the "economic predominance" of the Jews while preserving their lives and physical integrity. This predominance, "especially in the spring months," was "burdensome and displeasing to the self-sacrificing workers" who labored so hard to survive.

The "Jewish element" was more conspicuous in Lutcza than in other parishes: The manor and associated land had passed to "the hands of Jews . . . to the distress of the impoverished rural population."[136] The owner, Chaskel Wallach, acted as a moneylender and had people work on his land to redeem their debts, while he alone judged and recorded the value of their work. Furthermore, over a dozen local Jewish families were principally occupied with usury. Hersch Felber, the patriarch of one of them, had been taken to court for his activities.[137]

In the light of the local situation, then, the public prosecutors found it hardly surprising that the news of attacks on Jews and their property had been "eagerly received" and fallen on "fertile ground" in Lutcza. But they did not connect the locals' sympathetic reception of the news with the rumors that had sparked each instance of rioting. They considered the rumors to have been spread by "some agitators" who easily duped the simple, uneducated folk. The reasons for the public prosecutors adhering to the notion that there were agitators outside the naive masses, even after hearing numerous personal accounts to the contrary under questioning, will be explored below.

The statements given under interrogation confirmed the picture drawn by Chciuk and disproved the notion that the uneducated people had been manipulated. The Christian community shared a desire to terrorize and rob their Jewish neighbors, which disposed them to believe the talk. They, in turn, were personally responsible for perpetuating the talk, as they provided the individual contexts that made the "malicious gossip" seem credible. References to a warrant were just one link in a chain of "arguments" used to convince potential co-attackers. Narrating the rumors was a mobilizing and synchronizing act—the first step to performing a collective action. There was no need to discuss whether it was right to assault the Jews or whether they would act on the warrant. That seemed to go without saying. Even if someone preferred not to take an active part in assaulting Jews, their mere presence served to indirectly support the acts of violence. The crowd gave encouragement and assured the perpetrators that a majority tolerated this violation of the normal rules of conduct. Women, for instance, were mainly involved in confiscating the booty, enticed by the prospect of selling it straight-away outside the tavern.

Official Authorization in Lutzca: The Narrative Context

The seventh count of the indictment described a situation that frequently arose that summer and explained why Jewish citizens sought police protection prior to the holidays. Feliks Obodziński and Wojciech Kurcoń had gone to the Diamonds' tavern in the early evening of 18 June, before there had been any lootings in Lutzca. They ordered brandy from Chaja Diamand and told the seventy-year-old barmaid about the disturbances in the neighboring parishes and the rumor of a warrant. They then prophesied that the same thing would happen in Lutzca and that "the peasants would strike." While scaring the elderly lady by suggesting that violence might erupt at any time, they continued to order brandies from her, for which they refused to pay. In this situation, the barmaid's service functioned as a pacifying act or a form of protection payment. The peasants, for their part, used their knowledge of the riots and the rumors to conjure a credible scenario of intimidation and gain material advantage without inflicting actual violence. The two men then repeated the scenario in the tavern run by Hinda Mützer. In summer 1898, several cases were reported of Jews being threatened with violence to make them lower their prices or allow the perpetrators to avoid paying entirely—even in East Galicia, where there was less unrest.[138] Antisemitism functioned by means of narrators compounding rumors with actual events, thus asserting superior knowledge. By speaking in the third person, moreover, the narrators denied any blame; they were merely passing on information. Yet the rumors served to intimidate the Jews even before they were personally affected by any disturbances. They confronted Jews with their impending misfortune, often in surprisingly harsh terms. In direct contact with Jews, narrators spoke of disturbances involving killings and bloodshed. Under interrogation, however, they played them down as just "letting off steam" and insisted that it was always clear that killing was forbidden. The threat of violence compelled many Jews to leave Lutzca on the evening of 18 June. Most of them were men, who were more likely to be physically attacked than their wives or children.

But above all, the warrant rumor was part of the "pickup game,"[139] serving to mobilize more peasants to take part in the riots. A peasant name Jędrzej Szurlej repeated the story of the barber's assassination plot and the merciful Empress Elisabeth on several occasions. He was consequently charged with insulting the monarchy, as the story implied His Majesty acted on vengefulness, hatred of Jews, and other base motives and damaged his reputation.[140]

Mateusz Urban, the local policeman who had guided the marauding procession in Lutzca with his trumpet-playing, was another perpetrator who used false authorization to agitate. He had been tasked with delivering a notification by the district captain in Strzyżów on the disturbances and measures to prevent further riots to the mayor of Lutzca, a certain Nowakowski. Before he performed his task, Urban showed the notice to a group of presumably illiterate peasants and called out, "See, lads? We're allowed to beat the Jews." The mayor later claimed to have personally rebuked him for this. But the message could not be retracted. The news started to spread that the local policeman had shown a notice from the district captain, authorizing the public to beat the Jews. Several more people went on record as passing on this information in the days preceding the lootings.[141]

Attempts to publicly refute the rumors were futile or even counterproductive, since the information they conveyed was always interpreted in the light of the receivers' own interests. The desire for a warrant to assault and rob Jews still prevailed, the bloodshed and military interventions notwithstanding. Even after the riots had occurred in Lutcza and armed forces had appeared in Domaradz to prevent further attacks, Jędrzej Szurlej insisted they were officially authorized. He referred to an encounter with the district inspector, Bronisław Librewski, who had stopped for an after-work drink in Moses Freifeld's tavern in Domaradz. Here, a guest had complained about the local council's involvement in military deployments. At this, Librewski advised the peasants to stop believing the agitators' "whispers" about a warrant. He was not aware that these men were not duped by agitators; they were agitators themselves. After this encounter, they proceeded to spread the news that "some commissioner or inspector" had also mentioned the emperor's authorization.[142]

Mobilization Scenarios: Competitive Pressure and Opportunity through Authorization

Disturbances in any given place were almost always a reaction to riots in neighboring villages or towns. In late June in the Limanowa area, the violence spread along a stretch of railroad, suggesting that information and probably ringleaders were conveyed by train (see figure 2.3).[143] Almost all disturbances occurred on holidays or Sundays and the preceding evenings.

Figure 2.3. Map showing the spreading of riots and rumors from Frysztak to Lutcza. Thomas Rettig with courtesy of the David Rumsey collections.

Chciuk and others had described how people had heard eyewitness reports about the disturbances in other areas. Events within a radius of about forty kilometers (twenty-five miles) were considered relevant and significant for developments in other villages. While the rumors of the early summer of an impending reckoning with the Jews were received with interest, they were regarded as wishful thinking and far removed from reality.[144] Reports of incidents in neighboring communities, however, brought these wishes into the realm of the possible. What happened in one town or village could happen in the neighboring village, too.

The warrant rumors were then updated and adapted to the local circumstances, lending the news of disturbances further relevance and significance. At the same time, people learned that such attacks were feasible and went unpunished, leading them to conclude that they really were authorized. Agitators also adapted information about the period of validity to the situation. The two-week period, as most often mentioned in Galicia, was rarely referred to in Lutzca. Here, most people spoke of a three-day time limit. Jan Janusz is alleged to have said that the local police had tickets that permitted the holder to beat one Jew over a period of three days. To obtain a ticket one should go to Mateusz Urban on 18 June. Interested parties gathering at Urban's door then actualized his role as ringleader. The tendency in Jasło County to refer to a three-day period suggests that the main trigger for disturbances here was the bloodshed in Frysztak.

A stretch of almost thirty kilometers (eighteen miles) lies between Lutzca and Frysztak. The two towns were just within the radius of communication in which information was regarded as reliable because the sources were familiar. News of the disturbances and "outrageous behavior" of Jews and gendarmes in Frysztak on Corpus Christi Thursday sparked attacks in eight other places in the surrounding area that night.[145] Four of these occurred on the road between Frysztak and Lutzca. People observing the developments in the area to plan assaults on Jews in their own village chose the Saturday as the earliest opportunity before a holiday. If the attacks were to comply with the warrant rumor, which was important for mobilization purposes, they should last three days. That explains why the people from Frysztak and the surrounding area launched their assault on a Thursday. There were further disturbances on Friday, and the third day had marked the last opportunity for the people of Lutzca. Had they spoken of a two-week warrant, they could equally well have launched their assault the following weekend. That would have given them more time to mobilize participants; after all, as large a group as possible was required for conducting a successful raid. The following Saturday, the rumors surrounding Świnicki et al. seemed to suggest, would be the only and last opportunity to acquire some booty or satisfy a desire for destruction.

Most people were not unshakably convinced of the truth of the warrant rumor but added the information pragmatically to an aggregate of further arguments and claims to motivate a large section of the majority to participate in attacks on the minority. Another of the rumors circulated to mobilize potential accomplices will be considered below. It provides insight into the relations between the Christian peasantry and the Galician Jews.

Antoni Koszarski said that the people who had assaulted the Jews of Niebylec the previous day had announced their intention to come to Lutzca to carry out more lootings.[146] This "news" was certainly realistic; Lutzca was targeted by looters from several other places, as will be shown below. But the information had above all an appellative function; it was intended to advise the locals to rob their "own Jews" before others did so. In a conversation on the morning of 18 June, a man named Jakób Marczak persuaded an obviously hesitant villager named Wojciech Wnęk that it would be unbearable if the peasants from Lutzca went "into the woods" while "strange peasants" raided the Jews in Lutzca.

During this troubled summer, peasants frequently demonstrated a sense of entitlement to rob the Jews in their own village, as if they were a natural local resource. Later, instances were documented of peasants even protecting their local Jewish taverns from rampaging itinerant peasants, only to loot the bars themselves afterward. This form of assault was not motivated by anti-Jewish ideology. It articulated material interests informed by a conceptual horizon that placed equal importance on geographical origins as on ethnicity. Despite the conflict between peasants and Jews, the two sides were bonded by a familiarity that generated rules to which both sides could adhere. This familiarity was apparent in the way the barkeepers spoke to their guests and in Samuel Feiner's attempt to calm the cacophony-makers outside his house by explaining that his wife had just had a baby. He obviously had reason to expect his appeal to be heard. Interaction such as this did not occur in any of the incidents in East Galicia, where migrant workers conflicted with local Jews. When the disturbances escalated into extensive gang raids in southern Galicia, the residents of the affected villages feared the worst.

Authority and Agitation: Who Leads the Pickup Game?

The public prosecutors' indictment gave credence to Chciuk's statement that certain actors had played leading roles as agitators before and during the raids.[147] Charges were pressed against seventeen individuals for inciting violence and aiming to provoke and justify violent acts. They were accused of spreading false information about impending "antisemitic disturbances" and attacks on Jews in Lutzca and the surrounding area without having verification of their accuracy, and so "alarming the public." The indictment named them "moral perpetrators" and "intellectual leaders."

These agitators were also charged with threatening hesitant bystanders. They had allegedly declared that peasants would set fire to the houses of anyone who refused to join in the raids on the Jews. Unlike the threats that Chciuk reported ringleaders to have made during the raids, this was a mere rumor rather than a concrete accusation.[148] Though only hearsay and entirely anonymous, people such as Jan Krupski, who told it to his nephew Jędrzej Krupski, used it to mobilize others and exert *imagined* peer pressure. Another charge was leveled at six individuals who had lowered the threshold for collective violence by the offences they committed. They had thrown the first sticks and stones at the Diamands' tavern and animated the crowd to join in with their calls of "Where are you?" Mikołaj Chciuk was not the only one who later remembered their actions as setting off the violence in Lutzca.

Chciuk's description of the crowd gradually shrinking as the night progressed was also confirmed in the indictment. While the group that raided the tavern run by Salomon Diamand and his family comprised fifty people, all identified by name, the attacks on Izaak Steinmetz and Moses Ritter were committed by thirty-nine. Thirty-eight people took part in the subsequent robbery of Salomon Rieder, and only thirty-three were involved in the raids on Jakob Eisner and the Mützner family. But the core group of six ringleaders, all of whom were among the seventeen individuals who had previously agitated for violence, were present at all these attacks. During the raid on Chaskel Wallach's estate, the crowd grew again, bolstered by the arrival of women to take the booty away.[149]

It is true, then, that certain men took prominent roles in leading the group of perpetrators. They were the first to throw stones and to charge into buildings. They guided the group to the next target and ensured it stayed together by keeping aggression levels high. But it would be wrong to claim that the less active offenders and hangers-on were effectively held hostage by these ringleaders, although some of those questioned suggested as much to play down their own responsibility. Rather, the follower-perpetrators looked up to the perceived leaders for guidance. Several people had gone to Mateusz Urban's house to find out more from him about the permit cards. Ringleaders such as Urban were also authorities in other aspects of village life; their word was respected, whether because of their role as local policemen or as uncles. To some extent, these leaders found themselves confronted with the expectations of those who held them in esteem. This is especially vividly illustrated by the statements of two leaders from Godowa, who had planned to attack Jews in Lutzca, four kilometers away. The accounts they gave under interrogation painted a picture of the pickup game as a dynamic blend of expectation, observation, and the initiative of individual village spokespeople.

"I know nothing about agitators, and I don't read any newspapers": The Case of Izydor Moskal

A forty-year-old farmer from Godowa who was married with children, Izydor Moskal made a statement under questioning that clearly aimed to minimize his own involvement in the local raids. He only confessed to what Krzyszkowski, the court secretary leading the investigations, could prove anyway from the statements of others.[150] Moskal told the interrogator how Władysław Rokita, a signalman from Strzyżów, had appeared in the afternoon of 18 June, asking him to assemble a group of people to go with him and "his men" to the Godowa tavern that evening to "beat up and rob" the Jews. They planned to go on to Lutcza and Żyznów afterward. He had also mentioned "some unknown Sokols"[151] who would go with them and insisted there was now a warrant to attack and rob Jews and destroy everything. He alleged that some unnamed "princes" and "lords" had spoken of it. He had assured Moskal that it was now permitted to beat and rob Jews.

Moskal had not told anyone. When he went out in the evening, he found some acquaintances gathered in his front yard. He identified eight of them. He claimed not to have participated in smashing Naftali Kramer's windows. This attack had involved a violent assault on a Jewish woman, for which reason he had purportedly left the scene.[152] Afterward they all went to Gorgel's bar, who called the initially peaceful crowd "robbers and thieves." Consequently, they started smashing his windows. Moskal then went home. Asked to name the agitators, he denied knowing any. He claimed he did not read any newspapers and could not say any more on the matter.

In prison a few days later, he mentioned that a certain Piotr Matłosz had told him of pamphlets he had distributed even before the controversial military intervention in Strzyżów. Moskal suggested these might have motivated "the people" to go on the rampage. Although Krzyszkowski's comments are not recorded, Moskal's latter statement shows that he was prepared to mention things he had probably never seen in order to improve his standing with the authorities. While claiming not to know anything about the agitators during his first interrogation, and refusing to comment on the popular newspapers, it seems curious that after two days' imprisonment he remembered some pamphlets. It is likely that Krzyszkowski had been seeking confirmation of the role of the *Jewish Secrets* pamphlet, which had previously been found to have fueled incidents in Wieliczka, inciting violence in other places. Moskal told him what he wanted to hear: extreme agitation had provoked the disturbances.

"Everyone was armed with sticks—and I had a stick in my hand, too": The Case of Wojciech Moskal

Izydor's elder half-brother, the local councilor Wojciech Moskal, gave a slightly different account of events. Wojciech claimed that Izydor had persuaded him to assemble "his people" while Izydor did the same. Then they would go together with the Sokols. Izydor, he said, had told the villagers that everyone should gang up against the Jews. The Moskal half-brothers lived at opposite ends of the village and were both spokesmen for their immediate neighborhoods. When Wojciech went out into the yard in the evening, he found several people gathered there, including his farmhand, all armed with sticks. Izydor's gang went to Naftali Kramer while Wojciech waited with his gang. Then they all went to Chaskel Gorgel together. At this point in the narrative, Wojciech repeated verbatim Izydor's statement about the barkeeper's insults provoking the crowd to throw stones. The interrogator then asked him directly what the perpetrators' source of information might have been. Wojciech assumed the newspapers and above all Stojałowski had motivated Izydor Moskal to gang up on the Jews. He, however, claimed never to have seen Stojałowski or to read the newspapers.

But he did recall how a strange gentleman with an "elegant moustache" had spoken to him two weeks previously in the tavern in Strzyżów, claiming to be an agent for Jan Stapiński, the chairman of the secular peasant party. He had told Moskal about narrowly escaping a thrashing from peasants while agitating in Sieklówka. He had also said that things would soon "heat up" for the Jews, that they would be attacked and that this was "now allowed." This occurred before the news about Frysztak reached Godowa; people here knew only about the events in Kalwarya.[153]

The Perpetrators' Perspectives: An Attempted Generalization

Virtually everyone had heard the rumors about an alleged warrant to beat Jews, issued by a high authority. Information about the disturbances—how they developed and the consequences they had—was freely and eagerly exchanged between neighboring parishes. Each fresh item of news caused the rumors to gather momentum. Those concerning a warrant seemed to corroborate those predicting a crackdown on the Jews, and vice versa. And whenever lootings occurred in a familiar place, perhaps just a few hours' walk away, the rumors turned into current affairs. Then, the emperor's supposed word echoed in the nearby villages, and spokesmen tried to rally support to copy what their neighboring villagers had done. They knew they needed to accumulate a critical mass in which the individual could immerse himself to be capable of attack. After all, their opponents would be people who spoke the same language and whom they encountered in everyday life. They had to quash the normality of their relations to make a confrontation possible. Nobody seemed to want justification for the raids or to discuss whether it was morally defensible. With sets of different, to some extent contradictory, arguments and rumors, the ringleaders prepared their accomplices for the strike.[154]

An adequately large group could only be assembled on a holiday or the preceding evening. Only then would people have the time to walk long distances in search of adventure and diversions while consuming large amounts of alcohol to lose their inhibitions. The Sokols' appearance in Godowa and Stojałowski's meeting were initial mobilizing factors. Subsequently, the warrant rumor was updated to coincide with the next holiday. This generated a sense of unique opportunity. The news of peasants from elsewhere coming to attack local Jews also precipitated action. Most crucially, however, since Kalwarya and Frysztak, people knew they needed to outmaneuver the law enforcement agents, who would try and stop riots and were likely to use firearms.

The gendarmerie was known to be understaffed. Lutzca did not have one single gendarme; the nearest unit was stationed far away. But the military would approach as soon as the disturbances in a neighboring parish had been reported. Once a unit had arrived in a neighboring village, it would not take long to get to Lutzca. It might even arrive while an attack was in progress. This intensified the sense of urgency to raid the Jews before the opportunity had passed.

Those eager for a share of the loot from "their Jews" heeded the local spokesmen, the men who stood at the vanguard and who had a certain standing in the community—the fathers and uncles of younger men, for instance. The local councilor and the policeman mentioned above were no exception. Even mayors and, in some small towns, the intellectual elite, teachers, priests, and organists were arrested as ringleaders. Francois Guesnet suggests such literate people—including the aforementioned daughter of a teacher, the monk, or the priest—be understood as a subgroup of these "pogrom-specialists" in Paul Brass's description, distinct from members of the peasant communities who led groups of plunderers.[155] They had access or connections to the written and official world and used it to translate antisemitic beliefs into the peasant world. They functioned as transmitters of antisemitism as well, yet with the clear agenda to make violence happen by legitimizing future deeds with their authority as members of the clergy or of the educated local elites.[156] These people moved oftentimes together with the mobilized peasants, armed with sticks, toward their targets. Others joined them along the way, perhaps hesitantly, or out of curiosity, or with determined urgency, forming the anonymous crowd that would prepare the target for storming when the right words of encouragement were spoken. Hurling stones to mark out and damage the targeted building, they did not so much have to break in as step into a ruin. Even women and children joined in, jeering and acting as an audience for the men's antics, as well as carrying booty home. The presence of the entire Christian community made the looting seem like a public festival rather than a criminal offence committed under the cover of darkness.[157]

Nevertheless, there were rules about how to act toward the victims. The desire to let off steam and seize some booty was checked by the conventions governing everyday conduct in the tavern. Though not all the rioters knew the Diamands, Ritters, and Kramers and their bars, they were familiar with the roles played in the barroom situation. Feiga Diamand and Naftali Kramer were brave enough to appear before the crowds of rioters and try to dissuade them from criminal acts. Hardly any of the rioters would have regarded themselves as robbers despite their actions on this occasion. By naming them such, the barkeeper Kramer reminded them of the common rules they were in the process of transgressing. The ringleaders perceived such reminders of familiarity, often conveyed as advice from a sober barkeeper to his or her drunken guests, as a provocation.[158] Conventions had to be broken to allow familiar figures to be made victims. To mark the transgression of normality and create menacing scenarios, not to mention drum up courage, rioters threw stones and banged sticks and tried to maintain darkness inside the tavern. While willfully accepting the possibility that even women and children might be injured during the first phase, when they came face to face with the inhabitants, they usually acted with consideration. Most objected to direct physical attacks, such as occurred in Godowa. Physical attacks jeopardized the group's cohesion, and the community of violence could only profit at the Jews' expense as a collective. Whenever a member of a group challenged the collective goal by not participating, the group's aggression could turn toward its own community. Insults and threats of beatings were as much a part of its arsenal as the rumors of authorization.

A majority tolerated the attacks, regarding them as anonymous phenomena that inexorably befell the Jews. But they were neither frenzied nor routine acts. Time and again, instigators were needed to encourage the groups and motivate them to join in and carry on. It was not only a matter of forming a superior mass to overwhelm the Jews, nor of turning witnesses into co-perpetrators to ensure their later silence. By jointly committing crimes against the others, the Christian peasants experienced themselves as a community. They became a village unit. Even beyond the borders of their own parishes, the Christian peasantry generated a sense of powerful community that could hold sway over the Jews. The raids yielded symbolic capital. They demonstrated the strength of the peasant class, despite the antisemitic discourse on "Jewish predominance" and talk of politicians manipulating the peasants.

Peasants did not eliminate the Jewish competition, or combat the curse of alcohol, as the peasant movement demanded, by wrecking Jewish taverns and looting stores and workshops. They had a different relationship with Jewish property and felt it was their prerogative to loot their "own" Jews. This attitude perhaps stemmed from the notion that local wealth came originally from the land and that the Jews had unjustly appropriated it by monetary means. But no such ideas were articulated or used to steer the raids. The riots were not a reaction to an economic conflict between two colliding worlds. Rather, they were part of a conflictual process of negotiating power within a common rural world of experience. The encounter between Feiga Diamand and the peasants shows that a common language prevailed even during the riots, indicating that they did not mark a complete break with tradition.

The Jews in Lutzca evidently did not have connections with the military and were not accused of having bribed soldiers as they were in Kalwarya and Frysztak. The town's Jewish inhabitants adhered largely to the traditional script, trying to keep the peace by avoiding confrontation. Many left the village for the same reason. They no doubt knew they could not rely on the swift help of the military because of Lutzca's geographical location and sought other ways of averting disaster. After the riots, the Jewish victims assisted in the criminal investigations, gave testimonies in court, and identified culprits.

The accused, meanwhile, could try and influence their fate by their statements under interrogation. Naturally, they initially tried to defend themselves by playing down their roles and denying involvement in certain incidents. But their scope in this respect was limited due to the bulk of information gleaned from the statements of fellow suspects and victims. Still, they could use their statements to settle accounts with others in the village or the community of violence, or to reward loyalty. Mikołaj Chciuk is a case in point, who reported the threatening behavior of certain of his co-perpetrators but refused to incriminate any who were his friends.

Gradually, while under interrogation or in custody, the accused peasants deciphered what the investigating judges wanted to hear. They realized that, because illiteracy was widespread among the peasantry, the public prosecutors from Rzeszów and the investigating judge from Strzyżów regarded them collectively as simpleminded. The situation had not changed since the Ritter trial. The accused peasants consequently let the interrogators think they had been duped by notices and false warrants, although investigations had shown that the warrant rumors were never the sole motive for the riots.

The accused drew advantage, then, from the stories of unknown agitators whispering incitement, and of newspapers and pamphlets putting the idea to attack the Jews in their heads. Agitators of the first order such as the Moskals and known perpetrators of violence like Chciuk assured the officials they were right in thinking that Stapinski and Stojałowski—the usual suspects—had not only sown unrest but also sent their agents to instigate violence when, in fact, they themselves had observed developments in the area and seized the opportunity to agitate, to rally their fellow villagers to overrun the Jews.

In this respect, the peasants utilized politicians for their own anti-Jewish practice, like they did the emperor, the pope, and Archduke Rudolf. They portrayed themselves as gullible and simpleminded in contrast to the educated "gentlefolk." But in fact, they twisted every comment and every printed report to suit their own wishes and intentions. Their statements satisfied the investigating officials, who could then report to Krakow and Lemberg what the authorities wanted to hear: the peasants were not yet educated or responsible enough to choose their own representatives or make decisions about their own welfare. They were manipulated by populist politicians, who incited them to riot. Consequently, they needed to be protected from their own elected representatives.

Most urgently, though, Galician parishes needed to be protected from rampaging gangs, for in Jasło and Nowy Sącz counties, huge groups were forming and carrying out nocturnal raids.[159] In the night of Sunday to Monday 13 June, "almost 400 peasants" from Jasło county overran the small town Biecz; three days later, oil workers from four different places marched into Gorlice. Here, a riot was prevented as an infantry unit from Nowy Sącz raised the alarm just in time. However, the frustrated men then vented their aggression on the taverns in the surrounding area. In response, the Jasło district captain placed the large distilleries under protection but declared military protection for the taverns and stores to be unfeasible as they were too far apart. He described the population being gripped by a mass panic, which had long since spread beyond the Jewish communities to affect the Christians, too. There were increasing incidents of arson in taverns, with a danger of the fires spreading to the surrounding buildings. The robbers, moreover, threatened to attack any Christians who came to the Jews' aid. Made unwitting co-victims in this way, the Christian population's attitude to the riots changed. These new disturbances were not like the boisterous excursions to Jewish neighbors around Żywiec, Kalwarya, or Strzyżów, where people threw stones, made commotions, and enjoyed free vodka and tobacco along with a sense of power, all from the safety of the crowd.

The raids had started on the realization that law enforcement agents rarely preempted attacks but tended to march in wherever disturbances occurred.

Knowledge of the military's logistics made swift raids seem possible and, in view of the high frequency of attacks, almost natural. Many people in Jasło district, too, were keen to rob the Jews and saw it as within their rights, in a sense, to do what people in other areas had already done. Material gain was clearly the prime motive here. The idea prevailed that one could seize another's property not because it was legitimate but simply because it was possible. The persistent rumor that the attacks were legal had generated an alternative reality with a fluid definition of legality, since the state did not enforce its claim to a permanent monopoly on power. In this respect, the disturbances were not dissimilar to the pogroms in southwestern Russia two decades previously. Here, too, the knowledge that one could rob and terrorize Jews without the state interfering had motivated ever more copycat offenders and launched a wave of pogroms in the region.[160] Only inquiry into developments in the ensuing years in Galicia would reveal how far the violence spread here and whether it led to repetitions and a new tradition of increased violence, as John Klier has described with regard to Russia.[161]

Certainly, two crucial factors contributed to the disturbances: first, a sense that limited violence against (or lootings of) Jews was considered legitimate, at least if all the participants of a community benefited—that is, if the "resources" were distributed equally; and, second, the valuable symbolic capital gained from the experience of power over both a minority and the authorities.

The Empire Strikes Back: Official Explanations of the Violence

Not only politicians and residents but also the government needed to make sense of the unprecedented wave of peasant violence. When the state eventually changed its policing strategy, it distinctly altered the nature of the disturbances. The Galician authorities and the military had long since become significant actors in the conflict. But they did not form a discrete group in the confrontation, with coherent interests. Agendas diverged among all the groups involved, including the state and its agents.

Szajnowski, the trainee in the district governor's office who had been sent to Kalwarya, brought back the first government inquiries into the causes of the violence. His superior in Wadowice, who had reported visits from Jewish delegations, sent word to Lemberg that they had found the people to have been "duped and incited to violence" (*obałamucony i podburzony*). The "general hatred of Jews," stemming from religious or economic differences, and the "arrogance of the Israelites," their "provocative behavior in very many cases," and the fact that the "current price rises" and shortfalls in revenue were popularly attributed to Jewish speculation provided the explanation for people being persuaded to believe the "incredible rumors." It was not known who had started the rumors.

The Wadowice district captain assumed there was a natural antagonism between Christians and Jews, echoing the peasant movement's claims of religious and economic conflicts. Expressing understanding for the peasants' actions, albeit without approval, he showed a clear bias toward the Christian population. Similar comments appeared in the Galician newspapers, from the nationalist *Gazeta Narodowa* to the conservative *Czas*. But despite the district captain's conviction that Jews as a collective shared the blame for the disturbances, he gave unequivocal instructions to suppress the violence, as it posed a threat to government rule and public order. He also left no doubt that it had been agitators who had led the people astray. His report implied that unnamed strangers had used a stratagem to incite people to attack the Jews. Although most of the Christian population were impoverished and resentful, he believed they would never have turned on the Jews on their own initiative.

It was precisely these findings that the authorities referred to in their German-language correspondence with the ministries in Vienna on the causes of the violence. The disturbances had been the work of "fervently active agitators," who had aroused the "basest instincts" in the peasants.[162] A movement was suspected behind the riots, a movement that had given the "agreed signal" to attack.[163] The sudden eruption of disturbances pointed to the fact that someone had conducted "purposeful agitation," which had fallen on "fertile ground" in the minds of impoverished peasants. The district captain responsible for Kalwarya, the governor's office went on, had immediately taken all the necessary steps and so prevented greater harm from being done, despite the involvement of "2000–3000 malefactors."[164]

The Imperial Ministry of the Interior accepted this reading of the events and wrote that the riots had threatened not only "order and property" but also the entire "social organism." Orders were given to suppress the violence, expose the "prime movers," and prevent further disturbances: "The penalties issued [should] in every respect [have] a deterrent effect."[165]

The Galician authorities' reports did not mention the role of the Jews or any "general hatred" that was felt to exist. Staff in the governor's office knew that anti-Jewish views would not fall on sympathetic ears in Vienna. It was more expedient in this context, then, to emphasize their efforts to ensure the safety of all the crownland's citizens. Domestic autonomy in return for loyalty on an imperial level and a guarantee of peace in the crownland—these were the mainstays of the "minor compromise" which the Galician conservatives sought to maintain. Now the pressure was on them to keep their end of the bargain, especially in the light of accusations of election fraud and criticisms of Kasimir Badeni's government policies.[166] The troubles were an acid test for the Galician administration, and the entire empire was looking on. Since the deadly disturbances in Frysztak, the German-language newspaper *Pester Lloyd* had run a regular column titled "Anti-Semitic Unrest in Galicia."[167] It publicized the view that the Galician authorities demonstrated incompetence and inertia, and that the situation called for a state of emergency to finally allow the imperial armed forces to take control.[168]

State Strategies against Violence: Militias in Response to Frysztak

The task of pacifying the crownland fell to Governor Leon Piniński. He had to show the rampaging peasants and the entire empire that the Galician authorities were in control, ideally without any help from without. The strategy he pursued in response to the tragedy in Frysztak and the violent gangs in Jasło district started a new chapter in the history of Galician unrest. He aimed to decentralize and expand the law enforcement agencies in the land—and at the same time blur the lines of conflict between Jews and Christians, and between the state and its subjects—by enlisting residents to keep the peace in their local communities. In

Figure 2.4. K.u.k. (imperial and royal) Gendarmes in Krakow, *Nowiny Illustrowane*, no. 32, 1907. Public domain.

this way, belligerent peasants would be confronted by their "own" people rather than anonymous soldiers.

Piniński had instructions issued to form militias on 18 June 1898. Community elders, magistrates and estate owners were made personally responsible for ensuring that groups of men guarded their communities day and night. Ten men were to patrol the streets during the day, and twenty at night. Wearing armbands in the imperial colors, black and yellow, to signalize they represented the emperor, they were authorized to arrest any perpetrators of violence and hand them over to the judiciary.[169] In addition to invalidating the warrant rumor, the militias disrupted the previous group dynamic. Now it was no longer possible for an entire Christian local community to turn on the Jews, or to look away passively. Anyone conscripted to a militia was forced to oppose even looters. Indeed, the militias could be made up of both Jews and Christians, obliging them to cooperate to prevent acts of violence. Thus the lines of conflict no longer ran along ethnic-religious boundaries but between the men on guard and "malefactors," or between the local community and the looters from out of town, regardless of their religion.

The militias raised the importance of personal responsibility and harnessed the dynamism of former ringleaders. It was hoped that enlisting them to lead groups combating the violence would put an end to the "cat-and-mouse chase" that had hitherto characterized the disturbances and been so critically observed in other countries.[170] And it substantially boosted the potential for law enforcement beyond the limited capacity of the state's meager resources. Previously, units had only been pre-emptively deployed on market days or holidays, and the presence of anonymous guards had often aggravated the situation. It was hoped that the appearance of familiar figures to ward off attacks would help defuse tensions instead.

The militias were an especially effective instrument against raids in rural areas. For one, they allowed even remote communities to offer organized resistance. Second, they prevented the formation of local gangs intending to attack the Jews in their own community. They gave local councils, mayors, and district captains new scope for responding to the violence.[171]

The district captain of Łańcut, having been warned of impending disturbances in the Kaniczyga parish by a Jewish delegation, convened a meeting not only of the local council but also the "more important and respectable citizens of Christian and Jewish faith." These residents assured him there was no serious dispute between the local Jews and Christians and that they themselves would ensure order was maintained. They obviously hoped to avoid a military intervention. As a precaution, the district captain ordered the local mayor to ensure the taverns closed early in the evening for the next few days, to double the number of nighttime guards, to keep a close watch on the local youth, and to immediately penalize any who acted conspicuously. Furthermore, he banned the fair that had been due to take place on 5 July.[172]

In the area around Nowy Targ, peasants thronged to join the local vigilante groups when news broke of the approach of a "gang from Sandez."[173] Gangs of between twenty and fifty nonlocal peasants roaming the area around the small town Brzesko in late June were successfully repelled by resistance groups organized by Mayor Jakub Piekarz in Miłkowa.[174] Similarly, on 24 June, raiders in Paleśnica were prevented from attacking, although they were said to have been a hundred strong and possibly an amalgamation of several different gangs. Days later, this gang was still lurking in the nearby woods. The rough terrain in the mountainous region around Limanowa made the disturbances a different affair from those in the north. Here, where the state was normally absent, the military struggled to safeguard the scattered population.

Three patrolling soldiers were attacked by five peasants. Shots were fired and the soldiers pursued the fleeing peasants into the forest. They found a gang of some thirty men, armed with "guns," at whom they aimed their rifles and fired, prompting the men to flee deeper into the forest. Reporting on the incident to the detachment's commanding officers, the governor explained that the area was barren and rocky and the people were "poor and rough" and tended to "banditry" not only when unrest was rife. In terms of administrative staff, the region had been neglected, but he had dispatched two "capable officials" to ensure order was restored. He assured the command that the army would not have to fear such archaic conditions in any other regions.[175]

Gangs like this, the governor went on, could neither be tolerated nor left for militias to deal with.[176] Admittedly, the "neglect in terms of administrative staff" and the rough terrain placed the gangs at an advantage. They had, moreover, threatened to cut the telegraph lines, worrying both the authorities and the (Jewish) residents.[177] The governor's office relied on telegrams to keep abreast of gang movements. Crucial information, such as gang plans and projected targets, was often sent by members of Jewish communities to the government officials in far-off towns. Gang leaders, meanwhile, chose their targets by calculating the distance to the next telegraph office and the distance from the next garrison to the nearest railroad station and on to the target in terms of the time it would take for a detachment to travel it. The result was a confusion of suspected plans, threats, and calls for help.

In such a situation, rumors could be used as an instrument to thwart the telegrams and trains or to increase the threat of violence in the absence of law enforcement agents. Military routine then gained acute relevance for the safety or otherwise of Jewish citizens.[178] Rumors about ultimatums for attacks, rather than mythical warrants, were circulated to play on the others' fears and seemed only too realistic against the background of widespread rioting.

While roving gangs went on the rampage in the wake of the disturbances in Frysztak, the rumor reached Wielopole that a gang from Strzyżów district was one day's walk away. The Jewish community did not fear attacks from the local Christians; the priest, estate manager, and parish leader had all vowed to maintain peaceful relations. But if attackers arrived from elsewhere, they could not rely on any swift help. There was no telegraph office in Wielopole; the nearest stations were ten and seventeen kilometers away in Wiśniówca[179] and Ropczyce.[180] In the latter town, there was talk that "malefactors" were planning to walk the fourteen kilometers from Frysztak to Wielopole. Many Jewish residents of Wielopole started to pack their belongings and flee. The Jewish Community requested military protection from the district captain and promised to bear the cost. The gang that had been rumored to be on the way to Wielopole was then stopped by the military before it even got to Strzyżów, which, as we have seen, had been the scene of several previous attacks.

However, local populations and itinerant gangs did not always conflict. Sometimes they formed unholy alliances that, compounded by the incompetence of the local authorities, could have disastrous consequences for the Jewish population. This is illustrated by an incident in Stary Sącz.

Raids on estates in the area around Nowy Sącz and the arrival of a visiting mission, expected to attract a public of two thousand, set a foreboding scene. To make matters worse, several raids had recently been carried out along the railroad line between Limanowa and Nowy Sącz[181] in neighboring Limanowa County. Rumors had been broadcast, probably in a bid to mobilize potential co-perpetrators, that socialists were planning attacks on Jews here.[182] The district captain in Nowy Sącz dispatched three infantry companies and half a cavalry squadron to try to tackle three trouble spots simultaneously.[183]

Relations at a Nadir: Lootings in Stary Sącz

Two thousand peasants, including women and children, allegedly took part in the lootings in Stary Sącz. In addition, residents of the town itself, of all income and age groups, seized the opportunity to plunder their Jewish neighbors. Thirty-one houses around the market square, where Jews lived or ran businesses, were looted in a mass raid that lasted several hours. The material damage caused was estimated at a terrific 80,000 guilders. The conservative *Czas* newspaper commented on this first visible instance of middle-class townspeople participating in collective robbery with obvious disgust: "The world has surely never seen such a shameful night. The wives of wealthy citizens and aldermen, ladies in hats, overloaded with stolen goods hidden under their coats and jackets, spent the entire night prowling around the market square amongst the animalistic crowd. They piled laundry starch, soap, coffee powder, sugar, tea and other items into their skirts to carry them home."[184] The sun rose the next morning on a devastated market square. Window panes were smashed, and store interiors demolished. The floors of the looted buildings and the market square itself were covered in broken glass and trampled items of food, sodden with water that the fire brigade had hosed on to the many lit matches people had strewn.[185]

This unprecedented collaboration between townspeople and rampaging peasants in a veritable frenzy of looting and destruction was prompted by several factors. For the past month there had been almost daily riots; lootings had virtually become normal. Jewish traders had been marked out as victims, and few Christians wanted to miss the opportunity to join in taking some booty. All the soldiers billeted in Stary Sącz had set off in the direction of Gorlice to deal with the disturbances in neighboring Limanowa and other raids in the area. Only a few gendarmes were left in the town. At least three agitators had passed through the surrounding villages in the morning on their way to Stary Sącz, where they had earmarked the Jewish stores as their next target. They were joined by a huge crowd of people who came into the town equipped with carts, baskets, and cloths to transport their booty home. The disturbances mutated into acts of collective robbery, and open season was called on Jewish property.[186] However, the Christian burghers left the ransacking to the peasants and participated only in the robbery. And Christians who lived on or near the market square placed candles and pictures of saints in the windows so that rampaging peasants did not throw stones at them.

Another factor peculiar to Stary Sącz and the surrounding area was the deep impact of the conservative peasant party on relations with Jews, similar only to those in Żywiec. The party's extreme anti-Jewish newspaper, *Związek Chłopski*, had a large and enthusiastic readership in the Sącz area. Representing the more prosperous farmers, the party press organ disseminated Jewish-hostile fantasies of violence and conspiracy theories in explicitly brutal language. Its commentaries no doubt played a part in mobilizing the rural population in the surrounding area.

Furthermore, the municipal authorities had been paralyzed for years by an incompetent and virtually powerless local council. Council elections the previous year had not ended the stagnation. The district captain responsible for the town, Lewinksi, based in Nowy Sącz, complained that none of the town's intelligentsia was prepared to assume political functions and that the existing council could not agree on a single issue. Charges should have been pressed against the mayor, in his opinion, for abuse of power and public acts of violence.[187] He was referring to a recent incident and striking example of an alderman abusing his office to fight professional Jewish competition, which also illustrated the extremely tense relations between local and government authorities. In the light of this incident, it is not surprising that Stary Sącz was left to be raided despite the many warnings; cooperation between the municipal authority and the military administration was strained, and the few gendarmes stationed in the town were hopelessly overchallenged.

Gliński, the mayor of Stary Sącz, was also the proprietor of a restaurant in town that was obviously not prospering. When a group of visitors from Nowy

Sącz, consisting of three officers, an industrialist, and the forest ranger, went to dine in the only restaurant in town run by a Jew (a certain Mr. Finder) and parked their five carriages in front, the mayor and rival of the Jewish restaurateur ordered the latter to have the carriages moved as they were supposedly blocking the thoroughfare. But this was obviously not the case. Two gendarmes were called in to clear the street. A crowd of onlookers gathered, in the middle of which stood the mayor's wife, Rosalia Glińska, who called out, "They only go to the Jew's, they're parked outside the Jew's, and they're all inside at the Jew's." When the visitors left the restaurant after their meal, they found themselves facing a crowd of two to three hundred people. The gendarmes refused to remonstrate with the high-ranking gentlemen about their parking, angering some people in the crowd, who proceeded to climb on to the coachman's seat. The police officers held the crowd back and managed to prevent the situation from escalating. But by doing so, they earned the animosity not only of the crowd but also of the mayor, whose orders they had defied. Although it is likely that many onlookers were merely curious and that the protests were directed at the upper-class men from the larger town of Nowy Sącz and their perceived arrogance rather than at the Jewish restaurant-owner, the situation showed that the mayor could not be relied on to maintain order. He had obviously abused his office to try to gain economic advantage.

On the morning of 26 June, the situation on the market square had exceeded anyone's fears of disorder. When the governor Leon Piniński arrived to see the devastation for himself, he called for the imposition of a state of emergency. It had been discussed in the ministry some weeks previously and was now declared with immediate effect. It was to be the most drastic suspension of parts of the constitution within the Habsburg Empire until World War I.[188]

State of Emergency! Military Rule and the Restoration of Order

A state of emergency was declared in thirty-three districts. In all West Galicia and in the neighboring parts of East Galicia, several constitutional guarantees were suspended.[189] Anyone arrested could now be held in custody for up to eight days without a court order or even questioning. House searches could be made without a warrant. The right to mail privacy was revoked. The government was entitled to suspend the printing of periodicals and tighten censorship. Public gatherings were banned; special permission was required from the authorities to hold election meetings. Summary court martials were installed in the Limanowa and Nowy Sącz districts to hear cases of murder, robbery, arson, and vandalism of alien property. Any major arrested committing one of these offences would be summoned before one and, in the case of a unanimous verdict (which could not be repealed), sentenced to death, to be enforced within three hours.[190] The gravity of the situation under emergency law was underlined by the arrival of the executioner Selinger and his two assistants from Vienna, who stayed in Tarnów at the ready. In this way, the state regained its authority. It showed the population that the consequences of being caught "letting off steam" in the districts under martial law far outweighed any prospective benefits. But it took more than knowing that an executioner named Selinger had been installed in Tarnów to make the threat of a death penalty credible.[191] The likelihood of arrest also had to increase. For this reason, in late June, a new policing strategy was introduced. Rather than the decentralized approach of local law enforcement agencies acting on council orders, responsibility was now assumed by the army, supported by cavalry units from other crownlands.

Under the state of emergency, the Galician authorities were forced to surrender some of their autonomy to the imperial government. Major General von Schulheim took over the task of pacifying the region. From the outset, he made no secret of his low opinion of the Galician government, whose response to the disturbances he felt had been far too hesitant.[192] As soon as he entered the field on 24 June, even before the state of emergency had been imposed, he sought to extend his remit. Seizing the initiative from the local officials he regarded as incompetent, he set about building a dense network of soldiers across the region. They would be able to act both preventively, by patrolling, and correctively, by intervening swiftly at any trouble spot. His dual approach was based on the premise that disturbances erupted wherever state control was lacking, and wherever disturbances erupted, visibly vigorous action needed to be taken. In the ensuing weeks, the major general drew ever-increasing circles on maps of Galicia, marking out the growing radius he had brought under state control. Whether he had just perfunctorily stationed troops for the sake of progress reports to Vienna or also created functioning communicative spaces is not known. Perhaps it was immaterial; in any case, the campaign sent the right signals and made an impact on the ground.

This was certainly true for Jasło, one of the most troubled districts. In his report to the governor's office, the district captain Waydowicz agreed that the local police forces would never have been able to bring the vast, mountainous terrain under control alone. He blamed understaffing and incompetence equally for the region's weak governance. A mere twenty-one gendarmes were responsible for the 122 communities scattered across the county. At any given time, an average of three or four of them were on vacation or sick. Six commanding officers were required to remain permanently at their posts. That left just twelve officers to be deployed in trouble spots. The municipal police in Jasło were fundamentally passive, Waydowicz went on, and the situation was not likely to improve under the hopelessly divided council. The riots in the county had only been suppressed with the help of two infantry battalions and order maintained due to one of the companies staying to conduct patrols and intervene where necessary.[193]

Waydowicz's report not only spelled out the uncomfortable truth about conditions in Galicia to the crownland's government; it also explained why the rioting had become so rampant. Most of the assaults were symptomatic of the de facto absence of government. People did not need to act clandestinely to conduct coordinated attacks. Anyone unscrupulous enough to be interested in robbing and victimizing Jews had the opportunity, so long as the state acted powerless. The imposition of emergency law did not spell an abrupt end to the rioting, but incidents became less frequent and spatially isolated. By September that year, they had completely abated.

The "troubles" provided a lesson in the connection between state control—that is, the credibility of the permanent threat of using monopolistic force—and public safety. Although violence did not erupt every time the state's law enforcement agencies were absent or incapacitated, the state's weakness was highlighted by the riots that occurred. While this was of no concern in everyday life, so long as routines proceeded as usual, during the disturbances it was different. Word-of-mouth news of lootings, soldiers being bribed by Jews, and peasants being shot conveyed to everyone that Galicia truly was in an exceptional state, which many interpreted as a unique opportunity. By intervening to contain the disturbances and imposing tangible sanctions on public life, the state reminded Galicians of its existence. Unlike the pogroms in Tsarist Russia, the disturbances in Galicia were answered with a severe governmental crackdown. The riots and the long process of combating them were a lesson to all citizens about the meaning of state rule.

From the point of view of the ruling Galician Conservatives, the state of emergency was tantamount to a defeat. It was bad for the image of the crownland and cast a negative light on their administration, which was not only criticized in *Pester Lloyd* but also discredited in military reports to the imperial capital about incompetent officials and woods teeming with bands of robbers. Yet the governing elite nevertheless managed to draw some benefit from the situation.

Aftermath: Restrictions on Peasant Parties and Social Democrats

The imposition of emergency rule forced the Galician Conservatives to admit they were not capable of maintaining order by conventional means or with their own resources. But it allowed them to crack down not only on the perpetrators and ringleaders of the violence but also on their own political rivals. Under emergency law, they could impose more effective—and entirely legal—restraints on the latter's work. Consequently, as soon as the state of emergency was declared, the Conservatives set about beleaguering all the opposition parties, including the Social Democrats, who were not even remotely involved in the disturbances.[194] In public debate, the Conservatives focused on the virulent rumors and newspapers printed in Hungary as causes of the disturbances, which had incited the masses to violence.

This legitimized the forms of repression that the crownland had been practicing for years. In their internal Polish-language communications, however, they made no secret of the prevalent view, shared even by the governor, that the Jews and their "anxious nature" were a harmful influence. Although the Galician government knew about local understaffing and communication difficulties, they did not assume responsibility for it, and mentioned it only incidentally in their reports.

Restoring Trust: Punishment, Restitution, Assistance

Despite the dismissive attitude of local officials toward the "Jewish delegations" who sought help when attacks were threatened, the Jewish public was assured that the military would take resolute action against rioting peasants once it arrived on the scene. Unlike some local policemen and parish leaders who participated in the robbing, no armed gendarmes or soldiers collaborated with rioting mobs. Knowing justice would prevail was crucial for Jews to continue coexisting with their Christian neighbors. This knowledge was affirmed when the damages suffered were publicly recognized and at least symbolically mitigated, and when the perpetrators were made accountable for their crimes.

It has often been said that the Galician judiciary was not consistent in its jurisdiction. But it made concrete efforts, following instructions from the Ministry of Justice, to reconstruct the circumstances of the crimes and to punish the perpetrators, which should not be overlooked. Victims contributed to investigations, quantifying the material damage they had suffered and testifying in court. Restitution was afforded partly by the return of stolen goods and partly in the form of payments from third parties, chiefly Jewish organizations. Victims could not expect any money from the perpetrators. Martial law was expedient to locating stolen goods as it facilitated house searches. Gendarmes could identify suspects from witness statements, track them down in their homes, and compel them to produce the loot. They were known to act with some brutality, threatening violence to ensure the loot was handed over or its whereabouts revealed.[195] Sometimes looters could be persuaded by priests or other local leaders to return stolen goods.

The Jewish community sought to provide unbureaucratic monetary assistance to Jews who had suffered damages, to deter them from suing for compensation. It was feared that civil proceedings against the impoverished peasants, many of whom had been imprisoned, would only serve to exacerbate tensions between Christian peasants and Jews.[196] Hence, in early July, prominent members of urban Jewish communities, including the parliamentarians Rapaport and Emil Byk, set up a fundraising committee to compensate Jews affected by the riots. Donations were also collected from the Austrian Israelite Union and private individuals across the empire. They hoped to offset another rumor—namely, that Jews had provoked the outbreak of peasant violence in order to demand excessive compensation afterward. It was a bitter realization that to avoid ongoing conflict, it was prudent to relinquish legitimate demands. The pogroms in Tsarist Russia in the 1880s, which had compelled many Jews to migrate to Central and Western Europe, were a cautionary example. Another lesson learned from the disturbances in Galicia was that it was better for Jews not to exercise their rights as equal citizens if they were at all concerned to restore peaceful relations. Even calling the police when under threat was something to be given careful consideration, not only because of the arrogance of certain district captains.[197]

Jewish Reactions: The Double-Edged Sword of State Protection

In the above-mentioned telegram from the Jewish community in Tłuste in East Galicia, the authors thanked the council for sending the armed forces to ensure that order was restored. But they also pointed out that their withdrawal would likely renew the risk of disturbances. The Jewish citizens feared Christians acting on their threats to set fire to buildings and cut the telegraph wires in revenge for them calling for the military's help. Most Jews had already left town; trade was suspended. The remaining Jewish residents therefore requested the billeting of fifty infantrymen until completion of the railroad, the extra costs of which they offered to meet themselves.[198] Their request was turned down, so the Tłuste Jewish community sent another telegram to the Landtag member Emil Byk to the same end, and another on 6 June to the governor's office, requesting reinforcements for the gendarmerie.[199] In Wielopole, too, the Jewish Community paid 193 guilders and 54 kreutzers to the royal-and-imperial captain on his company's withdrawal.[200] If soldiers were billeted at the prompting of a Jewish community, even if there were several indications of impending criminal disturbances, it was customary to make the Jewish community bear the cost. This sent a fateful signal to the Christians in the local community who sought a "reckoning" with the Jews. Although they obviously did not welcome the presence of the military if they were planning robberies or severe harassment, they approved of Jews paying to have their fears—roused by rumors of impending attacks—assuaged by a military presence. This was no universally approved procedure. In Prussia in the German Empire, for example, the billeting of soldiers to suppress disturbances was publicly funded. Hence Christians contributed to the costs if they attacked their Jewish neighbors.[201]

It was common knowledge that Jewish communities in Galicia paid for their own protection. This information was then twisted not only into tales of "bribed soldiers" but also to some extent by local officials. The district captain of Wadowice mentioned at the start of the chapter, who emphasized his diligence to the public prosecutors but described his displeasure at Jewish requests for assistance to the governor's office, regarded it as a matter of course that Jewish communities paid for the billeting of soldiers whom they had requested. He informed the governor's office, moreover, that he had instructed local leaders to publicly display the bills that Jewish communities were required to pay so that "all Jews can see how great the expense of exploiting their fellow believers." There is no record of whether anyone followed his instruction. It would certainly not have helped defuse the situation. But the district captain obviously presumed that staff at the governor's office would approve of his antisemitic machinations. Publicly displaying billeting bills would in fact primarily have conveyed a message to the Christian population. If the mayor of Kalwarya, for instance, displayed such a bill, it would have shown the Christian townspeople that they were not required to meet the cost of protecting the Jews, but only the Jews themselves. In the light of the rumors about official warrants and soldiers bribed by Jews, ordering such bills to be publicly displayed was an insidiously anti-Jewish act. The district captain even confirmed the antisemitic narrative when justifying it by claiming that exploitation by Jews was the root cause of the disturbances, so when they paid for military protection, they simply paid the price for exploiting others. The Jewish communities that requested protection always agreed to pay for it themselves. But displaying the bills would have conveyed the impression they were unsettled and would have inscribed this reading in the public consciousness.

Galician Jews suffered humiliation not only at the hands of local officials. Even the military, which most Jews experienced as reliable and trustworthy in summer 1898, could act with ambivalence and occasionally distinct hostility.

Powerbroker Arrogance: The Strzyżów Cemetery

An incident that caused a major stir that summer occurred in Strzyżów during the state of emergency. Billeted hussars left their horses to graze on the old Jewish cemetery. The caretaker of the graveyard, Jacob Hagel, was offended by this disregard for religious sensitivities and suggested to a hussar that the horses graze on the Christian cemetery.[202] He was subsequently sentenced to one year's imprisonment, later reduced to two months, for this "defamation of religion."[203] The officer who had shown a blatant disregard for the repose of the dead was not penalized. This incident and the subsequent hearing made waves as far away as Vienna.[204]

The Poisoned Priest

Another episode during the summer of unrest vividly illustrates the contradictory signals sent by the different institutions and echelons of the state to the people operating with rumors and violence, and those targeted by them. On 12 June, there had been several incidences of looting in different parts of the Brzostek parish, for which forty-five people were later sentenced.[205] Earlier that month, the local priest had died, and it was widely suggested that he had been poisoned by Jews.[206] The rumor was so persistent that eventually the court ordered an exhumation to investigate the cause of the priest's death. Quite apart from how the exhumation of a priest would have been received under normal circumstances, it is easy to imagine the passions it roused when the rumor was abroad that he had been poisoned by Jews and unrest was rife. The soldiers of the "assistance squad" were reluctant to guard the cemetery and protect the Jewish population as it delayed Major General von Schulheim's marching plans.[207] No matter whether the exhumation confirmed or disproved the theory that the priest had been poisoned,[208] the mere fact that the judiciary gave credence to the rumors of a poisoning when talk of plots to murder the pope and the emperor had sparked mass attacks on Jews was astounding. Investigations were not even dropped when locals started looting Jewish property and arrests were made.

The rumor of the poisoned priest is easily exposed as part of the justification and mobilization strategy pursued during the disturbances. The allegation was perhaps an act of revenge on the Jewish community, who were often portrayed as provoking the disturbances. Even if there had been indications that the priest had not died of natural causes, it must have been clear that his exhumation would only add more grist to the gossip mill. Those who held the rumor to be credible and who passed it on must have seen the act of exhumation as a confirmation of their suspicions. By the same communicative process by which various rumors were interwoven and chronologies suspended, the causality of the disturbances could be inverted. In retrospect, then, the lootings could be interpreted not as acts of Christian aggression but as a reaction to the murder of a priest by Jews. The exhumation exacerbated tensions between Jews and Christians; military reports show that the conflict reignited in the area. Unfortunately, there are no files on the case in the Ministry of Justice. The terse comments of the military authorities do not reveal how the rumor became a criminal complaint or what the preliminary investigations found. Whether the subsequent attacks were motivated by a desire for revenge or an attempt to obstruct the course of justice must remain conjecture. But it is significant that the local authorities investigated the allegations despite the volatility of the situation and so became an instrument in the conflict between Christians and Jews and an obstacle to the military.

Last Opportunity for Violence? Dragoons on the Rampage in East Galicia

Two incidents in summer 1898 served to shake Jewish trust in the Austrian state. In the night of August 1–2, imperial Austrian dragoons committed several offences against Jewish citizens in the small town of Strusów and the village Warwarzynce in East Galicia, apparently echoing the anti-Jewish riots (see figure 2.5). Small groups of soldiers roamed the streets, smashing windows with their sabers

Figure 2.5. K.u.k. Dragoners at a race in Przemyśl, *Nowiny Illustrowane*, no. 34, 1907 Public domain.

and tailstocks, and demanding free food and drink in the taverns.[209] Only a concerted effort by the gendarmerie, fire brigade, and night watchmen could stop them. The soldiers were of the 10th Dragoon Regiment "Fürst von Liechtenstein," which was on its way back to Moravia following a deployment in Galicia. Some of them seized this last opportunity before returning to their barracks in Olmütz/Olomouc to wield their apparently incontestable power and do what had almost become normal in Galicia over the last weeks—harassing, blackmailing, and robbing Jewish citizens. Unfortunately, this was not the only instance of the military abusing its power in Galicia.[210]

In spring 1896 and late January 1897, soldiers of the 13th Dragoon Regiment had raged against Jews in the small town Łańcut, smashing the windows of Jewish houses and the synagogue and beating an old man unconscious.[211] Again, these incidents occurred before some of the unit left Galicia. The soldiers of the 13th regiment were mostly from Bohemia, with some recruits from Vienna. Their drunken rituals to celebrate the end of their period of service, when years of disciplinary pressure were lifted, combined with the sense of detachment they felt from their supposedly benighted and primitive surroundings, gave rise to a short tradition of violence. It was directed at Jews. The soldiers had not failed to notice their precarious situation within a predominantly Christian environment.

The soldiers of the 10th Dragoon Regiment wrote another chapter in the story of disturbances in summer 1898. They came from Bohemia, a region unfamiliar with Jewish shtetls.[212] Soldiers of the royal-and-imperial army followed the rioters' lead and seized the rare opportunity to plunder and let off steam on Jews. No political agitation was needed to motivate them. The context of violence and absence of state sanctions were enough to prompt them to assail a minority. Although these were only isolated incidents, they compounded the Galician Jews' insecurity and sense of risk attached to relying on the military stemming from the widespread violence, the cost of billeting, and allegations that they bribed officers.

Nevertheless, the traditional script of coexistence largely retained its validity. It offered guidance not only for dealing with violence but also for restoring symbiotic neighborly relations between Christian peasants and Jewish artisans, tradespeople, and barkeepers. The riots had, of course, altered relations between the two groups—in some places, irrevocably and fatally, compelling Jews to leave their homes. An even more significant factor impacting Christian-Jewish relations, however, was the government's intervention. The restrictions imposed under emergency law, sentencing of offenders, and the experience of an uncompromising military had an enduring impact on life together. The "anti-Semitic riots" were remembered as an event that changed the structures of coexistence. The individual incidents, which varied in character depending on local traditions of coexistence, topographies, and the point in time during the wave of violence, became tellable experiences. The politicians of anti-Semitism contributed to this process by applying different interpretations to the various incidents and turning them into political narratives. This transformation of anti-Jewish violence into anti-Jewish politics will be explored in the following chapter.

Notes

1. Publications dealing with different aspects of the riots are Golczewski, *Polnisch-jüdische Beziehungen*; Jobst, "Die antisemitischen Bauernunruhen"; Keely Stauter-Halsted, "Jews as Middleman Minorities in Rural Poland: Understanding the Galician Pogroms of 1898," in Robert Blobaum (ed.), *Antisemitism and Its Opponents in Modern Poland* (Ithaca, 2005), 39-59; Unowsky, "Peasant Political Mobilization"; Buchen, "Herrschaft in der Krise"; Soboń, "Polacy wobec Żydów."
2. See Robert Darnton, "Reading a Riot," *New York Review of Books*, 22 October 1992. John Klier speaks of a "dialog of violence" conducted by Christians and Jews. John D. Klier, *Russians, Jews, and the Pogroms of 1881–1882* (Cambridge, 2011), 104. See also the introduction in Werner Bergmann, Christhard Hoffmann, and Helmut Walser Smith, *Exclusionary Violence: Antisemitic Riots in Modern Germany* (Ann Arbor, 2002).
3. Anyone confronted with violence is forced to react and interact. Limiting the inquiry to the aggressors' part would therefore impede an understanding and interpretation of the dynamics of the riots. The question of who was responsible is not affected or relativized by extending the inquiry in this way. Even if all contemporaries become perpetrators by their actions, and their deeds influence the further course of events, the categories of perpetrator and victim in terms of guilt, responsibility, murder, and justice remain in place.

Similarly, descriptions of the "dialog of violence" should reflect the suffering, pain, and gravity of the drama.
4. In his fascinating book about communities of violence, David Nirenberg suggests that in modern capitalist societies, competition between all individuals has replaced violence between groups. Nirenberg, *Communities of Violence*, 9.
5. The violence explored in this study was not frenzied, such as Wolfgang Sofsky describes in his treatise on violence. Rather, it was in line with what Rogers Brubaker and David Laitin write on the nature of ethnic and nationalist violence: "culturally constructed, discursively mediated, symbolically saturated, and ritually regulated." Wolfgang Sofsky, *Traktat über die Gewalt* (Frankfurt a. M., 2005); Rogers Brubaker and David D. Laitin, "Ethnic and Nationalist Violence," *Annual Review of Sociology* 24 (1998): 423–452, 441.
6. Struve, "Gentry, Jews, and Peasants"; Levine, *Economic Origins*.
7. As Bourdieu proposed, "social action" can create nonreflective "social meaning." Cf. Lutz Raphael, "Habitus und sozialer Sinn: Der Ansatz der Praxistheorie Pierre Bourdieus," in Friedrich Jaeger and Jürgen Straub (eds), *Handbuch der Kulturwissenschaften: Paradigmen und Disziplinen* (Stuttgart, 2004), 266–276, 270.
8. William W. Hagen, "The Moral Economy of Popular Violence: The Pogrom in Lwów, November 1918," in Blobaum, *Antisemitism and Its Opponents*, 124–147; Helmut Walser-Smith, "From Play to Act: Anti-Jewish Violence in German and European History during the Long Nineteenth Century," in idem, *Continuities*, 115–166.
9. As such, it is not a phenomenon limited to premodern societies but can be observed in every variant of community including the modern constitutional state, such as in interaction between law enforcers and protesters. Nevertheless, inquiries into the symbolic dimension of violence in modern, Western community formations are commonly based on methods of analyzing "foreign" cultures, whether they be anthropological descriptions of non-European peoples or European societies in the Middle Ages and early modern period. Cf. Marshal Sahlins, *Inseln der Geschichte* (Hamburg, 1992); Arlette Farge and Jacques Revel: *The Vanishing Children of Paris: Rumor and Politics before the French Revolution* (Cambridge, 1991).
10. Anthony Giddens, *Die Konstitution der Gesellschaft: Grundzüge einer Theorie der Strukturierung* (Frankfurt a. M., 1984), 51–90.
11. "Gewalt, die sich Zeit nimmt, wird zur Macht" (Violence that takes time becomes power). Cf. Elias Canetti, *Masse und Macht* (Hamburg, 1960). Violence is not, however, the language of power. On the contrary, violence can indicate a sense of powerlessness, as it is an attractive option for making one's voice heard when one feels it would otherwise not be heard. Jörg Baberowski, *Räume der Gewalt* (Frankfurt a. M., 2015).
12. Signifiers included the judiciary and parliamentarianism. See chapter 3.
13. Such people in uniform should not, however, be regarded as tools of a bureaucratic authoritarian state but as individuals with their own agenda. Their behavior was influenced by various factors including loyalty to their employer, personal ambition and weaknesses, and religious, national, or dynastic loyalties.
14. This triangular constellation therefore has a major impact on the outbreak, course, and goals of violence. Werner Bergmann, "Ethnic Riots in Situations of Loss of Control: Revolution, Civil War, and Regime Change as Opportunity Structures for anti-Jewish Violence in Nineteenth and Twentieth Century Europe," in Willhelm Heitmeyer, Heinz-Gerhard Haupt, Stefan Malthaner, and Andrea Kirschner (eds), *The Control of*

Violence in Modern Society: Multidisciplinary Perspectives, From School Shootings to Ethnic Violence (Berlin, 2010), 487–516, 489.
15. Cf. Bergmann, Hoffmann, and Smith, *Exclusionary Violence*.
16. John Klier and Shlomo Lambroza (eds), *Pogroms: Anti-Jewish Violence in Russian History* (Cambridge, 1992); Donald L. Horowitz, *The Deadly Ethnic Riot* (Berkeley, 2001).
17. Canetti, *Masse und Macht*, 14f.
18. Cf. Clifford J. Geertz, *Dichte Beschreibung: Beiträge zum Verstehen kultureller Systeme* (Frankfurt a. M., 2002); William Sewell, *The Logics of History: Social Theory and Social Transformation* (Chicago, 2005), especially the section "A Theory of Structures: Duality, Agency, and Transformation," 123–151.
19. Andreas Würgler describes several cases during the eighteenth century of peasants claiming that a royal patent, privilege, or other ruling existed that had been suppressed by the authorities. Andreas Würgler, "Fama und Rumor: Gerücht, Aufruhr und Presse im Ancien Régime," *Werkstatt Geschichte* 15 (1996): 20–32, especially 23f.
20. Research into the early modern period sees the emergence of rumors as a reaction to the repressive communicative conditions of the Ancien Regime and its secret politics, which left an information gap that was filled by rumors. The function of rumors as both "counter-publicity" and "improvised news" are considered here in analyses of case studies. Joachim Eibach, "Gerüchte im Vormärz und März 1848 in Baden," *Historische Anthropologie* 2 (1994): 245–264, 264; Würgler, "Fama und Rumor," 23f.; Tamotsu Shibutani, *Improvised News: A Sociological Study of Rumor* (Indianapolis, 1966); Jean Delumeau, *Angst im Abendland – Die Geschichte kollektiver Ängste im Europa des 14. bis 18. Jahrhunderts* (Reinbek, 1989).
21. In both cases, the target was the same social group, but its relationship to the peasants changed after the abolition of serfdom and the constitution of 1867.
22. Rumors arising in dictatorships or in times of revolution often have this quality. See Orlando Figes, *Die Flüsterer: Leben in Stalins Russland* (Berlin, 2008); Jörg Baberowski, "Gerüchte und Gewalt im Zarenreich und in der Sowjetunion," *Humboldt-Spektrum* 1 (2009): 46–48.
23. Orlando Figes and Boris Kolonitskii, *Interpreting the Russian Revolution: The Language and Symbols of 1917* (New Haven, 1999).
24. Hans-Joachim Neubauer, *Fama: Eine Geschichte des Gerüchts* (Berlin, 2009), 211.
25. While the analogy seems apt, as both epidemics and rumors are spread via close interpersonal contact, the epidemic metaphor should nevertheless be avoided in reference to rumors. Rumors are not an abnormal form of communication, not a social "disease," but part of "normal" communication and therefore by no means more harmful per se than other forms of social communication. Among the authorities and elites wishing to educate the people, however, a tradition of pathologizing "gossip" and branding it disruptive misinformation developed. Brigitte Weingart, "Kommunikation, Kontamination und epidemische Ausbreitung, Einleitung," in idem, Jürgen Brokoff, Jürgen Fohrmann, and Hedwig Pompe (eds), *Die Kommunikation der Gerüchte* (Göttingen, 2008), 241–251, 243f.
26. "Was alle sagen, ist noch kein Gerücht, sondern das, von dem man sagt, dass es alle sagen" (What everyone is saying is not a rumor in itself but whatever people say everyone is saying). Neubauer, *Fama*, 12.
27. This self-referentiality is perceived as the communication becoming autonomous, the participants in which appear as "instruments of the rumor." Weingart, "Kommunikation," 247.

28. Hedwig Pompe, "Nachrichten über Gerüchte: Einleitung," in *Die Kommunikation der Gerüchte*, 131–143, 131.
29. Theodor Adorno, *Minima Moralia* (Frankfurt a. M., 2001), 200.
30. Historical events are understood here in the sense of Marshal Sahlins as a relationship between a certain occurrence and a given symbolic system. Sahlins, *Inseln der Geschichte*, 150.
31. During the transmission process, rumors are often reduced to their essence. In the long term, only those "survive" which are both concise and open, thus allowing them to be understood by many speakers while still having meaning and currency. In each individual speech situation, a version can be told with different information or explanations. The concept of the meme as a cultural gene provides a vivid illustration of this "selective pressure" to "survive" among the mass of what is told. Weingart, "Kommunikation."
32. Rumors should not be regarded as chains but rather as networks, as each speaker generates a rumor not just once, but several times, and they are processed in a nonlinear way.
33. "Gerüchte erzeugen . . . die Welt und deren Wirklichkeiten und verwalten individuelle oder kollektive Ansprüche auf innerweltliche Teilhabe an diesen Wirklichkeiten" (Rumors generate . . . the world and its realities and administrate individual or collective claims to inner-worldly participation in these realities). Pompe, "Nachrichten über Gerüchte," 132f.
34. Rumors should be analyzed not only in terms of content, as texts, but also in relation to their communicative potential and impact, triggering discrimination on many levels. See Neubauer, *Fama*, 170.
35. The peasant parties sought to take over the landowners' political legacy. While the Greek Catholic priest Kaluzniackyi could rely on the votes of the Ruthenian peasants, the Christian People's Party candidate Witold Lewicki and the chairman of the secular People's Party Jan Stapiński competed for the Polish peasants' votes.
36. The attack was rumored to take place on his journey to Vienna. Report by the district captain of 13 March, CDIAL/146/4/3117, 1. It was perhaps the death of Wysocki that sparked this "news."
37. Report by the district captain to the governor's office, CDIAL/146/4/3117, 3.
38. [Omawiał także kwestyę żydowską] report of 15 March, CDIAL/146/4/3117, 8.
39. The Krakow public prosecutors launched investigations into thirty-seven persons. AGAD Min. Spraw. 310, 55.
40. CDIAL/146/4/1337, 6.
41. The rumor was most often circulated among church-goers. The correspondent for the *Neue Freie Presse* wrote that many nonresidents who had come to the town evidently took the rumor back to their villages. "Die antisemitischen Excesse in Wieliczka," *NFP*, 17 March 1898, 5.
42. The same was reported to have occurred in Zabawa and Taszyce, AGAD Min. Spraw. 310, 50.
43. CDIAL/146/4/3117, 8. *Głos Narodu*, 15 March 1898.
44. According to the district captain's office in Wieliczka. CDIAL/146/4/3117, 6. On the pamphlet by Mateusz Jeż in the same Kahal-Talmud genre, see chapter 1.
45. Similar rumors had also spread following anti-Jewish disturbances in Tarnów in 1870, linked with the Galician Landtag elections. Cf. Soboń, "Polacy wobec Żydów," 281ff.
46. Much to the annoyance of *Prawda*, which maintained the ban proved the truth of the allegations against the Jews. *Prawda*, 25 March 1898 and 5 June 1898; Unowsky, "Peasant Political Mobilization."

47. The Austrian Israelite Union in Vienna complained to the minister for culture about the pamphlet's use in religious instruction. CDIAL/146/4/3117, 15. On the AIU, see the subsection "Counter-Rumors: Female Abduction and Clericalism in Galician Political Discourse" in chapter 3.
48. Jews in Wieliczka feared there would be further unrest after Easter during the army's recruitment campaign, which attracted many young men to the town. *Neue Freie Presse*, 17 March 1898, 5.
49. The rumors in circulation during the pogroms in Russia following the murder of Alexander II also spoke of a "Jewish crime" because one of the assassins had been Jewish. The Tsar's successor Alexander III, moreover, gave his permission to beat Jews following an incident in which a Jew had not been duly respectful. Klier, *Russians, Jews, and the Pogroms*, 114.
50. Most peasants had accepted the Habsburg monarch as part of their world and referred to him affectionately as "Our Emperor." Franciszek Józef not only had the same name as many Galician peasants, he was also a Catholic and was looked upon as the wealthiest countryman. Cf. Anna Kowalska-Lewicka, "'Cysorz' w folklorze galicjskim," in Ewa Fryś-Pietraszkowa and Anna Spiss (eds), *Przed 100 laty i dzisiaj: Ludoznawstwo i etnografia między Wiedniem, Lwowem, Krakowem a Pragą* (Krakow, 1999), 141–153.
51. The only exception evidenced by sources from 1898 was a case from the area immediately surrounding Krakow: a bricklayer named Józef Gajewski from Nowa Wieś Narodowa incited "the population to violent acts" against the Israelites, calling on them to defend the fatherland with scythes and flails and "burn down" the Jews and the local judges.
52. *Kurier Luwowski*, no. 169, 19 June 1898. Golczewski, *Polnisch-jüdische Beziehungen*, 82.
53. AGAD Min. Spraw. 308, 242.
54. Each imperial family member took a different role in mediating the various nationalities' diverging claims. Empress Elisabeth, for instance, was famous for her affinity with Hungary, while Franz Ferdinand was known for his trialist ideas.
55. Unowsky, *Pomp and Politics*.
56. I am grateful to Stefan Wiese for pointing this out to me.
57. Richard Wortman, *Scenarios of Power, Myth and Ceremony in Russian Monarchy* (Princeton, 2000).
58. Indeed, there is evidence of privileges being guaranteed to rob Jews for a limited period in the pogrom region of 1881. In the seventeenth century, Cossack hetmen allowed their hired soldiers to loot conquered towns for three days. I owe thanks to Marcin Soboń for drawing my attention to Władysław A. Serczyk, *Na płonącej Ukrainie: Dzieje Kozaczyzny 1648–1651* (Warsaw, 2007). In a bid to delegitimize this practice, the Cossacks were accused of attempted regicide by various commentators, including the Jewish history writer and eye witness Nathan (ben Moses) Hanover in his work *The Abyss of Despair (Yeven Metzulah): The Famous 17th Century Chronicle Depicting Jewish Life in Russia and Poland during the Chmielnicki Massacres of 1648–1649* (London, 1983). My thanks go to Daria Starcenko for pointing out these correlations in the early modern age.
59. Ivan Franko describes the connection between a wave of emigration by Ruthenian peasants to Brazil with the rumor that Rudolf had resettled in South America to build a new state and would bestow land on his loyal Ukrainian subjects. Ivan Franko, *Beiträge zur Geschichte und Kultur der Ukraine: Ausgewählte deutsche Schriften des revolutionären Demokraten 1882–1915*, ed. Eduard Winter and Peter Kirchner ([East] Berlin, 1963).
60. In Lubsza on 13 July. CDIAL/146/4/3125, 69.

61. The same story was told by a maidservant of a railroad official in Kalwarya. Cf. note 38.
62. On this point, see Daniel Unowsky, "Staging Habsburg Patriotism: Dynastic Loyalty and the 1898 Imperial Jubilee," in Judson and Rozenblit, *Constructing Nationalities*, 141–156.
63. Witnesses questioned after the disturbances in Lutcza alleged that a certain Józef Janusz of Ruślówka had said that "all over the world the Jews will be attacked." AGAD Min. Spraw. 308, 68. News of the developments in France naturally also reached Galicia. Cf. Grzegorz Krzywiec, "Między kryzysem a odrodzeniem. O odgłosach afery Dreyfusa w polskich środowiskach radykalnej inteligencji," in Borkowska and Rudkowska, *Kwestia żydowska*, 423–438, 425.
64. The motif of the assassination plot was an effective mobilizer. It not only stirred strong emotions such as fear and anger but simultaneously offered an outlet for them by justifying assaults on Jews. Horowitz, *Deadly Ethnic Riot*.
65. The prevalent claim that "the Jews had murdered the tsar" during the pogroms in Tsarist Russia, 1881–1882, was an extremely significant factor in mobilizing and justifying the violence here, and hence a vehicle of self-empowerment. It may, then, have inspired the Galician rioters of 1898 to conduct a preemptive strike against Jews supposedly planning an assassination attempt. Cf. Klier, *Russians, Jews, and the Pogroms*, 118.
66. Speaking in the tavern of Radłów, a court clerk named Stanisław Religa claimed that the parliamentarians Szajer and Stojałowski had told him about the imperial warrant in Vienna. AGAD Min. Spraw. 309, 390.
67. Cf. the subsection "Antisemitic Interpellations Connecting the Villages to the Capital" in chapter 3.
68. Puns such as this had been widespread since the eighteenth century. Wolff, *Idea of Galicia*.
69. Każdego żyda powstałego z atramentu może zmyć nowo wynaleziony środek Statim, AGAD Min. Spraw. 307, 3.
70. A monument to the poet was erected on Krakow's main square in the same year. Eight years previously, Mickiewicz's remains had been transferred from Paris to the cathedral catacombs of Wawel Castle. On the centenary celebrations, see Patrice M. Dabrowski, *Commemorations and the Shaping of Modern Poland* (Bloomington, 2004).
71. AGAD Min. Spraw. 307, 3.
72. "As the uneducated folk apart from a very few exceptions have no understanding . . . for what purpose a celebration in honor of the poet Mickiewicz, about whom they had hitherto known nothing, [should take place] . . . malicious people gave the said celebration a different interpretation and because the ill-will of the rural population toward the Jews is growing, nourished by the antisemitic papers that are also being read in the country, talk that the said celebration in fact represents the enactment of a hunt on the Jews fell not only on credulous but also on sympathetic ears." This was how the Kalwarya police chief assessed the situation; cited from a report by the imperial-and-royal prosecutor Sułkowski in Wadowice, AGAD Min. Spraw. 307, 3.
73. Handwritten notices appeared on Jewish houses and the municipal offices, signed by a "Kalwarya social committee," calling for violent acts against Jews in Maków, Myślenice district, on 29 May. The municipal secretary Pieróg was suspected of being the author. Interestingly, the notices did not mention any official permission but were formulated as internal communiqués within the peasant community: "Attention! Get rid of the Jews, those Christian leeches, because if we do not fight these locusts, we will be ruined—Onwards, peasants, take up your sticks and scythes to fight the locusts! By the Kalwarya social committee. We will meet soon." Another notice read, "The Jews have drunk enough of

our blood. The time has come to put an end to them. We will soon come to meet you, the Kalwarya social committee." CDIAL/146/4/3126, 45f.
74. CDIAL/146/3117, 40.
75. "Znając jednak tchórzliwą naturę żydow i skłonność ich do stwarzania bajek na tle narodowościowem, nie wierzyłem im tembardziej, że najmnisza wiesci o zajść mających rozruchach, ani też o przygotowaniach w tym kierunku czynionych niedoszla mnie."
76. CDIAL/146/4, 40.
77. The public prosecutor Sułkowski played down the incident in his report to the Ministry of Justice, writing that "some scallywags [who] joined in the music" had also smashed windows. AGAD Min. Spraw. 307, 3.
78. They used the word *chłopi*, which can mean "countryman/peasant" or "boy."
79. Report by the district authority in Wieliczka of 28 May 1898, CDIAL/146/4/3117, 42–43; *Czas*, no. 123, 1 June 1898, 2.
80. Another peasant had called the disturbances a *rebulacja*, a term combining *rabacja* (referring to the "Galician Slaughter" of 1846, in which the peasants attacked the nobility) and *rewolucja* (revolution).
81. Some women had brought baskets with them to Kalwarya specifically to transport their booty home.
82. Otto was not the only man of the cloth to cause trouble. A priest named Peter Burczak and two other clergymen were arrested for throwing stones and inciting the crowd to violence. Szponder also reported drunken gendarmes and a Jewish police officer in his article "On the Unrest in Kalwarya" in *Głos Narodu*, no. 130. The district captain in Wadowice then wrote a counterstatement, stressing that the gendarmes had been sober and had not been given any liquor by Jews. If they consumed alcohol at all, it was only beer, which they bought from the above-mentioned Christian store owner Leo Kakol. Officer Wilk was not a Jew, he stated, but a Catholic. CDIAL/146/4/3118, 84 and AGAD Min. Spraw. 307, 3.
83. Cf. *Kurier Ludowski*, no. 173, 24 June 1898, and no. 228, 28 August 1898. The motif of the drunken, bribed gendarmes also appeared in a request for compensation for the fatalities. Cf. CDIAL/146/7/4488, 14ff.
84. *Prawda* of 5 June 1898, 3, quoted from Unowsky, "Peasant Political Mobilization." The report echoed the outrage expressed at the pogrom of Smela, after the tsarist army opened fire on the *pogromschki*. Klier, *Russians, Jews, and the Pogroms*, 114.
85. *Głos Narodu*, no. 130, 9 June 1898. This issue was confiscated by the Kraków public prosecutor. Soboń, "Polacy wobec Żydów," 307.
86. CDIAL/146/4/3120.
87. Report by the district captain in Myślenice of 2 June 1898, CDIAL/146/4/3117. Public prosecutor Sułkowski of Wadowice received a telegram on 1 June from a Mr. Fischfreund and Mr. Rosenbaum of Myślenice, asserting that the Jews of Sułkowice had been robbed and beaten. AGAD Min. Spraw. 310, 4 & 76f.; also "An das Bezirksgericht in Skawina," 1 June 1898, CDIAL/146/4/3117, 87f.
88. Barkeepers were insulted and threatened with robbery and murder: "You know Yankiel that you only have until Sunday to live. Somebody will come to slay the Jews and he will move in here." Cited (transl. C. H.-K.) from a witness statement in Czarna, AGAD Min. Spraw. 310, 176.
89. AGAD Min. Spraw. 307.
90. As occurred in Trzinica near Jasło and in Ujanowice. Cf. Soboń, "Polacy wobec Żydów," 318.

91. Golczewski, *Polnisch-jüdische Beziehungen*, 75.
92. AGAD Min. Spraw. 308, 58.
93. *Czas*, no. 166–167, 23–24 July 1898, cited from Golczewski, *Polnisch-jüdische Beziehungen*, 72.
94. AGAD Min. Spraw. 308, 88ff.
95. In this respect, the riots can also be regarded as "exclusionary acts" by means of which the perpetrator collective assured itself of its affiliation and rights. Werner Bergmann: "Exclusionary Riots: Some Theoretical Considerations," in idem, Hoffmann, and Smith, *Exclusionary Violence*, 161–186, 179f., 187.
96. Eventually the obstinate peasant's farmhand and wife came to his aid. The latter joined in the verbal abuse, shouting at Körbel, "You son of a bitch hit my husband?" and the farmhand struck Körbel with the whip. CDIAL 146/4/3127, 37.
97. Cf. Edward P. Thompson, *Plebejische Kultur und moralische Ökonomie: Aufsätze zur englischen Sozialgeschichte des 18. und 19. Jahrhunderts* (Frankfurt a. M., 1980).
98. AGAD Min. Spraw. 309, 126.
99. "Hurrah against the mayor, let's play for the Jewish mayor!" ("Hurra na wójta, pod kolana wojta, grać żydowskiemu wójtowi. Ty żydowski wójcie!") AGAD Min. Spraw. 307, 126.
100. "Żydy [*sic*] my was porrezamy [*sic*] i będziemy solą solić." See AGAD Min. Spraw. 307, 126.
101. Cf. the subsection "Against Jewish Assimilation: The Second Phase of Anti-Jewish Agitation 1889–1898" in chapter 1.
102. AGAD Min. Spraw. 307, 126.
103. Ibid. There were also incidents of *katzenmusik* in the bordering parish of Sułkowice Jeleśnia.
104. AGAD Min. Spraw. 309.
105. CDIAL 146/4/3120, 35.
106. Report by the district captain of Drohobycz of 9 June 1897, CDIAL 146/7/4688–4689, 10ff.
107. Around the turn of the last century, Austro-Hungary was the fifth largest oil producer in the world. Most of the oil came from East Galicia. Cf. Alison Fleig Frank, *Oil Empire: Visions of Prosperity in Habsburg Galicia* (Cambridge, 2005). For a comparison with growing industrial cities in Tsarist Russia and their ethnic and social conflicts, see Charles Wynn, *Workers, Strike, and Pogromes: The Donbass-Dnepr Bend in Late Imperial Russia, 1870–1905* (Princeton, 1992); Jörg Baberowski, "Nationalismus aus dem Geist der Inferiorität: Autokratische Modernisierung und die Anfänge muslimischer Selbstvergewisserung im östlichen Transkaukasien 1828–1914," *Geschichte und Gesellschaft* 26 (2000): 371–406.
108. An interesting account of the oil-boom years in East Galicia from the perspective of a Jewish entrepreneurial family is provided by the historical novel, based on the correspondence of the family of Claudia Erdheim, *Längst nicht mehr koscher* (Vienna, 2007).
109. An attack by several hundred workers in Borczszów was prevented. CDIAL 146/4/3124, 138.
110. CDIAL 146/4/3130, 78.
111. Such as in Zagórza near Sanok, where seven participants were Roman Catholic and nine Greek Catholic.
112. CDIAL 146/4/3120, 18ff.

113. Report by the district captain of Lisko of 2 July 1898. CDIAL 146/4/3124, 66.
114. AGAD Min. Spraw. 310, 178.
115. AGAD Min. Spraw. 310, 181.
116. CDIAL 146/4/3126, 47ff.
117. The military authority's report stated that the head of the unit, Winiarski, had not given any order to shoot but had been in the process of sending a telegram asking for further reinforcements when the violence escalated.
118. Shortly before the clash, people on the market square had shouted that the gendarmes' weapons were only loaded with blanks, thus encouraging an outburst. Cf. *Kurier Luwowski*, no. 226, 16 August 1898; also, a report by the Strzyżów district administration of 20 June 1898, CDIAL/146/4/3120, 7; Soboń, "Polacy wobec Żydów," 313.
119. CDIAL 146/4/3120, 7.
120. Interpellation by Danielak, Szponder, and comrades of 30 September 1898. Sten. Prot. AH 3. Sitzung der XV. Session am 30. September 1898, 138f.; cf. the subsection "Galician Anti-Semites in the Imperial Diet in Vienna" in chapter 3.
121. *Kurier Luwowski*, no. 173, 24 June 1898, and no. 228, 18 August 1898; Soboń, "Polacy wobec Żydów," 314.
122. Daniel Unowsky presumes that at least some peasants sincerely believed the rumors to be true. Unowsky, "Peasant Political Mobilization."
123. AGAD Min. Spraw. 308, 296f.
124. For the indictment relating to this raid, see AGAD Min. Spraw. 308, 296f.
125. When questioned, Chciuk admitted he had never seen any such notices himself. But a certain Jędrzej Pitera had said on his arrest that he had seen and torn off the printed notices. But they had been so sticky with glue that he had not kept them.
126. "Co wy ludzie chcecie, czy to jest rozbój?" AGAD Min. Spraw. 308, 296f.
127. My thanks go to François Guesnet for pointing this out.
128. Haumann, *Juden in der ländlichen Gesellschaft Galiziens*.
129. While taking tobacco, money and candy, the unwelcome guests also smashed glasses.
130. See the introduction.
131. "Co psiakrew chodź, jak dzisiaj nie zrobisz, to jutro też nie zrobisz, bo ci nawala wojska."
132. AGAD Min. Spraw. 308/300f.
133. The indictment comprises seventy-one pages and is preserved in its entirety under AGAD Min. Spraw. 308/242.
134. Twelve persons (eight male, four female) were under twenty; five men were over fifty. Thirty-four were single; thirty-seven childless. The sixty-one majors (twenty-four or older) had on average 2.3 children.
135. Sixty-five from Lutzca, fifteen from Domaradz, one from Czortków, and another from Gwoznica górna.
136. AGAD Min. Spraw. 308/249.
137. Members of the Felber family were also arrested in the context of the "Ritter trial."
138. Jakub Fest and Mojszesz Verständig of Lezajsk reported that the mayor of Giedlawra near Leżajsk was alleged to have stood in Benjamin Goldmann's store and said, "We will do the same with you as they did in Jasło" (my wam tak zrobimy jak w Jaśle). The district captain came to the defense of the mayor, Antoni Chmura, claiming that in fact he had said, "You here in Lezajsk have your peace but in Jasło there are riots" (wy tu w Leżajsku macie spokój, a w Jaśle rozruch). If he had made the former comment, it was only with the intention of convincing the storeowner to reduce his price slightly. He had certainly

not had any malicious intentions as he was known to be a good mayor—according to the mitigating report on behalf of the mayor by the district captain of Łancut to the governor's office of 21 June, CDIAL/146/4/3120. In Rudanicy, a certain Jan Rak threatened the barman Mejer Leiba with the words "The emperor has now allowed [us] to beat the Jews so I have to kill you," after being refused any more vodka. CDIAL/146/4/3127, 16f. In Ceperowa, two peasants threatened a barman named Hersch Mohrer on 5 July, saying, "In Jaryczów Nowy the gendarmerie and the townsfolk are going around and calling for trouble, because they're going to beat up the Jews, the warrant to beat the Jews was issued by the emperor. They just haven't got to Ceperowa yet. When they get here, you Hersch will be the first to be killed." CDIAL/146/4/3127, 17f.

139. This is how Donald Horowitz describes the process by which a community of violence is formed and tries to win further perpetrators for the group. Cf. Horowitz, *Deadly Ethnic Riot*, 266ff.

140. Such a warrant would not be issued by any "civilized state" or modern government, the indictment stated. It would obviously be in violation of "religious doctrine," the "constitution," "reason, the heart," and a "healthy sense of love for one's neighbor."

141. All the narrative situations reconstructed here are documented in the indictment by the Rzeszów public prosecutors of 30 July 1898, AGAD Min. Spraw. 308/242, 67–71.

142. Ibid., 69.

143. See also the study by Christhard Hoffmann, "Political Culture and Violence against Minorities: The Antisemitic Riots in Pomerania and West Prussia," in Smith, Bergmann, and Hoffmann, *Exclusionary Violence*, 67–92.

144. An exception was news concerning the area around Wieliczka, where attacks had in fact previously occurred.

145. Namely Niewodna, Szufnarowa, Wojaszówka, Ustrobna, Żarnowa, Niebylec, Kamienica, and Czudec. Cf. Soboń, "Polacy wobec Żydów," 315.

146. According to a statement by Jan Kozimor. AGAD Min. Spraw. 269f.

147. On the last count, Jędrzej Szurlej was accused of insulting the monarchy as he had alleged the emperor harbored base motives such as revenge and hatred against the Jews.

148. "J. K. told him that the peasants had threatened those who did not join in the arson and pillaging."

149. Counts 10 and 11 were leveled at Agata Stachowicz and Anna Gosztyła, with individual charges of robbery.

150. For this statement, see CDIAL/146/4/3125, 41–43.

151. Sokół (English: falcon) was a nationalist and (later) paramilitary gymnastics movement among Poles, Ukrainians (Sokil), and Czechs (Sokal) in the Habsburg Empire. Jan Snopko. "Oblicze ideowo-polityczne 'Sokoła' galicyjskiego w latach 1867–1914," *Kwartalnik Historyczny* 99, no. 4 (1992): 35–55; Alojzy Zielecki, "Zaryz dziejow wiejskiego ruchu paramilitarnego w Galicji w latach 1908–1918," in Stanisław Dąbrowski (ed.), *Chłopi, naród, kultura*, vol. 2: *Działalność polityczna ruchu ludowego* (Rzeszów, 1996), 167–183.

152. There is no information on record concerning this statement. Neither the press nor the authorities found any evidence of rape or manslaughter, as the confessions suggest.

153. Wojciech Wnęch, allegedly the only other person in the bar, confirmed this incident under interrogation. He, however, was slightly deaf and had not heard all that was said.

154. Horowitz describes the preliminary phase before violence as a "rough sequence . . . that characterizes the transition from peace to mass violence and back. The riot is preceded by

a chain of identifiable precipitants, events, that persuade people that violence is necessary and appropriate." Horowitz, *Deadly Ethnic Riot*, 71.
155. Paul Brass, "Introduction: Discourses of Ethnicity, Communalism, and Violence," in idem. (ed.), *Riots and Pogroms* (Basingstoke, 1996), 1–55, here 42f.
156. Francois Guesnet, "T. Buchen: Antisemitismus in Galizien," review, *H-Soz-Kult*, 6 March 2015, www.hsozkult.de/publicationreview/id/reb-18986.
157. Similarly, the pogroms in Tsarist Russia often had the character of recreational amusement. See Klier, *Russians, Jews, and the Pogroms*, 99.
158. Magdalena Opalski, *The Jewish Tavern Keeper and His Tavern in Nineteenth-Century Polish Literature* (Jerusalem, 1986); Józef Burszta, *Wieś i karczma; rola karczmy w życiu wsi pańszczyźnianej* (Warsaw, 1950); Haumann, "Juden in der ländlichen Gesellschaft."
159. CDIAL 146/4/3122, 20ff.
160. In Russia, too, the rumor of a Jewish plot to assassinate the emperor was used to organize violence and referred to an actual incident in which the tsar had been targeted by an attack. On literature concerning the pogroms in Tsarist Russia and their reception and repercussions in Galicia, see the section "Galician Anti-Semites in the Imperial Parliament in Vienna" in chapter 1.
161. Klier, *Russians, Jews, and the Pogroms*.
162. Transcript in AGAD Min. Spraw. 307.
163. Cited from Jobst, "Die antisemitischen Bauernunruhen," 139.
164. This version contradicted the district governor's report, which stated he had not responded to the Jewish delegation's application until the last day. On the other hand, these precautions were also seen to have "contributed to the physical outburst of hatred directed at the Jews," as the latter had acted in a provocative manner having attained the requested protection. Governor's office to the Ministry of the Interior, AGAD Min. Spraw. 307, 49.
165. Ibid. By this time, the incidents in Rzeszów district and Nowy Sącz had occurred.
166. See the section "Galician Anti-Semites in the Imperial Parliament in Vienna" in chapter 3.
167. Later the column was titled "Troubles in Galicia" (Exzesse in Galizien). Cf. *Pester Lloyd*, nos. 145–160, 1898. Soboń, "Polacy wobec Żydów," 325.
168. This article provoked angry responses from some Polish newspapers in Galicia. Cf. the headline "jüdische Unverschämtheit" [Jewish impertinence], *Gazeta Narodowa*, no. 180, 1 July 1898.
169. CDIAL/146/4/3121, 39–48.
170. In addition, "measures against the antisemitic and other excesses in Galicia" had been issued by the minister of justice to the president of the regional court and the senior public prosecutors in Lemberg and Krakow. AGAD Min- Spraw. 310/8, no. 14392, 8.
171. District captains in East Galicia, too, intervened in the conflicts. An imperial chancery trainee named Kazimierz Przybysławski brought the curfew forward and set price limits for meat, bread, and milk. This successfully prevented attacks on Jews in protest of their alleged exploitation of monopolies and extortionate prices. The district captain of Borszczów tried to prevent riots by railroad workers by involving the Greek Catholic priest, talking to the Jewish population about their safety, and restricting licenses to serve alcohol; CDIAL 146/4/3124, 32. The unfamiliar groups who overran communities in the Limanowa and Grzybów districts and often had no contact with the local Christians were not only opposed by the militias but also by much of the local population.

Sokół members, veterans, and firefighters agreed to support the twenty gendarmes in Borszczów if necessary. There had been indications that Ruthenian workers planned an assault, which the urban Poles hoped to prevent. CDIAL 146/4/3124, 36.
172. Because a ban on livestock trade was already in place due to an outbreak of disease, there was little objection to the cancellation of the fair. CDIAL 146/4/3124, 69ff.
173. CDIAL 146/4/3124, 6.
174. Report by the district administration in Brzesko of 26 June 1898, CDIAL/146/4/3123, 1; report by the royal-and-imperial public prosecutors in Krakow, 19 July 1898, AGAD Min. Spraw. 305, 431. Indictment in Nowy Sącz of 16 September 1898, AGAD Min. Spraw. 309, 597.
175. CDIAL 146/4/3124, 16–18.
176. In the event, they were not able to apprehend this gang. CDIAL 146/4/3124, 50.
177. Telegram from the Israelite community of Tłuste, CDIAL 146/4/3117, 71.
178. In Sambor in East Galicia people said there would be a "reckoning" with the Jews as soon as the local garrison went on maneuvers. CDIAL 146/4/3126, 47ff.
179. On the line between Rzeszów and Gorlice.
180. On the line between Dębica and Rzeszów.
181. Soboń, "Polacy wobec Żydów," 323.
182. Some of those arrested claimed they had only gone to the scene of the crime to see the socialists' uniforms and the soldiers. Indictment, Nowy Sącz, 18 November 1898, AGAD Min. Spraw. 309, 518.
183. CDIAL 146/4/3124, 36, and AGAD Min. Spraw., 307, 23. In the jurisdictional district of Wisnirz and Woynirz, some two hundred peasants from Dzierzaniny were found marching toward the small town of Zakliczyn to conduct lootings, led by their parish head Franciszek Malisz. They scattered when the gendarmerie intervened, but Malisz was arrested. During the annual fair in Zbyszyce on 23 June, a "gang of hundreds of unknown peasants" raided the Jewish stores, causing damage said to amount to 6,265 guilders. The perpetrators escaped.
184. *Czas*, no. 149, 3 July 1898, 2, cited from Soboń, "Polacy wobec Żydów," 320.
185. Indictment, Nowy Sącz.
186. A 44-year-old peasant named Józef Bukowice asked a few young neighbors to let him know when they "went for the Jews." When they told him they were setting off for Rozdziele because nobody had raided the tavern there yet, he followed them with his horse and cart to transport the booty home. But when he got there, he found that the Jews in Rozdziele were "not as terribly rich" as he had supposed and did not yield any more booty than he could carry in his own hands. *Czas*, no. 169, 27 July 1898.
187. Report from Lewinski to the governor's office, CDIAL 146/7/4682, 20ff.
188. Cf. Unowsky, "Peasant Political Mobilization," 413f.
189. Cf. *Wiener Zeitung*, no. 147, 29 June 1898, 2.
190. Soboń, "Polacy wobec Żydów," 324f.
191. Selinger left Galicia again on 11 July, without having conducted any executions. Soboń, "Polacy wobec Żydów," 325. *Czas*, no. 147, 1 July 1898, 3, and no. 156, 12 July 1898, 2.
192. ÖStaA Wien, KA, MKSM, Kart. 734 (1898), Konv. 28-4, 4, no. 11.
193. Report from the district captain to the governor's office, CDIAL 146/4/3125, 98ff.
194. Buszko, *Polacy w parlamencie*, 220; see the section "Krakow Clericalism: Christian Socials against Liberalism and Social Democracy" in chapter 1.

195. This phenomenon is explored in chapter 3.
196. Żbikowski, *Żydzi krakowscy*, 153.
197. In later parliamentary and press debates on the situation and conduct of the Jews in Galicia, nationalist Jews and Zionists criticized this avoidance of provocation as counterproductive to equality. Emil Byk, especially, was a frequent target of their attacks. Cf. the sections "Galician Anti-Semites in the Imperial Parliament in Vienna" and "Beyond the Canon: Accusations of Ritual Murder in Galicia" in chapter 3.
198. CDIAL 146/4/3117, 71f.
199. CDIAL 146/4/3117, 102 and 120.
200. CDIAL 146/4/3120, 10.
201. Cf. Hoffmann, "Political Culture."
202. *Czas*, no. 152 of 7 August 1898, 2.
203. Unowsky, "Peasant Political Motivation," 24.
204. The newspaper *Neue Freie Presse* reported on the trial and quoted the public prosecutor, who justified the charge by saying that not only Poles but also Jews were responsible for the violence due to their provocative behavior. *NFP*, late edition of 6 July 1898. For more press coverage, see Unowsky, "Peasant Political Mobilization," footnote 83.
205. "Extract aus den dem Justizministerium vorgelegten Berichten der Staatsanwaltschaften," 3. AGAD Min. Spraw 287.
206. ÖStaA, MKSM (1898), 28-4, 4, no. 11. On 21 January 1899, *Obrona Ludu* ran a report claiming that a priest had said on his deathbed, "I think the Jews have poisoned me," *Obrona Ludu*, no. 5, 1899.
207. ÖStaA, MKSM (1898), 28-4, 4, no. 11.
208. The absence of comment in all the sources suggests that no evidence of poisoning was found.
209. CDIAL 146/4/27, 21f.
210. On this problem, see the section "Galician Anti-Semites in the Imperial Parliament in Vienna" in chapter 3.
211. *Dziennik Krakowski*, no. 354, 7 March 1897, and *Prawda*, no. 5, 1896.
212. The regiment had a historical link with Galicia: until 1893, it also conscripted soldiers from East Galicia. Georg Schreiber, *Des Kaisers Reiterei: Österreichische Kavallerie in 4 Jahrhunderten* (Vienna, 1967).

Chapter 3

POLITICS

National Isolation: The Language Dispute and Representations of Protest

In 1897, members of parliament representing the general class of electors joined the Imperial Diet for the first time.[1] Right at the beginning of the new term, prime minister and former governor of Galicia Kasimir Badeni caused a controversy by introducing a new language regulation to Bohemia, making Czech an official language of administration in Bohemia alongside German. The ensuing dispute between Czechs and Germans precipitated a major parliamentary crisis.[2] While Czechs welcomed the regulation, in the nationalist climate of the day, Germans perceived it as an attack on the supremacy of "the German culture and language" in Central Europe and the "German character" of the Habsburg Monarchy.[3] What came to be known as the "Badeni crisis" facilitated an impressive political comeback by the German nationalist Georg von Schönerer and led to violent clashes in Bohemia, which permanently scarred relations between the Germans and the Slavic nations in the Austro-Hungarian Empire.[4] The crisis impacted political antisemitism in two respects: it summoned national conflicts that impeded transnational antisemitic policy, and it created conditions of political and parliamentary tumult in which Galician members of parliament were required to operate.[5]

The language dispute exacerbated a tendency to bury supranational commonalities under national arguments and claims of a fundamental difference between Slavs and Germans. This is illustrated by the failure of Austrian Christian Socials and Galician anti-Semites to form an alliance. The two factions might have been unified by their opposition to Kasimir Badeni.[6] But the Christian Social mayor of Vienna Karl Lueger offended the Poles by derogating the prime minister as a

"Polack" and railing against the "Polish economy" and "Jewified Galicia."[7] Karl Hermann Wolf, a German National member of parliament, claimed that Austria had been "poisoned" by the "Galician export" of "*Schlazizen*, Jews and ministers" with even graver repercussions.[8] When Wolf topped his comments by calling the language regulation "Polish drudgery," Badeni challenged him to a duel.[9] It was not the only duel Wolf was to fight: he was also challenged by Polish Club member of parliament Włodzimierz Ritter von Gniewosz, who was injured in the confrontation. Polish Club and Young Czech party delegations of parliamentarians visited von Gniewosz during his convalescence to pay tribute to his efforts to "restore Slavic honor."[10] These duels illustrate the vehemence with which national conflicts were fought at the time. Personal and national honor played a crucial role in political argument. Honor was not only restored in parliament or through legal channels in verbalized forms of exchange, but also physically, in armed single combat.[11] Galicia's political culture was shaped by anachronistic ideals of chivalry that conservative aristocrats such as Badeni and Gniewosz upheld and exploited to generate publicity. Meanwhile, politicians of the Karl Hermann Wolf school, to whom personal standing within the imperial elite was immaterial, used provocations and insults to rally support "from the street."

While the conflict between German Nationals and the Polish Club Party or the Young Czechs proved the fiercest, relations between Christian Socials and the Christian People's Party also suffered under the nationalist uproar caused by the language dispute. Eventually, the Polish members of parliament refused to cooperate entirely when the Christian Socials declared their support of Emperor William II in the wake of his blatantly anti-Polish speech at Marienburg in June 1902.[12]

Though antiquated, the duel was at least a form of conflict settlement that involved consensus and agreement. The language dispute, in contrast, marked the loss of a generally accepted "language of negotiation." In the Imperial Diet, the many voices of the multinational empire yelled their respective views at each other, each in their own language. It was not the decibels that demonstrated the limits of parliament as a "place to parley" but the fact that the content was linguistically incomprehensible to many of the parliamentarians.

It was perhaps inevitable that a language dispute would plunge the Habsburg Monarchy into crisis. Along with a range of languages, numerous sociocultural spaces came together in Austria. Their hierarchical arrangement was negotiated in Vienna. In the multilingual context of the Austro-Hungarian Empire, many individuals developed considerable language skills, acting as translators for and mediators between the various linguistic-cultural contexts within which they operated.[13] These imperial actors contributed to forming a supranational culture and personified the idea of the state as more than the sum of its lands and kingdoms. Yet the Imperial Diet in Vienna revealed the other side of the multilingual coin—mutual incomprehension and struggles for cultural hegemony—to the public.

With each extension of voting rights—in 1883, 1896, and 1906—the composition of the Reichsrat changed. Formerly influential German Liberal dignitaries were gradually replaced by politicians of various national and social leanings. Many of them became transmitters of misunderstanding.[14] Parliamentarians who did not understand German were excluded from several means of exchange, as the Peasant Party members from Galicia found to their dismay. But language is not only a medium for exchanging information about the world, understanding it, and making oneself understood in it.[15] Language also conveys the world of its speakers.[16] In the politicized fin-de-siècle world, language became the "primary identifier" for individuals and groups.[17]

During the language dispute, the Imperial Diet was the scene of unprecedented filibustering. Parliamentarians twisted the house rules and blocked proceedings by stonewalling and proposing countless motions concerning banal issues. Language barriers were also used obstructively, symbolically inverting the relationship between the center and the periphery.[18] Provincial Czech parliamentarians would speak for hours in their native language to demonstratively exclude the members who did not understand it from the debate. At the same time, the strategy could be regarded as a democratic act, echoing Czech voters' negative experience of the German-language administration, and demonstrating the necessity of the Bohemian language regulation.

Figure 3.1. Imperial Diet (Reichsrat) in Vienna, *Nowiny Illustrowane*, no. 28, 1907. Public domain.

As well as problems of exclusion due to linguistic barriers, parliamentarians also addressed conflicts due to cultural differences, such as between state bureaucracy and Galician village life. Each culture's values and concepts of justice were enshrined in their language. Antisemitic speech, using neologisms and memorable watchwords that condensed complex systems of reference, could concur with a range of milieu-specific conceptual worlds. Antisemitic agitation appealed to the emotions of the listeners by suggesting an actual or impending threat to their milieu, using references that were specific to them. The concept of representations of incomprehension and multilingualism, then, is also helpful for understanding the potential and various functions of antisemitic policy.

All a Song and Dance? Performances of (In)Justice in Parliament

Barrages of tabletop banging, stamping, and catcalling, frequent scuffles, and thirteen-hour speeches no doubt dismayed many and deterred them from attending sessions of the Imperial Diet.[19] But they did not serve to depoliticize the public or disinterest them in the goings-on in Vienna.[20] Parliament remained the key arena for representing the various groups and nationalities of the Austro-Hungarian Empire.

Representation involves not only performance but also medial interpretations of and reactions to performances and their repercussions for the various publics. Parliamentary debates were media events.[21] They satisfied the demands of a politically and socially fragmented society for the political representation of their interests and worldviews.[22] Sometimes Reichsrat sessions also offered fantastically theatrical entertainment to the inquisitive public.[23]

Honorable presidents chaired sessions ringing with insults, whistling, and jeering. So long as a policy of obstruction prevailed, chaotic scenes were common, with parliamentarians appealing to the house ad absurdum. The minutes printed at the end of every session read like stage directions for dramas, recording in shorthand the tumultuous interchange of verbal cut-and-thrust, melodramatic avowals, and raucous laughter. The reader soon comes to recognize the characters who most persistently caused disturbances, reiterated the same points again and again, or held particularly passionate speeches. Parliamentarians from the peripheral crownlands presented their concepts of national identity and culture, and the capital's press played with the notions of idealization and exoticism they represented. The newspaper *Neue Freie Presse*, for instance, ran an article admiring Tomasz Szajer, a member of parliament for the Galician Peasant Party, for his "youthful, vigorous appearance in Polish national costume, with broad red stripes and sulfuric yellow embroidery on the collar and the breast. A light-colored, brightly embroidered waistcoat rounded off the colorful costume and made the handsome figure of the rural parliamentarian stand out favorably." Descending entirely into tabloid mode, the newspaper added a comment concerning the Galician's effect on the female Viennese public: "All the eyeglasses of the ladies crowding the galleries were pointed at Szajer."[24]

News from the Reichsrat was never merely dry political reporting but contained vivid descriptions of the actors' dramatic entrances and exits. It was ideal material for the burgeoning fin-de-siècle newspaper market, along with sensational court hearings.[25] And just as reports from the Imperial Diet were not confined to relaying the content of debates and bills, press coverage of trials was by no means limited to discussing the legal aspects of the cases. Both parliament and the courts were read and interpreted in the light of theatrical conventions as performance.

Frequent press exploitation was not the only thing court hearings and parliamentary sessions had in common. The cultural impact of court hearings on contemporaries' reading of parliamentary practice is a key to understanding parliamentary antisemitism. Anti-Semites used the Imperial Diet as a symbolic courtroom, where they accused Jews of crimes and advanced the construct of a specifically Jewish brand of delinquency. Parliamentarians so often discussed and criticized Galician courts and their rulings that it seemed at times as if the Reichsrat were a court of appeal. Most did so to reiterate an antisemitic concept of "Jewish crime" and be seen to represent a "Christian" concept of justice. The Reichsrat, indeed, would have been the place to appeal the Supreme Court's decision in the Mnich murder case, had Merunowicz not been the only antisemitic member at the time. It was not without reason that Galician populists drew an analogy between the imperial seat of legislation and sites of jurisdiction. Both were public venues for adjudication processes. Accusations were made in the Reichsrat as well as in the courts. Hostile motions could turn ministers into "defendants" called upon to justify their actions. Whatever the outcome, such motions brought internal parliamentary affairs into the public eye and shed light on the goings-on behind the scenes of government. Although there was no judge in the Reichsrat—sessions were chaired by the president and judgments pronounced by the parliamentarians—speakers were expected to provide information in their defense and present convincing evidence, like witnesses in a trial. The public was always present, both in a direct sense in the galleries, and in an indirect sense via the newspaper reports they read and on which they based their own judgments. Newspaper reports from the courtrooms resembled coverage of parliamentary sessions, speculating on who was honest and who was concealing the truth. Both echoed theater criticism, not only recalling the content of the drama but also describing and interpreting the gestures, facial expressions, and reactions of the performers and public.[26] More than the traditional Viennese love of theater and operetta, this was due to the fundamental similarities.[27]

Court rituals and judicial symbols represented the state order, norms, and hierarchies. Judges, prosecutors, and lawyers all donned costumes. Though still recognizable as individuals, they were assessed according to how well they played their roles. Their role in the courtroom drama was to preserve the public's faith in a fair and independent judiciary. The Imperial Diet, where the state staged the representation and participation of its citizens, functioned in a similar way. The representatives of the government embodied temperance and a sense of responsibility, while the opposition administered control by expressing doubts and criticisms and conveying any dissatisfaction with the government or, indeed, the system. The difference between theater, courts, and parliament lay in the consequences that bad performances in each could have.[28] Every court hearing assures that the state will deliver justice; every session of parliament purports to acknowledge the wishes of the electorate and regulate those in government. If the audience does not believe the roles that the performers are playing, but sees only a charade, they will lose faith in the performance. If citizens lose faith in the state's justice and controllability because of incredible performances in the courtroom and parliament, the state acquires a legitimacy problem.[29]

The Galician opposition's strategy consisted of arguing to the parliament-as-court that their "clients" had lost faith in the autonomy of Galician office holders. The tools they used were debate and above all interpellation—parliamentary questions to the ministries. Listening to their repeated accusations, the public must have found their representation of Galician law and order to be a very poor performance. Their interpellations concerning Jewish crime were characterized by recurring patterns and motifs, the impact of which will be considered below.

The Antisemitic Canon

An analysis of the thematic canon used in antisemitic interpellations reveals the core issues of antisemitic research. The term canon indicates the influence antisemitic politicians exerted to convince the Reichsrat to address such topics—that is, their active role in the process of negotiating the relevant problems. A comprehensive consideration of the idea of canonization must extend the field of inquiry to include the occurrences that were disregarded and reflect on what went unsaid as well as what was said. In the light of literature studies, a canon is understood here as a selection of texts distinguished from a large, indeterminate mass.[30] Canonization implies the forgetting and censoring of those texts that are not selected. Canons are formed via communicative processes by participants who can be regarded as "active and communicative authorities" and assessed in terms of their influence on discourse. The interest of the actors in such processes is of central importance.[31] Members of parliament, with the attendant enhanced social status and opportunities for communication via party newspapers, used the practice of interpellation to become leading authorities on canonization. They dictated which incidents were addressed, signaling their authority, and censored others. The incidents that they chose to address, presented as part of an emerging complex of motifs, became selected texts—the canon—by their representation in interpellations. The Galician opposition's interpellation practice acted, then, as a filter on speech about Jews.[32]

The first filter can be regarded as pragmatic and subject to the constraints and logics of parliamentary politics. To pass this filter, motions had to be feasible and sayable in terms of the prevalent conditions in the Reichsrat.

The second filter could be described as semantic. Antisemitism was not only a new concept that changed people's way of talking and their positioning of themselves and the other with respect to Jewish questions. Antisemitic agitators tried to find new reasons for being against the Jews, to break away from the image of harboring an ancient religious prejudice. They needed to make their accusations against Jews consistent with the political agenda. In this secular, constitutional state, where believers in all religions were legally equal and traditional ideas of the status of Christians and Jews were blurred, emphasis shifted on to conceptualizations of "Jewish crime" and away from the idea of Jewry as a fanatic minority that performed criminal religious practices.[33] In view of this, this question is raised: to what extent did parliamentary policy influence the selection of anti-Jewish motifs to be circulated or dropped?

No canon is ever undisputed. Even antisemitic politicians operated in fields covering a wide range of worldviews and concepts of meaning. Deviant views could exist and exert influence alongside the political canon, even within a politician's own group of supporters. The expression and application of these deviant views must also be examined, insofar as the sources allow. It might emerge that old anti-Jewish motifs were abandoned by political antisemitism but endured in everyday encounters between Jews and Christians. Did politics contribute to establishing "modern" ideas of the harmfulness of Jews, and discarding others? What was caught in the interpellation filter but continued to circulate through other channels, such as rumor and gossip, over which the politicians of antisemitism had no control? The motif of Jewish ritual murder is a case in point, which the present book will contrast against the political process of establishing the idea of "Jewish crime" via the practice of antisemitic interpellation. Ritual murders were not the subject of any of the Galician interpellations, though several preoccupied the public and the administration for some time.[34] Can the gulf between the rural population and the media and political spheres, which became so apparent in the Mnich murder case, be explained by the two sides' divergent views on the motif of ritual murder, which simply did not correspond with the peasant parties' agenda? Certainly, the politicians of antisemitism should not be seen to have had exclusive influence on anti-Jewish discourse. The fact that politicians and voters cooperated on antisemitic representations of Jewish crime does not mean that they inevitably agreed on all issues. By fathoming the extent of antisemitic policy in speech and acts targeting Jews, this chapter brings together the questions explored in chapters 1 and 2.

Potential Antisemitic Policy: Pragmatic or Programmatic?

By examining interpellation practice as a multilayered form of political communication, insight can be gained into the possibilities and limits of antisemitic mobilization. A broad consideration of the whole process—from the populace's articulation of complaints to requests for inquiries in the Reichsrat, responses to the interpellations in the press, and subsequent government action—sheds light on the conditions in which antisemitic patterns of interpretation became established and people rallied against Jews. It is no coincidence that popular writing and speech about Jews and their role in society changed qualitatively and quantitatively just as broad sections of the population were included in political processes for the first time.[35] A process of communitization in a specific historical space then took place, fueled by positive self-identification as an in-group in opposition to a perceived common enemy. The "Jewish issue" was an important topic, but not the principal one, for Galicia's political opposition. To understand it, one must consider the context of the province in which the parliamentarians were based, and their tasks of selecting, interpreting, and translating mostly oral sources into written processes.[36] The influence of newspapers and representational politics, supported by a constitutional administration, on the nature and popularity of "rumors about Jews" must also be explored. And another, familiar, question must be asked: to what extent did politicians manipulate "the masses" or exploit antisemitism to win votes? Or was hostility toward Jews already commonplace and merely made public and brought into parliament by the extension of suffrage? Was the antisemitic process an aspect of the "dark side" of democracy, as it addressed the possibility of practicing hate in society, or because by the logic of political rivalry it was inevitably radicalized and taken to extremes? When and how did antisemitism change relations between Christians and Jews around the turn of the century? And could the answers to these questions bring history more clearly into focus, especially with respect to the developments that followed in the twentieth century?

Dual Opposition in the Reichsrat: Galician Social Democrats, Populists, and Antisemitic Alliances

After Galician Social Democrats and populists took seats in the Imperial Diet, they formed an opposition to the Galician Polish Club, whose members were closely linked to the governor's office and supported the Cisleithanian government.[37] The Christian Social faction had hoped to use the newly discovered theme of antisemitism to unite not only the German anti-Semites but also the members of Stojałowski's party, the secular Stronnictwo Ludowe (SL), and the Ukrainian radicals.[38] However, the opposition to the 58-seat-strong Polish Club and its coalition partner, the Ukrainian conservatives of the Slavic Christian National Union (six seats), split into different parliamentary groups, including the Polish Christian Social Club (six seats) and the Polish People's fraction (three seats).

The two initially "clubless" Ukrainian radicals named themselves the "Independent Ruthenians" in 1899. Jan Potoczek, representing the conservative Peasants' League, joined forces with the Polish Club. The two Polish Social Democrats and their Ukrainian counterpart were the only Galician newcomers to become part of a supranational group, the Social Democratic Union, with a total of fifteen seats. Despite the fragmentation into separate clubs, there was lively cooperation both within the Galician opposition and with opposition groups from other crownlands. The opposition's preferred means of participation was interpellation, which required the endorsement of a minimum of fifteen parliamentarians. Social Democrats from Austria could initiate interpellations independently if they cooperated. But the Galician oppositionists (with a total of fourteen seats) needed support from other lands. When seeking to propose motions with an anti-Jewish thrust, as will form the focus of this chapter, the German Christian Socials were the obvious allies for them to call on. And following the Polna affair and the by-elections of 1900, Czech parliamentarians such as the lawyer Baxa also showed a keen interest in the "Jewish issue" and sought to use it to draw public attention across the empire to Galician concerns. Discussion of the antisemitic riots and the state of emergency imposed in consequence certainly succeeded in generating a high level of publicity.

Antisemitism and the Antisemitic Riots in Reichsrat Debate

In late November 1898, the disturbances in Galicia dominated parliamentary debate in Vienna for two days in succession. This marked the second time that Galician parliamentarians were able to get their interests on the imperial agenda.[39] Motioning to impeach the ministers for their part in the military brutality and imposition of emergency rule in Galicia, the Galician opposition symbolically put the government on trial. They turned the Cisleithanian parliament into a court of law, negotiating who was to blame for the unrest in Galicia. With their audacious proposal for an inquiry committee to investigate the imperial ministers' decisions, the newcomers in the Reichsrat deployed the heaviest ammunition available to parliamentarians and drowned out any other issues and debates for some time.[40]

The proposal was submitted by a Social Democrat, Ignacy Daszyński, and contested the legality of the state of emergency. It was an indictment against the "rulers" of Galicia and reiterated the Galician opposition's main allegations against the nobility and the high clergy. The opposition accused the former, whom they labeled *Schlachziz*,[41] of egotism, making a mockery of the Galician citizens' constitutional rights and abusing their authority to silence their political rivals, the people's parties and Social Democrats.[42] It charged "clericalism," which the ruling Conservatives had promoted during their electoral campaign, with causing the riots. Using antisemitic arguments to fight socialism and divert attention from their own wrongdoings,[43] the Conservatives had motivated the population to unleash on the Jews the anger and frustration that should have been vented at the *Schlachziz*.[44] Daszyński even termed the anti-Jewish disturbances "clerical riots" in a bid to overwrite their common labeling as "antisemitic riots."[45] The latter term, adopted from bureaucratic communication, focused equally on the victims and the cause, on Jews and political agitation. To use this term was to perpetuate the notion that the violence had been triggered by popular agitation against the Jews. With his alternative definition of the disturbances as "clerical riots," Daszyński not only took the victims out of the equation, but also shifted the focus of attention on to political Catholic propaganda as another of the Conservative's weapons in their fight for supremacy in Galicia.

Daszyński was right to assert antisemitic tendencies in Krakow's clerical press in the run-up to the 1897 elections. But he failed to mention similar currents within the peasant parties, which were inclined to distribute writings such as *Jewish Secrets* among rural communities. At no part of his long speech to the Reichsrat did Daszyński go into the significance of winning votes with antisemitism. Perhaps he did not want to remind parliament of his own inconsistencies: he himself had agreed to an electoral alliance with clerical anti-Semite Stojałowski in 1897. Neither did he say a word to acknowledge the suffering of the Jewish victims of the unrest. It was strategically important to gloss over the perspective of the Jews, many of whom were his supporters, to not jeopardize the chance to consolidate the heterogenous Galician opposition. Apart from resistance to the Polish Club, the oppositionists shared the opinion that the ruling class abused its power and had entered an unholy alliance with Jewish businesspeople to the detriment of the Christian population:

> Who is to blame [for the disturbances]? [The gentlemen of] this large bloodsucking caste, . . . this historically branded caste, which devastated and sold its fatherland (lively agreement from his party comrades) . . . which forever cheats behind the scenes here with Vienna, with the centralist or any other government, which is omnipotent in the land, and where some issues are concerned, across the empire. . . . (applause from his party comrades) You will no doubt remind us of the Jewish moneylenders, of the odd Jew's kaftans and earlocks. I will show you that the Jews are bloodsucking among your ranks too, that the Jews are your right-hand men in your economy, I will show you that not by my own words but by the words of one of your fellow class members, Prince Puzyna, that what the Jews do in our country, they do only with your approval and under your generous patronage."[46]

What Does Antisemitism Mean?

Reporting on the debate a few days later, the newspaper *Neue Freie Presse* criticized Daszyński's arguments and maintained that suppressing populist parties and social democracy under emergency law was a legitimate means of combating anti-Jewish violence. But it conceded that, judging by the comments of subsequent speakers, "the political administration in Galicia is steered more by political than administrative considerations" and that the privileged ruling class used antisemitism to redirect the population's hatred on to the "middlemen," the Jews.[47]

Across the party landscape, then, a consensus prevailed that antisemitism had caused the summer's disturbances. Views diverged greatly, however, on who was to blame for antisemitism or even how to define it. The Social Democrats accused Galicia's ruling Conservatives of antisemitism. A Secular People's Party member named Winkowski spoke of "state-sanctioned antisemitism." He described himself as a "semi-anti-Semite" who supported assimilation and combated only the "malicious Jews" who had "grasped too much power" in his hometown Tarnów, in contrast with the Christian-social movement under the aegis of Bishop Ignacy Łobos, which tried to pass on the population's hatred of the *Schlachziz* to the Jews. Winkowski defined "full" antisemitism as exploiting hostility toward Jews for other purposes, and dehumanizing Jews with intent to murder or expel them. In his view, "full antisemitism" could be observed not only in the clerical movement in his own crownland but also in the Vienna Reichsrat and in the Dreyfus affair in France:

> I am of the opinion that—I don't know if one can say this so openly in the Austrian parliament (general merriment)—Jews are human too, whatever others may claim (more general merriment; heckling). As Jews are humans, one cannot solve the Jewish question by slaughtering them like cattle. One could at most drive them out, if they don't voluntarily emigrate, but Austria has no Devil's Island, and Franz Josef Land is rather far away (laughter), and if one should send the Jews over the border, it would perhaps precipitate a war, so we should seek to exploit the Jews' positive sides for the general good and eliminate their negative characteristics (quite right!). That is the only way to solve the Jewish question, there is no other in my view.[48]

Another Secular People's Party member, Jan Stapinski, also argued in support of the proposal. The eloquent party chairman and later editor-in-chief of the party newspaper *Przyjaciel Ludu* had, as mentioned above, gained his seat in the Reichsrat after the turbulent by-election of summer 1898. He, too, held the *Schlachziz* responsible for the disturbances and accused them of allowing the raids on Jews to take place, despite being informed of the rumors, to be able to subsequently suppress all unwelcome political movements under the banner of combating violence.

Stanisław Stojałowski also defended the proposal. Although widely held to be the driving force behind anti-Jewish agitation in Galicia and the mastermind behind the "movement,"[49] he, too, condemned the violence. Being a member of the Christian People's Party, he naturally did not hold clericalism responsible for the riots. Neither did he blame the Galician government, but the Jews themselves.[50] Indeed, he proudly acknowledged his leading role in antisemitism: "In contrast, I postulate that our party has thank God been active for over 20 years and throughout that time has consistently fought the Jews and was always antisemitic, but never physically set upon the Jews. When it came to riots, then, it was not our party that encouraged or incited the people to violence, but Dr. Byk's fellow nationals and believers themselves."[51]

Diverging Counter-Opinions: Emil Byk and Jan Potoczek of the Polish Club

Before Stojałowski spoke, Emil Byk argued against the proposal. A member of the Polish Club and chairman of the Jewish Community of Lemberg and the Schomer Israel association, Byk was the only parliamentarian to acknowledge the suffering of the Jews of West Galicia.[52] He defended the state of emergency as safeguarding the security and property of equal citizens of the crownland. On balance, he argued, it was more important to protect such assets when in dire risk than to ensure the free expression of political opinions. In this context, he noted ominous developments in "mass politics," away from the ideal of "uplifting" and "enlightening" the populace and toward a populist tendency to "stoop" to the level of "mob instincts." Such politicians were no longer role models but agitators of the masses to whom they "promised the moon." Byk denied that hostility toward Jews had come to pervade everyday relations between Jews and Christians in West Galicia and stressed his enduring commitment to the Polish nation and assimilation. Poland, he said, was the land of religious tolerance, which deserved the Jews' gratitude, as it had received them when they fled persecution in Germany. Antisemitism had not grown on "Polish soil"; Stojałowski had "imported coarse Viennese antisemitism" with dreadful consequences. The latter's politics, he argued, did not deserve the names "Polish and Christian Social."

Byk received some support from his party comrades for his mention of Jewish equality and Poland's history of tolerance. Few supported him in his view of Jews as victims, and certainly no non-Jewish speakers. Not even Minister President von Thun found any words of sympathy when he addressed the Reichsrat to defend the state of emergency. Byk had gone out on a limb to describe antisemitism as imported from Germany, overlooking the substantial movements behind the secular and the Christian-social peasants parties, for whom a national community exclusive of Jews was party policy. The Ukrainian Radicals, meanwhile, contradicted the notion of "Polish soil" and assimilation to the Polish nation by their mere presence. In short, Emil Byk's speech invoked values and ideas that would have been applauded in the Galician Landtag in 1868.[53] But thirty years later, his vision of Jewish Polishness did not appeal to many. And the lack of support from the majority of Christian Galicians became glaringly apparent.

Speaking next, Stojałowski denied Byk the right to define what it meant to be Christian. He was followed by the Viennese anti-Semite Georg Pattai, who echoed Stojałowski and added mockingly that he did not meddle with the Poles' treatment of Jewish views of Polishness.[54] In 1868, Pattai would have been overruled by the liberal majority in government, but by 1898 he had the majority behind him. Karl Lueger had completed his gradual march to victory and arrived in Vienna's City Hall, defeating liberalism. The allegation of "crude Viennese antisemitism" could, then, be refuted with a list of antisemitic successes in the imperial capital.[55] Pattai went so far as to justify the persecution to which Byk had referred and laid the blame on the Galician Jews themselves for the summer's disturbances. They would not have happened, he argued, if the Poles had driven the Jews out of Galicia as the Germans had done. Pan-German Party member Karl Wolff had fired a similar salvo during a debate on the constitutional situation in Galicia two weeks previously, when he denigrated the Polish nation as a "nation of parasites."[56] He had not only kindled fears of a Slavic-Jewish threat to German Austria by repeating the familiar slogan that Galicia was "Jew-infiltrated," but also hampered efforts toward an international antisemitic alliance in Vienna.[57]

Not all speakers who supported the proposal blamed Jews for the unrest. And not all who voted against it held "rabble-rousers" responsible for antisemitism. Jan Potoczek of the conservative Peasant League registered to contradict the motion. But he did not entirely defend the state of emergency, arguing that it should be lifted as soon as possible to minimize the negative economic consequences for Galicia. In his view, the Jews had provoked the Galician people into rioting by "sucking their blood." His rural-rooted antisemitic rhetoric echoed the Peasant League's policies and programmatic use of language. But since he was not a social revolutionary, like the members of the secular peasant party or the Christian People's Party, and cultivated good relations with the governing elite, he had joined the governor-loyal Polish Club.[58] Exercising caution, Potoczek did not vote in favor of impeaching the government, although he had an obvious affinity with the "semi-anti-Semites" and anti-Semites of the peasant parties and Christian People's Party. Potoczek did not link the Jews' allegedly harmful influence with government failings. But when he spoke about Jews, he sounded much like the opposition.

Potoczek's stance highlighted the vulnerability of Jewish members of the Polish Club in parliament. As well as avowed anti-Semites such as Teofil Merunowicz, there were also politicians like himself among its ranks, who held more subtly anti-Jewish views and poured scorn on the memory of a Polish tradition of tolerance. Potoczek showed that the idea of brotherly Polish-Jewish cooperation, not only in the kingdom of Poland but also in Galicia, had by this time become a dream that had lost much of its allure.[59]

Potoczek and Byk were members of the same party; one voted against the proposal, the other abstained. While Byk stressed the equality of all citizens before the law and their equal right to safety, Potoczek spoke of an ethnic conflict caused by the Jews in Galicia, to which Christians had responded by rioting. Their voting was dictated by party-political demands, which took precedence even over antisemitic convictions. In a sense, antisemitic policy positively thrived under these conditions, as parliamentarians utilized it as an inclusionary—and exclusionary—device.

Broader Use of Antisemitic Interpellation

The debate surrounding Daszyński's proposal illustrates the opposition's efforts to form a united front against the state of emergency and the conservatives in Galicia by focusing enmity on the Polish Club. But their views on issues such as clericalism, the role of Jews in inciting the violence, and antisemitism diverged starkly. Certainly, with German anti-Semites being such a strong force in the Reichsrat and in Vienna, antisemitism was not stigmatized. On the contrary, playing the anti-Jewish card was the easiest way to win the support of prominent imperial parliamentarians. And that was sure to attract press interest and thus raise public awareness of Galician concerns throughout the empire.[60]

None of the parliamentarians or commentators participating in the debate pointed a finger at the actual perpetrators of the riots. Time and again, it was said that the rural population had been manipulated by opinion makers. The political game consisted of attributing responsibility for the violence to one's current chief opponent, whether that be the ruling party, the people's parties, or the Jews. The riots of 1898 became political capital that even Czech and German Bohemians could exploit in parliament.[61] Speakers often digressed completely from the traumatic events in West Galicia and seized the opportunity to give voice to their ethnocentric understanding of politics and to practice antisemitic politics.

Interpellation in Political Practice

Parliamentary politics consisted not only of speaking in parliament; there were more ways of representing one's electorate in the Reichsrat. Indeed, Galicia's most active antisemitic politician, Secular People's Party member Franciszek Krempa, never spoke in parliament.[62] Parliamentarians chose to address the house if they had a talent for public speaking and a mastery of German. But Krempa did not speak any German.⁶³ For the same reason, most Galician People's Party members were disqualified from the mainstay of parliamentary activity, in-house debate. Those parliamentarians who could not contribute by rhetorical means represented their Galician electorates via textual channels and so established a new form of antisemitic politics. With written interpellations—questions to the ministers—members of parliament created public arenas where modern antisemitism took place, without having to speak any German themselves. Galician politicians contributed to the controversial debate surrounding the "antisemitic riots" by having their interpellation texts read out in the Reichsrat.

Interpellation as a Means of Representation

Interpellations were not merely texts that were read out in parliament. They involved a whole process of channeling messages back and forth between rural Galicia and the imperial capital. To initiate interpellations, politicians needed a substantial body of information on local events. The people's parties benefited from the procedure's reminiscence of bygone days' appeals to the lord of the manor or ruler, an option that was familiar to peasants. Since the Josephine reforms, the law had guaranteed legal recourse for every subject. This was only hesitantly realized by the peasant population,⁶⁴ who even after the Ausgleich of 1867 mostly felt that public servants acted in the interests of the landowners rather than in accordance with the law. Feeling that officials treated them with contempt and disregarded their concerns, peasants had little confidence in the

Figure 3.2. Peasants from Tarnobrzeg accompany their recently elected deputy to the train station on his way to Vienna, *Nowiny Illustrowane*, no. 25, 1907. Public domain.

Odjazd posła: Ludność z pod Tarnobrzega żegna p. Wiącka na dworcu kolejowym.

Figure 3.3. Farewell to the deputy at the train station in Tarnobrzeg, *Nowiny Illustrowane*, no. 25, 1907. Public domain.

official channels. They were more inclined to place their trust in the emperor, whom they believed to be just and to heed his subjects' concerns. Often, peasants confronted by arrogant officials invested all their hopes for attaining justice in going straight to the highest authority and informing the emperor of their predicaments.[65] This was especially true in remote areas where the state was represented by one single—unpopular and mistrusted—gendarme.

The myth of the good emperor was also useful for the parliamentarians' practice of interpellation. As the parliament was in Vienna, many Galicians assumed its members had preferential access to the emperor, on whom they pinned their hopes for solutions to their problems.[66] Politicians then called on the public via party newspapers to write to them or approach them personally with their concerns,[67] which they pledged to bring forward in Vienna.

Despite the large turnout for Reichsrat elections and high level of politicization since the extension of suffrage, many provincial voters still associated Vienna primarily with the Habsburg court rather than with the imperial parliament.

Politicians needed to inform their voters they could voice their concerns via interpellations that were read out in parliament. Their efforts were to some extent undermined by the colorfully attired clerical newspaper editor Tomasz Szajer, who liked to play on his readers' expectations that Emperor Franz Joseph would personally deal with the problems in their villages.[68] Meanwhile, the newspaper's correspondents advised emboldened readers not to go to Vienna themselves, ensuring them the parliamentarians could better represent their interests.[69]

Politicians made efforts to be accepted by their readers and potential voters as representatives and thus mediators between the villages and the capital. When conveying the voters' concerns to parliament, they acted not only as messengers and translators but also as politicians with their own agendas. Between an issue being told to a politician and read out in parliament, it went through several changes, due to the translation process and the politician's conscious efforts to be perceived as a "people's attorney." This incongruence between the voters' concerns and how they are represented affects every kind of political representation. The stage of transforming oral into written information is usually a key moment of change. Yet it was precisely this service of translating the needs and fears of rural voters from their oral vernacular into the textual grammar of the Reichsrat that constituted the Galician parliamentarians' main appeal.[70] It meant they could bridge the cultural gap between the provinces and the capital, between the life-worlds and problems of their voters and the seat of power. Interpellations influenced realities in Vienna, Lemberg, and Krakow and returned to affect the places where the complaints had been raised. By the process of translating local, oral culture into that of political representation, the form and sense of the original text was altered, as occurs with every translation.[71] The translations, moreover, reflected the balance of power between the parliamentarian and the voters.[72] The parliamentarian embodied power during the process of interpellation. But he also relied on his electorate's information and votes. Despite the imbalance, then, voters and politicians were linked by mutual interests and mutual dependence, analogous to the process of political agitation and rumor-circulating.

By selecting which points to include in an interpellation to represent the cares and concerns of the *lud*, the parliamentarian or newspaper editor acting as "town crier" created a concept of the problems and ideals of their community. An interpellation negotiated one specific situation. But when several, similar complaints were made, a narrative pattern was formed. This form of representation proved a reliable way of portraying conflicts between Christians and Jews, or between peasants and officials, which party circles could find acceptable and relatable. Originating in oral reports, interpellations on the Jewish issue integrated voters and politicians in one text. These texts condensed what their authors considered to be collective notions by charging the key points with emotion and incorporating narrative conventions familiar from fables, fairytales, and rumors. They illustrate the semantic structure of antisemitism. Considering the originator communities' reception of the thusly constructed meanings in the light of the interpellation scenario, one gains an impression of the communicative potential of antisemitic policy.

Politicians orchestrated series of similar questions as a strategy of political communication. In this way, the individual cases accumulated to form a bigger picture, lending them greater credibility and inscribing their view of the causes of "Galician misery" into the public consciousness.[73] Once a topic had become a firm talking point, it was raised again and again. Newspapers informed readers on how questions were received and which topics were addressed in interpellations. Some readers were no doubt encouraged to likewise seek the help of a member of parliament. Word was spread that anyone with a problem relevant to a peasant party agenda could attempt to solve it this way. In the interplay between reporting, selecting, and publicizing issues, a catalog of problems was collated that might be addressed in parliament. The entire interpellation process was an act of representing citizens—electoral groups or individuals—in the context of the parliamentary state. If the state pursued the questions, its bureaucracy had an impact back on local realities via its officials. There had been no such links between the villages and the capital at the time of the Franka Mnich "ritual murder" case, and it was all observed and commented on by the party-political press and other newspapers. Interpellations can therefore be regarded as performances, as meaningful actions.[74] The political representation of Galician voters by means of interpellations wove a complex fabric of communication that will be described in ideal terms below.

The Interpellation Process and Its Impact

Members of the public reported offenses they had observed or experienced and rumors they had heard to a member of parliament, who then translated the information—by a process of selection, interpretation, and ordering—from its "infinite" verbal form into a written form. From this raw material, the parliamentarian formulated a text describing an explicable grievance, or several related grievances, and concluding with a question to a minister. The questions were translated into German, and at least fourteen other parliamentarians sought to endorse the query with their signatures. For Galician parliamentarians to initiate interpellations, then, the issue needed to be relevant to several parties and avoid offending a variety of potential signatories. This was the first pragmatic filter, as mentioned above. However, in view of the heterogenous nature of the opposition, united mainly by its hostility toward the Polish Club, getting this far was no easy task. Criticism of the Galician government was sure to garner attention and find approval but did not necessarily address the "Jewish question." Issues popular with the clericals and religious questions would have a divisive effect, as would equating socialism with Jews. Addressing the idea, widely held among Ukrainian nationalists, that the Poles and Jews held the Ukrainian people in a stranglehold would have spelled the end of cooperation with Polish oppositionists.[75] The Galicians did not have enough contacts among German anti-Semites to win their signatures. And criticizing the purported alliance between the emperor and the Jews would have amounted to lèse-majesté. Tomasz Szajer, who was said to have deeply impressed the ladies of Vienna, had lost his immunity at the start of his mandate by claiming that the emperor "curtseyed before Rothschild." Completed interpellations were submitted at the start of a parliamentary session and checked against the formal requirements. The leader of the session then read out the questions before handing them to be copied for the records. The questions were not usually debated in the same session but sent straight to the relevant ministry. On the rare occasions that a minister answered a question directly, his answer was also put on record.

What potential lay in raising a question in parliament if it was only read out—along with many others—but not debated? Mere questions naturally did not receive as much coverage as full-blown debates.[76] Yet the practice of interpellation nevertheless reached the public. For one, party newspapers printed the questions to prove the parliamentarians' commitment to defending the interests of their readers and voters.[77] Citations from the parliamentary records were, moreover, officially exempt from censorship. As many interpellations contained direct attacks on the Galician governors and their usually strict policy of censorship, citing the records enabled publishers to run criticisms of the Galician government's authoritarian practice yet remain within their constitutional rights. Textualizing and printing the questions to the ministers also added symbolic significance to the peasants' grievances, presenting the information gleaned from informal oral contexts in the authoritative language of parliament. The place and date on the bottom line indicated when they had been read out in the Imperial Diet. That alone raised their importance in the eyes of oral communication communities.

In terms of communication theory, by textualizing the peasants' oral reports, the newspapers fed more information into the gossip cycle.[78] While gossip is an "infinite" network, gaining authority through self-referentiality and conveying a constantly changing flow of speech, its textualizations are "finite" and legitimized by the name of the author or publisher. The interpellations were authorized by the parliamentarians and shorthand records of parliamentary sessions.[79] Many more people received the reports, appropriated them, embellished them with their own emphases or interpretations, and passed them on, altering the tales and adding renewed momentum as they did so. Antisemitic interpellations not only drew on rumors about Jews but also influenced the rumors by consolidating various strands of gossip, feeding new gossip in, and offering multilayered interpretations.

The various tales were further compounded when the ministries tasked the local authorities with conducting investigations in response to the questions. This of course was a main objective of antisemitic interpellations. To members of local communities, the public prosecutor calling for witnesses and conducting interrogations seemed to prove there was some truth to the talk. Witnesses were then emboldened to add knowledge gleaned from gossip or press coverage of the interpellation texts to their statements. Information and allegations were constantly reinterpreted and reorganized in the minds of members of the communication network.[80] The dynamic thus generated gave rise to an interpretative space between government action, the "official" news printed in the newspapers, and the population's stock of readings. Seen in this light, nobody had any control over what was said, not even newspaper publishers or parliamentarians. But they could influence it by feeding in new information and offering different interpretations of it. The instrument of parliamentary review was frequently used to generate antisemitic realities.[81] Additionally, by initiating a series of interpellations on the same theme, parliamentarians helped construct and consolidate the notion of a specifically Jewish brand of criminality in Galicia.[82]

Parliamentary Debates on the State of Emergency and Police Brutality

The Galician opposition relied even more heavily on the interpellation practice when the disturbances broke out in Galicia. From 2 June to the end of the year 1898, Galician parliamentarians submitted thirty-seven requests for a government response to issues concerning Jewish crimes, unjustified censorship, or abuses of power by the Galician rulers.[83] As the self-proclaimed "attorneys" of the rural Christian population, they used two strategies to defend their clientele against negative public opinion.

First, they portrayed the peasants as helplessly immature and, as such, unaccountable for their actions. Daszyński maintained that "the people could not be directly blamed" for their "ignorance and gullibility, habitual drunkenness and uproariousness."[84] The peasants' vices, though regularly pilloried by reformers, worked to their advantage "before the law," as they mitigated the circumstances of their crimes and diminished their guilt in the public eye.[85] A second defense strategy consisted of explaining or even justifying the peasants' rage against Jews and the armed forces by accusing the latter two groups of violence and other offences. In this way, the interpellators turned the tables and suggested that the rural population was itself existentially threatened by military brutality and Jewish profiteering and fraud. Many interpellations drew a horrific picture of police brutality in response to the disturbances. Allegations of military violence against peasants were nothing new; it was the subject of a long list of protests and interpellations by the people's parties. Indeed, a glance at the Krakow military court files shows that gendarmes and especially soldiers frequently subjected civilians to physical abuse. An interpellation on 30 September addressed a string of assaults by the military, committed since the imposition of emergency law. The civilian population was accustomed, it claimed, "to various forms of unbridled conduct on the part of the military," but now the latter's "sense of liberty was degenerating into such brutish behavior, yes, even acts of violence, that the entire Galician press can hardly keep up with the coverage, and the populace, lacking weapons, is literally overcome with panic."

Most reports of military abuse concerned cavalry units, hussars, and lancers, who could have inflicted serious wounds with their sabers and often needed restraining by gendarmes. Interpellators explained the military's misconduct by the inherent tension of their situation: while required to obey strict inner rules under pain of severe penalties, they were not bound by any sense of obligation toward the civilian population. Recruits, moreover, were subjected to grueling, sometimes inhumane, rites, as had also been addressed in several interpellations.[86] The alarmingly high suicide rate[87] in some garrisons due to abuse in the barracks was no secret.[88] Interpellations and newspaper articles often reported officers who were not from Galicia insulting and striking civilians.[89] Preserving honor was essential to the officer class. While dueling was an honorable way to challenge offenders of equal rank, they had no ritual method of dealing with slights from civilians.[90]

In the multiethnic context of the Habsburg crownland, misunderstandings caused by linguistic and cultural differences were frequent. Nationalist ideas and a traditional understanding of honor turned individual conflicts into a question of national pride. It was the imperial army's task to hold the empire together, partly by suppressing national movements. The supranational officer corps, which used German as the language of command, represented unity beyond national borders.[91] But to Poles especially, German symbolized oppression and the domination of countrymen by the German Empire, as well as their own domination by the Austrian emperor and army. The interpellations against military brutality not only articulated concerns about nationally interpreted conflicts around the periphery of the empire but also highlighted the complex nature of establishing a liberal legal order. An autocratic spirit lingered longer in the military than in the administration, as the former resisted the judiciary's claim to be sole arbiters. Members of the Galician opposition addressed this inconsistency of imperial rule in the context of the 1898 riots in order to shift blame from their clientele.

Andrzej Szponder, representing the Christian People's Party, directed a question at the minister president, inquiring whether he intended to initiate any measures to support the widows and orphans of peasants killed by the armed forces in Galicia.[92] He estimated the number of fatalities caused by military deployments at thirty and declared all the victims to have been "completely innocent."

The only other description he included in his interpellation text was of two of the victims, aged seventy and seventy-two, who had been sitting on the church steps, holding their prayer books, when they were shot. These details became a popular motif in accounts defending the *lud*, the people. The information from the people's elected "attorneys" conveyed the impression that soldiers had fired at a gathering of peaceful geriatrics without any provocation by a scythe-wielding, angry mob.

In the next interpellation, Michał Danielak and Andrzej Szponder addressed the incidents in Frysztak.[93] They repeated the motif of the innocent peasants holding prayer books before turning their attention to the Strzyżów district captain Winiarski, who had allegedly given the order to shoot. The following lines purportedly echoed the popular opinion at the time: "In the blood of this district captain there is something that drives him to murder: His brother murdered his young wife and his elderly uncle, the priest in Dydnia, with a knife at Easter this year. . . . The public is right to demand atonement. The innocently shed blood is a disgrace that calls for revenge." The residents of Fryzstak processed the tragedy and the shock at the loss of their family members by feeding the local rumor mill.[94] They vented their anger at the armed forces' brutality in defamations of the district captain's family. At the least, the interpellation aimed to convey this impression to the Reichsrat in Vienna.

At the next session, Andrzej Szponder was joined by Jan Kubik in broaching the riots in Kalwarya[95] and continuing the fight for the definitive explanation of the disturbances. Having collated "public opinion" on them—a selection of voices identifying Jews and gendarmes as the cause of the violence—Szponder and Kubik claimed to have personally assessed the situation on the ground and made a considered analysis before bringing the matter to parliament in Vienna. In the process of assigning meaning to concepts, certain terms emerge as useful. Szponder and Kubik introduced the linguistic convention of referring to the "*so-called* antisemitic riots" to distance themselves from the popular assumption that the riots had been motivated by anti-Jewish feeling. They contrasted their interpretation against the opposing view with the following lines:

> And what was the cause of this bloody tragedy, which touched our people to their very core? The newspapers seemed to know. Antisemitic disturbances. Major convergence of peasants to beat the Jews and rob them. The gendarmes intervened, opened fire. Two casualties. The crowd was dispersed, calm, order restored. So much for the newspaper coverage. And now, shifted into the light of truth and by eye-witness statements, which can conjure this at any time, the whole story appears as follows:
>
> A few days previously, the Jews in Kalwarya had provoked the peasants and said to them: "Now they will beat the Jews too, on May 26 the fight with the Jews will start." At the same time, they sent a delegation to the district captain in Wadowice to ask for reinforcements of the gendarme unit in Kalwarya, and possibly a detachment of soldiers, as their lives were allegedly under threat. Without reviewing the necessity

of such measures, the district captain gave the order to reinforce the gendarmes and dispatched the inspector there already on the eve of the celebrations, on May 25. . . . Although they [the peasants] acted utterly peacefully, and although there was not a trace of preparation for an attack on the Jews, the inspector proceeded to interrogate the people without having the slightest grounds, thus only embittering the peasants.[96]

Szponder and Kubik went on to describe the subsequent disturbances, during which some "urchins and apprentices [had] imprudently smashed quite a few windows in Jewish houses" while "the people [had] acted quite calmly and . . . gone home in the evening." The shots had been fired well after the crowd had started to disperse. This summary of the events portrayed not the Christians but the Jews as having caused the violence and asserted that the deployment of armed forces was "in no way justified . . . because it only encouraged the provocative and impudent behavior of the Jews." Later interpellations supported the criticisms of the state of emergency raised during the Reichsrat debate described above.[97]

Unfortunately, the police continued to use violent methods once order was restored. They were instructed to ensure the material damages suffered were swiftly compensated to allow Jews and Christians to return to peaceful coexistence following the ravages of the summer. But although their actions met the Galician Jews' need for justice and security, they were not conducive to building the Christian population's trust in the law enforcement agencies.

An interpellation of 13 October, cited below, illustrates the opposition's linguistic experience of, and the populace's perception of, police methods of investigating the attacks on the Jewish population and affording compensation.

> When performing arrests of the alleged participants in the so-called antisemitic riots in Galicia, terrible acts of cruelty were carried out against the population by both the gendarmes and the military detachments deployed in the villages . . . :
>
> 1. Marianna Nowak of Moszczenica, district of Neu-Sandec, was assailed by a soldier early in the morning of July 2, slapped in the face and confronted with the words: "Give back the things you robbed!" At this the soldier hit her behind the ears and demanded that she tell him where the stolen goods were hidden; eventually he started to administer such heavy blows with his rifle butt that he broke her arm, as well as giving her nine-year-old son Franz punches to the head to induce said person to reveal where the stolen goods were, and all this occurred although the persons thus maltreated had not participated in the robbing. . . . The injured party went to the lieutenant colonel to complain; there, the military surgeon examined her broken arm and she also discovered that the soldier in question was named Bleimann and a Jew.
>
> . . .
>
> 4. Johann Majewski of Moszczenica, in the afternoon of July 3, following a search of the house of his brother Peter Majewski and the confiscation of objects found there, was bound with handcuffs and thus detained at a cart for over an hour; hereupon the gendarmes apprehended his nine-year-old son, dealt him punches and threatened to stab him [with bayonets] if he refused to say where his father had hidden the stolen cache.

The boy in his fright said that his uncle Johann Majewski might have the cache, ... upon [the uncle's] explaining that he did not possess the stolen goods and had not been at any looting raids, a gendarme leapt at him, dealt him a blow and shouted: 'Give it back you hound!'

...

7. Sieniec and Zielinski said that on the same day, the gendarmes and soldiers had struck an aged, 80-year-old woman named Anna Talarczyk in the home of Michael Korna in Cyganowice, in order to extract from her information on the whereabouts of the stolen goods. ... he was bound and tied to the cart and when he confessed that the loot was in a bush by the mill stream, the aforementioned mounted him as if he were a horse and made him carry them over the mill stream, whereupon they subjected him to further abuse in the bushes.[98]

Although these reports were tendentious and probably exaggerated, there is no reason to doubt that police used violence to elicit confessions and induce people to return stolen goods. Consequently, the stories of military brutality against the civilian population came to overshadow the original conflict between Christians and Jews. Politicians also shifted the focus of their portrayals of the disturbances in their interpellations. To the Reichsrat in Vienna, they glossed over the raids on Jewish houses and taverns with accounts of riotous bands of soldiers—deployed by the power-hungry conservative elite—beleaguering the impoverished rural population. But "the Jews" continued to play an important role.[99] In the populist narrative, not only were they provocateurs and beneficiaries of the punishments suffered by the people; they had also managed to get the state apparatus on their side and make it serve their purposes.

This view was clearly reflected in the next day's interpellation by Jakub Bojkos of the People's Party. Making a connection between the riots and the military's conduct,[100] he stressed that the people had "until very recently" held gendarmes in high regard because "no offender" eluded "their vigilance"; they exercised "control over the barkeepers" and enforced "restrictions on the bloodsucking profiteers." But since the end of the "blessed term of office of Count Kasimir Badeni," they had been primarily deployed to suppress the Conservatives' political opponents and obstruct the work of the people's parties. The riots in Galicia were the consequence of harnessing the police for political purposes:

> Disturbances, in several Galician districts this year, are doubtless the first large-scale effect of the inappropriate use of the police. Preoccupied with political agitation, they had no time to deal with the rumors circulating among the peasant population about an imperial warrant to attack Jews, [or] to investigate the sources and prevent the unfortunate riots.... Regrettably, the gendarmes who bear the blame for the above-mentioned abuses are triumphant. Not just that none of them have been punished, they have all been rewarded.... And the neglect of their proper duties can already be felt. The profiteers are raising their heads ever more boldly; alcoholism is flourishing again due to police compliancy toward barkeepers. Card games of chance are tolerated in

many areas. The [people's] favorable opinion of the police is generally reversing into a hatred of the institution. It is high time we put an end to this aberration.[101]

Bojkos's text inverted the governor's view on the causes and perpetrators of the riots. His explanation of the disturbances played down the many crimes committed against Jews and echoed the perpetrators' denials of responsibility. By this reading, the gendarmes—being the extended arm of the ruling conservatives—were responsible for inciting the riots, not the "fervently muck-raking" socialists and populists. The main problem, the oppositionists claimed, was the decline in public approval of the gendarmes. Their image had not only suffered from their misappropriation to combat the people's parties but also because of their increased tolerance of the evils of alcoholism and usury, which were unquestionably associated with Jews. Having become instruments of the Stańczyks, they had stopped quelling criminals, offensive barkeepers, and "bloodsuckers." In this argument, the accusation resonated that the gendarmes were on the side of the Jews. Furthermore, it pointed to a connection between government officials and the crimes committed by Jews, the most fruitful motif of antisemitic interpellations.

Antisemitic Interpellations Connecting the Villages to the Capital
The Kleinmann Case

The first interpellation concerning Jewish crimes was initiated by Franciszek Krempa on 28 May 1897.[102] Krempa called on the Minister of Justice to urge the judicial authorities to more stringently enforce the law against usury to free "the population from the plague of loan sharks." There were still many moneylenders abroad, he maintained, at liberty to "ruin and exploit the peasant population." A concrete example he referred to in his text was that of a "certain Abraham Klainmann" who had been causing trouble in the district of Mielec for several years. Twelve years previously, he had lent twenty-seven guilders to a peasant named Wojciech Ciemięga of the village Jaślany, who had paid him back four hundred guilders but whom he had still sued for distraint equivalent to twenty guilders. Krempa cited three further examples of Abraham Klainmann suing peasants from Jaślany despite receiving redemption and interest payments far in excess of the amount he had lent them. The local police, Krempa wrote, had filed several complaints of usury, but the public prosecutors in Tarnów had either soon abandoned or never opened investigations.

Krempa's interpellation text was obviously based entirely on village gossip and the complaints of debtors seeking revenge on their creditor. The grotesquely exaggerated back payments without reference to repayment periods, as well as the vague mention of complaints without specification of dates or procedure numbers or reasons for closing the proceedings, all point to the fact that Krempa had not conducted any documentary research. He relied exclusively on oral sources, collecting rumors about the local moneylender and his "victims," Wojciech Ciemięga, Jan Pszczenicy, Józef Trella, and "Wojciech the Pawlusiak." Nevertheless, the interpellation brought together a reliable stock of signatories, keen to raise the issue of a Christian-Jewish conflict in Galicia in the Reichsrat and discuss it in a broader context of usury and exploitation.

The Blasbalg Case

The following interpellation, initiated by Krempa on 29 November, provides intriguing insights into antisemitic political strategy, as well as into the Austrian authorities' handling of antisemitic interpellations on a local and a ministerial level.[103] Alongside the typical accusations of fraud on the part of a Jew and passivity on the part of the judiciary, it addressed the controversial issue of peasant land loss due to the commercialization of agriculture, which had led to the wave of foreclosure auctions in Galicia mentioned above.

This interpellation told the story of the heirs of Michał Kosmala of Chmielów, who were left penniless by a combination of his granddaughter Maria's imprudence and Chaim Blasbalg's exploitative moneylending methods while the Rszeszów district court and the judicial authorities in Tarnobrzeg failed to intervene.

The interpellation text was framed by two narrative settings. The outer frame placed the events in a general context. It asserted that the "ignorance of the peasant population" was still being exploited by "notorious leeches" due to the courts' failure to protect the peasants despite their legal obligation to do so. And it warned that the case was "likely to undermine the population's faith in the legal authorities."[104] Thus it followed the familiar strategy of portraying the Jews' crimes and the authorities' inactivity as a double misfortune for the Christian population, inscribing this view in the public consciousness. Correspondingly, the question ran as follows: "Does his Excellence the Minister of Justice intend to have these circumstances and especially the above case of Blasberg investigated, and to urge the relevant legal authorities to protect the peasant population against such dangerous elements?"

The inner frame embedded the events in a melodramatic story following fairy-tale conventions. It started at an unspecified point in the past: "In the parish of Chmielów ... some time ago, a peasant named Michael Kosmala ... passed away." The frame closed in the present day with an account of the heirs' poor mother, who died of "heartbreak over the affair" while her son—robbed of the land of his ancestors—led a desperate struggle to survive. Chaim Blasberg, in contrast, "continued to cause havoc unhindered." By describing the issue in this fairytale mode, the interpellation asserted a claim to general relevance. And by citing actual names and places, it turned a story of Jewish fraud, peasant imprudence, and state passivity into a ministerial question.

The clerk assigned to process the query, a certain Mr. Klein, read the "notorious leeches" and "nuisances to society" mentioned in the text to be Jews. Consequently, he formulated the title of the interpellation as "concerning the exploitation of the peasant population of Galicia by the Jews" before passing it on to the Ministry of Justice. The text itself had not referred to "the Jews." Klein's "reading" of the interpellation is, then, persuasive evidence that antisemitic discourse had already come to dominate discussions of "Galician ills." Anyone in Vienna reading about a case of fraud in Tarnobrzeg or Rzeszów would have involuntarily envisaged capitalist exploitation, and anyone translating "leeches" into nonmetaphorical language was likely to imagine "Jews." Even if they did not consciously subscribe to such stereotypes, they helped to perpetuate them, just as Mr. Klein did when he sent the request on its journey through the official channels.

The end of that journey was marked, on 9 April 1899, by Chaim Blasbalg's sentencing to six years' dungeon imprisonment with one day of fasting per month for fraud.[105] The ministry file on the case provides insights into the interpellators' methods, strategies, and successes. The repeated misspelling of the culprit's surname—it was Blasbalg, not Blasberg—indicates that the interpellators drew their information from hearsay rather than documents.

Answering the Ministry of Justice's inquiry, the Krakow senior prosecutor confirmed that the Blasbalg case went back a long time—in fact, sixteen years.[106] In February 1882, Blasbalg had bought Maria Klimczykowa's quarter-share of the inheritance from a third party, Elias Birnbaum. But the property had not been auctioned until 12 January 1887.[107] The public prosecutor had not intervened because nobody had pressed charges. The family had not raised any objections—either to the sale of Maria Klimczykowa's share of the inheritance, to the property's auction, or to their later eviction. The public prosecutors did not act because the family did not lodge any complaints.[108] Yet over the years, the Kosmala family had by no means remained passive victims, as the interpellation text had suggested. Barbara Kosmala had herself convinced the appraisal commission sent to value the property to estimate it lower than its actual worth. The files do not reveal how she managed to persuade the committee men Antoni Motyka, Jan Rytwiński, and Jan Ordon to declare the property to be worth only 690 guilders.[109] But she did so with the intention of paying less to Chaim Blasbalg for his quarter-share of the property. As they were not able to agree on a price, Blasbalg turned to the courts to secure his share and sued for a public auction. He then purchased the property at auction for the relatively small amount of 820 guilders, thanks to the artificially low entry-level price. Barbara Kosmala's attempt to falsify the property's value had backfired on her.

It was not until 1896 that Blasbalg's allegedly fraudulent activities against the Kosmala family, and others, were reinvestigated. Blasbalg eluded pretrial detention on 19 September by going into hiding.[110] His wife, Malke, requested "safe conduct" on his behalf in March 1897 but was refused by the Ministry of Justice.

After paying two thousand guilders bail money in July 1898, Blasbalg came out of hiding, and the investigations were resumed. Now, several other complainants leveled charges against him for a range of offences, from embezzlement and fraud to incitement to commit perjury. Some of them had long since been time-barred and to all intents and purposes forgotten.[111] Public opinion had obviously turned against him, and any reluctance to press charges thrown to the wind.

Although this new trend was undoubtedly linked to Krempa's interpellation, we can no longer know whether Krempa became aware of the case through the flood of complaints or whether news of the interpellation encouraged people to press charges. Certainly, the many complaints served to enrich the gossip concerning Blasbalg with concrete "facts." The dimensions of the case against Blasbalg grew exponentially as more and more victims came forward and described their experiences to the public prosecutors, and no doubt in everyday conversation. The Ministry of Justice only recorded the complaints that were included in the Rzeszów public prosecutors' indictment of February 1899. The many others can therefore not be precisely dated. But charges were still being pressed in December, and the minister was forced to postpone his response, scheduled for mid-December, until they had all been investigated.[112] In the event, only four charges appeared in the public prosecutors' indictment, of which only the cases of fraud against the Kosmala family were negotiated in court, resulting in the sentence of six years' dungeon imprisonment.

The indictment reveals that plaintiffs and prosecutors used the same strategies and concepts as antisemitic interpellators. The public prosecutors referred to anti-Jewish stereotypes and invoked the image of passive Christian victims. They based their evidence partly on the statements given by Kosmala and his witness, although they were unfounded and could easily have been exposed as untrue. The indictment then echoed the popular assumption that Blasbalg won the foreclosure auction because he had a secret business arrangement with the two other bidders, David Wiesenfeld and Israel Sprirno, by which they bought up peasant holdings—information drawn only from the words of villagers.[113]

The charge that Blasbalg had merely simulated a willingness to sell part of the property to Antoni Kosmala was based on witness statements that incorporated all the clichéd images of "Jewish business methods." In Salomon Korn's tavern, it was claimed, Blasbalg had made Antoni Kosmala an offer for his share of the inheritance, amounting to 300 guilders. Rafał Steinhardt and Ignacy Rutyna had been present. The latter confirmed—a full eleven years later—Kosmala's account of the meeting: when Kosmala had said he could only pay 270 guilders, Steinhardt had tried to convince Blasbalg to lower the price by 10 percent in order to secure an agreement. Blasbalg had answered "in Jewish" (po żydowsku) that he was just trying to stop Kosmala from taking him to court. This version was confirmed by Ignacy Rutyna, who also stated that the very next day Blasbalg asked for 700 guilders. Another witness, Jakub Karpf, now also came forward with the information that Blasbalg had admitted to him his intention to prevent Kosmala from seeking "recourse" by making these offers. If the accounts were true, Steinhardt and Karpf had become accessories to the fraud by failing to translate Blasbalg's Yiddish comment for Kosmala, and not warning him of Blasbalg's true intentions. Blasbalg's former accomplices testifying against him opened the floodgates for numerous others to press charges against him. Yet precisely the detail in which they recalled Blasbalg's words after such a long lapse of time casts doubt on their statements.

The public prosecutor put forward additional arguments, which no doubt corresponded less with the views of the peasant plaintiffs than with those of the "people's attorneys" in Vienna. "As a woman and an unenlightened peasant at that," he opined, Barbara Kosmala had not been able to properly defend her interests. Similarly, he contrasted Kosmala's vulnerability with Blasbalg's fraudulent intent: Blasbalg had purposefully sought out victims who were not his intellectual equal in order to ruin them. The indictment echoed the language of Galician interpellations, reinforcing misgivings about Jewish businessmen using fraudulent methods. While the courts may not have generally treated Jews differently, they can be seen to have used narrative strategies against Jews that were—if not established—at least updated by interpellations.

What part did Krempa's interpellation play in Chaim Blasbalg's conviction for fraud? The minister of justice never answered the question in parliament since the session was over before the verdict was announced. The verdict was, then, the only answer. It was left to the individual to interpret the minister's silence on the matter as they saw fit. A written response in the Ministry of Justice files contains the court's verdict and the comment that the courts had acted correctly, as they had initiated investigations as soon as the first complaint had been lodged. No neglect of duty had, then, been committed. As the public were not informed of this comment any more than they were of the many untruths and half-truths in the interpellation text, the remark with which the caseworker, a certain Holzknecht, closed the file on the Blasbalg case revealed an unintentional, deeper truth: "The interpellation by the Members of Parliament Krempa & Co. was a complete success." In the eyes of their clientele, it appeared as if the interpellation had prompted the authorities to act while leaving their own shortcomings unexposed.

Krempa addressed a similar case of peasant land loss in the Reichsrat some two-and-a-half years later. Luckily for posterity, the Ministry of Justice files on this case, too, have survived.

The Grün Case

This interpellation was based on a complaint from the village Dulcza in the district of Mielec, Krempa's constituency. Again, it recounted an isolated incident as if it illustrated a general problem of Jews driving Christian peasants to financial ruin in Galicia. It was not only signed by politicians from the Christian People's Party, the Radicals, and the Ukrainian National Democrats, but also endorsed by the Lower Austrian anti-Semite Pattai.[114]

Again, Krempa framed the grievance it described with a portrayal of Galicia— in more pronounced terms than in the interpellation concerning Blasbalg—as a hotbed of usury. He explicitly declared the Christian victims to be of unsound mind, identified the complicit notary by name, and unequivocally branded the culprits Jews. "Jewish fraud and profiteering" were tolerated in Galicia, he claimed, and had the potential to ruin the peasant population. This interpellation not only played on popular associations with the word "leech" but also explicitly asserted that the crimes of profiteering and fraud were the specialty of Jews. It opened with these sentences: "Galicia is that site and breeding ground of usury in every form, where fraudulent deals are hatched by Jews to plague materially and intellectually degenerate peasants. Thousands of peasant families have been forced to emigrate or reduced to beggary by one or other form of Jewish profiteering."

The question took an outsider's view of Galicia, considering it from a distance—from a Viennese perspective. Using metaphors like "breeding ground" and "hatching," it evoked images of pests and parasites. Indeed, Galicia was regarded among Viennese anti-Semites as an inexhaustible reservoir of (Jewish) people liable to flock to Vienna and become a burden on the capital. Krempa's interpellation drew on this antisemitic discourse to deliver reasons for the Galician misery and large-scale migration, confirming the prevalent notion in Vienna of a Galicia "infiltrated by Jews."[115] The Galician opposition's interpellations in the Reichsrat intersected with other Galician and Viennese debates and influenced them.

Figure 3.4. Viennese cartoon depicting Galicia as a parasite, *Kikeriki*, 20 November 1898. Public domain.

The subject of this interpellation is easily summarized. It concerned the fate of the Wątroba family, who had been plunged into debt and subsequently cheated out of their property by the Jewish businessman Israel Grün, with the help of a certain Süßel Chrząszcz and a royal-and-imperial notary. Mr. and Mrs. Wątroba had signed the sales contract for their farm, which had been drawn up by the notary Krasicki, in the belief they were taking out a mortgage. Unlike in the Blasbalg case, then, where the notary merely failed to help the victims, the notary in this case had actively participated in the deception.

If the interpellation text concerning the Blasbalg case read like a melodrama, the interpellation on Wątroba versus Grün was the kind of grotesque farce that might have been shown at a Galician folk theater. Laurenz Wątroba being carried into the chancellery to seal his fate with his signature certainly has elements of comedy:

> Some Jews and an illiterate man named Martin Sządoł were called up as witnesses. After summation of the debt and interest, the amount of 300 florins was set in the contract and the bloated Wątroba, feeble and mentally ill as a result of illness, was carried in. As he was bloated, however, he could not hear anything, and as he was imbecilic, he could not understand anything either. Wątroba's wife was with the horses at the time. As the contract was being read out by the notary, the farmer Martin Druga remarked to Wątroba: "Stop! It won't turn out well!" at which Grün pushed him out the door and ordered Wątroba to pick up the pen.[116]

The interpellation portrayed the parties to the contract as adversaries, each with their entourage, like duelists with their seconds. The fault line of the conflict ran neatly along a religious divide, but the two sides' potential for securing a good deal was extremely imbalanced. On one side, there was the mentally and physically weak Wątroba with just an illiterate peasant to support him once his other advisor had been forcibly ejected. Grün and Chrząszcz, meanwhile, obviously had close links with the notary and used a group of nameless Jewish accessories to shield their intrigues from the critical gaze of Martin Druga.

The upshot of Krempa's request was that the minister of justice should declare the contract by which the Wątroba family mistakenly sold their farm and lost their means of existence to be null and void. It could not be legally valid as the signatory Laurenz Wątroba was not of sound mind, Krempa argued. Like many other interpellators in the Imperial Diet, he pleaded his case like a lawyer in court. In addition to Wątroba's illness, Krempa cited his practice of taking on another's cattle as evidence of his "imbecility": "The fact that Grün and Wątroba collaborated in business for several years, and in such a way that the latter was required to raise the former's cattle, for which the Jew pocketed money, proves that Wątroba was not of sound mind and *eo ipso* did not possess the competence to conclude a contract." While suggesting that doing business with a Jew was evidence enough of mental instability, Krempa elsewhere claimed that Grün had "fobbed off" the Wątroba family with "brandy . . . and fine words" in exchange for them raising his cattle. But the ultimate perfidy, by this account, was accomplished by the act of signing the contract. Wątroba had been coerced into the deal by the Jews, who were the only ones who stood to benefit from it, as from the cattle business. Laurenz Wątroba's signature on the contract finally precipitated the family's downfall.

Because the Jew's fraudulent deal—the culmination of long-term profiteering and a deceptive contract—had been committed before the eyes of a government official, in formal terms it was legally valid. The message the interpellation conveyed, then, was that Jews did business by unfair means and that peasants were not only hopelessly overchallenged by their contracts and deals but also let down by the corrupt officials. If you agreed to a cattle-raising deal with a Jew, you inevitably faced poverty and alcoholism, so the antisemitic narrative went. Its strategy was to construct discrete groups of actors, distinguished by inequality and mutual otherness. It portrayed Jews and Christians as irreconcilable opponents, and business as a zero-sum game rather than an arrangement seeking mutual benefits. Seen in this light, Grün could only secure an advantage at Wątroba's expense. Relations between Jews and Christians were characterized as an ongoing history of deception and conflict in which the naïve peasants were always the losers. Krempa's interpellation added another chapter to this narrative, along with the explicit claim that it was just one of countless similar cases. The incidents in Mielec served as examples of real social situations to project onto the peasant parties' agitation, as well as proof of the severity of the situation.

Following inquiries to the Krakow public prosecutors, the Ministry of Justice found a "state of affairs that considerably diverged from the account in the interpellation," as the minister of justice put it in his response to the Reichsrat on 25 October 1901.[117] Krempa had only indirectly mentioned, when quoting the notary's statements, the fact that the contract had been the subject of previous investigations. These investigations had culminated in a trial, lost by Wątroba in January 1897. He had not appealed. Several witnesses had testified that Mr. and Mrs. Wątroba and Israel Grün had done business for many years. They had started in 1888 when Grün lent the Wątrobas sixty guilders. A year later, they paid him back forty guilders. Having added interest of five guilders to the twenty outstanding guilders for the first year, at an interest rate of 8.3%, Grün could hardly be accused of usury.[118] Obviously Grün's priority was not to make money fast but to build a basis of trust for future cooperation. While there was conflicting information on some points—Wątroba claimed he paid off the debt and interest in kind with "potatoes, chickens and geese," which Grün denied—there was agreement over the fact that Grün had lent the Wątrobas a further fifteen guilders and more goods had been exchanged.

In 1891, the two parties started collaborating on a cattle-breeding venture. Grün bought calves and cows and installed them on the Wątrobas' farm. The latter fed and milked the cattle until they were sold on, when the proceeds of the sales were shared between them. The Wątrobas made over fifty guilders from this arrangement. They continued to cooperate even when a dispute over a hundred guilders, mostly money owed, led to Grün pressing charges in 1892. The Wątrobas had not only borrowed from Grün but also from Kasimir Schab (whom the interpellation had also mentioned), to whom they had pledged land as collateral. When Katharina Wątroba turned to Süßel Chrząszcz for help paying their mounting debts in 1896, the latter found out "from people in the village" that the four acres of land he had asked for as security were already pledged and that the Wątrobas also owed Israel Grün money. The three creditors then joined forces. They took Katharina Wątroba to make several visits to the notary until eventually a contract was concluded, by which the field was sold to Chrząszcz and the proceeds of the sale went to the creditors Schab and Grün. Another contract was drawn up for the Wątrobas to lease the field.

When questioned by the public prosecutor, the notary had said he had advised Laurenz Wątroba (whom he saw for the first time on the day the contract was signed) against the deal and recommended he wait for a foreclosure sale to be initiated. That would at least allow him to cultivate the land for a few more years. Otherwise, without the land and without any money, he would be reduced to beggary. Yet the physically ailing but by no means deaf or imbecilic Wątroba brushed him off and signed the contract. The money was immediately handed to the creditors.

This perspective on the case showed the Wątrobas' struggle with crippling debts. But usury was not the cause; they had neither been required to pay an extortionate amount of interest nor had the loan been designed to ruin them. Grün had clearly been more concerned to continue their joint cattle-breeding venture than to acquire their property. He had never at any point suggested seizing their land. Grün and Chrząszcz had not started to collude until Chrząszcz had learned that the land the Wątrobas had offered him as security was already pledged—to a Christian. It was not a case of Jewish perpetrators afflicting their Christian victims in the notary's office. There were people of both religions seeking the money back which they had lent and who relied on information from the same sources. Just as in the Blasbalg case, where the witnesses Steinhardt and Rutyna were not altruistically loyal to their fellow believers, the Christian creditor Schab put his personal interests first.

As interpellator, Krempa told the tragic but complicated story according to a familiar narrative: defenseless, passive peasants were exploited by an unscrupulous Jewish cartel to whom Galician government officials were no obstacle, and with whom they even colluded. As "the people's attorney," Krempa withheld the information about the previous trial and the involvement of Schab, who also profited from the sale. Neither did he mention the options open to the Wątrobas, such as waiting for a foreclosure sale. Rather, he proceeded like a lawyer in court, arguing that the contract was not valid because the signatory was not of sound mind. He reiterated the theory that peasants were reliant on guardian figures, who needed to be honest—that is, Christian, and not "Jewish," as the interpellation text labeled the creditors Chrząszcz and Grün.[119]

We can only speculate whether members of the Wątroba family, such as the son who had still been a minor at the time of the events leading to the sale, had approached Krempa and supported the interpellation. It is quite possible that Krempa heard of the case through village gossip. Both the witness statements from the first trial and the account given in the interpellation point to village communication as a source. The recounting of Matrin Druga's interjection "Stop! It won't turn out well!" is especially typical of verbal information. Although it had no impact on the outcome, the interjection, spoken in the future tense, anticipated the coming disaster. It was a prophetic statement that lent the story the aura of legend, suspending the chronology and conveying a deeper truth. It marked a fusion of Catholic peasant culture with parliamentary practice.

By presenting the gradual decline of the Wątroba family as "the Grün case," Krempa wrote another chapter in the story of Jewish crime that negated the possibility of business deals being mutually beneficial to Christians and Jews. In this drama, the local administration did not take the role of helper but of a biased, Jewish-loyal force. A hostile complex consisting of the state and dishonest businesspeople was said to run circles around the helpless peasants. But the ministry responded in the negative to the interpellation concerning the Grün case.

Krempa's Collected Cases before and after the Elections of 1900

On 17 March 1900, toward the end of his first term in the Reichsrat, Krempa initiated an interpellation addressing the alleged crimes of Mendel Groß of Tarnobrzeg. It described three cases in which Mendel Groß bought bills of exchange that he immediately tried to redeem. His tactic was to report debtors to the court to achieve the seizure or foreclosure sale of properties, which he then bought and sold on. The first incident, in which the heirs of a certain Maciej Smykła had lost their land, had occurred a full twenty-eight years previously.[120] Krempa gave the file number for each lawsuit, though all the charges against Mendel Groß had been dropped by the Galician public prosecutors. Krempa's text ended with the warning that

> a legion of people is prowling Galicia, exploiting the ignorance, inexperience and recklessness of our peasant population in the most shameless way, reducing entire families to beggary, and abusing certain legal formulae to prevent their heinous operations and forays from conflicting with the law. Among these leeches, the abovementioned Mendel Groß is especially prominent and it is high time we put a stop to these profiteering and fraudulent dealings."[121]

A request Krempa made twenty-four months later was similar in structure and content. Again, it concerned a case of fraud in Tarnobrzeg, committed against a farmer named Martin Ordon by "two Jewish leeches," Josel Lachmann and Israel Neuwirt.[122] They were at liberty to commit their persistent crimes, Krempa claimed, because the royal-and-imperial public prosecutors in Rzeszów refused to prosecute them. But the minister of justice's response on 2 June revealed that no charges had ever been leveled against the two men. Ordon himself had been sued by Neuwirt for the money he owed but had failed to appear in court.[123]

The same month, Krempa requested the review of an "unjust verdict made by the Mielec district court, as well as the damages thereby caused to Mr. and Mrs. Grzelak of Trzciana in Galicia."[124] Berl Honig of Mielec had bought a cow from the farmer Grzelak but wanted to return it the next day. Justin Grzelak objected to the return and so was sued by Honig.

The Mielec district court ruled that the cattle trader had a right both to return the cow and to make seizures if he did not receive the purchase price plus five crowns and thirty hellers for "additional expenses" within fourteen days. According to the account given in the interpellation, however, Honig sued for garnishment without giving the cow back to Grzelak. He had sold the cow to his son for fifty-six crowns and demanded the remaining forty-five crowns and fifty hellers from Grzelak. The latter sued him for selling the cow below its value but lost the trial and was therefore required to pay the legal costs as well. The Grzelaks were plunged into "great financial difficulties, so that the Jew sold all their furnishings and literally brought them to the brink of bankruptcy." Krempa took this isolated incident to direct a generalizing question at the minister of justice: "What measures does his Excellency intend to take to avoid such Jewish mendacity?" In his response of 18 June, the minister tersely stated that the courts had acted correctly and there were no legal grounds for putting the matter to the Mielec district court.[125]

Finally, Krempa presented an interpellation concerning the "fraudulency committed by Pfachie Honig of Mielec" to the Reichsrat.[126] Once again, it concerned a crime committed many years previously—in this case, over thirty. According to the interpellation, a certain Josef Skoroś had approached Pfachie Honig to borrow a hundred guilders. "The shrewd Honig naturally started plotting a scheme and made Skoroś sign a bill of exchange first, saying he would then give him the money." But he staved off Skoroś with just one guilder to start, with which the latter set off back home to Rozniaty. The next day, Skoroś fell ill with plague and died. Honig then visited his widow with a signed debenture for one hundred crowns and asked for the money to be paid pack in full. The matter went to court, which ruled in his favor, allowing him to seize the Skoroś' property. He then sold it to a certain Anton Raś for 430 guilders.

Krempa's interpellations negotiated cases of Jewish usury and fraud against Catholic peasants. The many examples he mentioned seemed to explain the phenomenon of "dismembration": peasant land being appropriated and divided up, apparently by a combination of Jewish cunning and government indifference. Yet most of the incidents Krempa mentioned had occurred decades previously. By the 1890s, foreclosure sales had in fact become a rare occurrence.[127] The politicians and their informers seized upon antisemitic interpellations, then, in the hope of reversing what they saw to be the negative consequences of the previous decades' economic restructuring.

At the same time, they updated the discourse on usury and fraud and portrayed it as an ongoing problem, demanding a change in peasant relations with Jewish businesspeople. Beware, the interpellations said, of the dire consequences of doing deals with Jews. And not only the peasants were warned against such evils but also the state, which would lose the peasants' trust if it failed to act. Referring once again to the "voice of the people," Krempa urged the Viennese government to take steps against the situation in Galicia. If it did not, he cautioned, the otherwise loyal province would cause serious trouble for the multinational state. Addressing the entire state via an interpellation in the Reichsrat, he conveyed an impression of public opinion in the province, over the heads of the Galician administration:

> In the interests of the court personnel's good reputation, it must be brought to the judicial administration's attention that in the area around Głogów, there is much whispering of the corruptibility of the court clerk Królikowski and the public prosecutors' functionary Schodnicki. It is, however, possible that these rumors are the consequence of malicious gossip, but then it would still be in the interests of the proper administration of justice to have the matter cleared up.[128]

Here, Krempa touched on a fundamental problem facing the Galician authorities, which had worsened since Galician politicians entered the Reichsrat and discovered the instrument of interpellation. It was immaterial whether rumors were based on truth or malicious gossip, they reflected the people's mistrust of the "Stanczyks' rule," which could give rise to conspiracy theories and even riots. The rumors could not be checked by repressive means; on the contrary, popular gossip burgeoned when the state interfered in the peasant sphere. Conveying the rumors to the parliament in Vienna, oppositionist politicians acted as constant reminders of the lack of peasant trust in the state. Their anti-Jewish tales of profiteering and fraud were inscribed with the peasants' negative experiences with the police and legal system.

As well as Krempa, a farmer and member of parliament for the SL, the clerical parliamentarians Szponder, Danielak, and Stojałowski made interpellations concerning Jewish crime.[129] They, too, used them to explain the economic plight of the peasantry, albeit in Christian-social terms. Although their policies naturally differed in some respects to those of the Secular People's Parties, they displayed an affinity in their use of antisemitic politics as a means of representing the peasant camp within the political landscape of the empire.

Stanisław Stojałowski presented his first two interpellations in the Reichsrat on 2 June 1898. By this time, news of the disturbances in Kalwarya and the districts of Myślenice and Podgórz had already broken.[130] Stojałowski's first question concerned the awarding of a pharmacist's concession to a "baptized Jew, [the] former Moritz Goldmann, now known as Martin Górzycki."[131] Stojałowski's main complaint was that the Ministry of the Interior had unjustly favored a former Jew over a Christian. By emphasizing the fact that Martin Górzycki was previously Jewish, and had merely changed his name, as it were, he proceeded as if exposing a wrongdoing. Being Jewish by birth, Stojałowski suggested, Górzycki would naturally tend toward dishonest business practices and have links with the ministry. Indeed, he had apparently used these to gain an advantage over the other, better qualified—Christian—applicant, Aleksander Żurawski. This narrative strategy updated familiar suspicions of Jewish conspiracies and articulated the unease that Jewish-hostile Catholics felt about converts. To them, the baptism of Jews signified a loss of clarity as it blurred the once solid boundary between the Christian and Jewish communities. Stojałowski aimed to restore this boundary by recalling the neophyte's "true name" and so protect unknowing Christians against his fraudulence.[132] This kind of religious motif, playing on people's fears about the new ambiguity surrounding Jews and Christians, was not to be found in Krempa's rhetoric.

Rumors Surrounding Judge Wiatr

Stojałowski's second interpellation of 2 June once again linked the topic of usury with criticisms of the state and brought Judge Wiatr and the "outrages" he had committed before the tribunal in the Reichsrat. Here, too, Stojałowski condemned the blurring of the boundary between Jews and Christians and the subversion of stable social relations based on religious loyalty. The text started with a general complaint about the usury that was plaguing the peasant population in the Jasło district. Under the cloak of a "Jewish lending consortium," it asserted, Szyja Parnes, Abraham Landau, and Isaak Lichtig had spun a "web of Jew-profiteering." In typical antisemitic style, it made it quite clear from the outset that this concerned a "Jewish problem."[133] Its concrete associations with Jews and allegation that the accused, Wiatr, was an "intimate Jew-friend" and "protector of extortioners" underlined the link between Jews and usury. Composite nouns prefixed with the word Jew not only had a derogatory function that turned the sense of the attached word on its head; the term "Jew-profiteering" also morphologically reflected antisemitic agitation's construct of "Jewish crime."

With his question of 2 June, Stojałowski aimed to articulate a section of the population's dissatisfaction with and resentment of Judge Wiatr, using a tried-and-tested strategy of attack for a community that felt disadvantaged by the state and held out no hope of gaining redress through the official channels: he spread rumors about Judge Wiatr. The query was composed of a blend of malicious gossip, hearsay, and accusations incorporated into the framework of an interpellation text, complete with introduction and a question to the minister of justice.[134] It echoed not only the content of the rumors but also their semantic structure, thus attaching as much importance to the verbal messages from Dukla as to bureaucratically recorded facts. Stojałowski made no attempt to prove the truth of the anonymous accusations by naming witnesses or document numbers, nor did he try to place them in any legal or administrative contexts. To him, the fact that Wiatr was "by the mouths of the entire neighborhood [said to be] an intimate Jew-friend and protector of extortioners" was proof enough of the truth of the accusations.[135]

He then gave two reasons for the popular opinion of the judge, packaged in a succinct rumor: "The secretary of the honorable Judge Wiatr is the scribe Südwärts, a Jew, who acts the almighty in court." Having an employee who was Jewish made Wiatr a Jew-friend and a supporter of "the others" in the eyes of the peasants. And a Jew presiding over Christians was an intolerable presumption, which Stojałowski magnified by the term "almighty," usually reserved for (the Christian) God and indicating a positively blasphemous arrogance on the part of a "heretic."

Legal Scandal and Murder: The Färber Case

Another instance of alleged judicial bias toward Jews was addressed in an interpellation by Stojałowski's fellow party members Michał Danielak and Andrzej Szponder on 20 October 1898. It concerned the case of Chaim and Salomon Färber, who had been accused of the "treacherous murder" of Josef Chudoba.[136] It had resulted in a protracted lawsuit, which the interpellators regularly reported on in their newspaper *Obrona Ludu*, established after the split from Stojałowski. One controversial point was whether the cause of death had been violence or a hemorrhage. Bungled forensic examinations, conducted days later, pointed to a murder, but a medical report by two (Christian) doctors, paid for by the family of the deceased, did not find any evidence of violence. However, by this time—eleven days after the time of death—Chudoba's body was in an advanced state of decay. The senior official in Nowy Sącz cleared Chaim and Salomon Färber of the charge, had them released from custody, and declared the matter to have been "the product of antisemitic machinations." Chudoba's widow appealed for a retrial in Krakow. According to the interpellation text, her request was granted, following an "investigation by the honorable Regional Court Judge Dr. Bajut" which he conducted with "great vigor and especial skill." Yet because one of the appraisals was financed by the family of the suspects, the interpellators claimed that "the courts were under the sway of the Jews." The text also described how the Färbers came to be suspected of murdering Chudoba. At 10:00 a.m. on 22 August 1897, Chaim Färber, owner of a brewery in Szaflary, had contacted Judge Brożek to say there was a "killed peasant" lying next to his house and people were accusing him of the murder. It did not take long for witnesses to come forward with evidence against him. A certain "Małezkowa, a peasant woman from Nowy Targ, [saw] two people who were carrying a person out of Färber's brewery in Szaflary. Małezkowa recognized one of the men as Chaim Färber."[137]

The idea spread "among the Galician folk" that Brożek was responsible for the bungled forensic examinations and that they had been deliberately subverted to protect the true culprits. Consequently, witnesses came forward who contradicted the judge's version of events under oath. A certain Ujivary, a "sixty-eight-year-old geriatric ... claimed quite resolutely that he had seen Färber [on the night Chudoba died] at around 4 am, entering the house in Nowy Targ where Mr. Brożek lived."[138] He presumed that during Färber's short stay of ten minutes in the judge's home, they had held a conspiratorial meeting on how to cover up the murder.

The Ministry of Justice's response to the interpellation on 22 November pointed out that it could not comment so long as proceedings were still ongoing. Although the case partly negotiated the shortcomings and failings of the judicial authorities, they did not necessarily affect all of Galicia.[139] The Färber case continued to be observed by all the popular newspapers until it finally ended in a conviction based on incriminating testimonies.[140]

The case marked an exception among antisemitic interpellations concerning Jewish crimes.[141] Neither violent crime nor the manipulation of forensic reports was a typical theme of the antisemitic canon. The most frequent allegation was that the Galician judiciary was not interested in prosecuting crimes of fraud and usury. While the claim that Jews manipulated the legal system was a central motif of German anti-Semites, as the Berlin pamphlet about the Ritter trial and the writings of Daniel Vyleta on Vienna illustrate, it was a marginal interest among Galician anti-Semites. This distinction can be explained by the different target groups of antisemitic politics in the respective communities and their diverging ideas of the position of Jews in society.

Galician interpellations portrayed Jews as traders and moneylenders who colluded with government officials to defraud peasants of their property. The officials appeared in this scenario as mere instruments and agents of the Stańczyks, who were ignorant of the peasants' situation and used by the seditious Jewish businesspeople to lend their dealings a sheen of legality. As we have seen, such portrayals were constructed by means of omitting and twisting facts and by making false generalizations and assertions. Nevertheless, they referred to real experiences of conflict encountered by their voters. Unlike the popular newspapers, the interpellations did not allude to an abstract Jewish force but to individual "fraudsters and racketeers," regardless of whether their conduct was illegal or not. Referring to "Jewish business methods" was an act of antisemitic practice, intended to discredit Jews in general.

Aside from the roles of the "scribe Südwärts" and the Färbers in the above interpellations, the judiciary and the media were not generally portrayed as Jewish-controlled spheres in Galicia. The finger here was pointed chiefly at the Galician authorities who allegedly tolerated violations of the law. In Vienna, in contrast, the "Jewish press" and "Jew-infiltrated medical profession" were the bogeymen of anti-Semites, believed to influence appraisals and manipulate public opinion. This theory not only provided anti-Semites with an explanation for the high proportion of Jews in the liberal professions but also enabled them to rationalize their anger and incomprehension at various court rulings. Whenever science or the legal system contradicted their antisemitic truths, they alluded to the Jewish influence. Non-Jewish and mid-ranking government officials were another important part of the equation, not because they were alleged to exert a negative influence, but because German anti-Semites relied on their votes. In Galician interpellations, meanwhile, public servants were portrayed as part of the problem and clearly marked out as "others." Galician antisemitic interpellations were distinctly peasant representations in which white-collar groups had no place. The election of 1897 in Krakow had shown that the urban clientele from the (lower) middle class did not participate in anti-liberal political antisemitism. They felt better represented by Democrats or Conservatives such as Merunowicz, who still echoed Mochnacki's and Gorzkowski's resentment of Jewish conspiracies and found a political home in national democracy after the turn of the century.

The Canon of Jewish Crime

Interpellation texts canonized the motif of Jews harming the Christian peasant population by their racketeering and fraud and linked it with the accusation that Galician court officials were effectively—whether consciously or unconsciously—accessories to these crimes. This specifically Galician construct of "Jewish crime," based on concrete examples from Galician constituencies, was supported by various opposition parties and earned the interest and endorsement of several German Christian Socials and Czech anti-Semites.[142]

German anti-Semites received the narrative as evidence of Galicia's "Jew-infiltrated Polish economy," which in view of the large proportion of Galician ministers in the cabinet, posed a threat to all Cisleithania. To Galician populists, meanwhile, it was a reminder of the unholy alliance between the "Schlachziz" and the Jews, who continued to get rich at the expense of the peasants in the constitutional era.

The interpellations painted a picture of the constant violation and erosion of the usury law, drafted in Galicia and later applied to all Cisleithania, by Jewish businesspeople. Interpellators were aware that to prompt the ministries to deal with their questions, they needed to cite concrete examples of criminal offences. Their accounts of fraudulent contracts and property auctions from the injured parties' perspective also conveyed the widespread outrage at the foreclosure sales. Interpellations were, then, a highly productive means of disseminating and visualizing the antisemitic narrative of Jews fraudulently profiting from the sale of peasant land simply because they were Jews. They focused on crimes of deception and officials' implication in them for a reason. Highlighting usury as the cause of Galicia's misery became the foremost motif in the antisemitic canon. Usury and fraud, often leading to foreclosure sales, was a central theme in the peasant parties' antisemitic repertoire.

The interpellations continued this program; when news of them returned the narrative to the village context, it conveyed to the peasants the implicit advice to stay away from Jews and to not borrow any money or agree to raise their cattle, especially since the state could not be relied on to help. The exploitation and downfall of Christian peasants could only be averted by not doing any business with Jews at all. By convincing people that usury and fraud were the beginning of the end for peasant families, politicians aimed to raise awareness of pro-Polish behavior among the *lud* (and pro-Ukrainian among the *narod*), or pro-Christian, and the need to boycott Jews. From the many interpellations with individual tales but a similar overarching moral, a canon grew that could be used for agitation purposes and to motivate peasants toward antisemitic consumer behavior and business conduct in everyday life.

The Usefulness of Interpellations

Agitation toward inducing voters to display "antisemitic behavior" in their daily lives was just one goal of antisemitic interpellation. The entire interpellation process, from villagers offering information, to politicians reading out the texts in parliament and witnesses testifying, was an opportunity for everyone involved to represent the political peasant community. Accounts of Jewish mendacity and government disdain served both Christian voters and their political representatives. Against a backdrop of Jewish crime, their own work and business ethics seemed superior, and a purely Christian or national economy the only way out of Galicia's misery. By addressing the gossip and rumors about Jews and their accomplices in the Reichsrat, parliamentarians demystified the process of representing political interest groups and let the public participate. Above all, they hoped their accounts of the situation in Galicia would strike nerves among the Galician administration and Cisleithanian politics. At the very least, they would place the onus on the state and its representatives to react and prove to the populace they could still trust the courts despite the persistent rumors to the contrary.

Accounts of negative experiences of dealing with Jewish businesspeople should not be equated with the views of the "the people"—these did not exist as a discrete category beyond those accounts. The interpellations were ultimately the work of individual politicians, though they drew on many sources. And many people became involved in the interpellation practice in the hope of gaining psychological, symbolic, or material benefits. Considering the number of individuals involved in spreading rumors and disseminating gossip about businesspeople such as Pfachie Honig, Süßel Chrzcząszcz, and Mendel Groß, as well as the writers of reports in party newspapers and the politicians' informers, a picture of a large circle of beneficiaries emerges.

Anyone who managed to turn their story into an interpellation that received serious consideration by the Ministry of Justice and resulted in a court action that they won certainly stood to make a material profit. In this respect, it is irrelevant whether people really believed that Jewish moneylenders were more likely to cheat them than Christians. If it came to a dispute with a Jew or if a deal transpired to be unpropitious, the dissatisfied party could use the antisemitic canon to add credibility to the claim they had been ruined by a "Jewish profiteer." Even after years of doing business together, as in the case of Wątroba and Grün, citing Jewish crime could be an attractive option.

Another use of participating in the gossip about Jewish criminals was seized upon by those who testified as witnesses, enticed by the prospect of a share in the material benefits or even just some precious attention. Having consolidated belief in the accused Jew's guilt within their verbal communication community, they then affirmed as much—with legal significance—in their statements. The multitudes of people who pressed charges against Chaim Blasbalg participated in spinning the story of his many swindles, climaxing in the trial he lost, which incorporated various motifs and arguments from the interpellators' arsenal.

Armed with a regularly updated stock of information that was familiar to both Jews and Christians and could always be presented as fact, Christians symbolically relegated their Jewish business partners to positions outside the community. The entire interpellation process—transmitting supposed knowledge, gleaned from village gossip, of a fraudulent Jew and his offences, and recalling the news of previous interpellations and incorporating witness statements—can be regarded as a discriminatory practice. The fact that testimonies were accepted even decades after the events was a warning to Jewish moneylenders. It cautioned that rumors should be taken seriously, as the "tale" of the warrant to rob and beat Jews that had propelled the riots had shown. A bad reputation could prove critical if an interpellator seized upon it and managed to initiate a trial through a request to the Ministry of Justice based on witness statements. Seen in this light, interpellations were the *katzenmusik* of modern politics. They marked the first time that antisemitic politicians backed by Christian peasants tried to involve the state in the imagined conflict of interests between Christians and Jews. Although they rarely achieved their primary goal, they provided the satisfaction of forcing the government to respond to those who felt disadvantaged by the state's alleged bias toward the Jews during the disturbances.

Beyond the Canon: Accusations of Ritual Murder in Galicia

Interpellations were not the only means of involving the state in disputes between Christians and Jews, and usury and fraud not the only topics negotiated in situations of Christian-Jewish conflict. The following section will consider the forms of "Jewish crime" that were not mentioned in interpellations, especially ritual murder. These cases were not turned into interpellations by antisemitic politicians and therefore not assumed into the canon of antisemitic politics. But they nevertheless demonstrate how the practice of interpellation influenced the way Christians approached Jews.

The Child in the Box

The following report of 27 March 1898, sent by a Krakow judge to the Ministry of Justice, shows how a superstitious tale like that of the ritual murder myth could become endowed with meaning and apparent credibility. The incident it recalls occurred at a time when the disturbances in Wieliczka had abated and before they escalated into the riots of the early summer.

> Two or three days ago it was heard in Nowy Sacz that a Christian child was robbed from an unspecified place and that it was packed in a box marked with the address of a certain Jew and sent by train to Nowy Sacz. According to the rumor, the box was opened by coincidence at said railway station and a living child found within it. The rumor is connected to the opinion among the lowest classes of the population that in view of the forthcoming Easter holidays, the child was intended to be murdered by Jews for ritual purposes.
>
> Initially I did not pay any heed to the rumor or attach any importance to it, since we all know that such rumors arise from time to time and—without causing any disturbance or annoyance to the public—expire again.
>
> In the meantime, however, namely yesterday afternoon, I received notification from the district court in Mszana dolna that the 2-year-old daughter of a certain Sophie Jackowiec, Marie, resident in Lostówka, had inexplicably gone missing, and that the rumor was abroad in Mszana górna that the child had been robbed by Jews for ritual purposes.
>
> In consequence to this notification, I immediately called on the district court in Lostówka to perform the necessary inquiries without delay. This day, a police report

from the same district court—concerning the same matter—arrived on my desk, expressing the opinion of the court official Ptaś, who yesterday ascertained the disappearance of the child at the scene, that the findings hitherto of the inquiries justified the assumption that a crime had been committed in the given case.

Allow me to draw the attention of the royal-and-imperial senior public prosecutor to this circumstance and to add that since I learned from the local district police that the above-mentioned incident involving the box is said to have occurred in Krakow, I intend to request further information this day from the Krakow police department.[143]

The judge's report indicates that the police and judiciary were quite familiar with rumors of kidnappings and ritual murder. These evidently tended not to have legal consequences and only rarely caused tangible disruptions in Christian-Jewish relations. From this perspective, it is easy to understand why the rumors of riots were often ignored by the authorities. The rumors in this case stemmed from the lower classes' superstitions concerning the Jewish Passover festival. As the story named neither the crime nor the victim, the police had nothing to go on. The rumor of the missing child from Łostówka had covered the thirty-five miles to Nowy Sącz faster than the court message from Mszana dolna sent via the official channels. The investigations in Krakow showed that the story of the child in the box was "completely unfounded."[144] It was a fabrication of elements of the ritual murder myth interwoven with the specific cultural and topographical characteristics of West Galicia. In the missing child's remote home village of Łostówka in the Carpathian foothills, nobody suspected a case of Jewish kidnapping. There were no reports of riots or disturbances, and no Jews lived there.[145] The report concerning Marie Jackowiec's abduction came from Mszana dolna (Lower Mszana), a town with a district court and a train station. But the rumor stemmed from the far smaller village of Mszana górna (Upper Mszana) further up the mountainside, which travelers from Łostówka passed through on their way to the district town. As Marie had not yet been found and not been seen in Mszana górna, and news of a missing child in the run-up to Easter evoked tales of Jewish rituals, the tellers of rumors in Mszana górna came up with the story that the child had been sent to the town in a box. Since the news of the missing child reached Nowy Sącz in such a short time, it is likely that one or another rumor-teller also took the train. Nobody here was familiar with the village of Łostówka and nobody was missing a child. But the story of mysterious human freight just before Easter was appealing enough to be passed on. As it mutated into a contextless urban legend, the rumor-tellers described how the child had been sent even further, to Krakow.[146] The chance opening of the box and the miracle by which the child had survived the hundred-mile train journey inside it made the story sensational. On a subliminal level, it also articulated fears of the consequences of unchecked modernization: how many more children might be abducted from apparently safe places and sent far away in a matter of hours? This case distinctly echoed the widespread tales of the abduction of young women and female trafficking.[147] And it conveys the Mszana górna residents' sense of being left behind by progress: while the similarly named neighboring town was directly connected by rail to Nowy Sącz and the world beyond, Mszarna górna remained a backwater. The ritual murder myth may have been ancient and an impulse suggestion—one of many possible explanations for a child disappearing just before Easter—but its loose structure made it applicable to very modern fears. When the people in Nowy Sącz spread the story of the child in the box without making any concrete accusations, they not only recalled the topic of ritual murder and updated the idea that certain Jews killed little children, but also affirmed popular notions of otherness and anonymity.

"Silent screams": The Case of Karolina Siedlaska

In November 1899, the parish priest of a village named Nowotaniec placed great hopes in the power of interpellation. He wrote to Count Jan Potocki, who had recently been elected to the Reichsrat, to report the tragic story of a young girl named Karolina Siedlaska. His letter was archived in the Ministry of Justice as the "Bart case."[148] The story was covered by the newspapers and retold many times, illustrating the reciprocation between the press and political initiatives "from below." It also sheds light on the conditions in which prejudices about Jewish ritual murder thrived and seemed plausible.

Karolina Siedlaska was twelve years old when she went with other children from the village to see the wedding of the Jewish cattle trader Berek Bart's daughter on 28 August 1898. Guests came from far and wide, some traveling the seventy-five miles from Nowy Sącz and others all the way from Hungary. The children watched the Jewish dances with curiosity and were given small gifts by the hosts. Karolina was different from the other children because she could not hear the music to which they were dancing or say thank you for the gifts—she was, in the words used at the time, "deaf and dumb."[149] But she was not at all shy, and promptly made friends with the bride's niece, the daughter of David Leib Bart of Nowy Sącz.

The next day, the bride's mother asked if Karolina would like to come and play with the guests. Later that evening, she asked the deaf girl's mother Katarzyna if Karolina could serve in her son's house in Nowy Sącz during the preparations for and celebration of the forthcoming Feast of Tabernacles. She promised Karolina would be well looked after and paid. Katarzyna, by her own account a poor widow, eventually agreed under the proviso that her daughter would soon be returned home. The next day, Katarzyna accompanied her daughter to the railway station in Nowosielec. She was never to see her again. Karolina probably left the house of David Leib Bart, a baker, two days later, plagued by homesickness, and she disappeared without a trace.[150]

The Bart family launched a search for Karolina and were rumored to have offered a reward of 250 guilders for the finder. But they did not tell her mother she had disappeared. When Katarzyna went to Berek and Reizla Bart in October to ask for her daughter back because she needed her help at home, they assured her she would soon see Karolina again. Some days later, Reizla Bart brought a girl to the Siedlaskas' house. She was deaf, but she was not Karolina.[151]

While Katarzyna was understandably indignant, Reizla Bart insisted it was the girl who had served in her son's house. A fight ensued in which Katarzyna's neighbors soon became involved. The senior public prosecutor described the dynamic of the conflict in his report almost a year after the events:

> It is easy to understand why Siedlaska and the inhabitants of the village Nowotanice, far away from Neu-Sandez [Nowy Sącz], who had not received any substantial information from the Jews about Carolina Siedlaska and who were left in the dark about her fate and embittered by the impudent claims made by Reizla Bart, sought to explain the cause of Carolina Siedlaska's disappearance themselves, and as they found no other expedient, simply accused the Jews of ritual murder in the first moment. The sheriff in Nowotanice expressed the villagers' general outrage by filing a complaint the very same day with the public prosecutor and police in Neu-Sandez, pressing charges of ritual murder. In Neu-Sandez, however, where the missing girl had resided in the house of Leib Bart and where the people of Nowotanice presumed the ritual murder to have taken place, no suspicions of ritual murder had arisen at all. The neighbors of Leib Bart (even the Christians) view his explanation [that Karolina left the house of her own account and did not return, T. B.] as most likely.[152]

The author apparently based his report on local administration documents. By referring to "the Jews" rather than the Bart family, and "impudent claims," it echoed the language of the local mayor and Christian inhabitants. Its reasoning that ritual murder seemed a possible explanation for the Barts' attempt to return the wrong child when there was no other obvious explanation is convincing. The village community found itself in an extraordinary situation and the Bart family was acting highly suspiciously. Ritual murder was the explanation on which most could agree in the initial moment of outrage, including the police who arrested Berek Bart. In the "knowledge" that there were Jews who murdered children for ritual purposes, the child's disappearance in connection with Jews was turned into a clear case of ritual murder.[153] The local cattle trader's family suddenly became "the Jews." Under normal circumstances, the villagers would surely not have accused their neighbors of such practices. According to Karolina's mother, Jewish and non-Jewish children had played together at the wedding; such a celebration was a major event for the entire village, though there was no record of adult Christian neighbors attending. Indeed, by referring to the peculiar "Jewish dances," Katarzyna underlined the cultural differences between the neighboring Siedlaska and Bart families. Yet they knew and trusted each other. After all,

Katarzyna had agreed to let her daughter work for the Barts in distant Nowy Sącz. True, by her own account, she was persuaded above all by the prospect of some money, certainly a vital consideration for a poor widow. But Karolina's new friendship with David Bart's daughter and the family's promise to send her back soon had also convinced her. Katarzyna believed she was placing her disabled daughter in good hands.

When she found her daughter was missing and the Bart family seemed to be deliberately trying to foist the wrong child on her, she feared the worst. Records do not show who uttered the allegation first, but soon the girl's mother and her neighbors were all convinced that the Barts had abducted Karolina to perform a ritual murder. The Christian local mayor lent the theory further weight by having Berek Bart arrested. Without even asking his colleagues in Nowy Sącz to make inquiries in the house of David Leib Bart, he immediately pressed charges of ritual murder.

In Nowy Sącz, too, Christians and Jews lived side by side. But Karolina had only been in the town for two days when she disappeared, so nobody knew her, and her disappearance did not cause a stir. Bart the baker, however, was well known and obviously well liked. His Christian neighbors found it quite implausible that a ritual murder might have taken place in his house; whether because they knew the family was not very religious and only potentially "fanatical" Jews were suspected of ritual murders, or whether they could not imagine him personally acting so cruelly, is not known.[154] In any case, the police here, too, relied on the neighborhood opinion and cited the Bart family's explanation as the most feasible in their report. And the town prevailed over the village: the senior public prosecutor in Krakow ruled that the Nowy Sącz version, blaming Karolina herself for walking out, was the royal-and-imperial judiciary's official verdict and closed the case. But the villagers found other channels to make their version heard.

The dark tale of the deaf Christian girl who was taken from her mother by Jews, who then tried to replace her with another girl, was a highly saleable news item. Journalists added chilling detail by suggesting that the murderer deliberately selected a "dumb" child while planning the abduction as she would not be able to alarm the neighbors with her screams. It is not surprising, then, that a variety of newspapers, including the *Nowa Reforma* from Krakow and the *Gazeta Warszawska* and the notoriously antisemitic *Deutsche Volksblatt*, based in Vienna, all seized upon it.[155] On 10 January 1899, under the heading "A mysterious story," the latter recounted the tale of the missing deaf girl in an article that contrasted the official *Gazeta Lwowksa*'s "dry and empty" coverage against the anger of the Christian population, whose side the author took. The government newspaper, it wrote, had merely reported that a deaf girl was missing and another, whose identity had not yet been clarified, had appeared. The governor's report had kept the crucial aspect quiet that "suspicions were inevitably roused that this might be a case of ritual murder committed by Jews."[156] The *Deutsche Volksblatt* article went on to mention further unfounded rumors in a similarly evocative way: "There is reason to believe that the replacement *dumb girl is a Jewess*."[157] Its frequent use of words such as "mysterious," "puzzling," and "strangely" conveyed the author's delight in conjecture and echoed conspiracy theories. The newspaper used the story from Galicia to spin a scandalous yarn that had little connection with the actual events or actors.

Many members of the public approached the police, claiming they had either seen the missing child or knew who was behind the impostor.[158] One *Gazeta Warszawska* reader believed the girl to be identical with one found in a field in his parish six months previously, whom they had nursed and who after a time had set off "in the direction of the Austrian border." This was reported by the mayor of Pałecznica in the kingdom of Poland in a letter to the parish priest of Nowotanice. The letter and the concurrent Hilsner affair in Polna, which caused a scandal across the empire, motivated the priest to try to restart proceedings against the Bart family by addressing an interpellation to the Ministry of Justice. In his opinion, there was "no doubt that a child was murdered for ritual purposes, as none had ever been murdered for any 'other purposes.'"[159] The priest took the suspicions of ritual murder as fact, claiming to know that the murder of a child always indicated ritual murder and thus inevitably pointed to Jews as the perpetrators.[160]

Originally, it had been the other way around. Because the suspects were of the Mosaic faith, their neighbors had suspected a ritual murder. The priest, however, concluded from the fact that the victim was a Christian child that its murderer was Jewish. His letter of interpellation went on to accuse the "high government" of indifference and even of protecting the culprits [zbrodniarzy], just as it did in the Hilsner case. He demonstrated a clear talent for antisemitic demagogy, asserting the authority—as an expert on religious questions—to present suppositions and personal interpretations as facts and fully exploiting the potential for analogy offered by the scandalous case in Bohemia. In this light, ritual murders and their concealment seemed the eternal antitheses shaping Christian-Jewish coexistence. The missing child was one example; Agněžka Hrůbesova, the victim from Polna, another. The priest tried to win the aristocratic parliamentarian Count Potocki for his cause by implying that his decision whether to support it or not would be a test of whether he, too, was indifferent and therefore co-responsible for violating the truth, or whether he was a man of integrity. The priest's goal was to initiate a new trial, but not at the court in Nowy Sącz. With the politicians' help, he hoped to circumvent the small-town officials and present his village's interpretation of events in the imperial capital, Vienna. He shared the Galician opposition's mistrust of the local judiciary and faith in the power of interpellations. Indeed, he even composed his letter as if it were an interpellation, opening with a description of the scene and victims of the crime, then recounting the circumstances, and lastly making general comments about the failings of the court and the government, which had allowed such a crime to occur. The letter ended, just like a parliamentary request, with a list of signatures. These included his own, that of Karolina's mother, and Bukowski, the local mayor. Below them were the signatures of twenty-six women and men from Nowotanice—some clumsily scrawled, presumably by illiterate villagers, some fluently penned—who all supported the ritual murder theory and the bid for an interpellation. It was not a matter, then, of the people of Nowotanice accusing the Jews of ritual murder merely "in the first moment," as the public prosecutor had suggested.

Eleven months later they still believed it. Or did they believe it again, in the light of the Polna affair? There are no reports of violence in Nowotanice, either during the riots in summer 1898 or later that year, when Karolina went missing. Neither do the files mention any changes in the Bart family's situation over the years. How could a cattle trader continue living in a small village where he was suspected of murder for a whole year? Presumably life carried on as normal, occasionally interrupted by situations that reminded the villagers of Karolina's story. The reports on the affair in Polna and the priest reading out his letter before collecting signatures would have been such situations, in which the villagers' prejudice about Jewish ritual murder was updated and also given special credence by a clerical authority figure.

Jan Potocki did not incorporate the priest's letter into an interpellation. The popular perspective it took and the attacks on the government and judiciary it made would have suited the rhetoric of a member of the opposition in the Reichsrat but not a representative, like him, of the Galician elite and conservative member of the Polish Club. It is not known whether the priest appealed in parallel to any of the Christian anti-Semites, such as Szponder, Danielak, Szajer, or Stojałowski. Perhaps he had noticed that ritual murders were never the subject of the opposition's interpellations. But he nevertheless achieved his goal of relaunching investigations since Potocki passed his letter on to the minister of justice. The latter ordered further inquiries, which produced the above information behind the antisemitic imaginings. The officials in Vienna accepted the senior public prosecutor's findings, and the Bart family were not put on trial. Still, the attempt showed that the practice of interpellation had become firmly established as a way of creating publicity and connecting the most remote backwater with the seat of imperial politics. While the local community used the story to vent its anger at the loss of a child, which was never explained and never atoned for, it served the newspapers in Vienna as a sensational scoop from the murky depths of Galicia.

Fantasy and Conspiracy: The Case of Katarzyna Tabaka

Six years later, the *Deutsche Volksblatt* again described an incident in Galicia of alleged attempted ritual murder, which deserves closer consideration. This time, the version of events published in Ernst Vergani's newspaper prompted Galician officials into action, turning the carousel of antisemitic politics.[161] Like the previous case, it shows that antisemitism not only traveled from the center to the periphery but that Viennese anti-Semites also observed and received developments in the provinces. Stories concerning "Eastern Jews" committing ritual murder in "backward" Galicia suited the *Deutsche Volksblatt*'s profile. Its variety of reports vilifying a range of Jews, from emancipated "stockbroker Jews," lawyers, and doctors to the masses of unprogressive, fanatical, and diseased Jews from the East, lent the imperial capitals' antisemitic campaigns a decidedly explosive thrust.

At 6:00 p.m. on Sunday, 19 March 1905, Katarzyna Tabaka, a thirteen-year-old maid from Mytoczka, reported to the gendarme Jakub Król that on her way to church in Żmigród that morning she had been abducted by five Jews who had taken her to the house of Zimel Sender.[162] Her kidnappers had laid her on the straw-covered floor of Sender's cellar while they sat enthroned on white armchairs, eating bread rolls, she claimed. She had managed to escape in the evening, leaving her shoes and shawl behind. These pieces of clothing were later found in the cemetery. The gendarme apprehended the suspects Josef, Zimel, Malte, Chana, and Rhyma Sender and remanded them in custody.

The rumor started to spread that Katarzyna had been kidnapped for ritual purposes. Missionaries were active in the area in the pre-Easter period, giving live enactments of the Passion of Christ, and the authorities in Jasło feared that the situation might escalate into violence against Jews. The mood, they noted, was very tense. However, a search of the Senders' house did not produce any evidence of straw or breadcrumbs in the cellar, let alone white armchairs. Katarzyna could not pick out Zimel Sender from a lineup, and the gravedigger Piotr Wątkowski admitted having been given the clothing that he was supposed to have found in the cemetery. The senior public prosecutor in Krakow ordered the suspects' release and the launch of investigations into Piotr Wątkowski and Katarzyna Tabaka on charges of deception.[163] Katarzyna then admitted not having headed for church at all but visiting her mother in Poraj, six miles away. She had made up the story as an excuse to her employers for returning late. She was an adolescent girl seeking the attention she was denied in her daily life as a maid. In this regard, her lies and her vividly embellished story of white armchairs, bread rolls, and clothes symbolically buried in the cemetery served their purpose.

The case of Katarzyna Tabaka is one of hundreds of examples of ritual murder allegations in Catholic areas of Europe in the late nineteenth century.[164] If it had not come to the attention of the public prosecutor via the newspaper article, the story would probably soon have been forgotten. But the authorities were concerned not only to ensure that the true culprits were convicted at the end of a trial but also that the public received truthful information. They contested the version given in the *Deutsche Volksblatt* of the events and, even more significantly, of the royal-and-imperial public prosecutor's investigations. They therefore demanded that an alternative account was published. Of course, this was not enough to convince the readers of the *Deutsche Volksblatt*, or to restore the Jewish public's trust in the Galician police and judiciary, which had allowed a teenage girl's tales to result in an entire family being imprisoned and their hometown turning against them.

The clerical newspaper *Głos Narodu* was the first to report on the case of Katarzyna Tabaka under the heading "A suspicious incident."[165] It recounted that an adolescent girl had been sent to buy provisions from a "Jewish store" in Żmigród. Here, she had been dragged into a small room "by Jews." They had undressed and washed her and "shut her in the rearmost basement." When another Jew had gone to check on her, she had managed to escape and call for help. The rumor of a planned ritual murder had immediately started to circulate among the local population, and anger at the Jews rose to dangerous levels. While the accused Jews were remanded in custody, the other Jewish residents had called on the Franciscan monks in Krosno to cancel their planned mission to avoid inciting violence among the crowds it would attract.

That very evening, the *Deutsche Volksblatt* published its own coverage of the incident under the heading "A strange Jew-affair." This turned the childlike escapade into a sexually charged scandal, with a subheading that suggested rape was the motive behind the alleged abduction rather than ritual murder: "Jews indecently assault Christian girl." It described the thirteen-year-old maid as a "full-grown schoolgirl" who had been sent to a Jewish general store to buy provisions. "The Jews present in the store pulled the girl into an outlying parlor, where they *stripped her naked*, washed *her whole body* and locked her in a rear-facing basement." The article's use of emphases made sure the reader envisioned a rape scenario, in which men had their way with a physically mature girl, undressed her, touched her all over, and then kept her hidden away under lock and key. Under a thin veneer of news reporting, consisting of references to a "reliable source" and the geographical location, the actual purpose of the "strange" and "positively scandalous" story was to reflect male fantasies of power. It did not adhere to the conventional components of the ritual murder myth. The author left it up to the Galician peasants to interpret the events in terms of ritual-religious activities, while he focused the readers' attention on the naked, defenseless girl, who remained unnamed.

Having first been at the mercy of her kidnappers, she was then exposed to the scrutiny of the Christian residents:

> When after a while another Jew came into the cellar to check on the girl, she slipped out of the cellar door in the darkness, ran to freedom and started crying pitifully. The neighbors heard the cries and, seeing the naked girl, went to her rescue. The news spread through the village and the surrounding parishes as fast as lightning, causing an angry crowd to gather. As the Jewish Eastertime festival is approaching, people were speaking of nothing but the planned ritual murder. The mood among the peasants was extremely threatening and the afflicted Jews fled to nearby Krosno to the Franciscans, whom they begged for protection and at the same time asked to cancel the scheduled

popular mission, as this would attract a large gathering of people, which appeared very dangerous to the Jews. Meanwhile, however, the incident also came to the attention of the authorities and the suspicious Jews were detained in the prison in Jaslo. At the same time a judicial commission was delegated to Żmigród and made a record of the offense. The girl's clothing is said to have been found buried in Jewish ground.[166]

Two days later the *Deutsche Volksblatt* returned to the incident. Now it described the "strange Jew-affair" as a "mysterious" one, with a subheading that cited a recurring motif of antisemitic agitation in Vienna—the claim that the Alliance Israelite had attempted to cover up the crime. What had started as the fantasy of a girl in the Galician provinces who had duped a police constable in Żmigród became another chapter in the grand tale of the Jewish manipulation of law and order in the Habsburg Empire.

Apparently confirming its earlier report in the first sentence, the newspaper then went on to contradict its previous coverage of the incident.[167] It changed "schoolgirl" into "maid," and the charge that the kidnappers had "stripped her naked" into "removed most of her clothes," since she had left only her shoes and shawl behind. It did not attempt to explain the gravedigger's involvement but, building suspense, recounted it as a "peculiarity" and hinted in the style of a rumor ("people think . . .") that he had been bribed by Jews. The article was unequivocal, however, about the much more serious charge of Jewish manipulation, evident in the "Alliance Israelite in Vienna" dispatching the "advocate Dr. Friedmann" to act as attorney for the imprisoned Zemel family. This, it asserted, was to "hush up the affair"—with success, as it transpired: the senior public prosecutor ordered the family's release after some days. The author writing for the *Deutsche Volksblatt* juxtaposed the rulings by the public prosecutors in Jasło and Krakow, based on police findings following house searches and an identity parade, against the outrage of the perturbed "Christian population." In this way, he constructed a bond of solidarity between the newspaper's readers and the people in Żmigród, who had been powerless in the face of the shadowy "cover-up efforts" hat had lasted "several days," and which must have insulted their sense of justice in view of the near certainty that the suspects were guilty. Lastly, on 4 April, the *Deutsche Volksblatt* wrote that Wątkowski and Tabaka had been charged with giving false evidence and proceedings initiated on orders from the Austrian Israelite Union, which had sent a telegram to the Ministry of Justice.[168]

There is no record in the Ministry of Justice files of either the involvement of a Viennese advocate named Friedmann or a telegram from the Austrian Israelite Union. Nor is there any mention of either in internal communications. A letter from the Union, dated that September—after the first judgments had been pronounced—has survived. It demonstrates how sensitively justice was administered in Galicia and that fears of a biased judiciary were also widespread among Jews in Galicia.[169] On 4 September 1905, Siegfried Fein of the Austrian Israelite Union wrote to the privy councilor, announcing in laconic terms "two additions to the chapter on 'Galician justice.'" The first concerned the Jasło county court's overturning of the Żmigród district court's conviction of Katarzyna Tabaka, which Fein criticized. Indeed, a report by the senior public prosecutor in Krakow to the Ministry of Justice of February 1906 shows that, in the end, Piotr Wątkowski was sentenced to one week's imprisonment, and Katarzyna Tabaka, having first been sentenced to three months in the dungeon, was acquitted due to her young age at the time of the incident.

Again, it is unclear whether the Union's intercession had any impact on the courts. Certainly, the lawyers working for them were successful insofar as their clients in Galicia trusted them to have a decisive influence and believed it was ultimately thanks to their advocacy that the Sender family was released and the slanderers put on trial and sentenced.

In this regard, it is interesting that the Austrian Israelite Union echoed the Galician opposition by criticizing "Galician justice." But while the people's parties condemned the legal system's perceived tendency to support the Jews' unethical business practices to the detriment of the peasants, in the eyes of the Union, the shortcoming of Galician justice was its failure to penalize crimes against Jews. The second case that Siegfried Fein described in his letter concerned the failure to convict the alleged murderer of a certain Adam Edelman of Sokołów, Wladyk Pajak. "To the horror of all Jews," he was still at large. While members of the Austrian Israelite Union criticized the discrimination against Jews by the Galician judiciary, oppositionist interpellators tried to prove that the Galician courts were corrupted by Jews. The two groups referred to each other, used similar terminology, and communicated via the same channels of interpellation and newspaper coverage to condemn alleged crimes and the maladministration of justice. The interplay between antisemitic politics and groups representing Jewish interests is apparent in the similarity and entanglement of their major discourses, using allegations of Christian disadvantage or Jewish discrimination, respectively, to assert their interests in the context of a public that was highly sensitive to the struggle between nations and government efforts to hold the multiethnic empire together.

Counter-Rumors: Female Abduction and Clericalism in Galician Political Discourse

As the Austrian Israelite Union's telegram to the Ministry of Justice shows, Jewish actors also referred to the concept of "Galician justice." However, they did not use it to imply that the Galician authorities gave Jews preferential treatment. On the contrary, they used it to allude to the discrimination against Jews. The Austrian Israelite Union and its founding father, Reichsrat member and editor of the *Österreichische Wochenschrift* (Austrian Weekly News) Joseph Samuel Bloch, tried to construct an anti-antisemitic image of "Galician justice," so to speak, from the fabric of interwoven rumors, press coverage, and interpellations, akin to the antisemitic view.[170] The tale of "female abduction"[171] was an especially strong antidote to the antisemitic canon of Jewish crime and biased judiciary as it lambasted Galicia's uncompromising clericalism. The story of Jewish girls being forcibly baptized was a direct riposte to the ritual murder allegations, with their implications of sexual slavery. It, too, could be presented to the Viennese public as the credible reality in backward Galicia, just like the tales of ritual murder in the *Deutsche Volksblatt*.[172]

Joseph Samuel Bloch (1850–1923) was a member of the Reichsrat representing the conservative Polish Club from 1883 to 1895 and the first to promote decidedly Jewish political interests.[173] Along with his experiences as a traveler between Western and Eastern European Jewry, a Viennese rabbi and a member of the Polish Club had convinced him that the various national assimilation projects only served to disunite Jews, while the Christian majorities would never completely accept Jews as full members of their nations. It was no coincidence that Bloch came to this conclusion in Vienna in the early 1880s.[174] Populist politicians were increasingly harnessing a sense of hostility toward Jews and discussions of the "Jewish question" for their purposes. Bloch, in turn, used their antisemitism to propagate his own political concepts. He made his first appearance in the public arena as a critic of August Rohling and his "expertise" for the Tiszaeszlar trial.[175] Bloch's high-profile debunking of the German professor followed the conventions of a libel action. He not only defended the honor of the Jews but did so on all the platforms that anti-Semites used for their agitation. He argued with the enemies of the Jews before the court, in the Reichsrat, in his newspaper, and in the union that he founded.

"Girl Stealing"

Similar to female trafficking, "girl stealing" was a complex phenomenon and an expression of the major upheavals that were changing the lives of Galician Jews.[176] The term denoted the (attempted) conversion of underage Jewish girls to Catholicism in Roman Catholic convents, against the will of their parents.[177] It mostly concerned lower-middle-class girls from small towns in West Galicia who went to secular schools and were close friends with their Christian classmates.[178] Their motives for changing their religion, which often meant severing contact with their families, diverged widely.[179] Under Austrian law, it was legal to change one's religion without parental consent from the age of fourteen.[180] However, parents had the right of custody of their children up to the age of twenty-four. Hence, they could not legally stop their children from receiving baptism, but they could forbid them to live in a convent. The convents were breaking the law, then, by accommodating conversion-willing minors against their parents' will. In terms of the law, this was deemed abduction even if the girl explicitly wished to stay in the convent. The young women's motives and the psychological and social consequences of their converting were not discussed in public debates. The girls were not perceived as actors but as victims. The issue of girl stealing in Galicia first came to the public eye with the disappearance of Michalina Araten in the winter of 1899 and her father's untiring efforts to find her. This story, which even involved the emperor, drew a broad public's attention to the phenomenon, which the Austrian Israelite Union and other opponents of antisemitic politics incorporated into their campaign against antisemitism and clericalism.

The Araten Case

Michalina (Mechtsche) Araten left her parents' home in Stradomska Street in Krakow on 30 December 1899 to prepare for baptism in the Felician Sisters' Convent.[181] Her father Israel Jakob Araten went to the police to report his underage daughter missing. When he found out that Michalina was living in a convent, he demanded her release. He claimed that Michalina was not yet fourteen and therefore not eligible to change her religion without his consent. But Mother Superior Rozalia refused to let him see his daughter, and the police proved reluctant to help him and his wife. So, the Aratens turned to higher levels of government and published a photograph of Michalina (see figure 3.5) to appeal to the public for help getting her back. It showed a girl in a white dress, with melancholy, faraway eyes—undoubtedly still a child, not yet mature enough to make life-changing decisions.[182]

Israel Araten also carefully chose the words he used to describe his daughter, and how the convent brushed him off, to the police. His descriptions were so eloquent that some politicians and journalists repeated fragments of them word for word when discussing subsequent cases. Three interpellations, a speech by Julius Ofner in the Lower Austrian Landtag in 1900, and two requests by the National Jewish parliamentarian Benno Straucher of the Bukovina used quotes from Israel Araten's accounts.[183] He drew a picture of Rozalia as a hard-hearted and fanatically religious nun with absolutely no pity for him, the girl's despairing father. She admitted to him she was playing for time and keeping Michalina hidden in various places until she was old enough to be converted.[184] She responded to the information that Michalina's mother had fallen severely ill and would only recover if she saw her daughter again by saying that they would "see each other in heaven."[185] When Israel Araten fainted at the news, the Mother Superior said it was "a sign from God."[186]

As the police would not help Michalina's parents, her father wrote to the governor for assistance. He also went to see the minister of justice, the minister for Galicia, the minister of the interior and eventually Emperor Franz Joseph himself to appeal for intercession.[187] While the minister of justice, the minister of the interior, and the emperor all promised to send telegrams to order Michalina's immediate release, the minister of Galicia, Piętak, went down in history as say-

Figure 3.5. The picture of Michalina Araten her father gave to the police, AGAD Min. Spraw 287. Courtesy of the Archives.

ing "Secular power ends at the walls of the convent!" Reichsrat member Kareis vehemently objected to Piętak's anti-constitutional statement, sparking a minor parliamentary scandal.[188] But all Michalina's parents' efforts were in vain as the police and judiciary merely cautioned the mother superior that she was violating the law and refrained from taking any further action. When Israel Araten tried again to see his daughter in Smoleńska Street, she had already left the convent and gone into hiding. Various leads pointed to convents in Łagiewniki, Binczice, Morawice, Wola Justowska, Stanislau, Wielowieś, and Kenty.[189] A search of the Capuchin monastery in Kenty by two policemen, accompanied by Israel Araten, elicited a public outcry. The Krakow Curia complained; clerical newspapers railed against the disturbance of the monks' peace; and the antisemitic Reichsrat member Andrzej Szponder initiated an interpellation in protest.[190] The judiciary responded indecisively, first sentencing the policemen to ten days' imprisonment for overstepping their authority, but in the second instance annulling the decision.[191] Israel Araten claimed that the police commissioner in Krakow had told him he knew where Michalina was but it was not his job to bring young Jewish runaways back to their parents.

The Austrian Israelite Union attributed the same statement to the police inspector in Wieliczka, who brushed off another father, Marcus Weiss, when he reported that his daughter, Rochme, was missing.[192] Analogous to the antisemitic interpellations considered above, by a process of alteration and adaptation, the plaintiffs' accounts were shaped into texts that had repercussions on the situation in Galicia via interpellations and newspaper reports. The story of Michalina Araten established a template for the parents of runaway children to portray their fate as victims of fanatical Christians and the Galician police and judiciary. Mothers publicized their suffering and begged for information from the populace. Many claimed to have spoken with their daughters through a window or a crack in a fence.[193] Their daughters, they claimed, begged to be freed or told of their mistreatment at the convent.[194] Fathers took the official path and confronted the convents in question. The accounts of their experiences told of police ignorance of, and nuns' contempt for, their legal rights.

If victims told their stories according to the above narrative, they were assured of the attention of politicians and journalists, especially in Vienna, and so increased the chances of getting their daughters back. Like the construct of Jewish crime used in other interpellations, the "stolen girl" narrative was applied to individual grievances, which were then investigated, assessed by numerous mediators, and presented to the public. The newspapers of the empire publicized notions of the authorities' negligence in dealing with the issue of "girl stealing" in "clerical Galicia."[195] The mere headings of their articles, such as "New cases of girl stealing in Galicia"[196] and "Another girl stolen in Galicia,"[197] informed readers that there were many such cases. The articles portrayed the girls as the victims of kidnappings by simple Christian men and coldhearted nuns and priests, determined to conduct "enforced baptisms" despite the distress it caused both parents and children.[198] Although most of the affected were in fact young women, their absconding to a convent was rhetorically described as "child stealing"[199] to make the victims appear helpless and unknowing. At the same time, it called to mind parallels with the ritual murder myth. Rather than portraying the girls as active subjects who had decided to leave their parents' home, the stories focused on the motives of the kidnappers and nuns, who allegedly regarded the children as "spiritual booty."[200] Galicia, it was claimed, was the scene of "conversion agitation,"[201] "over-zealous tendencies to convert the young," and even "religious fanaticism."[202]

These counter-stories showed that not only Talmud-studying Jews could be accused of fanatical traits. Among Christians, there were apparently similar tendencies toward abusing people of other religions for their own plan for salvation, disregarding the legal equality of all citizens.[203] The reports of enforced baptisms in Galicia became media sensations, injecting anti-clerical viewpoints into political debate. They fell on fertile ground in Vienna, where the stereotypical view of fanatical Galician peasants was widely held. After all, the riots of summer 1898 had shown the peasants to be superstitious, anti-Jewish, and brutal. In a polemic published in Bloch's weekly, the historian Leo Herzberg-Fränkel even alleged that Christians were conducting "systematic child abduction" and that missing-persons cases were portrayed differently to the public depending on whether they concerned Jews or Christians:

> Who of us is still tempted to believe we live in a constitutional state, . . . when reaction inundates us from all sides and all that remains of the achievements of previous decades, all that remains of freedom and equality is thrown overboard? . . . Whoever knows of a grave sin against God and man simply grabs the first Jewish child he comes across and carries it off as a sin offering to the priest or the nearest convent, where [the child] remains irrecoverably entombed. . . . What does he care about earthly justice, which he never sees; what does he care about the parents' lamenting, they are only Jews! Oh, if it were the other way around! Woe betide not only the guilty Jew but all blameless Jewry if one of us is condemned for abducting a Christian child in order to raise it in the Mosaic religion! It is currently enough for a Christian boy or a Christian girl to be missing for some or other rowdy, swag-seeking individual to cast suspicion, no matter how vague, on a Jew and so unleash a whole revolution. Easter-blood! That nonsensical word turns women into harpies, draws the most infamous lowlifes out of their holes, drives dissolute journalists to act as presumptuously as public prosecutors and exposes entire communities to robbery and looting. And once this wild popular beast is released, nothing can help anymore, not even if the missing child or the girl who stayed too long with her lover returns home, safe and sound.[204]

Leo Herzberg-Fränkel had contributed the entry on Galician Jews to the 1898 edition of the *Kronprinzenwerk*, the Austro-Hungarian Monarchy's encyclopedia of regional studies.[205] Here, he had hegemonically placed "German knowledge" over the life-worlds of Eastern European Jews.[206] But now, in the postliberal era, he felt that the ideals of the constitutional state had been trampled underfoot by the clericals' bigoted regime. While the Mortara case had still elicited cries of outrage throughout Europe, treating Jews and Christians differently had now become normal. Herzberg-Fränkel himself noted a parallel between the narratives of "girl stealing" and the ritual murder myth.[207] Reporting on the abductions as if they had taken place against the will of the young women lent a cloak of reportage to the broader criticism the reports aimed to convey. Bloch's *Wochenschrift* published various commentaries on the ills of clericalism and the anti-Jewish mood in Galicia. One edition of the weekly newspaper ran a feature headed "The convent affair in parliament," which juxtaposed the text of Straucher's interpellation against an article taken from the *Arbeiter Zeitung* and a letter to the editor of the newspaper *Pester Lloyd* from a Protestant priest in Racz-Kozar. This priest denounced what he saw as an essentially un-Christian practice among many Catholics of converting girls to turn them into nuns.

The Galician convent stories were regarded by the opponents of clericalism of all religions as evidence of a change in the political climate in Austria. Increasingly, the Catholic church refused to submit to the authority of the state. Crucially, however, most of those who spoke out on the issue lived in Vienna, not Galicia. Their comments on the situation in the empire's largest crownland were, in a sense, repressive acts—colonial observations on a backward province.[208] A speech by Julius Ofner to the Lower Austrian Landtag is a good illustration:

> And the cases have another thing essentially in common: the convents' successful fight against the authority of the state. . . . We live in Europe, but one does not hear of such cases anywhere else in Europe, only here. And in Austria fortunately only in Galicia. . . . The [cause] lies in the conditions in Galicia. The rule of the schlachta, representing unadulterated clerical feudalism, has left its imprint on this unfortunate land. Eloquent and diplomatically clever, but domineering, self-serving and capricious, the schlachta, having ruined its own realm [the Polish-Lithuanian Commonwealth], now rules over Galicia and Austria. . . . The schlachta is joined by the Galician bureaucracy. . . . The Josephine official may not be a democrat . . . and he is motivated by a sense that he is able and destined to rule over the people. But he is law-abiding, unbiased, a protector of the weak and a defender of government authority, especially against church intervention. . . . But this tradition has suddenly been broken in Galicia. . . . Officialdom in Galicia is, then, not Austrian but stanczykish, and an order from Vienna is received and evaluated quite differently in Galicia than in the rest of Austria. The . . . cause of our cases lies in the ominous general tendency, which started in Austria in the eighties and has recently greatly intensified, toward a boom in clericalism. . . . Step by step, paragraph by paragraph, the achievements of the progressive era are drowned out by an all-oppressing clericalism. . . . We can surely surmise from the toleration of such a missionary hotbed . . . that the power of the clericals has in these years experienced an especially vigorous upturn.[209]

Ofner's speech is one of the many that referred to abduction stories to convey broader criticisms. The stories evoked associations with the ritual murder myth but portrayed Jews as the victims of fanatical Catholics and a hostile judiciary. They acted as a counternarrative to the canonized accusations of Jewish crimes and newspaper coverage of alleged ritual murders. Both discourses worked by communicatively interconnecting the center and the periphery and branding them mutually alien. Ofner considered the achievements of the Austrian administration in Galicia to have been undermined since the "minor compromise" by the Stanczyks' conservative-clerical rule. Hence his idealization of the hegemonial, centralist Josephine regime. Since Eduard Taafe's term as minister president, the Polish nobility and clergy had made ever more inroads into imperial policy, asserting the "backward" province's powers against the central government. The negative image of Galicia not only served as a contrast to the "civilized" center of the monarchy; it also performed an anti-conservative and anti-clerical function in imperial discourse. The large number of conservative Galicians in the Austrian parliament was portrayed in threatening terms as the "Galicization" of the monarchy. The achievements of the constitutional state seemed to be endangered by reactionary forces all over the empire. Enforced baptisms taking place before the eyes of the government in distant Galicia could be regarded as an indication of the creeping prevalence of conservative cabinets, ruling over the heads of parliament via emergency laws.[210]

Clearly, local officials bent the law when they refused to help parents get their children back, even if it would have been against the will of the children. But the problem was not that orders from Vienna were understood differently in Galicia than they were in the rest of Austria.[211] Rather, the problem was the loopholes that the orders from above contained. While the government aimed to ensure that justice was obtained, it left scope for avoiding trouble in the convents. In a three-page letter to the Galician governor of 11 December 1900, Minister of the Interior Koerber stressed that in the eyes of the law and the "case-law of the Supreme Court," the missing-child cases involved crimes of abduction and "no special emphasis" was necessary to know that "even if the abductee changes religion . . . it does not [protect] either the kidnapper or his accomplices from being accountable before the law." But a few lines later, he wrote that the authorities should decide whether to "accede to the wishes of the fathers for the return of the absconded children (§145) . . . or whether it would be more in the interests of the children to allow them the possibility, against the wishes of their fathers, by staying in a new environment (children's home, convent) of a better education and upbringing and so to build the foundation for a happier future."[212]

In this way, Koerber conceded options for sidestepping the law. Although the authorities might not have wished to deliberately disadvantage Jewish parents, they did so to avoid the unpleasant task of disturbing the convent peace. Many observers believed, moreover, that the girls were better off in a convent than in their family homes. Such opinions influenced the governor's decision on whether to help the parents of missing children obtain justice, as an internal document of 1909 shows: "The cases of the abduction or escape of Jewish girls to convents are caused above all by their being prevented from marrying Catholics, for which reason the former leave their parents' home seeking protection and supervision in convents and voluntarily enter in to the bosom of the Catholic church to facilitate a marriage. . . . These facts never surface in public."[213] The governor's office, then, cast doubt on the prevalent reading of the conversions in the Viennese press and by the girls' parents. Several escape helpers were nonetheless put on trial, some receiving sentences of several months' imprisonment, but the nuns and priests in the convents and monasteries were consistently spared. Yet it was not a cast-iron Galician tradition to avoid searches of convents or actions against the clergy, not even in "clerical" Krakow. The famous case of Anna, alias Barbara Ubryk,[214] can serve as an illustration of the situation in 1900.

A Liberal Interlude: Anticlerical Protests and the Rule of Law in Krakow

In July 1869, the Krakow district court received a tip-off that a nun was being kept in inhumane conditions in the convent of the Discalced Carmelites. The police were granted a search warrant on condition of confidentiality, but the shocking findings of the search surfaced nonetheless: a mentally ill woman from the kingdom of Poland (Barbara Ubryk) had been living in a tiny, unheated cell, with one window that was almost entirely bricked up, for twenty-one years.[215] She received a paltry amount of food through a hatch in the permanently locked door to her cell, and was found to be emaciated and covered in injuries from throwing herself at the cell walls.

The rumors of the mistreated nun spread like wildfire, mobilizing thousands of Krakow citizens to protest. On 24 July, they tried to storm the convent in Wesoła Street. Hussars were called in to fend off the anti-clerical hordes, who also threatened to attack the Jesuit and Norbertine monasteries. Mother Superior Maria Wężyk was taken to court but was eventually acquitted. Neither opinion makers nor the state regarded the action against the convent to be a breach of taboo. On the contrary, broad sections of the population joined in the protests at the smug complacency and arrogance of the clergy in "little Rome."[216]

Karakow Clericalism around 1900

By the late 1890s, the climate had changed in favor of the clericals and against the liberals' advocacy of the rule of law. The two highest-profile cases of convent internment, outlined above, differed not only in terms of the zeitgeist with which they coincided, but also because the Araten case involved a Jew crossing the threshold of a convent. In an interpellation concerning the latter case, anti-Semite Andzrej Szponder described Araten's entry into the convent as a brutal intrusion that injured the "sacred feelings" of the Catholic population. Summarily equating the "Catholic population" with the church, he shifted the focus away from the relationship between the state and the church to negotiate the relationship between the state and Christians or their antagonists, the Jews. By this antisemitic reading of the abduction, to demagogically attack Araten and the judiciary was to defend the Christian community against a Jewish-obedient press and courts:

So, it has come to this, that in a *Catholic state* even the quiet of the convent is defiled and profanely treated! If Christians did something like that in a synagogue, the entire Jewish press would howl with anger and attack everything that is Christian, with the consequence that the Christian daredevils would be fettered in chains and sentenced to hard dungeon imprisonment. But this only concerned a Catholic convent, in that the convent of the poor Felicians was violated by *Jews and their accomplices*, who are unfortunately permitted to do anything in Austria. The high royal-and-imperial government might take note that if it tolerates such acts of Jewish violence and even supports them, if it continues to leave all the Jews' terrible abuses unpunished, it must seriously fear that the Christian population will feel compelled to defend itself, which might pose a substantial risk to the public order and peace."[217]

Szponder advised the minister of the interior to "make violent acts such as these impossible, and to protect the Christian population against insult and provocation by Jewish misdeeds.[218]

This was an unadulterated expression of clerical antisemitism, enriched with an alternative interpretation of the riots of summer 1898 as self-defense. Yet the sense of outrage elicited by a Jew entering a convent with the assistance of public servants was by no means limited to anti-Semites. Regardless of the citizen's right to speak to his child, even members of the Upper House were motivated to sign a protest interpellation by the conservative parliamentarian Bilinski. Signatories Stanisław Badeni,[219] Stanisław Tarnowski, and Tadeusz Dzieduszycki were among the most prominent representatives of Galician conservatism. While superficially moderate, like Szponder's interpellation, the text placed the majority population's religious feelings above the law and asserted that Israel Araten had committed acts of defilement:

> The Mother Superior was forced to bow to the stronger force; the search was not only stringently carried out in the cells of all the convent inhabitants but in the presence of Araten, who is said to have loudly cursed and ranted about the convent institution in the process. The result of the search was wholly negative as the missing person was not in the convent. However, the entire procedure caused grave offense and outrage among the Christian-Catholic population as it violated article 9 of the basic state law of 21st December 1867 and especially as the entering of a convent enclosure by an Israelite made a mockery of the convent rules. The upset of the Christian-Catholic population must have been all the greater for the fact that the very next day, in a busy alley in Krakow, an incident occurred in broad daylight that provides clear evidence of the kind of brutish violence to which a female Israelite who has converted to the Christian-Catholic faith is exposed from her closest Jewish relatives.[220]

The interpellators concluded by asking the minister president and the minister of justice how they intended to prevent "similar excesses by fanatical Israelites." The minister for Galicia was not alone in his objection to secular laws being applied beyond the convent walls—the conservative leadership of the land naturally agreed with him, asserting they had the backing of "the Catholic population." From this perspective, the Jews' legal equality also ended at the convent walls. Terms such as "fanatical Israelites" were appropriated from the anti-Jewish discourse that accused Jews of practicing arcane rites, learned from the Talmud. They followed a strategy of defamation, previously used to argue against legal equality, and now reapplied to attack Jews whom the predominant Christian community considered to be acting presumptuously by making an issue of female abductions to convents.

The "brutish violence ... in broad daylight" mentioned by the interpellators was a reference to the attempted blackmail of Lea (or Stanisława, or Maria) Jacob of Wieliczka by her brother-in-law Bernard Bernstein and her brother Adolf Jacob, as reported by the major newspapers.[221] Lea had converted to Christianity and become engaged to a Christian clerk, Stanisław Świerczek. While out looking for furniture for their home, she had been lured into a trap by the furniture dealer Saul Selzer of Tomasz Street. Here, her brother and brother-in-law demanded that she either return to Judaism or give back her share of the inheritance from her late parents. The cries for help of a friend who had accompanied Lea/Stanisława attracted a crowd of people and a gendarme, who freed her.[222] The attack seemed to confirm the rumors that female converts faced mortal danger if their families caught up with them.[223] And the interpellators' references to it clearly illustrated how rumors based on stereotypes steered individual readings of factual information; to a large extent, the rumors and the readings were mutually dependent. The "fanaticism" of the nuns was regarded as a reaction to Jewish religious fanaticism, and vice versa. The narrative of convent abduction generated publicity not only for the opponents of clericalism. It was also used by anti-Semites and conservatives as evidence of "Jewish arrogance." Tales of conversions and the reactions they elicited could be exploited by different groups to publicly claim a collective disadvantage. Ultimately, both Jewish accusations of discrimination and antisemitic complaints of "anti-Christian feeling" negotiated the role of the state as a mediator between the religions and the influence of the church. Over time, the debates changed the way people spoke about Galicia, Jews, and clericalism.

On an imperial level, Galicia served as an example of the negative effects of a conservative government turning away from secular principles. But within Galicia, the stories of convent abductions lent a voice to precisely those Catholic circles who condemned the "impertinence" of the "liberal central government" and the Viennese press. The debate on female abductions and clerical justice also bonded the Jewish community—both within Galicia, as a minority that was de facto denied legal equality in some areas, and across the empire, as a mutually supportive community. Interest groups, assistance services, and supraregional parliamentary representation promoted a sense of community, offering a way forward from Central Europe's nationalism dilemma.[224] This development put pressure on the Jewish politicians in the Polish Club, who campaigned for assimilation into the Polish nation. In view of the close intermeshing of the Catholic religion and the Polish nation, they were doomed to remain silent in the dispute over convent abductions. Antisemitism and public reactions to the discrimination of Jews changed the way in which the future of Christian-Jewish coexistence in Galicia was discussed—for everyone involved.

Notes

1. Cf. chapter 1 in the present book, section "The Christian-Social Movement in the City"; also Józef Buszko, *Polacy w parlamencie Wiedeńskim 1848–1918* (Warsaw, 1996), 214–239. On the political system in general, see Karl Ucakar, *Demokratie und Wahlrecht in Österreich* (Vienna, 1998); Hans Peter Hye, *Das politische System der Habsburgermonarchie* (Prague, 1998).
2. On these events, also known as the Badeni Crisis, see Hannelore Burger and Helmut Wohnout, "Eine polnische Schufterei? Die Badenischen Sprachenverordnungen für Böhmen und Mähren," in Michael Gehler and Hubert Sickinger (eds), *Politische Affären und Skandale in Österreich* (Vienna, 1995), 79–98; Hans Mommsen, "1897: Die Badeni-Krise als Wendepunkt in den deutsch-tschechischen Beziehungen," in Detlef Brandes (ed.), *Wendepunkte in den Beziehungen zwischen Deutschen, Tschechen und Slowaken 1848–1989* (Essen, 2007), 111–118.
3. Julia Schmid, *Kampf um das Deutschtum: Radikaler Nationalismus in Österreich und dem Deutschen Reich 1890–1914* (Frankfurt a. M., 2009).
4. Andrew G. Whiteside, *Georg Ritter von Schönerer: Alldeutschland und sein Prophet* (Graz, 1981). Especially in Prague, Jews were caught in the crossfire between the opposing nationalities. See Michal Frankl, *"Prag ist nunmehr antisemitisch": Tschechischer Antisemitismus am Ende des 19. Jahrhunderts* (Berlin, 2011).
5. See Peter Bettelheim and Robert Harauer (eds), *Ostcharme und Westkomfort: Beiträge zur politischen Kultur Österreichs* (Vienna, 1993), especially the chapter by Ernst Hanisch, "'An erlaubten G'spaß – ka Silb'n Politik?' Die historischen Grundlagen der politischen Kultur Österreichs," 15–41.
6. The Galician opposition coined the term "Badenismus" (Badenism) to sum up the political situation they condemned. Badeni was also critically viewed by Vienna's anti-Semites since he had opposed Karl Lueger's appointment as mayor of Vienna.
7. He was referring to the strong presence of Poles in the Cisleithanian government and the appointment of Heinrich Ritter von Halban-Blumenstock, a man of Jewish faith, as director of the Parliamentary Office. See Adam Wandruszka, "Die Krisen des Parlamentarismus 1897 und 1933: Gedanken zum Demokratieverständnis in Österreich," in idem and Rudolf Neck (eds), *Beiträge zur Zeitgeschichte: Festschrift Ludwig Jedlicka zum 60. Geburtstag* (St. Pölten, 1976); Binder, *Galizien in Wien*, 352.
8. German-nationalist circles' perception of Galicia as an "export land" will be considered below. Sten. Prot. 6. Sitzung der 12. Session vom 9. April 1897, 239–243.
9. On the duel and reactions to it, see Łazuga, *Rządy polskie*, 181–183.
10. Buszko, *Polacy w oarlamencie*, 222; Binder, *Galizien in Wien*, 356.
11. Dagmar Burkhart, *Eine Geschichte der Ehre* (Darmstadt, 2006).

12. Binder, *Galizien in Wien*.
13. Moritz Csáky argues that the linguistic, ethnic, and cultural diversity within the relatively small area of Central Europe called for and promoted a "pragmatism of coexistence" over the centuries. "Paradigma Zentraleuropa: Pluralitäten, Religionen und kulturelle Codes; Religion-Mythos-Nation; Einführende Überlegungen," in idem and Klaus Zeyringer (eds), *Pluralitäten, Religionen und kulturelle Codes* (Innsbruck, 2001), 9–18. See also Wolfgang Müller-Funk, "Kakanien revisited: Über das Verhältnis von Herrschaft und Kultur," in idem, Peter Plener, and Clemens Ruthner (eds), *Kakanien revisited: Das Eigene und das Fremde (in) der österreichisch-ungarischen Monarchie* (Tübingen, 2002), 14–32.
14. Cf. Peter Stachel, "Ein Staat, der an einem Sprachfehler zugrunde ging: Die 'Vielsprachigkeit' des Habsburgerreiches und ihre Auswirkungen," in Johannes Feichtinger and Peter Stachel (eds), *Das Gewebe der Kultur: Kulturwissenschaftliche Analyse zur Geschichte und Identität Österreichs in der Moderne* (Innsbruck, 2001), 11–45.
15. Scholars of media studies would therefore find regarding language as a medium problematic, while communication science does see language as a medium of communication. Kay Kirchmann, "Das Gerücht und die Medien: Medientheoretische Annäherungen an einen Sondertypus der informellen Kommunikation," in Manfred Bruhn and Werner Wunderlich (eds), *Medium Gerücht: Studien zu Theorie und Praxis einer kollektiven Kommunikationsform* (Bern, 2004), 67–85, 72.
16. Consequently, language is a reservoir of common memories, pasts, and interpretations of those on the one hand and a means to disseminate and harness the contents of this reservoir on the other. Cf. Karoshi, "Patriotismus und Staatserhalt," 12.
17. Stachel, "Ein Staat," 11.
18. On the policy of obstruction and the mechanisms and logics of the Reichsrat, see Lothar Höbelt, "Parliamentary Politics in a Multinational Setting: Late Imperial Austria," Working Paper by the Center for Austrian Studies 92-6, University of Minnesota, http://cas.umn.edu/assets/pdf/WP926.PDF, accessed 28 July 2015.
19. The notoriously bad behavior of many parliamentarians was immortalized by Mark Twain in his accounts of the session he attended in November 1897.
20. Dvořak, *Politik und die Kultur*.
21. Hanisch, *Der lange Schatten des Staates*.
22. Robert Kriechbaumer, *Die großen Erzählungen der Politik: Politische Kultur und Parteien in Österreich von der Jahrhundertwende bis 1945* (Vienna, 2001).
23. Carl Schorske, *Fin-de-siecle Vienna: Politics and Culture* (New York, 1981), 9.
24. *Neue Freie Presse*, 6 April 1897, Abendausgabe (Evening edition), 2.
25. Wood, "Sex Scandals"; Vyleta, *Crime, Jews and News*; Larry Wolff, *Ansichtskarten vom Weltuntergang: Kindesmisshandlung in Freuds Wien* (Salzburg, 1992).
26. Both the entertaining and the identity-creating dimensions of the press coverage of trials are described in the introduction.
27. Moritz Csáky, *Ideologie der Operette und Wiener Moderne: Ein kulturhistorischer Essay* (Vienna, 1998).
28. The theatrical presentation and depersonalization of the judge and public prosecutor is designed to instill the belief that where "law and justice" prevail, uniform, unbiased judgments will be passed. See also André Brodocz (ed.), *Institutionelle Macht: Genese-Verstetigung-Verlust* (Cologne, 2005); Oswald Schwemmer, "Die Macht der Symbole," *Aus Politik und Zeitgeschichte* 20 (2006): 7–14.
29. Interestingly, the temporary premises that preceded the Reichsrat building (1861–1883) in Vienna's ninth district were unofficially known as the Schmerling Theater, after the

liberal politician and Austrian minister president Anton von Schmerling. *Justitia fundamentum regnorum*, or, in the words of Friedrich Schiller, "Der Anker, an welchem die Staaten hängen, ist die Gerechtigkeit" (the anchor to which the states cling is justice), was emblazoned on Hofburg Palace. Since it was the constitutional era, Emperor Franz I, who chose the motto, no doubt implied the constitutional state. On the debate surrounding the constitutionality of the Habsburg Monarchy, see Adam Wandruszka, "Ein vorbildlicher Rechtsstaat?," in idem and Peter Urbanitsch (eds), *Die Habsburgermonarchie 1848–1918*, vol. 2: *Verwaltung und Rechtswesen* (Vienna, 1975), ix–vxiii.

30. Andreas Poltermann (ed.), *Literaturkanon-Medienereignis-Kultureller Text: Formen interkultureller Kommunikation und Übersetzung* (Berlin, 1995). According to Gregory Bateson, canonization is a distinction that makes a distinction. Cit. from Siegfried J. Schmidt and Peter Vorderer, "Kanonisierung in Mediengesellschaften," in ibid., 144–159, 144.
31. Schmidt and Vorderer, "Kanonisierung," 145.
32. The method by which interpellations functioned is more closely considered in the subsection "Antisemitic Interpellations between the Capital and the Villages" in this chapter, as it is connected to the specific context of the peasant parties and their relationship with their voters, which is described in chapter 1.
33. On the huge significance of crime and criminality for understanding society around 1900, see Vyleta, *Crime, Jews and News*, 14–39.
34. See the introduction.
35. This also coincided with a rapid change in the economic and legal situation of the Jews and their social and spatial mobility.
36. This process of translation constitutes the "extreme stretching of a formerly spoken situation." By writing down a spoken situation, it is stored, divested of its situational character, and turned into a text that can be retrieved any number of times. In other words, *one* spoken situation yields a potentially unlimited number. Cf. Jan Assmann, "Kulturelle Texte im Spannungsfeld von Mündlichkeit und Schriftlichkeit," in Andreas Poltermann (ed.), *Literaturkanon-Medienereignis-Kultureller Text: Formen interkultureller Kommunikation und Übersetzung* (Berlin, 1995), 270–292, 272.
37. On the Polish Club, see Philip Pająkowski, "The Polish Club and Austrian Parliamentary Politics, 1873–1900," PhD diss., Indiana University, 1989.
38. Staudacher, "Der Bauernagitator."
39. The previous time, they had accused the Polish Club of election fraud.
40. The opposing speaker, Ritter von Milewski of the Polish Club, then criticized what he condemned as an abuse of the right to interpellation, dulling this "sharpest of weapons." For the full debate, see Sten. Prot. 22. Sitzung der XV. Session 22 November 1898, 1426–1468, and of 24 November. For the full proposal text, see "Antrag betreffend die Anklage gegen die Minister der Gesamtregierung wegen der Verordnung vom 28. Juni 1898, 209 der Beilagen zu den Stenogr. Prot. Des Abgeordnetenhauses-XV. Session 1898," S. 1. Minister President and Minister of the Interior Thun, who was responsible for imposing martial law, defended himself and the Galician governor Piniński in a riposte following Daszyński's speech.
41. The term *Schlachziz* was derived from *szlachta*, the Polish word for the privileged noble class. During this debate, parliament agreed that the nature of the Polish *szlachta* was so specific that the German word *Adel* (nobility/aristocracy) did not capture "what the Schlachta is according to historical and Polish concepts." Emil Byk, Sten. Prot. 22. Sitzung der XV. Session, 24 November 1898, 1436.

42. The state of emergency had been imposed "merely at the request of one political party, and moreover for the notorious purpose of facilitating this party's political battle against other parties."
43. By way of evidence, he cited an article in *Czas*, which suggested preventing further electoral successes for social democracy by claiming it was a Jewish invention. The article ran under the heading "Poison against poison" and demonstrated the conservatives' manipulative exploitation of the Jewish issue: "And then [following the Social Democrats' electoral success in Krakow] along came their battle organ with a battle cry, a new slogan: 'poison against poison,' to inoculate the antisemitic, Christian Social poison against the social democratic, against the oppositionist poison. It was explicitly formulated thus in two leading articles: poison against poison! Gentlemen, how they have injected this poison! This poison was instilled drop by drop every day by their prostituted press. It regularly stirred up hatred and pelted every oppositionist with excrement, tirelessly and carefully, so that not one clean spot was left on a man." Bishop Puzyna of Krakow financially supported the newspaper *Der Antisemit*. Sten. Prot. 21. Sitzung der XV. Session am 22. November 1898, 1364.
44. "Every one of us knows . . . that these mighty schlachziz purloin thousands upon thousands of the net income from the public purse, and then shift all the contempt of the unknowing people on to their only accomplices, namely the village Jews." Sten. Prot. AH 21. Sitzung der XV. Session am 22. November 1898, 1361. Unowsky assesses Daszyński's indictment as a hypocritical charge: Unowsky, "Peasant Political Mobilization."
45. The *Neue Freie Presse* was the first to publicize this term in its coverage of the unrest in Wieliczka.
46. Sten. Prot. AH 21. Sitzung der XV. Session am 22. November 1898, 1481.
47. *Neue Freie Presse*, 25 November 1898, 2.
48. Alfred Dreyfus had been exiled to Devil's Island in French Guiana. Cf. Stephen Wilson, *Ideology and Experience: Antisemitism in France at the Time of the Dreyfus Affair* (Rutherford, 1982); Michael Burns, *Rural Society and French Politics: Boulangism and the Dreyfus Affair* (Princeton, 1984).
49. See chapter 2, section "The Empire Strikes Back."
50. Explicitly antisemitic conspiracy theories were most often alluded to in parliament by clerical members of the People's Party. One such incident had occurred a year previously in a debate in which the German anti-Semite Leopold Steiner (1857–1927) and the prelate Josef Scheicher (1842–1924) claimed that Jews had a bad influence on Galicia. Officially registered as an "actual rectification," the Greek Catholic priest Danylo Taniackevyć of the National Radicals had, with the consent of the antisemitic faction in parliament, described Jews as a "demoralizing and corrosive element." Andrzej Szponder (1856–1945), even after several warnings from the president, insisted on claiming that Jews were "either instigators or initiators" of "all despicable matters." "Theft," Szponder went on, "swindling of diverse kinds, false oaths" were "daily and common fare for the Jews." Jews, he maintained, were a plague on Galicia. Neither Szponder nor Taniackevyć used the term "antisemitism." Sten. Prot. 28. Sitzung der XIII. Session am 22. November 1897, 1777f.
51. Sten. Prot. AH 21. Sitzung der XV. Session am 22. November 1898, 1481.
52. Mendelsohn, "Jewish Assimilation," 581; Soboń, "Polacy wobec Żydów," 252.
53. Cf. chapter 1, section "The Debate on the Emancipation of Jews in Galicia."
54. Sten. Prot. 22. Sitzung der XV. Session, 24. November 1898, 1576f.

55. *Neue Freie Presse*, 25 November 1898, 2.
56. Buszko, *Polacy w parlamencie*, 221.
57. Häusler, "Zwischen Wien und Czernowitz," 67f.
58. He earned the criticism of his more radical brother Stanisław for this. Binder, *Galizien in Wien*, 215 and 354.
59. Theodore Weeks, "Poles, Jews, and Russians, 1864–1914: The Death of the Ideal of Assimilation in the Kingdom of Poland," *Polin: Studies in Polish Jewry* 12 (1999): 243.
60. In a parliamentary speech in March 1897, Andrzej Danielak cited his party comrade Tomasz Szajer as saying that the emperor must curtsey before Rothschild. Szajer lost his immunity as a result and was arrested for insulting the sovereign. Karl Lueger referred to the comment in a discussion, prompting further press coverage of the incident across the empire. Sten. Prot. 12. Session, 2. Sitzung, 31–32.
61. During the debate on the state of emergency in Galicia, a German Prague-based parliamentarian named Emil Pfersche and a member of the Young Czech Party named Herold argued over who was to blame for the unrest surrounding the language dispute the previous year in Prague, which had resulted in the local imposition of martial law. Sten. Prot. 22. Sitzung der XV. Session am 22. November 1898, 1483.
62. Franciszek Krempa (1853–1935) was a farmer from Mielec district and was voted by the fourth class of electors of the constituencies Ropczyce, Mielec, Radomyśl, Tarnobrzeg, and Rozwadów to represent the Secular People's Party (SL), defeating the candidate from the (conservative) Central Electoral Committee, Henryk Dolański. At the next elections in 1900, Krempa defeated both the conservative candidate, Adam Kopcyński, and the candidate for the Christian People's Party, Włodzimierz Lewicki, who had lost to Jan Stapiński in the by-election of 1898.
63. Non-German speaking parliamentarians only addressed the house to filibuster, not to make points. Binder, *Galizien in Wien*, 367. Krempa could have prepared a speech in Polish and had it translated into German. But under §55 of parliamentary law, only reporters and members of parliamentary committees were permitted to read out prepared speeches. Some members of parliament occasionally read off parts of their speeches despite the ban.
64. Rosdolsky, *Untertan und Staat in Galizien*.
65. Buchen, "Herrschaft in der Krise."
66. This is illustrated by the above-mentioned rumor circulated during the riots that the member of parliament Stojałowski had brought a warrant to beat Jews from the emperor in Vienna.
67. To this end, they announced when they would be in the editor's office in Krakow or visiting their constituencies. See "Help parliamentarians do their work" [Pomóźcie posłom w pracy] "your points must be well documented and supported by evidence," *Przyjaciel Ludu*, no. 26, 19 September 1898 and *Kronika* of 10 March 1898. In the clerical newspaper *Antysemita*, with its connections with the parliamentarians Szponder and Danielak, the call for letters in the masthead came with the appeal to "pillory every matter in public."
68. According to *Przyjaciel Ludu* of 10 March 1898, Szajer claimed that the emperor attended sessions in parliament. In fact, Franz Joseph never set foot in the Reichsrat. Hanisch, *Der lange Schatten des Staates*.
69. *Obrona Ludu*, 4 February 1899, 16; and *Obrona Ludu*, 11 November 1899.
70. Translation not only applies to "linguistic content" but also to the modes of thinking that are embodied in the content. Talad Asad, "Übersetzen zwischen Kulturen: Ein Konzept

der britischen Sozialanthropologie," in Eberhard Berg and Martin Fuchs (eds), *Kultur, soziale Praxis, Text: Die Krise der ethnographischen Repräsentation* (Frankfurt a. M., 1999), 300–334, 301. Seen in this broader context, translation theory is part of all cultural theory.

71. On the application of linguistic concepts to cultural theory since the "linguistic turn," see Doris Bachmann-Medick, *Übersetzung als Repräsentation fremder Kulturen* (Berlin, 1997).
72. In the view of ethnologist Stephen Tyler, "representation" always involves "repression," both in representational democracy and in the relationship between writer and speaker. Stephen Tyler, "Zum 'Be-/Abschreiben' als 'Sprechen für': Ein Kommentar," in Berg and Fuchs, *Kultur, soziale Praxis, Text*, 288–296, 288.
73. Repetition and "re-presentation" are requisite elements of successful political representation. Jonathan Fabian, "Präsenz und Repräsentation: Die Anderen und das anthropologische Schreiben," in Berg and Fuchs, *Kultur, soziale Praxis, Text*, 335–364, 339.
74. "Repräsentationen (im Plural) werden dann als Handlungen oder Sequenzen von Handlungen betrachtet, kurz: als *performances*. *Performances* benötigen Akteure und Publikum, Autoren und Leser." See ibid., 335ff.
75. In the term following the first general elections of 1906, Galician members of parliament, apart from the Social Democrats, completely disintegrated into national groups in the Reichsrat. The *Volksfraktion* joined the Polish Club in April 1908, with which the Christian Social Association, being the clerical "center party," had already merged during the previous term. The Jewish national politicians constituted their own club, and the "Ruthenian Club" went from opposing to filibustering after the disturbances at Lemberg University. Cf. Binder, *Galizien in Wien*, 431ff.
76. Nevertheless, the flood of interpellations addressing "Galician misery" impacted the Viennese public. Cf. Maner, *Galizien*, 149ff.
77. Frequently under headlines such as "Another successful interpellation by Dr. Danielak," *Obrona Ludu*, 27 May 1899, 12; "Interpellation by Danielak," *Obrona Ludu*, no. 4, 1899, 12; or "Successful interpellations," *Przyjaciel Ludu*, no. 14, 10 May 1898.
78. Pompe, "Nachrichten über Gerüchte," 133.
79. Thomas S. Eberle, "Gerücht oder Faktizität? Zur kommunikativen Aushandlung von Geltungsansprüchen," in Bruhn and Wunderlich, *Medium Gerücht*, 85–116.
80. On rumors as networks, see Neubauer, *Fama*, 254.
81. Not all interpellations by anti-Semites were antisemitic. They were in fact far more frequently concerned with issues such as river regulation, bridge construction, crop damage caused by military maneuvers, and abuses of power by Galician officials.
82. This was the second semantic filter in antisemitic discourse.
83. "Jewish crime" was the topic of twenty-five interpellations by the above-mentioned parliamentarians up to the first session of the Reichsrat following the general election in 1907.
84. Sten. Prot. AH 35. Sitzung der XV. Session am 27. Jänner 1899, 2288.
85. The mental incompetence of the peasants was stressed not only to win public favor but also to help attain pardons for those who had been arrested. To get penalties reduced, defendants emphasized the wrongdoers' remorse and claimed they had now realized that the warrant to beat the Jews had been a "fairytale."
86. Sten. Prot. AH 18. Sitzung der XVI. Session am 23. November 1899, 1157. For an account of military ordeals, see Sten. Prot. AH 5. Sitzung der XV. Session am 4. Oktober 1898, 291f. Cf. also Christa Hämmerle, "Dort wurden wir dressiert und sekiert und geschlagen . . .': Vom Drill, dem Disziplinarstrafrecht und Soldatenmisshandlungen im Heer (1868 bis 1914)," in Laurence Cole, Christa Hämmerle, and Martin Scheutz

(eds.), *Glanz – Gewalt – Gehorsam: Militär und Gesellschaft in der Habsburgermonarchie (1880–1918)* (Essen, 2011), 31–54.

87. The suicide rate in the royal-and-imperial army was the highest in Europe. István Deak, *Beyond Nationalism: A Social and Political History of the Habsburg Officer Corps 1848–1918* (Oxford, 1990), 107; Hannes Leidinger, "Suizid und Militär: Debatten – Ursachenforschung – Reichsratinterpellationen 1907–1914," in Cole, Hämmerle, and Scheutz, *Glanz – Gewalt – Gehorsam*, 337–358.
88. Allmayer-Beck, "Die bewaffnete Macht," 111.
89. This could perhaps be attributed to the crownland's negative image and stereotypical notions of "Polish economy," as well as the fact that being stationed in Galicia was regarded as a punishment. A request to the provincial defense and railways minister showed that the problem was not only a clash between the military and the civilian population but also a national conflict, defining Galicia as "Polish soil" on which "military persons and Germans" should approach the "Polish population" with "polite and humane conduct." Sten. Prot. AH 235. Sitzung der XVI. Session am 19. Juni 1903, 21462f. An insider's view of the military sense of honor and the difficult nature of restoring it vis-à-vis civilians is provided by Arthur Schnitzler's novella *Lieutenant Gustl*, which at the time of its publication was perceived as an affront to the officer's rank and cost Schnitzler, a reserve officer, the title of honorary council. Arthur Schnitzler, *Lieutenant Gustl* (Berlin, 1901); Hanisch, *Der lange Schatten des Staates*, 218.
90. Peter Hauser (ed.), *Säbel, Degen und Pistole: Zweikampfregeln für den k. u. k. Offizier* (Hilden, 2007); Hubert Mader, *Duellwesen und altösterreichisches Offizierseethos* (Osnabrück, 1983).
91. Deak, *Beyond Nationalism*; Hanisch, *Der lange Schatten des Staates*; Allmayer-Beck, "Die Bewaffnete Macht."
92. Sten. Prot. AH 3. Sitzung der XV. Session am 30. September 1898, 138.
93. Ibid.
94. As mentioned above, investigations showed that Winiarski had not given any orders to shoot. Cf. chapter 2 of the present book, section "The Riots from the Perpetrator Perspective."
95. Sten. Prot. AH 4. Sitzung der XV. Session am 3. Oktober 1898, 251ff.
96. The district captain's account should be remembered here, according to which he had rebuffed the Jewish delegation's first request and only agreed to reinforcements after their second appeal.
97. Sten. Prot. AH 2. Sitzung der XV. Session am 29. September 1898, 59; Sten. Prot. AH 10. Sitzung der XV. Session am 14. October 1898, 579. The request of 3 October for the exact figures on arrests and sentences seems to be owing to the Ministry of Justice's breakdown according to districts and localities; Sten. Prot. AH 4. Sitzung der XV. Session am 3. October 1898, 255f. AGAD Min. Spraw. 307.
98. Sten. Prot. AH 9. Sitzung der XV. Session am 13. October 1898, 513ff.
99. This viewpoint even reached the Vatican, where an anonymous defender of Stojałowski reported that Galicians held the Austrian government responsible for the disturbances and that "this agitating against the Jews [is] merely a ploy to repress the people." During operations to suppress riots, Austrian soldiers had killed thirty peasants "but did not lay a finger on a single Jew." All this occurred although the priests had testified "that in those places where disturbances had erupted, the Jews had provoked the people into them." Cited from Kertzer (transl. C. H.-K.), *Die Päpste gegen Juden*, 270.

100. Sten. Prot. AH 10. Sitzung der XV. Session am 14. October 1898, 543f.
101. Ibid.
102. Sten. Prot. AH des Reichsrates, 18. Sitzung der XII. Session am 28. Mai 1897, 1048.
103. A relatively comprehensive file from the Ministry of Justice, showing how the question was processed and answered, has survived, AGAD Min. Spraw. 287/6453.
104. Sten. Prot. AH 24. Sitzung der XV. Session am 29. November 1898, 1583f.
105. Rzeszów court of assizes, confirmed by the "royal-and-imperial High Court of Cassation and Justice" on 19 July that year, AGAD Min. Spraw. 287/6453.
106. The peasant Michał Kosmala referred to in the interpellation had a brother named Marcin and two sisters, Maria and Katarzyna. He and his wife Barbara had two children, Magdalena and Antoni. The "wasteful one" was his sister Maria and her "quarter-share" referred to the property inherited from Maria and Michał's father, who died in 1879 and was also named Antoni. The grandchildren's share then amounted to an eighth of Antoni Kosmala senior's bequest.
107. AGAD Min. Spraw. 287/6453, cited from the indictment, 2f.
108. Report by the Rzeszów public prosecutors to the Krakow senior prosecutor: "The allegations made to the judicial authorities in the interpellation can however be regarded as untenable and plucked from thin air. . . . the fact that proceedings were not initiated until the year 1896 is the fault of the heirs of Anton and Michał Kosmala themselves, as they did not press charges earlier."
109. Ibid., 9.
110. A warrant for his arrest was issued but the case closed on 2 November 1896. AGAD Min. Spraw. 287/6453 from the report by OStA. Krakow.
111. He was charged with fraud against Kacper Tos in October 1877; with inciting Chaim and Pescha Schreiber to commit perjury in September 1898; with three cases of embezzlement in March 1887, fall 1894, and October 1896. From the indictment in AGAD Min. Spraw. 287/6453.
112. The Krakow senior prosecutor to the Ministry of Justice on 19 December 1898, AGAD Min. Spraw. 287/6453.
113. "People everywhere are saying" (powszechnie mówino), page 6 of the indictment.
114. AGAD Min. Spraw. 287/2258.
115. The prelate and Christian Social member of the Reichsrat Joseph Scheicher fantasized about a solution in the following terms: "In Poland and Ruthenia [i.e., West and East Galicia] we have had to hang thousands . . . the fact that predatory humans must be treated just like predatory animals did not seem logical to these people. But now, by the way, we have no Jews anymore!" Joseph Scheicher, *Aus dem Jahre 1920: Ein Traum* (St. Pölten, 1900); Anton Szanya, *Der Traum des Josef Scheicher: Staatsmodelle in Österreich 1880–1900* (Innsbruck, 2009).
116. AGAD Min. Spraw. 287/2258.
117. Stenographische Protokolle 65. Sitzung der XVII. Session am 25. Oktober 1901, 6075.
118. Interest rates well over 12 percent were the norm. Tokarski, *Ethnic Conflict*.
119. For more on the guardian motif, see chapter 1.
120. Sten. Prot. AH 48. Sitzung der XVI. Session am 17. März 1900, 3299.
121. Sten. Prot. AH 48. Sitzung der XVI. Session am 17. März 1900, 3299.
122. Sten. Prot. AH 115. Sitzung der XVII. Session am 21. März 1902, 10857.
123. Sten. Prot. AH. 157. Sitzung der XVII. Session am 18. Juni 1902, 14468.
124. Sten. Prot. AH 102. Sitzung der XVII. Session am 4. März 1902, 9715.

125. Sten. Prot. AH 157. Sitzung der XVII. Session am 18. Juni 1902.
126. Whether he was any relation of Berl Honig of Mielec cannot be ascertained from the interpellation text. Sten. Prot. AH 277. Sitzung der XVII. Session am 3. Mai 1904, 24955.
127. Cf. chapter 2, section "The Riots from the Perpetrator Perspective."
128. Interpellation concerning "Rumors about the bribability of two court functionaries in Głogów," Sten. Prot. am 6. November 1906, Sten. Prot. AH 444. Sitzung der XVII. Session am 6. November 1906, 39496.
129. In 1900, he became a member of the Polish Club; he reconciled with the conservative forces in order to have his excommunication reversed. Buchen, "Herrschaft in der Krise."
130. On 28 May, the mayor had sent the governor's office a telegram concerning the riots in Tłuste. CDIAL/146/4/3117, 37. See also the report by the district captain in Zaleszczyce of 29 May, CDIAL/146/4/3117, 64ff.
131. Sten. Prot. AH 22. Sitzung der XIV. Session am 2. Juni 1898, 1362.
132. Cf. chapter 1, section "The Antisemitic Turn and the Invention of Antisemitism."
133. This interpellation was supported by a strong contingent of non-Galician signatories. Schneider, Schlesinger, Heller, and Lebloch were all German Christian Socials to whom Stojałowski had closer links than Galicians such as Danielak, Szponder, and the members of the Secular People's Party.
134. By incorporating the "discreet indiscretions" spoken against the judge, they were made rumors. Manfred Bruhn, "Gerücht als Gegenstand der theoretischen und empirischen Forschung," in Bruhn and Wunderlich, *Medium Gerücht*, 11–40, 16.
135. Sten. Prot. AH 22. Sitzung der XIV. Session am 2. Juni 1898, 1361.
136. Sten. Prot. AH 12. Sitzung der XV. Session am 20. October 1898, 665f.
137. Sten. Prot. AH 12. Sitzung der XV. Session am 20. October 1898, 665f.
138. Ibid.
139. Sten. Prot. AH 21. Sitzung der XV. Session am 22. November 1898, 1346.
140. *Przyjaciel Ludu*, 10 October 1899.
141. Another one concerned the murder of a soldier following a fight in a tavern.
142. See Michal Frankl, *"Prag ist nunmehr antisemitisch": Tschechischer Antisemitismus am Ende des 19. Jahrhunderts* (Berlin, 2011).
143. Nowy Sącz am 27. März 1898, AGAD Min. Spraw. 310/406, 98.
144. AGAD Min. Spraw. 310, 110.
145. *Słownik geograficzny Królestwa Polskiego i innych krajów słowiańskich*, vol. 5 (Warsaw, 1884), 737.
146. In German-language communication studies, these are also described as "moderne Sagen": Bruhn, "Gerücht als Gegenstand," 17.
147. Cf. chapter 1, section "The Christian-Social Movement in the City."
148. AGAD Min. Spraw. 287/6518.
149. In fact, she was not "deaf and dumb," but hard of hearing. The only words she had learned to say were "mama" and "papa." However, the records consistently described her as "deaf and dumb"—significantly, as it transpired.
150. This was considered a plausible explanation for her disappearance. She was known to walk off when angry. As she did not know the way home and could not ask for directions because of her impaired hearing, she was presumed to have "perished in the mountains."
151. The girl transpired to be the daughter of Jan and Katarzyna Ramza of Lasy Biegońskie. She must have looked very like Karolina as her sister Maria Rybczak "at first sight thought the girl that Bart brought to Nowotanice was her sister and led her to her mother and

only on the way starting doubting her identity and to make sure brought the girl to her mother Siedlaska, who immediately saw that it was not her daughter." Report by the senior public prosecutor in Krakow of 28 August 1899, AGAD Min. Spraw. 287/6518.
152. AGAD Min. Spraw. 287/6518.
153. The discrepancies with the "classic ritual murder" narrative—a girl rather than a boy had disappeared, and it was not shortly before Passover—were dismissed as irrelevant.
154. On the concept of "fanatical" Jews, see chapter 1, section "Failed Assimilation: The First Phase of Antisemitic Agitation, 1879–1883."
155. *Czas*, 5, 6, and 7 November 1898; *Nowa Reforma*, 5 January 1899; *Deutsches Volksblatt*, 10 January 1899.
156. *Deutsches Volksblatt*, no. 3601, 10 January 1899, 2.
157. Ibid., emphasis in the original.
158. Information was reported by the public in Nowy Sącz and Żywiec.
159. "Nie podlega bowiem żadnej wątpliwości, że dziecko to tylko w celach rytualnych zamordowane zostało, bo do 'innych celów' absolutnie nie nadawało się jeszcze."
160. There was not yet public awareness of the concept of pedophile crime. But the first cases of child abuse and killings were publicized by the Viennese press just a few months later, and, six years later, the Krakow public was confronted with the fact of sexually motivated murder in reports of the murder of nine-year-old Marya Kolasówna. Cf. Wolff, *Ansichtskarten*; also Nathaniel Wood, "Sex Scandals, Sexual Violence, and the Word on the Street: The Kolasówna Lustmord in Cracow's Popular Press, 1905–06," *Journal of the History of Sexuality* 20, no. 2 (2011): 243–269.
161. On Ernst Vergani, see Michael Wladika, *Hitlers Vätergeneration: Die Ursprünge des Nationalsozialismus in der k. u. k. Monarchie* (Vienna, 2005), 218–224.
162. AGAD Min. Spraw. 313.
163. Ibid., 492.
164. Rainer Erb, *Die Legende vom Ritualmord* (Berlin, 1993).
165. *Głos Narodu*, no. 89, 31 March 1905.
166. Deutsches Volksblatt Nr 3589, 31 March 1905.
167. Contrary to what Paul Nathan, a contemporary observer, wrote, the anti-Semites not only contradicted "civilized" countries such as Germany but also the Galician provinces. His alternative account did little to change the antisemitic message since the claim of "Jewish manipulation" of the truth and the judicial system had already been brought into play. Paul Nathan, *Der Prozess von Tiszla-Eszlar: Ein antisemitisches Culturbild* (Berlin, 1892), vi.
168. Another antisemitic newspaper, *Obrona Ludu*, speculated on the Union pulling strings behind the scenes during the affair in Polna, quoting a letter the Union allegedly sent its members to ask them for money. The article compared this with the Xanten case in which German Jews had raised over two million Reichsmarks for the defense of the Jewish suspect. The author then praised the *Deutsche Volksblatt* for posing the justified question of why they needed the money, as Hilsner had confessed to the murder. *Obrona Ludu*, 24 March 1900, 13.
169. AGAD Min. Spraw. 313, 535.
170. There is a relatively good stock of literature on Joseph Bloch and especially on the institution he founded. For more on Bloch's reaction to antisemitism, see Tim Buchen, "'Herkules im antisemitischen Augiasstall': Joseph Samuel Bloch und Galizien in der Reaktion auf Antisemitismus in der Habsburgermonarchie," in Ulrich Wyrwa (ed.),

Einspruch und Abwehr: Die Reaktion des europäischen Judentums auf die Entstehung des Antisemitismus (1879–1914) (Frankfurt a. M., 2010), 193–214; Jacob Toury, "Troubled Beginnings: The Emergence of the Österreichisch-Israelitische Union," *Leo Baeck Institute Year Book* 30 (1985); idem, "Josef Samuel Bloch und die jüdische Identität im österreichischen Kaiserreich," in Walter Grab (ed.), *Jüdische Integration und Identität in Deutschland und Österreich, 1848–1918* (Tel Aviv, 1984); Ian Reifowitz, *Imagining an Austrian Nation: Joseph Samuel Bloch and the Search for a Multiethnic Austrian Identity, 1846–1919* (New York, 2003); Katja Lander, *Josef Samuel Bloch und die Österreichisch-Israelitische Union: Initiativen zur Begründung einer jüdischen Politik im späten 19. Jahrhundert in Wien* (Saarbrücken, 1993).
171. This was referred to in the newspapers as "Mädchenraub" (literally: girl stealing), "Kindesentführungen" (child abduction) or "Mädchenentführungen" (abduction of girls).
172. Of course, the story of Galician female abductions was not equivalent to the ritual murder myth. The latter placed Jews under suspicion of murder, generated mistrust, and endangered the lives of countless people. It placed a severe strain on relations between Christians and Jews and was an outright lie. The female abductions were real in the sense that many young Jewish girls did enter convents, having been abducted in the eyes of the law.
173. He was elected to the Reichsrat three times: as successor to the deceased Szymon Schreiber in 1883, and again in 1885 and 1890 by voters of the predominantly Jewish East Galician constituency of Kolomea-Buczacz-Śniatyn. Lander, *Josef Samuel Bloch*, 138ff.
174. Bloch opposed both the assimilation campaign of the German liberal Jewish historian Heinrich von Friedjung and the standpoint of Polish Democrat Emil Byk. His newspaper, *Dr. Bloch's Österreichische Wochenschrift*, was a statement against Friedjung's *Deutsche Wochenschrift*. On Friedjung and his relationship to state and society, see Frederik Lindström, *Empire and Identity: Biographies of the Austrian State Problem in the Late Habsburg Empire* (West Lafayette, 2008). But it was not only his belief that no society would ever accept Jews as equals that caused Bloch to disagree with assimilation. As a religious Jew, it was important to him to preserve and cultivate Jewish tradition. He cannot then be reduced to his role as combater of antisemitism. He was equally a forerunner of modern Jewish politics, to whom discussing antisemitism was not just a matter of personal importance but also crucial as a political instrument.
175. Josef Kopp, *Zur Judenfrage nach den Akten des Prozesses Rohling-Bloch* (Leipzig, 1886); Lander, *Josef Samuel Bloch*, 92ff.
176. Teresa Andlauer, *Die jüdische Bevölkerung im Modernisierungsprozess Galiziens (1867–1914)* (Frankfurt a. M., 2001); Hödl, *Als Bettler in die Leopoldstadt*; Haumann, *Luftmenschen*; Rachel Manekin, "'The Lost Generation': Education and Female Conversion in Fin-de-Siecle Kraków," *Polin: Studies in Polish Jewry* 18 (2005): 189–219; Todd M. Endelman, "Gender and Radical Assimilation in Modern Jewish History," in M. L. Raphael (ed.), *Gendering the Jewish Past* (Williamsburg, 2002), 25–40.
177. Most conversions took place in the Felician Sisters Convent in Krakow. Jewish girls from the kingdom of Poland also converted to Catholicism there. Cf. APK DPKr 75, 1645; APK PMJ 71. Between 1887 and 1902, a total of 302 Jewish girls converted, while only 142 men converted to Catholicism in Krakow convents, half of whom were twenty years old or younger. In Lemberg, there were equal numbers of male and female converts. See Jakob Thon, *Die Juden in Oesterreich* (Berlin, 1908), 77f. Between 1902 and 1914, at least a hundred women converted; cf. APK PMJ 71. The case of Mendel Majer of Łopa-

tyn, in November 1913, is the only one known to this author in which a boy allowed himself to be abducted in order to be baptized; CAHJP HM 2/9333.
178. Their fathers were butchers, timber merchants, barkeepers, and landowners. Manekin, "The Lost Generation," 192.
179. The most frequent reason was to avoid an arranged marriage. This patriarchal practice was unacceptable to the young generation, who harbored romantic notions of marrying for love and aspired to a secular ideal of education and improvement. The ideal of romantic love was a powerful symbol of the new era, which girls asserted against their parents' life scripts, as it "transcended" national and religious boundaries. Manekin, "The Lost Generation," 190. It was, moreover, associated with the allure of city life, which provided an alternative to the "stifling" conditions in small towns. On 2 May 1901, for instance, a certain Gittla Schwimmer fled her parents' home disguised as a nun because she wished to marry her Catholic paramour, Józef Kordensz. Charges were later pressed against Kordensz. APK StT 60, 54 P; and AGAD Min. Spraw. 287, no. 21566. The case was widely publicized by a report in the *Wiener Tagblatt* of 8 May 1901. In another instance, the seventeen- and twenty-year-old daughters of a man named Wolf Kluger of Podgórze threatened to convert if he did not allow them to take up studies at the Jagellonian University; APK DPKr 75. A strikingly large proportion of converts of the years 1902 and 1904 were students at the faculty of philosophy; APK PMJ 71, p. 41–135.
180. Cf. Adam Wandruszka and Peter Urbanitsch, *Die Habsburger Monarchie 1848–1918*, vol. 4: *Die Konfessionen* (Vienna, 1985), 30–47. On its implementation and exceptional cases, see Andrzej Dziadzio, "Wolność wyznania I sumienia a przymus religijny w austriackiej monarchii konstytucyjnej (1867–1914)," *Czasopismo Prawno-Historyczne* (1993): 1–2.
181. Michalina Araten's story can be reconstructed in detail from several sources, including the history of the Felician Sisters Convent, the press, Ministry of Justice files, Kraków police files, Lemberg governor's office records, and a book written by her relative: Rachel Sarna Araten, *Michalina, Daughter of Israel: The True Story of a Jewish Girl Abducted by the Catholic Church* (Jerusalem, 1986). Rachel Manekin has retraced the historical source in an article about the story "Jacob Salomons Bett" by Nobel Prize-winner Samuel Joseph Agnon. Agnon came from Buczacz and was a youth during the wave of convent conversions. Rachel Manekin, "Tehillas Daughter and Michalina Araten" (Hebrew), *Ha'arets*, literature supplement, 27 June 2003.
182. AGAD Min. Spraw. 287. The photograph was most probably a few years old, as Michalina must have been sixteen at the time of her absconding. Her gravestone in Haifa shows that she was born in 1883.
183. There were five interpellations concerning the abductions in the years 1900–1909. Two were by Benno Straucher, one by Ferdinand Kronawetter (1907), one by Julius Ofner (1900), and one by Josef Steiner. Ofner's interpellation was published in *Dr. Bloch's Österreichische Wochenschrift*, no. 44, 780. Straucher's interpellation is recorded in Sten. Prot. AH 1900 and 1909.
184. *Dr. Bloch's Österreichische Wochenschrift*, no. 44, 817.
185. Ibid.
186. Interpellation by Straucher.
187. Letters to the royal and imperial governor in Lemberg of 4 and 15 February 1900, CDIAL/146/4/2427, 19; to the Minister of Justice of 4 February; to the Minister for Galicia of 14 February.

188. "Controverse Piętak-Kareis," Sten. Prot. HA-39. Sitzung der XVI. Session am 2. März 1900, 2561.
189. Soboń, *Polacy wobec Żydów*, 269. In a telegram to the governor, Israel Araten quoted the rumor that Michalina was dead; CDIAL 146/4/1162. In fact, Michalina had escaped to Belgium with the help of the Felician nuns, where she was baptized. She eventually married a Polish Catholic man in the Posen area. Maria P. Lenart, *Prowincja krakowska Zgromadzenia Sióstr Felicjanek*, vol. 2: *Leksykon domów* (Krakow, 2000), 223. Her father, Israel, emigrated to Haifa in Palestine in the 1920s. Michalina died in Haifa in 1969. Her matzevah bears the inscription "Michtsche Araten, daughter of Israel and Dvora." It does not mention her Polish husband and son but commemorates her sisters Lea and Malke-Ester, who were both murdered in Belzec.
190. See below.
191. Israel Araten also filed an unsuccessful complaint against the policeman Hartmann. The court ruled he had admittedly commented in a "tactless way . . . to Araten" but had otherwise shown flawless conduct. On 15 April 1901, Michalina's whereabouts were still unknown to the public prosecutors. Report by the president of the Higher Regional Court in Tarnobrzeg of 16 December 1900, CAHJP HM 2/9487, no. 7996.
192. "Kinderraub in Galizien," *Neue Freie Presse*, 4 July 1900, 4.
193. Such cases included that of Rosa/Rochme Weiß, Szalka Sobel, Deborah Sattler, Lea Altmann, and Franja Ledermann. Interpellatonen Ofner und Straucher, Sten. Prot. HA-130. Sitzung der XVIII. Session am 29. Jänner 1909, 14619.
194. When this was not the case, the narrators suspected the girls were manipulated or coerced by the nuns, such as in the case of Franja Widerschall. Interpellation Straucher 1909, 14629.
195. As well as *Słowo Polskie*, newspapers that reported on the Michalina Araten case included *Czas*, *Nowa Reforma*, *Dziennik Polski*, *Neues Wiener Tageblatt*, *Neue Freie Presse*, *Arbeiter Zeitung*, and *Pester Lloyd*. The Ministry of Justice also used the "Araten case" as a reference whenever a new incident of a girl fleeing to a Felician Sisters convent arose.
196. *Die Welt*, no. 37, 14 September 1900, 9.
197. *Die Welt*, no. 28, 13 July 1900, 11.
198. Benno Straucher wrote of "internments in convents" in his interpellation and "that the peasants [were] only pawns in the hands of the clergy and the convent directors." Sten. Prot. HA-130. Sitzung der XVIII. Session am 29. Jänner 1909, 14617–14633.
199. E.g., in Dr. Bloch's *Österreichische Wochenblatt* of 2 November 1900, 780–785; *Die Welt*, no. 27, 6 July 1900, 9; and an announcement by the Austrian Israelite Union.
200. *Dr. Bloch's Österreichische Wochenschrift*, no. 9, 2 March 1900, 163. An article in *Die Welt* prior to the Araten case had reported a "forcible baptism," without the participation of nuns, in which an "Austrian gendarme" had freed "the child from the hands of the fanatical peasants." *Die Welt*, no. 18, 5 May 1899, 12.
201. According to Julius Ofner in a speech to the Landtag, *Dr. Bloch's Österreichische Wochenschrift*, no. 44, 780.
202. *Dr. Bloch's Österreichische Wochenschrift*, no. 9, 163.
203. The record of one case has survived in which a girl was abducted against her will: Anna Łozińska pleaded guilty to luring ten-year-old Golde Reisler off the street in Zniesenie on 18 January 1901 and taking her to a convent. Łozińska was subsequently sentenced to three years' dungeon imprisonment with one day of fasting every two weeks. AGAD Min. Spraw. 287/1944, 162.

204. *Dr. Bloch's Österreichische Wochenschrift*, no 44.
205. Peter Karoshi, "Ein Versuch, Konzepte der Hybridität auf Quellen zum österreichisch-ungarischen Vielvölkerstaat anzuwenden: das Kronprinzenwerk," eForum zeitGeschichte, February 2001, www.eforum-zeitgeschichte.at/set2_01a4.htm, accessed 18 February 2010; idem, "Patriotismus und Staatserhalt," 4.
206. Karoshi, "Ein Versuch."
207. Benno Straucher also echoed the sexual connotations of the ritual murder myth by speaking of nocturnal "intrusions into bedrooms" and the forcible abduction of "sparsely clothed girls." Interpellation of 29 January 1909. Sten. Prot.HA-130. Sitzung der XVIII. Session, S. 14617-14633.
208. This hierarchical standpoint was also evident in some geocultural observations: "Now something Oriental occurred, the gendarme did not follow the orders of his superior to free a girl from a convent," in "Abermals ein Mädchenraub in Galizien," *Dr. Bloch's Wochenschrift*, no. 48, 824.
209. 1900, cited from "Kinderraub in Galizien," *Dr. Bloch's Wochenschrift*, no. 44, 780–785.
210. Rumpler, *Politische Öffentlichkeit*.
211. Such "orders" were sent to the district captains and the two police authorities following interpellations in the Reichsrat: by the minister of the interior on 16 February 1901, and by the governor after an interpellation by Kronawetter of 17 April 1900. APK DPKr. 75, 360.
212. CAHJP HM2/9333.
213. Notice of 29 August 1909 following an interpellation by Straucher in the Reichsrat, CAHJP HM2/9333. The governors' office displayed clear sympathy toward the Catholic church, not only by referring to the "bosom" of the church, but also in the fact that the governor's wife acted as godmother at a conversion ceremony in Lemberg cathedral, to the dismay of the Jewish population. Claudia Erdheim, *Längst nicht mehr koscher: Die Geschichte einer Familie* (Vienna, 2006).
214. Cf. Stanisław Salmonowicz, Stanisław Waltoś, and Janusz Szwaja, *Pitaval krakowski* (Krakow, 2010).
215. Barbara Ubryk had had fits of pious ecstasy and undressed during Mass while having visions. She was then placed in confinement in Rome under instructions from the superior general. APK SKKKr 231, 225. The case files (880 pages) remain in the archive in Spytkowice.
216. *Mały Rzym* (little Rome) is also the title of a four-volume history of the city written in the late 1930s by Juliusz Stanisław Harbut, criticizing Kraków's clericalism. The story of Barbara Ubryk was recounted in the light of numerous interpretations, some freer than others, but most with a propagandistically anti-clerical thrust. E.g., Adolf Söndermann, *Klostergeheimnisse oder Die lebendig begrabene Barbara Ubryk: Eine historische Erzählung nach authentischen Quellen frei bearbeitet* (Dresden, 1869); also *The Convent Horror: The Story of Barbara Ubryk; Twenty-One Years in a Convent Dungeon, Eight Feet Long, Six Feet Wide; From Official Records* (Philadelphia, 1869); a shortened version of the latter after the reprint in 1959 can be found at www.jesus-is-lord.com/barbara.htm, accessed 4 February 2010.
217. Sten. Prot. AH 40. Sitzung der XVI. Session am 3. März 1900, 2619. Emphases on the clerical, antisemitic terms and ideas placed by the present author.
218. Ibid.

219. Stanisław Badeni was land marshal of Galicia and brother of the former governor and Austrian minister-president Kazimierz Badeni.
220. Sten. Prot. AH 40. Sitzung der XVI. Session am 3. März 1900.
221. E.g., *Nowa Reforma*, no. 43, 23 February 1900, 2; also *Czas*.
222. A popular-science study of famous love stories in Galicia includes this tale, recounted from the perspective of the engaged couple and with reference to newspaper articles, under the title "The official and the beautiful neophyte." Bogna Wernichowska, *Tak kochali Galicjanie* (Krakow, 2005), 122–130.
223. In 1873, a convert named Józefa Geuzler was allegedly killed by members of her family. In 1898, a spate of violent attacks on neophytes caused the newspaper *Ojczyzna* to appeal to fellow believers to exercise reason. Cf. Soboń, "Polacy wobec Żydów," 274.
224. Rozenblit, *Reconstructing a National Identity*.

Chapter 4

Summary

The Antisemitism Years in Review

In 1868, the Galician Diet adopted legal equality for all its citizens, regardless of religion, in line with the imperial constitution—and over the heads of most of the population. Legal equality was primarily a concern of the secular elites and the liberal Jewish intelligentsia, who saw it as a way toward Jewish "assimilation." They hoped it would motivate Jews to abandon their cultural, linguistic, and economic particularities and becoming integrated in the Polish nation, or at least make them equal citizens within society. To some extent, they prescribed the same "civilizing process" to the Christian majority—the many illiterate peasants who lived "in darkness." At the time, the peasantry was largely excluded from political participation, and the church did not have its own media mouthpiece. The demand for assimilation encountered little open political opposition.

Yet the Galician Diet's formal ratification of legal equality could not put an end to age-old traditions of religious segregation across the crownland. In some places, equality never became a reality. Keeping Żywiec devoid of Jews was an integral part of the town's identity and culture, asserted by force if necessary, and by reference to Austrian decrees from bygone eras.

While the press delivered sensational coverage of the anti-Jewish Berlin movement and ritual murder trials in Hungary and Galicia, public figures such as the politician Teofil Merunowicz and the artist Jan Matejko played their part in popularizing negative images of Jewry. Criticizing the purported Jewish reluctance to assimilate, materialism, and lack of patriotism, and alleging that Jews used their religious institutions to outmaneuver Christians, they were among the nationalist liberals who propelled the first phase of anti-Jewish agitation. They called on Jews to realize their obligation to the (Polish) nation, having received equality and the "offer of assimilation."

The pogroms in Russia and the subsequent wave of Jewish refugees to and across Galicia added a sense of urgency to the "Jewish question." New solutions were sought, and various political schemes hatched. Thanks to international aid organizations cooperating with the government and advancements in modern communications and logistics, an unprecedented number of Jews were able to migrate overseas in a shorter time than ever before. Observing the popularity of this option among Jews, politicians came to regard the emigration of nonassimilated Jews as a viable "solution." Jewish otherness could be made to disappear, not only on a superficially visual level, by ensuring the carriers were physically removed.

Alarmed by the pogroms and fearing they might spread to Galicia, the provincial elites turned their attention to Christian-Jewish relations in the crownland. Their focus shifted away from legal and philosophical definitions and toward economic interrelations and social situations and conflicts in everyday life. This marked the start of the second phase of anti-Jewish agitation, ushered in by new actors on the political stage. With suffrage extended, populists and clericals appeared on the scene to represent the underclasses. Previously mere objects of discourse, the "masses" became a new political target group. Anti-Jewish politicians called on them to change their habits and attitudes toward Jews: to boycott or compete with Jews. Jews were excluded from this communication.

For the first time, the underprivileged and "benighted" elements in society gained a voice via an elected, upwardly open representative body. They could now reject the old elites' demand that they change and become similarly cultivated. Why should they try in vain to conform to a bourgeois society when they could legitimately constitute their own community according to their own traditions and designs? The trend in the latter nineteenth century toward viewing society and its development in terms of biological concepts, and the alternative picture of the world this generated, was expedient to populist politics. With humans conceived of as members of collectives, and personal welfare as dependent upon the prospering of the collective into which the individual was born, ensuring that society's natural collectives obtained justice became the task of the politician.

Increasingly, the new, secular people's parties and popular newspapers called for a Christian, or "ethnic Polish" (or Ukrainian), economy. Populist commentators urged the peasantry to set up and patronize their own stores, establish independent cooperatives, and run their own lending banks. In parallel, they were to boycott Jewish businesses. Addressing the populists' own non-Jewish clientele, this phase of agitation contrasted with the previous phase in that it was aimed at Christians, not at Jews.

Jews were no longer told to change their habits and become integrated in the majority society. They could emigrate. The carriers of alien cultures could remove themselves to their predestined homes. In the populist view, all Jews should heed Matejko's words. He had recommended those of his Jewish students who did not see Poland as their fatherland, or the Polish nation as the only community to which they belonged and had an obligation, to leave the country. But according to the populists' scheme, no more recommendations, arguments, threats, or pleas would be necessary. They envisaged the Jewish minority being compelled to migrate by sheer economic necessity when they were finally excluded from the economy and the Christian majority dissolved the ambivalent symbiosis. This program not only offered Christians the prospect of new fields of activity in the rural economy; it also shifted the popular notion of "Jewishness" out of the financial sector to become a cipher for all kinds of dishonest dealing and hostile intentions toward the majority society. By this logic, supporting the non-Jewish collective equaled combating the others. Defining the community in terms of ethnic criteria started a discourse and a practice of boycott, which in turn cemented the community. Antisemitism, communicated and promoted by the populist newspapers, became part of the collective peasant identity.

Clerical politicians also used antisemitic agitation in their political communication. Defining community by religious, national, and cultural criteria rather than by ethnic concepts, they tended to be more radical in tone and more focused on religious characteristics than secular anti-Jewish agitators. But all antisemitic camps shared the belief in a fundamental antagonism and irreconcilable rivalry with Jews and a sense of "natural" privileges over them (though for different reasons). "Liberation from the Jews" became a common goal, launching new ventures by non-Jews and supporting ongoing projects. Reformers who had long struggled to combat alcoholism welcomed the call to boycott Jewish taverns. Priests who helped Christians run community stores reinforced the church's influence on society. Christian storeowners advertising with slogans to the effect of "support your local (Christian) community" gained a commercial advantage. Meanwhile, unpleasant or traumatic experiences resulting from bad luck or incompetence, such as the loss of land or spiraling debt, were said to be the outcome of Jewish duplicity, profiteering, conspiracies, and fraud.

Jewish duplicity was also cited to discredit political opponents, to explain disunity among the peasant electorate, and to rationalize the newly ambiguous link between politics and the press. The slimmer a party's chance of victory—the wider the discrepancy between its claim to opinion leadership and its level of organized support and electoral success—and the fewer collectives on which its narrative of dissociation could be based, the more radical its anti-Jewish stance in critical situations, which were portrayed as matters of life and death. Asemitism and the antisemitic turn in Christian-social journalism lent the authority of the church to anti-Jewish feeling and called on readers to engage in anti-Jewish practice in everyday life. Demonizing Jews, its proponents inflamed tensions in the run-up to the elections of 1897 and the by-elections of 1898.

Election campaigns brought party politics to the villages with unprecedented intensity. Inter-party disputes, in which all sides accused their opponents of double-dealing, were often attended by violence. Stridently antisemitic publications, the "Jewish Secrets" pamphlet series, and the clerical daily press were combined with traditional anti-Jewish feeling in the pre-Easter period, were all fed into Szponder's sermons, and culminated in the disturbances in Wieliczka. The festival in honor of Mickiewicz and election campaign events were (in)auspicious occasions that attracted large crowds. They were perceived as a chance for peasants to wield their innate power—invested in them by dint of their sheer preponderance and hardiness—to acquire some loot and symbolically punish the Jews. Rumors in circulation convinced the peasant community of the legality of the imminent "attack on the Jews" and set its parameters. The rumors concerned the emperor as well as antisemitic politicians and referred to—sometimes fantastic readings of—incidents in which they had been involved or comments they had made. In this way, the rumors legitimized acts which, though hostile, were otherwise committed arbitrarily and often drunkenly and without any long-term goal in mind, such as expelling Jews from their communities. Yet the rumors had highly explosive potential. They turned the interaction between Jews, gendarmes, and aggressive peasant visitors at a national celebration into a deadly clash.

It was said that Jews had provoked the peasants by summoning the gendarmes, who in turn shot at the peasants. Gathering momentum in the communicative space of West Galicia, the scandalized talk eventually turned into rumors of an imminent anti-Jewish "attack," which proved self-fulfilling. The Jews had contravened the traditional script by not accepting their humiliation and seeking to pacify the peasants but provocatively calling on the authorities for help. In an antisemitic view, punishment was due, and it took different forms and dimensions from region to region. The gendarmes' disproportionately severe response marked the crossing of another boundary and a show of force that could not be left unanswered.

Seen in this light, the Frysztak tragedy seemed to be further evidence that the Jews and the military were fundamentally hostile toward the peasants. But an equally significant factor triggering violence was the many minor attacks on Jews, which no gendarme witnessed and against which no one intervened. As one incident followed the next, a consensus grew among the predominant majority in the rural Christian population—many of whom were in any case eager to get something for free for once—that it was legitimate to scare and punish Jews. At the same time, the rumors about attacks going unpenalized assured them it was possible within a certain timeframe. The understaffed police forces could not be everywhere at once. Disturbances erupting in several different places in quick succession exposed the state's weakness and the rural peasantry's strength. Village communities deliberately chose points in time when law enforcers were absent to punish the Jews and acquire some of their property. Galicia became the scene of a cat-and-mouse chase, steered by oral communication and the eagerness to make acquisitions at the Jews' expense, in which the gendarmes were always in the wrong place or arrived too late on the scene. The rural population as a collective created the opportunity structure, as it were, in which the state lost control over them.

Collective violence promoted a sense of community among the peasantry. It was organized in accordance with existing hierarchies, loyalties, and notions of belonging, and included and rewarded large parts of the Christian community. It also reflected the nature of relations between the perpetrators and victims. Situations of violence varied depending on whether the perpetrators and victims knew each other or not. If they did, the former not only located booty more purposefully but also showed more consideration for their victims. The two parties had a history of coexistence and presumed they would continue to live side by side in mutual dependence in the future. At the same time, Christian villagers felt they were more entitled to rob their "own" Jews than were people from elsewhere. Marauding mobs became a growing threat, to which situational agitators responded by increasing the pressure to mobilize. Peasants were encouraged to turn on their Jewish neighbors before any unpredictable strangers, who might not spare even the Christian households, did so. Here, a darker side of the ambivalent symbiosis between Christians and Jews emerged. None of the attackers intended to destroy the Jews' livelihoods or compel them to give up their taverns or stores. Although they sometimes used threatening rhetoric to this effect, their actions fell short of such radical goals. Rather, they sought to mete symbolic punishment, to teach the Jews a lesson for the future. The feeling of power and seizing some loot was satisfaction enough. They needed neither ideology nor politics. The Jews' stores and taverns were undisputed parts of village life. But by attacking the Jews, the Christians denied their equality and condemned their "provocative" actions. The disturbances did not, then, mark a violent end to the entangled consumer world of Christians and Jews. They did not put the peasant parties' policies into practice. Yet the latter's anti-Jewish agitation, advocating assaults on Jews per se, were a prerequisite for violence. Like rumors of imminent attacks, political agitation claiming Jews were "traitors" who were responsible for the plight of so many marked them out as prospective victims. At election meetings, potential ringleaders were mobilized and synchronized, and allegations voiced against Jews seemed to legitimize violence and so lowered the peasants' aggression threshold.

The importance of familiarity for local communities, causing visiting Christians to be perceived just as much as "others" as the Jewish stallholders on the market square, gave staff in the governors' office some leverage to tackle the crisis. Motivated by the need to avoid generating any more negative interest within the empire, local authorities tried several approaches to end the conflict. By setting up local militias and speaking with potential leaders of violent groups, Jewish citizens, and local officeholders, they managed to suppress several further attacks. Isolated incidents still occurred, the most brutal of which erupted when marauding gangs clashed with armed forces. This was the case in East Galicia, where migrant workers occasionally turned on Jewish storeowners, who were more likely to defend themselves by force against their belligerent short-term customers.

Local militias were not, however, able to restore order. The prospect of jumping on the mercenary bandwagon and robbing Jews proved too enticing. Moreover, in places such as Stary Sącz, the local administration was paralyzed by councilors who were more concerned with fighting the economic competition from Jewish businesspeople.

In mountainous regions, armed gangs fundamentally challenged the state's monopoly on the legitimate use of force. The government responded by declaring a state of emergency and introducing military rule. Under martial law, participants in collective robberies risked the death penalty. Cavalry units were strategically posted to intervene at short notice even in remote areas. Finally asserting its power, the state cracked down, using brutal means to identify and sentence perpetrators and compel them to return stolen goods. Sometimes military rule was a bitter experience even for the Jews who were threatened with attacks. Occasionally, they were at the receiving end of the soldiers' humiliating and violent methods; as a rule, they paid for the protection they required.

By and large, however, with financial support arriving from Vienna and the generally reliable deployment of Austro-Hungarian troops, Galician Jews found they could trust the state as well as Jewish interest groups in the capital to help. As no draconian penalties were imposed, the state avoided rousing resentment among the peasants and enabled neighborly Christian-Jewish relations to be restored in most places. The ambivalent symbiosis was continued, although it had been severely shaken. No doubt many more Jews considered emigrating. They had not only seen their Christian neighbors in a different and disturbing light, but some had also had ambivalent or negative encounters with local government representatives.

The ruling conservatives in and connected to the governor's office used the state of emergency to weaken the opposition, imposing bans and restrictions and tightening censorship to stifle its activities. The provincial government declared populists, Christian Socials, and Socialists to be directly responsible for the disturbances. Labeling them "antisemitic riots," the conservative opinion leaders popularized the concept that political agitation and violence against Jews were symptoms of antisemitism. Their political opponents, they maintained, used this antisemitism to manipulate the simple peasants.

Still newcomers in the Imperial Diet, the Galician opposition was accused of inciting major disturbances and so being more harmful than helpful to their supporters, many of whom were now imprisoned. Led by the Socialist Ignacy Daszyński, they in turn attacked the ruling Galician elite. The oppositionists criticized the military's excessive use of force and blamed the "Stańczyks," the conservatives, for the disturbances. They referred to the disturbances as "clerical" rather than "antisemitic" riots or spoke of "state-sanctioned antisemitism" to vilify Galicia's government on the imperial stage. The clerical parliamentarians Stojałowski and Potoczek claimed the Jews themselves were responsible for the violence. With the support of the anti-Semites who were already ensconced in Vienna's political mainstream, they portrayed themselves to their voters as steadfast opponents of the Jews.

In the Imperial Diet, Galician politicians promoted antisemitic politics by means of interpellations. By this method, they styled themselves attorneys representing their "clients," the voters. A recurrent issue they addressed was the harm caused by fraudulent Jewish traders and moneylenders, and the failure of the Galician judiciary to adequately respond. The imperial capital already held Galicia and its aristocratic ruling class in low regard. In view of the complaints made by Galician representatives, it seemed plausible that the summer's disturbances had been an attempt at self-defense and a cry for help by the oppressed peasantry. The interpellation process forged links between voters and politicians, overcame the distance between the center and the provincial periphery, and brought agitation to fruition when proceedings against Jewish businesspeople were initiated. It offered plaintiffs the opportunity not only to obtain compensation but also to generate some public attention and intimidate other Jewish moneylenders. In this way, they perpetuated the narrative of Jewish profiteering and fraud and of the Galician peasants' legal vulnerability.

Galician villagers, however, knew that the problems addressed in the interpellations were not principally due to a clash between Christians and Jews but between monetary and agrarian economy. They knew that Christians could be objectionable creditors, too, and that farmers and traders were mutually dependent, whatever their religion. Though political agitators drew on the antisemitic canon of cases of usury and deception for reasons to boycott Jews, doing so was in fact rarely a viable option for Christian peasants. Participating in building a discrete Christian branch of the economy, on the other hand, could have advantages.

Populists emphasized both options as ways to achieve "liberation from the Jews." But the Christian stock of knowledge of the Jews remained the same. The old story of ritual murder continued to be a useful device in various situations— as an excuse for returning home late, to explain the inexplicable, or to process and express anxiety about the effects of modernization. Popular resentment at the perceived lack of support from the judiciary was channeled and harnessed by members of the local intelligentsia, who imitated the interpellation practice to prompt the state into action in their interests. Initiatives such as the launch of investigations into the alleged poisoning of a priest precipitated administrative wrangling and antisemitic incidents. As the communicative network spanning the Habsburg Empire grew ever denser and the press more diverse, readers in

Vienna and Kraków were informed even of such absurd and marginal incidents. Various parties, camps, and organizations used conflicts between Christians and Jews, and the state's role in them, to legitimize their demands, and the attention thus generated to publicize their programs or vilify their opponents. "Galicia," "Galician Jews," "Galician peasants," and "Galician justice," along with "Galician voters" and "Polish economy," became the watchwords of the political community and the press. The political discourse woven around these concepts negotiated fundamental issues such as the influence of the church and state on social life, minority protection, and the nature of a liberal constitutional state. The antisemitic process changed both the political reality and Jewish-Christian coexistence in Galicia. It increased the pressure on Jews to assimilate in parallel with promoting various types of Jewish organization and collective identity-forming, including the national Jewish option. It reinforced Galician Jewry's tendency to align with Vienna and the imperial state. The intense antisemitic agitation used to build the peasant political community aggravated the sense of otherness between Jews and Christians. But it was not the only factor influencing everyday life in Galicia. It did not end the tradition of multifaceted neighborly relations. Rather, antisemitic agitation and politics extended the arsenal of hostile speech and, by association, hostile behavior toward Jews, which Christians fell back on in moments of conflict. Society was equally affected by the state's legal and military responses to the disturbances, which ruled out violence as a viable method of achieving political goals. Anti-Semites then attempted to harness the unrest among peasants without allowing it to descend into counterproductive riots by maintaining that "beating" was a metaphor for boycott. After the events of 1898, actual physical violence could no longer be advocated as a permitted practice. Later outbreaks of a similar nature under Habsburg rule never gathered the same momentum as the disturbances of 1898. Efforts to convince Christians to boycott Jews by cautioning negative consequences if they did not comply were doomed to fail. Five years after the disturbances, the limits of antisemitic agitation were made abundantly clear to local actors whose efforts to persuade Christians to spurn Jews came to nothing.

Prevention and De-escalation: Galicia in 1903

On 11 June 1903, the mayor of Nowy Sącz informed the district captain that he had learned—from a reliable source—of rumors predicting "antisemitic disturbances" in his town on 28 and 29 June, which would then spread across Galicia, to culminate in the "slaughtering of Jews."[1] It was also being said that villagers from the surrounding area would gather in Limanowa on the previous Saturday, 26 June, to "prepare." A delegation of Jews from Limanowa had already asked the mayor for "insurance," although the rumors had not yet reached their town.

But it was known that such talk could spread at a relentless pace, "especially among the rural population." The district captain duly visited Limanowa, where an annual fair was held on 15 June without incident. The Jewish population had installed its own guards and felt protected.[2] Mid-month, the Krosno district administration questioned Christians and Jews in the border town Dukla about rumors that a Jew from Dukla had intended to kill the emperor, for which reason it was being claimed that all the Jews in Dukla were to be killed. A certain Franciszek Żglusz was identified as having started the rumor and sentenced to six weeks' dungeon imprisonment.[3]

In Siedliska in the same district, gendarmes arrested two people for ruining the field of an agricultural worker because he had worked for a Jew.[4] Three other men were arrested for stirring anti-Jewish feeling among peasants. The district captain reported talk of Christians refusing to work for Jews, despite the double pay, and of Christians boycotting Jews. He had informed the residents of the harmfulness of such a boycott and the threat it posed to peace and order, and was considering taking steps against this "antisemitic movement" with the help of the gendarmes.[5]

Residents of the Rzeszów district complained to the police about a "certain kind of boycotting Jews" that was on the increase. Ever more people were claiming that "the court" had granted permission to drive out the Jews and whoever did not comply with the boycott would have their windows smashed.[6] People were also saying that Jews had thrown stones at the emperor, and the local mayor in Strzyżów had been informed that it was permitted to punish the Jews there in consequence.[7]

The district administration also received reports that Sokół members were visiting various mayors associated with the boycott campaign. This was confirmed by the local mayor of Polomya, who testified that four unknown men had approached him in his field and asked him several questions, such as whether there was a tavern in the village, whether Jews owned any land in the village, and whether the people from Polomya patronized Jews. Dressed in short black jackets and black hats, they had resembled returning migrants from America.[8]

A head of a gendarme unit in Tyczyn reported finding letters intended to be displayed in public, calling on any agricultural workers employed by Jews to put down their tools.[9] Andrzej Sitek, a father of eight, was allegedly being blackmailed into staying away from his work for a Jew. Notes had been attached to his door threatening to smash his windows and destroy the crops in his field before they could be harvested.[10]

On 30 June, police officer Josef Scholter of Strzyżów notified the police headquarters in Lemberg that people were "conducting aggressive agitation against the Jews" in six parishes in the area.[11] Residents were being told not to buy anything from Jews, sell anything to Jews, or work for Jews. The noncompliant were threatened with punishment. In Niebylec, Józef Błądziński and Jan Michoś were arrested for threatening to ruin the crops of another local man, Kajetan Lutak, if he mowed the field for a certain Dawid Salzman.[12] Furthermore, police officers seized a poster bearing the words: "Attention! July 3, 1903, 12 o'clock midnight, bring scythes to go tally-ho for the Jews!" It was signed "Sokół." The village blacksmith had torn the poster down and sent it to an acquaintance with a request to the Sokół president in Rzeszów not to display any more posters of the kind.[13]

In Pstrągowa in Rzeszów district, Vicar Leon Romański had preached that boys and girls should not work for Jews as it only made the latter rich.[14] The parish priest in Dukla, Jarek, also called on his congregations to "shake off Jewish exploitation," and the "social, Catholic intelligentsia" was spreading similar propaganda with the aim of breaking the Jews' majority at the local council elections.[15] Similar tendencies could be observed in Ropczyce.[16] This parish, led by a zealous, young priest named Antoni Kania, was a flashpoint of "antisemitic agitation."[17] Kania made repeated efforts to stop the peasants from working on Jews' fields. Locals were starting to complain about the anti-Jewish sermons he gave every Sunday and his confrontational behavior outside the church. If during the week he met a member of his congregation who worked for a Jew, he would say: "You go to work for a Jew? Then you likely go to a rabbi for confession, and when you're ill, you call the rabbi?"[18]

In the same period, unsettling news arrived in Lemberg from East Galicia that the Ukrainian-language newspapers *Hajdamak*, *Vola*, and *Dilo* were running biased coverage of the disturbances in Kišinev, designed to fire the "wild imaginations of the Hutsuls."[19] The reading halls run by the Prosvita association were said to be channeling incendiary ideas to the agitated population to the effect that it was time to murder the Jews and Poles. Ten thousand peasants had gathered at a Lenten mission event, where rumors had circulated that the Jews were to be dealt with like they had been in Kišinev, or that all Jews and Poles should be murdered on a certain date.[20] Attendees would have understood "Poles" to mean the intelligentsia and government officials. It was also rumored that a law had been passed permitting Galicians to murder Jews and Poles—or anyone who wore buttons on their hats—that is, officials.[21]

On 12 June, the Ministry of the Interior in Vienna instructed the local mayors and village leaders in Galicia to vigorously oppose the rumors that a high authority had granted permission to persecute the Israelites.[22] On 17 August, the governor's office notified the Ministry of the Interior of the "antisemitic boycott movement,"[23] explaining that it was most eagerly embraced by the youth and disseminated by means of posters and handbills. Rather than causing the Jews any notable damage, it had negative consequences for the Christians and peasants who worked for them, whose harvests and haystacks had been destroyed and windows smashed. Some of them had even been personally attacked. A total of fifty-four people had been arrested and thirty-three taken to court in connection with the boycott movement. A warning had also been issued to the Jews to not under any circumstances cause a provocation.[24]

As familiar as the above reports appear at the end of this study, on closer consideration, it is, above all, the differences to 1898 that are striking. Few people followed the countless calls to attack Jews in summer 1903, even though the agitation (that is, the communication intended to spur people into action), involving sermons, posters, letters, and even an organization promoting the boycott of Jews, was considerably more elaborate than five years previously, when it was based merely on rumors of a warrant. In 1903, demands were far more concrete. Signed notices called on the peasants to take violent action. They no longer needed to read between the lines of advertisements or festival announcements to find authorization.

Lessons Learned from 1898

The year 1903 did not see a repeat of the events of 1898, partly because Galicians had learned some lessons. After the disturbances of 1898, the military and judiciary had made it clear that the state not only did not issue permits to attack others but also that it punished the participants in such attacks—albeit after some delay—and ensured the loot was returned. This had not been forgotten.[25] Where the state was in control, it was inadvisable to riot. Galician Jews had learned that it was helpful to inform the authorities in good time of imminent attacks. Although this did not necessarily prevent riots, police intervention helped to contain them. Above all, the Jews of Galicia had noted the usefulness of appealing to Jewish interest groups with strong connections in the capital. They could be sure of the cooperation of the Galician authorities, who were eager for the approval of the Viennese public and the ministries. Arranging with the local council for the protection of market stalls and houses and the deployment of law enforcement officers in likely trouble spots proved reliable means of preventing violence toward property escalating into violence toward people. Police and councilors had realized the importance of responding to early warnings from Jewish citizens to maintain order and not be forced to surrender their powers to the military. They knew that the people's "tales," however absurd they sounded, were indicative of collective preparations to engage in lootings and to contest the authority of the state. Subsequent arrests and interrogations updated public awareness of the consequences of telling rumors.

Divisive Communication

Sources on the unrest of 1903 show that the rural population was by no means electrified—either within individual village communities or on a supra-village level—by the prospect of once again reckoning up with the Jews and acquiring property at their expense. There were isolated attempts to recreate a similarly riotous mood as in 1898, evidenced by the incorporation of new facts into old tales of warrants and punishments. The story of stones being thrown at the emperor was a new twist on the tales justifying cacophonies. The talk of permission from the courts was a sign that the judiciary's authority was now recognized, following the trials in the wake of summer 1898 and the actions initiated by the interpellation process.

But other attempts at agitation were not woven into rural communication. On an everyday level, individuals no longer situationally took the role of agitators, participating in mobilization and assuming the role of author from the rumors' originators by adding their own personal elements. The agitators and the agitated were clearly distinct in 1903. The agitators were others—nameless members of the paramilitary Sokól organization, re-migrants with experience of foreign lands who wore different clothes and had different financial circumstances, or vicars and priests. Their agitation did not guarantee benefits for the peasant community or legitimize its claims. Rather, it threatened the villagers who they deemed to have the "wrong" habits and targeted them with violence. It showed that symbolic punishment could just as well be inflicted on Christians as on Jews.

Though continuing the discourse of economic liberation, antisemitic practice in 1903 was fundamentally different from that of 1898. Rather than promising gratification and profit, it threatened restrictions and deprivation. Narrowing the choice of trading and business partners would have negative economic consequences for both producers and consumers, implying higher costs and longer distances. Boycotting employers who paid well resulted in income losses for the employees and allowed Christian employers to pay far less with impunity. Ending the ambivalent symbiosis and placing further constraints on rural Galicia's already limited business infrastructure, as the agitators demanded, was detrimental to most of the population of the Carpathian Foothills. And in any case, their inherent pride would not allow them to accept perfect strangers from the city dictating what they should and should not do. The antisemitic discourse of the interpellations and peasant newspapers, portraying Christian peasants as the victims of Jewish perpetrators, justified occasional backlashes against the "impudent Jews." But the latter-phase agitators' blackmailing and anti-Jewish preaching placed excessive pressure on the peasants. True, the boycott discourse had a certain usefulness for the Christian community. Supposedly founded in "scientific fact," it could be referenced to legitimize various anti-Jewish actions. But the element of compulsion proved offensive. A peasant involved in a dispute with a Jew might appreciate a priest sermonizing against Jews as a vindication of his own situation. But a priest making personal comments outside the church, reproaching members of his congregation on the street, was overstepping the mark.

Taking the boycott discourse to the level of everyday practice ran counter to the interests of most of the rural population. This antisemitic agitation did not fulfill any unifying, communicative function. It did not connect politicians with voters or create any possibilities for people to act. On the contrary, it limited their options. Consequently, the antisemitic process came to a halt. It worked to the peasants' disadvantage, exacting more than it promised, and was rejected. Peasants resisted the agitators' threats and refused to ostracize the Jews, which would have implied a significant loss of earnings for many. A strict separation of Jews from Christians could never be realized beyond the realm of catechisms and populist manifestos, and could only ever remain a fiction.

However severely the peasants were threatened and blackmailed, then, and however radical the language of violence became, it did not prompt them into action. Antisemitism that was de facto against Christians, because it demanded the unacceptable of them, was unpopular. It could not be used to invest plans and actions with meaning but, on the contrary, remained an impractical theory. Conversely, the rural population did not demonstrate the kind of anti-Jewish behavior that could be used in political discourse. Rather, Christians as well as Jews refused to be intimidated and reported any inflammatory posters and notices they saw to the authorities. The anti-Semites were isolated. They did not form a link between the Galician people and the imperial public, by which means they could have publicized their agenda. They remained alone with their demands for, and visions of, a Christian national economy. They were not on the side of the *lud*, against the military and the Jews, but stood alone, facing an ambivalent peasant world in which Christians and Jews lived side by side in a delicate balance of power and mutual dependency.

A Nationalist Process

Nationalist commentary played a far greater role in 1903 than five years previously. But rather than signifying the spread of nationalist viewpoints in rural Galicia, it highlighted the priorities of the actors now engaged in agitation. The Sokól, for one, was an actively nationalist organization that had also been involved in the disturbances in 1898. But while it had then joined in existing conflicts and appeared in rumors as an exotic mobilizing force, in 1903 it made autonomous attempts to enforce a boycott and spark a conflict in the name of the nation. These, however, failed.

Still, the agitators drew on a nationally charged dynamic affecting the crownland. There was major—and violent—agricultural action in East Galicia in 1902 and 1903, and strike was on many people's lips. Involving mostly Ukrainian peasants demanding higher pay from Polish or Jewish landowner-employers, it marked a social conflict that also ran along national fault lines. It could be read as a national boycott. Ukrainian agitators lumped together Jews and Poles as the Ukrainian peasants' adversaries, with whom they clashed on both social and national terms. The high number of Ukrainians in the statistics on the unrest of 1903 can be partly attributed to this circumstance. Also, officials in East Galicia now scrutinized the public more closely. Not because of the events of 1898— East Galicia had seen only isolated incidents—but because they themselves were increasingly targeted by peasant aggression. They were the Poles against whom the Ukrainian peasants rallied. To them, they represented the establishment and Polish landownership.

Polish nationalists in West Galicia responded to the events in East Galicia by trying to launch local strikes and boycotts. Roaming around in intimidating gangs, they chanted slogans and waved letters and notices. The Galician authorities, meanwhile, tried all they could to prevent the large-scale strikes in the east of the crownland from spreading to the west, increasing their efforts to suppress activists and troublemakers. The Jewish population feared above all echoes of the unprecedentedly brutal attacks that had occurred in Kišinev in Russia, which they had observed with horror as evidence of a new dimension in anti-Jewish violence.[26] With hindsight, new dimensions of aggression and violence can indeed be seen to have gripped Central and Eastern Europe around the time of the Russian Revolution and the murder of Governor Potocki. These events, which toppled the social order and precipitated violent social and national conflicts, marked turning points away from the past. The brutalization of language during and after the Russian Revolution of 1905 could also be observed in individual disputes between Jews and Ukrainian Christians, in which they articulated fantasies of radical social change and revolution.[27]

In the short period around 1903 to 1906, Galicia's political landscape became firmly entrenched as two opposing camps: social and national. The role of the church in political life was equated with the role of the nation, as the nation was defined in religious terms. With the introduction of universal equal (male) suffrage in 1907, the substantial Greek Catholic population, which made up 40 percent of the electorate, became a considerable force. To form a bulwark, the two clerical peasant parties merged with the Polish National Democratic Party until 1910. The resulting party refrained from taking an explicitly hostile stand on Jews since it relied partly on the votes and cooperation of Jews—as members or as coalition partners against the Ukrainian National Democrats. Teofil Merunowicz led the National Democrats' first election campaign after the introduction of universal equal suffrage. It was a decidedly anti-Ukrainian election campaign.

That is not to say that hostility toward Jews was banished from political rhetoric, let alone generally condemned. The secular peasant party and the Christian Social People's Center Party continued to be explicitly antisemitic. Anti-Jewish arguments were used less in political debate, but firmly incorporated into the respective nationalizing projects. As the national question rose in importance ahead of the Jewish question, boycotts were promoted as a means of fighting for the nation rather than primarily of combating the Jews. Ukrainians were called on to boycott Poles, and Poles were urged to boycott German products. Jewish businesspeople who traded with Germans were accused of national disloyalty rather than of Jewish profiteering or nepotism. The Germans of Galicia, meanwhile, founded a national umbrella organization in 1907 to uphold "German cultural work."[28] The world's first Jewish parliamentary faction, formed in the Reichsrat in the same year by politicians including Adolf Stand, Arthur Mahler, Henryk Gabel, and Benno Straucher, highlighted the national character of the Jewish question. It also shows that antisemitism cannot be regarded as integral to nationalism and that anti-Jewish feeling was certainly not caused by national conflicts. Still, the various nationalizing projects propounded ideas that were closely interwoven with the Jewish question and antisemitism. Yet this more intense nationalist agitation after the turn of the century did not cause a rise in antisemitic acts. On the contrary, the lessons learned from the riots of 1898 and the discrepancy between nationalist discourse and everyday life in rural Galicia ensured that the antisemitic process in Galicia never again gathered the same momentum under Habsburg rule as it had in the west of the crownland around 1900.

Remembering the Antisemitism Years

The various accounts and incidents outlined above do not lend themselves to cultivating the melancholy image of Galicia as the apotheosis of a lost country where life could be different. In this idealistic view, Galicia symbolizes an exotic, ambiguous, and nonperformance-oriented place, where diverse cultures with varying norms and conventions lived side by side, in contrast to today's standardized, bureaucratized, and commercialized nation-states.[29] Originating as far back as the interwar period, the tendency to mythologize Galicia grew after the carnage of World War II. In parallel, there is a tendency among those seeking the origins of human-made disasters in the past, and logical lines of development delivering comprehensibility, to regard the former Habsburg crownland as the breeding ground for negative developments.

It has emerged from this study of the antisemitic process that relations between Christians and Jews around 1900 were problematic. There is a very thin and by no means straight line connecting the disturbances of 1898 to the *Judenjagd*, or hunt for the Jews, of 1942 to 1945.[30] They happened in the same place, the Carpathian Foothills, and involved the same families. Their life worlds were shaped by accounts of their ancestors' experiences, most of which were oral, or written down from personal or verbally communicated memory. This form of history writing is still alive today, after the Holocaust. Do these witnesses make connections between 1898 and 1939–1945 in their accounts? How do they judge the relations between Christians and Jews in the antisemitism years in Galicia? The Memory Books recalling Jewish life in Galicia, written and compiled after the World War II by survivors of the Holocaust or those who managed to emigrate beforehand, mention conflicts between Jews, Christians, and representatives of the state prior to World War I. To assess these accounts, rather than meticulously checking them against the known historical facts—since communicative and individual memory are known to work differently than historical science—it is more illuminating to consider the recurring motifs that originated at the time of the disturbances and became so dominant that they structure and lend deeper meaning to various individual recollections.

The Book of Strzyżów and Vicinity, published in the United States in 1990, describes the main suspect in the Mnich murder case as having been seventy-year-old Itzhak Ritter. Emperor Franz Joseph himself later ordered his release after a delegation of prominent Galician rabbis and lawyers had informed him of the case, which had been conclusively solved when the murderer confessed.[31] He was the father of Franka Mnich's unborn child and a relative of the parish priest. Franka, a Ukrainian, had worked as a maid in his house. He had ordered her murder to avoid the dishonor of illegitimate fatherhood.

The same book contains a chapter on the "antisemitic riots," in which relations between Jews and Christians are described as having been generally good and peaceful, but distant. None of the Christians responsible for the riots was arrested, it recalls, with the exception of two Jews: the cemetery caretaker Jakob Hagel for complaining about the soldiers' horses grazing on the old Jewish cemetery, and a nameless man who had "dared to call the mob thieves."[32]

Similarly, "intercessions from Vienna" had been necessary to get the Jewish family released who were accused of planning ritual murder in the Katarzyna Tabaka case. The girl had quickly become a cult figure; many people from the surrounding area traveled to Żmigród to see the "holy virgin."[33] This account, portraying the local administration as anti-Jewish or at best idle, and the peasants as fanatically religious, illustrates the deep impact of political discourse and press coverage from Vienna. Justice had only been done thanks to the Jewish elites in and from Vienna appealing directly to the emperor, sidestepping the Supreme Court. Subsequently, the few known incidents of influential Viennese intervening to help blameless Jewish suspects were used to structure all tales of solved conflicts between Christians and Jews. Interestingly, their coexistence was described as largely respectful.

The Shtetlinks website summarizes the Frysztak tragedy in 1898 in one sentence, stating that "the Austrians" suppressed a "pogrom" and relations between Christians and Jews remained peaceful until World War II. In fact, the disturbances in Frysztak on 16 June 1898, which claimed eleven lives, became a milestone in the Christian peasantry's collective memory. This is reflected in the book *Bloody Evensong in Frysztak 1898* (in Polish) by Karol Marcinkowski, which recounts local memories of the bloody Corpus Christi holiday alongside a hagiography of Stojałowski.[34] Here, the Christians of Frysztak are portrayed as a community of mourning, victimized by the military and the Jews. Published long after World War II by the right-wing Polish National Democrat Jędrzej Giertych and written in the style of a Jewish Memory Book, Marcinkowski's book asserts the Poles' victimhood as rivaling that of the Jews. Appropriating Jewish memory culture, it contests established ideas of the identity and role of the "others" by not only giving an alternative account of events but also reinterpreting memory narratives in order to rewrite history. Significantly, the book was published in the United States, where the public had a different stock of knowledge about the murder of Jews in occupied Poland than people in the postwar socialist republic of Poland. Marcinkowski takes the obscure incident in Frysztak as the basis for a prehistory of the Holocaust in reverse. Instead of drawing a line of continuation from the "riots" to the *Judenjagd*, he portrays the royal-and-imperial gendarmes' crackdown on the peasant crowds under unit commander Winiarski, supported by the local Jewish population, as anticipating the German "evacuation commandos'" murder of Galician Jews.[35] After all, the order to shoot the innocent Polish peasants was said to have been given in German.[36] Almost one hundred years later, then, a nationalist author, to deflect guilt from his nation, seized on malignant rumors that arose in the immediate aftermath and were repeated as fact by newspapers such as *Głos Narodu* and *Prawda*.

In the overall view, such simplifying, idealizing, or dramatizing texts illustrate the ambivalent nature of the personal experiences of members of the various groups living alongside, with, and in opposition to each other in the Kingdom of Galicia and Lodomeria. The examples mentioned above all use narratives of hostility toward "others," the victimization of their "own kind," and the importance of a remote power for delivering justice to promote a sense of community. The narrative patterns with which rumors and interpellations operated shaped people's memories of the events they described and the circumstances in which they occurred. The experience of two traumatic world wars, Nazi occupation and murder in West Galicia, and German and Soviet rules of terror in East Galicia added further elements. The memories are now self-contained stories themselves, perhaps coloring our picture of antisemitism in Galicia. The historical reconstruction of the events in Frysztak, Żmigród, Stary Sącz, and Lutzca in the earlier chapters of the book paint a picture of antisemitism in Galicia around 1900. The accounts mentioned in this last section, in contrast, provide insight into how memories of history function and are harnessed for specific purposes. But neither knowledge of the events around 1900 nor later memories of them can explain the mass murder of the Jews in the former Austrian crownland of Galicia.

Notes

1. CDIAL 146/4/3128.
2. CDIAL 146/4/3128 B. 50; and CDIAL 146/4/3128, B. 84.
3. CDIAL 146/4/3129, B. 7.
4. CDIAL 146/4/3129/12.
5. Ibid.
6. CDIAL 146/4/3129/16, 24.
7. CDIAL 146/4/3130/7.
8. Ibid.
9. CDIAL 146/4/3129, S. 66. On 9 July, the district captain from Rzeszów reported calls for employees of Jews to strike, although Jewish employers did not pay any less in wages and could hardly be said to exploit their workforce. CDIAL 146/4/3129/68.
10. CDIAL 146/4/3129/68f.
11. CDIAL 146/4/3129/14.
12. CDIAL 146/4/3129, B. 5.
13. Ibid.
14. CDIAL 146/4/3130/5.330.
15. CDIAL 146/4/3130/7.
16. CDIAL 146/4/3130/40.
17. CDIAL 146/4/3130/31.
18. Ibid.
19. CDIAL 146/4/3130.
20. Threats that the Kišinev pogrom would be repeated in East Galicia were also reported by Jewish residents of Nowy Sącz in a letter of 8 June to the Ministry of the Interior. On 23 June, the governor's office received the news that two Ruthenians had robbed Jews in Skoly. One of them had returned to the region after a long period abroad, announcing his intention to kill Jews and Poles.
21. CDIAL 146/4/3130/1ff.
22. CDIAL 146/4/3130/60.331.
23. CDIAL 146/4/3130/67.
24. Ibid.
25. However, experiences gained in 1898 were inscribed in the rumors to make them seem more credible, as evidenced in tales such as those of Jews throwing stones or the court issuing authorization.
26. Hanna Węgrzynek, "Pogrom w Kiszynowie (1903): Reakcje na ziemiach polskich i wpływ na postawy Polaków," in Rudkowska and Borkowska, *Kwestia żydowska*, 453–462.
27. Ukrainian hostility was chiefly directed at the nobility and the Polish nation. Calls to hang opponents (na hak z nimi) or warnings of slaughter (budemo rizaty) were voiced at various events. Jews were frequently incorporated into fantasies of slaughter (teper Rusyny budut rizaty Polkiw I Zydiw) or threatened with scenarios such as having their "eyes gouged out like in Russia" or being "slaughtered like in Russia." The motif of authorization to rob Poles and Jews was also widely circulated in East Galicia during the Russian Revolution. In February 1906, Isaak Strumwasser of Strjy stated that Stefan Andruskow had threatened him with the words "Get out of here now, what are you doing in our village, go to Jerusalem. I have permission to cut your head off." (Ja maju dozwolinstwo

szozobym tobi holowu rizaw). All examples from AGAD Min. Wew. 314. Governor Michał Bobrzynski wrote to the war minister Franz Xaver von Schöneich in 1908 to request the installment of a permanent cavalry garrison in Śniatyn to be able to more swiftly suppress "riots and violent acts" consequent to "radical propaganda." AGAD Min. Wew. 25, S. 1114ff.
28. Maner, *Galizien*, 146.
29. Kerstin S. Jobst, *Der Mythos des Miteinander: Galizien in Literatur und Geschichte* (Hamburg, 1998); Dietlind Hüchtker, "'Der Mythos Galizien': Versuch einer Historisierung," in Michael G. Müller and Rolf Petri (eds.), *Die Nationalisierung von Grenzen: Zur Konstruktion nationaler Identität in sprachlich gemischten Grenzregionen* (Marburg, 2002).
30. See the detailed description of the murder of Jews in hiding in Dąbrowa Tarnowska district, formerly Galicia, and the system of blackmail, threats, and rewards with which the German occupying forces involved the local population in the hunt on Jews: Jan Grabowski, *Judenjagd. Polowanie na Żydów 1942–1945: Studiem dziejów pewnego powiatu* (Warsaw, 2011).
31. Itzhok Berglass and Shlomo Yahalomi-Diamond (eds), *The Book of Strzyżów and Vicinity* (Los Angeles, 1990), 58f.
32. Ibid., 58.
33. See Jewish Gen, https://kehilalinks.jewishgen.org/Zmigrod/zmigrod.htm, accessed 20 May 2020.
34. Karol Marcinkowski, *Krwawe Nieszpory we Frysztaku w 1898 r./Patriota Ks. Stojałowski* [Bloody Evensong in Frysztak 1898/The patriot Father Stojałwoski] (Philadelphia, 1983).
35. Unowsky sees the book primarily as an attempt to construct a Polish national history in which Jews were disruptive, foreign elements, and so negate the long history of coexistence. Unowsky, "Peasant Political Mobilization."
36. As outlined above, nobody had given orders to shoot and it is unlikely that unit commander Winiarski spoke German with the local gendarmes.

Epilogue

World War I turned Galicia into a battlefield, and its inhabitants into soldiers or other perpetrators and victims of violence.¹ In the wake of invading, occupying, and retreating armies, civilians were turned into refugees, potential spies, collaborators, or fellow travelers. Wherever a power vacuum arose, property owners were robbed and assaulted.² Rumors circulated that Jews had caused the war by murdering the emperor. Tens of thousands of Jews fled the advancing Tsarist army over the Carpathians.³ Further tens of thousands were deported during the Russian occupation of Galicia under suspicion of spying for the Germans, just as officers of the royal-and-imperial army executed Ukrainian subjects of the emperor for allegedly collaborating with the Russians.

Peace came late to Galicia and did not last long. The tsar had been murdered, and the emperor had died; their empires had crumbled, and their armies dissolved. Their former subjects tussled to secure as large territories as possible for their nations, encouraged by the American president. When Lemberg was conquered by Polish troops after a short period of Ukrainian rule, civilian inhabitants joined forces with soldiers of the Polish army to pillage and attack the Jews of the city. Seventy-one were murdered. Jews were now maligned as traitors to the nation rather than enemies of the House of Habsburg. Jews were robbed by their Christian neighbors in other parts of former Galicia too. There were no law enforcers to prevent it; armed men in uniform were themselves taking freely from storeowners, barkeepers, and private individuals.

The entire territory of Galicia was incorporated into the Polish Republic. While statesmen in Versailles were still negotiating constitutions and national borders, armies created precedents on Galician soil.⁴ The Red Army launched an unsuccessful attack on the Polish state. Once again, robberies and murders were justified with tales of Jews shooting at Polish soldiers. Jews were now often said to be Bolshevist sympathizers.⁵

By the early 1920s, state order had been re-established, and peace restored. Galicians became Polish citizens, and all men and women received the right to vote. Ten percent of the former crownland's population was still Jewish. A large proportion of them still worked in trade or crafts. Many of them spoke Polish and saw themselves as Poles, especially the city dwellers, but also increasingly the residents of small towns and villages between the Vistula and the Carpathian Mountains. Many artists and intellectuals of the Mosaic faith or with Jewish roots made contributions to Polish arts and culture; others helped create a modern Yiddish identity in Poland.[6] But priests and bishops preached more zealously than ever against the "damaging influence" of the Jews on Polish society. Among them were the notorious Stanisław Trzeciak and the primate August Hlond, who was ordained a priest in Przemysł and Krakow during the antisemitism years in Galicia. From the mid-1930s on, Christian and Jewish students increasingly disputed the issue of free access to education for the latter. The boycott movement against Polish Jews was revived, but the ambivalent symbiosis between Christian peasants and Jewish traders continued in the Carpathian foothills, even in Lutzca. Here, the manor was still owned by the Wallach family, though the proprietor Abraham had moved to Krakow. While several Jewish families lived in Lutzca, it was mainly inhabited by Catholic Poles, including the Mnich family. Some Ukrainian families lived on the outskirts near the village Krasna, such as the music and art teacher Jan Rusenko. Life was harmonious and peaceful in Lutzca in the late 1930s.[7]

On 11 September 1939, German soldiers arrived from Strzyżów on horses and bicycles. A few days later, German police reached the village. They beat up the Jews, shaved off their beards and earlocks, and spread mortal fear among them. On 4 November, they arrested the priest and vicar, the school's principal and three teachers, and the mailman.

In early summer 1942, the German occupiers deported the Jewish inhabitants of Lutzca, Strzyżów, and the surrounding area to the ghetto in Rzeszów. Only a few Jews of the Carpathian foothills survived the Nazis' extermination practice. Schlomo Wilmer managed to go into hiding in Lutzca. He was a cousin of Abraham Wallach, who likewise fled Krakow to seek refuge in his home village. But he was then shot by a German. The grandson of Moses Ritter suffered the same fate, having first managed to jump off the train that was taking 1,500 people on 15 November out of the Rzeszów ghetto to Bełżec extermination camp.

Notes

1. Alexander M. Prusin, *Nationalizing a Borderland: War, Ethnicity, and Anti-Jewish Violence in East Galicia, 1914–1920* (Tuscaloosa, 2005), 24–47.
2. Solomon Ansky, *The Enemy at His Pleasure: A Journey through the Jewish Pale of Settlement during World War I*, ed. and trans. Joachim Neugroschel (New York, 2002).
3. Salcia Landmann, *Erinnerungen an Galizien* (Munich, 1975); Minna Lachs, *Warum schaust du zurück? Erinnerungen 1907–1941* (Vienna, 1986).

4. Jochen Böhler, *Civil War in Central Europe, 1918–1921: The Reconstruction of Poland* (Oxford, 2019).
5. William W. Hagen, *Anti-Jewish Violence in Poland, 1914–1920* (New York, 2018).
6. Gertrud Pickhan, "Kulturelle Vielfalt und Mehrsprachigkeit: Jüdische Identitätskonstruktionen im Polen der Zwischenkriegszeit," in Rainer Kampling, *"Wie schön sind deine Zelte, Jakob, deine Wohnungen, Israel" (Num 24,5): Beiträge zur Geschichte jüdisch-europäischer Kultur* (Frankfurt a. M., 2009), 157–170.
7. Itzhok and Yahalomi-Diamond, *The Book of Strzyzow*; Franciszek Kotula, *Losy Żydów rzeszowskich 1939–44: Kronika tantych dni* (Rzeszów, 1999); Towarzystwo Przyjaciół Lutczy (ed.), *Lutcza w czasach okupacji* (Stalowa Wola, 1995).

Bibliography

Archives

AGAD: Central Archives of Historical Records, Warsaw
APK: Staate Archives, Krakow
CAHJP: Central Archives fort he History of the Jewish People, Jerusalem
CDIAL: Central Historical State Archives, L'viv
ÖStaA: Austrian State Archives, Vienna

Government Documents

Petition der Israelitischen Kaufmannschaft an Seine Majestät den Kaiser Franz Josef I. behufs gänzlicher Aufhebung der sonntäglichen Geschäftssperre oder dieselbe auf 6 Uhr Vorabends zu verlegen verfasst und argumentiert von Hendel Adler, Kolomea 1898.
Reichsgesetzblatt für die im Reichsrathe vertretenen Königreiche und Länder.
Stenografische Protokolle des Abgeordnetenhauses des Reichsrates.

Periodicals

Antysemita
Czas
Deutsches Volksblatt
Die Welt
Dr. Bloch's Österreichische Wochenschrift
Dziennik Krakowski
Dziennik Polski
Gazeta Krakowska
Gazeta Narodowa
Głos Narodu
Grzmot
Hasło
Izraelita
Kronika
Kurier Lwowski

Neue Freie Presse
Nowa Reforma
Obrona Ludu
Ojczyzna
Pester Lloyd
Pochodnia
Prawda
Przegląd Społeczny
Przyjaciel Ludu
Przyjaciel Sług
Pszczółka
Wiener Tagblatt
Wiener Zeitung
Wieniec Polski
Związek Chłopski

Secondary Literature

Adler-Rudel, Salomon. *Ostjuden in Deutschland 1880–1940: Zugleich eine Geschichte der Organisationen, die sie betreuten.* Tübingen, 1959.
Adorno, Theodor W. *Minima Moralia.* Frankfurt a. M., 2001.
Allmayer-Beck, Johann Christoph. "Die bewaffnete Macht in Staat und Gesellschaft." In *Die Habsburgermonarchie 1848–1918*, vol. 5: *Die bewaffnete Macht*, edited by Adam Wandruszka and Peter Urbanitsch, 1–141. Vienna, 1987.
Almog, Shmuel. "Alfred Nossig: A Reappraisal." *Studies in Zionism* 7 (1983): 1–29.
Anderson, Benedict. *Imagined Communities: Reflections on the Origin and Spread of Nationalism.* London, 1982.
Andlauer, Teresa. *Die jüdische Bevölkerung im Modernisierungsprozess Galiziens (1867–1914).* Frankfurt a. M., 2001.
Andreski, Stanislav. "An Economic Interpretation of Antisemitism in Eastern Europe." *Jewish Journal of Sociology* 5 (1963): 201–213.
Ansky, Solomon. *The Enemy at His Pleasure: A Journey through the Jewish Pale of Settlement during World War I*, edited and translated by Joachim Neugroschel. New York, 2002.
Araten, Rachel Sarna. *Michalina: Daughter of Israel: The True Story of a Jewish Girl Abducted by the Catholic Church.* Jerusalem, 1986.
Asad, Talad. "Übersetzen zwischen Kulturen: Ein Konzept der britischen Sozialanthropologie." In *Kultur, soziale Praxis, Text: Die Krise der ethnographischen Repräsentation*, edited by Eberhard Berg and Martin Fuchs, 300–334. Frankfurt a. M., 1999.
Assmann, Jan. "Kulturelle Texte im Spannungsfeld von Mündlichkeit und Schriftlichkeit." In *Literaturkanon-Medienereignis-Kultureller Text: Formen interkultureller Kommunikation und Übersetzung*, edited by Andreas Poltermann, 270–292. Berlin, 1995.
Augustynowicz, Christoph. *Geschichte Ostmitteleuropas: Ein Abriss.* Vienna, 2010.
Augustynowicz, Christoph, and Andreas Kappeler, eds. *Die galizische Grenze 1772–1867: Kommunikation oder Isolation?* Vienna, 2006.
Baberowski, Jörg. "Gerüchte und Gewalt im Zarenreich und in der Sowjetunion." *Humboldt-Spektrum* 1 (2009): 46–48.

———. "Imperiale Herrschaft: Repräsentationen politischer Macht im späten Zarenreich." In *Imperiale Herrschaft in der Provinz: Repräsentationen politischer Macht im späten Zarenreich*, edited by Jörg Baberowski, David Feest, and Christoph Gumb, 9–16. Frankfurt a. M., 2008.

———. "Nationalismus aus dem Geist der Inferiorität: Autokratische Modernisierung und die Anfänge muslimischer Selbstvergewisserung im östlichen Transkaukasien 1828–1914." *Geschichte und Gesellschaft* 26 (2000): 371–406.

———. *Räume der Gewalt*. Frankfurt a. M., 2015.

Bachmann, Klaus. "Antisemitismus." In *Deutsche und Polen: Geschichte – Kultur – Politik*, edited by Andreas Lawaty and Hubert Orłowski, 439–450. Munich, 2003.

———. *"Ein Herd der Feindschaft gegen Russland": Galizien als Krisenherd in den Beziehungen der Donaumonarchie mit Rußland (1907–1914)*. Vienna, 2001.

Bachmann-Medick, Doris. *Übersetzung als Repräsentation fremder Kulturen*. Berlin, 1997.

Baczkowski, Michał. "Prostytucja w Krakowie na przełomie XIX i XX w." *Studia historyczne* 43, no. 4 (2000): 593–606.

Bahr, Hermann. *Der Antisemitismus: Ein internationales Interview*. Berlin, 1893.

Bałaban, Majer. *Historia lwowskiej Synagogi Postępowej*. Lwów, 1937.

Beller, Steven. *Antisemitism: A Very Short Introduction*. New York, 2007.

Bender, Ryszard. "Wokół sprawy pobytce Ks. St. S. w Belgii w 1872/1873." In *Z zagadnień kultury chrześciańskiej*, edited by Stefan Wyszyński and John Paul, 465–471. Lublin, 1973.

Benz, Wolfgang. *Was ist Antisemitismus?* Munich, 2004.

Berg, Alexander. *Judenhyänen vor dem Strafgericht zu Lemberg*. Berlin, 1893.

Berg, Eberhard, and Martin Fuchs, eds. *Kultur, soziale Praxis, Text: Die Krise der ethnographischen Repräsentation*. Frankfurt a. M., 1999.

Berger, Peter, and Thomas Luckmann. *Die gesellschaftliche Konstruktion der Wirklichkeit: Eine Theorie der Wissenssoziologie*. Frankfurt a. M., 1987.

Bergmann, Werner. "Ethnic Riots in Situations of Loss of Control: Revolution, Civil War, and Regime Change as Opportunity Structures for Anti-Jewish Violence in Nineteenth and Twentieth-Century Europe." In *The Control of Violence in Modern Society: Multidisciplinary Perspectives: From School Shootings to Ethnic Violence*, edited by Wilhelm Heitmeyer, Heinz-Gerhard Haupt, Stefan Malthaner, and Andrea Kirschner, 487–516. Berlin, 2010.

———. *Geschichte des Antisemitismus*. Munich, 2002.

Bergmann, Werner, Christhard Hoffmann, and Helmut Walser Smith, eds. *Exclusionary Violence: Antisemitic Riots in Modern Germany*. Ann Arbor, 2002.

Bettelheim, Peter, and Robert Harauer, eds. *Ostcharme und Westkomfort: Beiträge zur politischen Kultur Österreichs*. Vienna, 1993.

Berglass, Itzhok, and Shlomo Yahalomi-Diamond, eds. *The Book of Strzyżów and Vicinity*. Los Angeles, 1990.

Bieberstein, Christoph Freiherr Marschall von. *Freiheit in der Unfreiheit: Die nationale Autonomie der Polen in Galizien nach dem österreichisch-ungarischen Ausgleich von 1867; Ein konservativer Aufbruch im mitteleuropäischen Vergleich*. Wiesbaden, 1993.

Binder, Harald. "Das polnische Pressewesen." In *Die Habsburgermonarchie*, vol. 8: *Politische Öffentlichkeit und Zivilgesellschaft*, edited by Helmut Rumpler and Peter Urbanitsch, 2037–2090. Vienna, 2006.

———. "Das ruthenische Pressewesen." In *Die Habsburgermonarchie*, vol. 8: *Politische Öffentlichkeit und Zivilgesellschaft*, edited by Helmut Rumpler and Peter Urbanitsch, 2091–2126. Vienna, 2006.

———. "Die Wahlreform von 1907 und der polnisch-ruthenische Konflikt in Ostgalizien." *Österreichische Osthefte* 38, no. 3 (1996): 293–320.

———. *Galizien in Wien: Parteien, Wahlen, Fraktionen und Abgeordnete im Übergang zur Massenpolitik.* Vienna, 2005.

———. "'Galizische Autonomie': Ein streitbarer Begriff und seine Karriere." In *Moravské vyronáni z roku 1905/Der Mährische Ausgleich von 1905*, edited by Lukás Fasora, 239–266. Brno, 2006.

———. "Kirche und nationale Festkultur in Krakau 1861 bis 1910." In *Nationalisierung der Religion und Sakralisierung der Nation im östlichen Europa*, edited by Martin Schulze-Wessel, 121–140. Stuttgart, 2006.

———. "Politische Öffentlichkeit in Galizien: Lemberg und Krakau im Vergleich." In *Stadt und Öffentlichkeit in Ostmitteleuropa: 1900–1939; Beiträge zur Entstehung moderner Urbanität zwischen Berlin, Charkiv, Tallinn und Triest*, edited by Andreas R. Hofmann, 259–280. Stuttgart, 2002.

Binnenkade, Alexandra, Ekaterina Emeliantseva, and Svjatoslav Pacholkiv. *Vertraut und fremd zugleich: Jüdisch-christliche Nachbarschaften in Warschau – Lengnau – Lemberg.* Cologne, 2009.

Bjork, James E. *Neither German nor Pole: Catholicism and National Indifference in a Central European Borderland.* Ann Arbor, 2008.

Blaschke, Olaf. "Wie wird aus einem guten Katholiken ein guter Judenfeind? Zwölf Ursachen des katholischen Antisemitismus auf dem Prüfstand." In *Katholischer Antisemitismus im 19. Jahrhundert: Ursachen und Traditionen im internationalen Vergleich*, edited by Olaf Blaschke, 77–110. Zurich, 2000.

Blobaum, Robert E., ed. *Antisemitism and Its Opponents in Modern Poland.* Ithaca, 2006.

Borkowska, Grażyna, and Magdalena Rudkowska, eds. *Kwestia żydowska w XIX wieku: Spory o tożsamość Polaków.* Warsaw, 2004.

Boyer, John W. *Karl Lueger (1844–1910): Christlichsoziale Politik als Beruf; Eine Biographie.* Vienna, 2010.

Böhler, Jochen. *Civil War in Central Europe, 1918-1921: The Reconstruction of Poland.* Oxford, 2019.

Bradley, Joseph. *Voluntary Associations in Tsarist Russia: Science, Patriotism, and Civil Society.* Cambridge, 2009.

Brafman, Jakob. *Żydzi i Kahały: dzieło wydane w języku rosyjskim w Wilnie w roku 1870 przez Brafmanná (żyda przechrzczonego).* Lwów, 1874.

Brass, Paul. "Introduction: Discourses of Ethnicity, Communalism, and Violence." In *Riots and Pogroms*, edited by Paul Brass, 1–55. Basingstoke, 1996.

Breitling, Rupert. "Populismus." In *Populismus in Österreich*, edited by Anton Pelinka, 26–33. Vienna, 1987.

Bristow, Edward J. *Prostitution and Prejudice: The Jewish Fight against White Slavery 1870–1939.* Oxford, 1982.

Brock, Peter. *Nationalism and Populism in Partitioned Poland.* London, 1973.

Brodocz, André, ed. *Institutionelle Macht: Genese – Verstetigung – Verlust.* Cologne, 2005.

Bronner, Eric Stephen. *Ein Gerücht über die Juden: Die Protokolle der Weisen von Zion und der alltägliche Antisemitismus.* Berlin, 1999.

Brubaker, Rogers. "Ethnicity, Race, and Nationalism." *Annual Review of Sociology* 35 (2009): 21–42.

———. "Myths and Misconceptions in the Study of Nationalism." In *The State of the Nation: Ernest Gellner and the Theory of Nationalism*, edited by John Hall, 272–306. Cambridge, 1998.

———. *Nationalism Refrained: Nationhood and the National Question in the New Europe*. Cambridge, 1996.

———. "Rethinking Nationhood: Nation as Institutionalized Form, Practical Category, Contingent Event." *Contention* 4, no. 1 (Fall 1994): 3–14.

Brubaker, Rogers, and David D. Laitin. "Ethnic and Nationalist Violence." *Annual Review of Sociology* 24 (1998): 423–452.

Bruhn, Manfred. "Gerücht als Gegenstand der theoretischen und empirischen Forschung." In *Medium Gerücht: Studien zu Theorie und Praxis einer kollektiven Kommunikationsform*, edited by Manfred Bruhn and Werner Wunderlich, 11–40. Bern, 2004.

Bruhn, Manfred, and Werner Wunderlich, eds. *Medium Gerücht: Studien zu Theorie und Praxis einer kollektiven Kommunikationsform*. Bern, 2004.

Buchen, Tim. *Antisemitismus in Galizien: Agitation, Gewalt und Politik gegen Juden in der Habsburgermonarchie um 1900*. Berlin, 2012.

———. "Die Sprache der 'Christlichen – Volkspartei' Westgaliziens und die Bauernunruhen von 1898." Master's thesis. Humboldt University Berlin, 2006.

———. "'Herkules im antisemitischen Augiasstall': Joseph Samuel Bloch und Galizien in der Reaktion auf Antisemitismus in der Habsburger Monarchie." In *Einspruch und Abwehr: Die Reaktion des europäischen Judentums auf die Entstehung des Antisemitismus (1879–1914)*, edited by Ulrich Wyrwa, 193–214. Frankfurt a. M., 2010.

———. "Herrschaft in der Krise: der 'Demagoge in der Soutane' fordert die 'galizischen Allerheiligen.'" In *Imperiale Herrschaft in der Provinz: Repräsentationen politischer Macht im späten Zarenreich*, edited by Jörg Baberowski, David Feest, and Christoph Gumb, 331–355. Frankfurt a. M., 2008.

———. "'Learning from Vienna Means Learning to Win': The Cracovian Christian Socials and the Antisemitism (1895–1898)." *Quest: Issues in Contemporary Jewish History* 3 (2012). Retrieved 29 November 2019 from http://www.quest-cdecjournal.it/focus.php?id=302.

Burger, Hannelore, and Helmut Wohnout. "Eine polnische Schufterei? Die Badenischen Sprachenverordnungen für Böhmen und Mähren." In *Politische Affären und Skandale in Österreich*, edited by Michael Gehler and Hubert Sickinger, 79–98. Vienna, 1995.

Burkhart, Dagmar. *Eine Geschichte der Ehre*. Darmstadt, 2006.

Burns, Michael. *Rural Society and French Politics: Boulangism and the Dreyfus Affair*. Princeton, 1984.

Burszta, Józef. "Kultura chłopska a ruch ludowy 1895–1949." In *Ruch ludowy w najnowszych dziejach Polski*, edited by Zygmunt Hemmerling, 201–237. Warsaw, 1988.

———. *Wieś i karczma: rola karczmy w życiu wsi pańszczyźnianej*. Warsaw, 1950.

Buszko, Józef. "Die politischen und sozialen Bewegungen der polnischen Bauern in Galizien am Ende des 19. und zu Beginn des 20. Jahrhunderts." In *Galizien um die Jahrhundertwende: Politische, soziale und kulturelle Verbindungen mit Österreich*, edited by Karlheinz Mack, 51–68. Vienna, 1990.

———. *Galicja 1859–1914: Polski Piemont?* Warsaw, 1989.

———. *Polacy w parlamencie Wiedeńskim 1848–1918*. Warsaw, 1996.

Buzek, Józef. "Rozsiedlenie ludność Galicji według wyznania i języka." *Wiadomości statystyczne o stosunkach krajowych* 21, no. 2 (1909).

Cała, Alina. *Wizerunek Żyda w polskiej kulturze ludowej*. Warsaw, 1992. [Engl. Version: *The Image of the Jew in Polish Folk Culture*. Jerusalem, 1995.]
Canetti, Elias. *Masse und Macht*. Hamburg, 1960.
Caro, Leopold. *Der Wucher: Eine socialpolitische Studie*. Leipzig, 1893.
———. *Die Judenfrage: Eine ethische Frage*. Leipzig, 1892.
———. "Lichwa na wsi w Galicji w latach 1875–1881." *Wiadomości Statystyczne o Stosunkach Krajowych* 8 (1883/1884).
Chotkowski, Witold, ed. *Księga pamiątkowa wiecu katolickiego w Krakowie odbytego w dniach 4, 5 i 6 lipca 1893 r*. Krakow, 1893.
Chvojka, Michal. "Zwischen Konspiration und Revolution: Entstehung und Auswirkungen der Revolution von 1846 in Krakau und Galizien; Wahrnehmung und Aktionsradius der Habsburger Polizei." *Jahrbücher für Geschichte Osteuropas* 58 (2010): 481–507.
Chwalba, Andrzej. *Historia Polski 1795–1918*. Krakow, 2001.
Ciesla, Maria, Jolanta Żyndul, and Sprawa Ritterów. "Aktualizacya legendy mordu rytualnego w Galicji końca XIX wieku." In *Kwestia żydowska w XIX wieku: Spory o tożsamość Polaków*, edited by Grażyna Borkowska and Magdalena Rudkowska, 439–452. Warsaw, 2004.
Clark, Christopher, and Wolfram Kaiser, eds. *Culture Wars: Secular-Catholic Conflict in Nineteenth-Century Europe*. Cambridge, 2003.
Cohen, Gary. "Nationalist Politics and the Dynamics of State and Civil Society in the Habsburg Monarchy 1867–1914." *Central European History* 40 (2007): 241–278.
Cohn, Norman. *Die Protokolle der Weisen von Zion: Der Mythos der jüdischen Weltverschwörung*. Baden-Baden, 1998.
The Convent Horror: The Story of Barbara Ubryk; Twenty-One Years in a Convent Dungeon, Eight Feet Long, Six Feet Wide; From Official Records. Philadelphia, 1869.
Corrsin, Stephen. "Aspects of Population Change and Acculturation in Jewish Warsaw at the End of the Nineteenth Century: The Censuses of 1882 and 1897." *Polin: Studies in Polish Jewry* 3 (1988): 122–141.
Cottam, Kazimiera J. *Bolesław Limanowski (1835–1935): A Study in Socialism and Nationalism*. New York, 1978.
Csáky, Moritz. *Das Gedächtnis der Städte: Kulturelle Verflechtungen; Wien und die urbanen Milieus in Zentraleuropa*. Vienna, 2010.
———. *Ideologie der Operette und Wiener Moderne: Ein kulturhistorischer Essay*. Vienna, 1998.
———. "Paradigma Zentraleuropa: Pluralitäten, Religionen und kulturelle Codes; Religion-Mythos-Nation; Einführende Überlegungen." In *Pluralitäten, Religionen und kulturelle Codes*, edited by Moritz Csáky and Klaus Zeyringer, 9–18. Innsbruck, 2001.
Czaplicka, John, ed. *Lviv: A City in the Crossroads of Culture*. Cambridge, 2000.
Czołowski, Aleksander. *"Mord Rytualny": Epizod z przeszłości Lwowa*. Lwów, 1899.
Dabrowski, Patrice M. *Commemorations and the Shaping of Modern Poland*. Bloomington, 2004.
———. "Cracow and Warsaw." In *Capital Cities in the Aftermath of Empires: Planning in Central and Southeastern Europe*, edited by Emily Gunzburger Makaš and Tanja Damljanović Conley, 189–207. London, 2010.
Dąbrowski, Stanisław. *Chłopi, naród, kultura*, vol. 2: *Działalność polityczna ruchu ludowego*. Rzeszów 1996.
Darnton, Robert. "Reading a Riot." *New York Review of Books*, 22 October 1992.
Davidowicz, Klaus S. *Zwischen Prophetie und Häresie: Jakob Franks Leben und Lehren*. Vienna, 2004.

Deak, István. *Beyond Nationalism: A Social and Political History of the Habsburg Officer Corps 1848–1918*. Oxford, 1990.
Die Debatten über die Judenfrage in der Session des galizischen Landtages vom J. 1868: Uebersetzt aus dem Polnischen nach den ämtlichen stenographischen Protokollen. Herausgegeben vom Vorstande der israelit. Kultusgemeinde in Lemberg. Lemberg, 1868.
Deckert, Josef. *Darf ein Katholik Antisemit sein?* Vienna, 1892.
Delumeau, Jean. *Angst im Abendland: Die Geschichte kollektiver Ängste im Europa des 14. bis 18. Jahrhunderts*. Reinbek, 1989.
Dembiński, Stefan. *Rok 1846: Kronika dworów szlacheckich zebrana na pięćdziesięcioletnią rocznicę smutnych wypadków lutego*. Jasło, 1896.
Dohrn, Verena. *Reise nach Galizien: Grenzlandschaften des alten Europa*. Berlin 2000.
Dunin-Wąsowicz, Krzysztof. *Czasopiśmiennictwo ludowe w Galicji*. Wrocław, 1952.
——. *Jan Stapiński: trybun ludu wiejskiego*. Warsaw, 1969.
Dvořak, Johann. *Politik und die Kultur der Moderne in der späten Habsburger-Monarchie*. Innsbruck, 1997.
Dziadzio, Andrzej. "Wolność wyznania i sumienia a przymus religijny w austriackiej monarchii konstytucyjnej (1867–1914)." *Czasopismo Prawno-Historyczne*, 1-2 (1993): 65–86.
Eberle, Thomas S. "Gerücht oder Faktizität? Zur kommunikativen Aushandlung von Geltungsansprüchen." In *Medium Gerücht: Studien zu Theorie und Praxis einer kollektiven Kommunikationsform*, edited by Manfred Bruhn and Werner Wunderlich, 85–116. Bern, 2004.
Eibach, Joachim. "Gerüchte im Vormärz und März 1848 in Baden." *Historische Anthropologie* 2 (1994): 245–264.
Eisenbach, Artur. *The Emancipation of the Jews in Poland 1780–1870*. Oxford, 1991.
Endelman, Todd M. "Gender and Radical Assimilation in Modern Jewish History." In *Gendering the Jewish Past*, edited by M. L. Raphael, 25–40. Williamsburg, 2002.
Erb, Rainer. *Die Legende vom Ritualmord*. Berlin, 1993.
Erb, Rainer, and Werner Bergmann. *Die Nachtseite der Judenemanzipation: Der Widerstand gegen die Integration der Juden in Deutschland 1780–1860*. Berlin, 1989.
Erdheim, Claudia. *Längst nicht mehr koscher*. Vienna, 2007.
Everett, Leila P. "The Rise of Jewish National Politics in Galicia, 1905–1907." In *Nationbuilding and the Politics of Nationalism: Essays on Austrian Galicia*, edited by Andrei S. Markovits and Frank E. Sysyn, 149–177. Cambridge, 1982.
Faber, Richard, and Frank Unger, eds. *Populismus in Geschichte und Gegenwart*. Würzburg, 2009.
Fabian, Jonathan. "Präsenz und Repräsentation: Die Anderen und das anthropologische Schreiben." In *Kultur, soziale Praxis, Text: Die Krise der ethnographischen Repräsentation*, edited by Eberhard Berg and Martin Fuchs, 335–364. Frankfurt a. M., 1999.
Farge, Arlette, and Jacques Revel. *The Vanishing Children of Paris: Rumor and Politics before the French Revolution*. Cambridge, 1991.
Feichtinger, Johannes, Ursula Prutsch, and Moritz Csáky, eds. *Habsburg postcolonial: Machtstrukturen und kollektives Gedächtnis*. Innsbruck, 2003.
Feldmann, Wilhelm. *Asymilatorzy, Syoniści i Polacy: Z powodu przełomu w stosunkach żydowskich w Galicyji*. Krakow, 1893.
Fellerer, Jan. *Mehrsprachigkeit im galizischen Verwaltungswesen (1772–1914): Eine historisch-soziolinguistische Studie zum Polnischen und Ruthenischen (Ukrainischen)*. Cologne, 2005.
Figes, Orlando. *Die Flüsterer: Leben in Stalins Russland*. Berlin, 2008.

Figes, Orlando, and Boris Kolonitskii. *Interpreting the Russian Revolution: The Language and Symbols of 1917*. New Haven, 1999.
Fischer, Jens Malte. *Richard Wagners: "Das Judentum in der Musik."* Frankfurt a. M., 2000.
Fischer-Lichte, Erika, and Doris Kolesch, eds. *Kulturen des Performativen*. Berlin, 1998.
Fleckenstein, Gisela, and Joachim Schmiedl, eds. *Ultramontanismus: Tendenzen der Forschung*. Paderborn, 2005.
Föllmer, Moritz. "Gewalt und Antisemitismus." Review of Nonn, Christoph: *Eine Stadt sucht einen Mörder: Gerücht, Gewalt und Antisemitismus im Kaiserreich*, Göttingen 2002, and Walser Smith, Helmut: *Die Geschichte des Schlachters: Mord und Antisemitismus in einer deutschen Kleinstadt*, Göttingen 2002. H-Soz-Kult, 8 January 2003. Retrieved 30 November 2019 from www.hsozkult.de/publicationreview/id/reb-3726.
"Forum: A City of Many Names: Lemberg/Lwów/L'viv/L'vov; Nationalizing in an Urban Context." *Austrian History Yearbook* 34 (2003): 57–109.
Frank, Alison Fleig. *Oil Empire: Visions of Prosperity in Austrian Galicia*. Cambridge, 2005.
Frank-Böhringer, Brigitte. "Angewandte Rhetorik." In *Sprache und Gesellschaft*, edited by Robert Ulshöfer, vol. 1, 158–161. Dortmund, 1972.
Frankl, Michal. *"Prag ist nunmehr antisemitisch": Tschechischer Antisemitismus am Ende des 19. Jahrhunderts*. Berlin, 2011.
Franko, Ivan. *Beiträge zur Geschichte und Kultur der Ukraine: Ausgewählte deutsche Schriften des revolutionären Demokraten 1882–1915*, edited by Eduard Winter and Peter Kirchner. (East-)Berlin, 1963.
Franko, Iwan. "Semityzm i antysemityzm w Galicji." *Przegląd Społeczny* 5 (1887): 431–444.
Fras, Zbigniew. "Die liberale Strömung unter den galizischen Demokraten 1848–1882." In *Liberale Traditionen in Polen*, edited by Hans-Georg Fleck and Ryszard Kołodzieczyk, 143–158. Warsaw, 1994.
———. "Mit dobrego cesarza." In *Polskie mity polityczne XIX i XX wieku*, edited by Wojciech Wrzesiński, 139–152. Wrocław, 1994.
Friedländer, Moritz. *Fünf Wochen in Brody unter jüdisch-russischen Emigranten: Ein Beitrag zur Geschichte der russischen Judenverfolgung*. Vienna, 1882.
Gąsowski, Tomasz. "From Austeria to the Manor: Jewish Landowners in Autonomous Galicia." *Polin: Studies in Polish Jewry* 12 (1999): 120–136.
———. *Między gettem a światem: Dylematy ideowe Żydów galicyjskich na przełomie XIX i XX wieku*. Krakow, 1997.
Gellner, Ernest. *Nations and Nationalism*. Ithaca, 1983.
Geertz, Clifford J. *Dichte Beschreibung: Beiträge zum Verstehen kultureller Systeme*. Frankfurt a. M., 2002.
Giddens, Anthony. *Die Konstitution der Gesellschaft: Grundzüge einer Theorie der Strukturierung*. Frankfurt a. M., 1984.
Gill, Arnon. *Die polnische Revolution von 1846: Zwischen nationalem Befreiungskampf des Landadels und antifeudaler Bauernerhebung*. Munich, 1974.
Glasenapp, Gabriele von. *Aus der Judengasse: Zur Entstehung und Ausprägung deutschsprachiger Ghettoliteratur im 19. Jahrhundert*. Tübingen, 1996.
Glassl, Horst. *Das österreichische Einrichtungswerk in Galizien (1772–1790)*. Wiesbaden, 1975.
Gmina Strzyzow (city website), www.strzyzow.pl.
Golczewski, Frank. *Polnisch-jüdische Beziehungen: Eine Studie zur Geschichte des Antisemitismus in Osteuropa*. Wiesbaden, 1981.

———. "Rural Anti-Semitism in Galicia before World War I." In *The Jews in Poland*, edited by Chimen Abramsky, 97–105. Oxford, 1986.
Goldenstein, Leo. *Brody und die jüdisch-russische Emigration: Nach eigener Beobachtung erzählt*. Frankfurt a. M., 1882.
Grabowski, Jan. *Judenjagd: Polowanie na Żydów 1942–1945; Studium dziejów pewnego powiatu*. Warsaw, 2011.
Grodziski, Stanisław. *Sejm Krajowy Galicyjski 1861–1914*. Warsaw, 1993.
Grodziski, Stanisław, and Irena Dwornicka, eds. *Chronografia albo dziejopis Żywiecki*. Żywiec, 1987.
Guesnet, François. *Polnische Juden im 19. Jahrhundert: Lebensbedingungen, Rechtsnormen und Organisation im Wandel*. Cologne, 1998.
———. "T. Buchen: Antisemitismus in Galizien," review. *H-Soz-Kult*, 6 March 2015. Retrieved 30 November 2019 from www.hsozkult.de/publicationreview/id/reb-18986.
Gurnicz, Antoni. *O ‚równą miarkę' dla chłopów: Poglądy i działalność pierwszej chłopskiej organizacji w Polsce Związku Stronnictwa Chłopskiego 1893–1908*. Krakow, 1963.
Hadler, Simon. "Von sprechenden Steinen: Die Mythologisierung des urbanen Raumes in Krakau." In *Galizien: Fragmente eines diskursiven Raums*, edited by Doktoratskolleg Galizien, 159–170. Innsbruck, 2009.
Hagen, William W. *Anti-Jewish Violence in Poland, 1914–1920*. New York, 2018.
———. *Germans, Poles and Jews: the Nationality Conflict in the Prussian East 1772–1914*. Chicago, 1980.
———. "The Moral Economy of Popular Violence: The Pogrom in Lwów November 1918." In *Antisemitism and Its Opponents in Modern Poland*, edited by Robert E. Blobaum, 124–147. Ithaca, 2006.
Hämmerle, Christa. "'Dort wurden wir dressiert und sekiert und geschlagen . . .': Vom Drill, dem Disziplinarstrafrecht und Soldatenmisshandlungen im Heer (1868 bis 1914)." In *Glanz – Gewalt – Gehorsam: Militär und Gesellschaft in der Habsburgermonarchie (1800 bis 1918)*, edited by Laurence Cole, Christa Hämmerle, and Martin Scheutz, 31–54. Essen, 2011.
Hanisch, Ernst. *Der lange Schatten des Staates: Österreichische Gesellschaftsgeschichte im 20. Jahrhundert 1890–1990*. Vienna, 1994.
Hann, Christopher, and Paul R. Magocsi, eds. *Galicia: A Multicultured Land*. Toronto, 2005.
Hanover, Nathan. *The Abyss of Despair (Yeven Metzulah): The Famous 17th Century Chronicle Depicting Jewish Life in Russia and Poland during the Chmielnicki Massacres of 1648–1649*. London, 1983.
Harbut, Juliusz Stanisław. *Mały Rzym*, 4 volumes. Krakow, 1937.
Harris, James. *The People Speak! Anti-Semitism and Emancipation in Nineteenth-Century Bavaria*. Ann Arbor, 1994.
Haslinger, Peter, ed. *Die Grenze im Kopf: Beiträge zur Geschichte der Grenze in Ostmitteleuropa*. Frankfurt a. M., 1999.
Haslinger, Peter, and Daniel Mollenhauer, "Arbeit am nationalen Raum: Deutsche und polnische Rand- und Grenzregionen im Nationalisierungsprozess." *Comparativ* 15, no. 2 (2005): 9–21.
Haumann, Heiko. *Geschichte der Ostjuden*. Munich, 1990.
———. "Juden in der ländlichen Gesellschaft Galiziens am Ende des 19. und zu Beginn des 20. Jahrhunderts." In *Deutsche – Juden – Polen: Geschichte einer wechselvollen Beziehung*

im 20. Jahrhundert, edited by Andrea Löw, Kerstin Robusch, and Stefanie Walter, 35–58. Frankfurt a. M., 2004.

———. "Jüdische Nation – Polnische Nation? Zur gesellschaftlichen Orientierung von Juden in Polen während des 19. Jahrhunderts." In *Kontexte der Schrift*, vol. 1: *Text, Ethik, Judentum und Christentum, Gesellschaft*, edited by Gabriella Gelardini, 442–457. Stuttgart, 2005.

———. *"Luftmenschen" und "rebellische Töchter": Zum Wandel ostjüdischer Lebenswelten im 19. Jahrhundert*. Cologne, 2003.

Hauser, Peter, ed. *Säbel, Degen und Pistole: Zweikampfregeln für den k. u. k. Offizier*. Hilden, 2007.

Häusler, Wolfgang. "Zwischen Wien und Czernowitz: Die Emanzipation des habsburgischen 'Ostjudentums' und der Antisemitismus." In *Identitätenwandel und nationale Mobilisierung in Regionen ethnischer Diversität: Ein regionaler Vergleich zwischen Westpreußen und Galizien am Endes 19. und Anfang des 20. Jahrhunderts*, edited by Ralph Schattkowsky and Michael G. Müller, 63–88. Marburg, 2004.

Hellwig, Isaak. *Der konfessionelle Antisemitismus in Österreich*. Vienna, 1972.

Hensel, Jürgen. *Polnische Adelsnation und jüdische Vermittler 1815–1830: Über den vergeblichen Versuch einer Judenemanzipation in einer nicht emanzipierten Gesellschaft*. Berlin, 1983.

Himka, John-Paul. "The Construction of Nationality in Galician Rus': Icarian Flights in Almost All Directions." In *Intellectuals and the Articulation of the Nation*, edited by Ronald Grigor Suny and Michael D. Kennedy, 109–164. Ann Arbor, 1999.

———. "Dimensions of a Triangle: Polish-Ukrainian-Jewish Relations in Austrian Galicia." *Polin: Studies in Polish Jewry* 12 (1999): 25–48.

———. *Galician Villagers and the Ukrainian National Movement in the Nineteenth Century*. London, 1988.

———. "Hope in the Tsar: Displaced Naive Monarchism among the Ukrainian Peasants of the Habsburg Empire." *Russian History/Histoire Russe* 7, no. 1-2 (1980): 125–138.

———. *Socialism in Galicia: The Emergence of Polish Social Democracy and Ukrainian Radicalism (1860–1890)*. Cambridge, MA, 1983.

———. "Ukrainian-Jewish Antagonism in the Galician Countryside during the Late Nineteenth Century." In *Ukrainian-Jewish Relations in Historical Perspective*, edited by Peter J. Potychnyi and Aster Howard, 111–158. Edmonton, 1988.

Höbelt, Lothar. "Parliamentary Politics in a Multinational Setting: Late Imperial Austria." Working Paper by the Center for Austrian Studies 92-6, University of Minnesota. Retrieved 28 July 2015 from http://cas.umn.edu/assets/pdf/WP926.PDF.

Hödl, Klaus. *Als Bettler in die Leopoldstadt: Galizische Juden auf dem Weg nach Wien*. Vienna, 1994.

Hoff, Jadwiga. "Stosunki wyznaniowe i struktura społeczno-zawodowa małego miasta galicyjskiego w dobie autonomii." In *Miasteczka Polskie: Z dziejów formowania się społeczności*, 131–146. Kielce, 1992.

Hoffmann, Christhard. "Christlicher Antijudaismus und moderner Antisemitismus." In *Christlicher Antijudaismus und Antisemitismus: Theologische und kirchliche Programme Deutscher Christen*, edited by Leonore Siegele-Wenschkewitz, 293-317. Frankfurt a. M., 1994.

———. "Political Culture and Violence against Minorities: The Antisemitic Riots in Pomerania and West Prussia." In *Exclusionary Violence: Antisemitic Riots in Modern German History*, edited by Helmut Walser Smith, Werner Bergmann, and Christhard Hoffmann, 67–92. Ann Arbor, 2005.

Holz, Klaus. "Die antisemitische Konstruktion des Dritten und die nationale Ordnung der Welt." In *Das bewegliche Vorurteil: Aspekte des Internationalen Antisemitismus,* edited by Christina von Braun and Eva-Maria Ziege, 43–61. Würzburg, 2004.

Holzer, Jerzy. "Zur Frage der Akkulturation der Juden in Galizien im 19. und 20. Jahrhundert." *Jahrbücher für Geschichte Osteuropas* 37 (1989): 35–59.

Hornowa, Elżbieta. *Ukraiński obóz postępowy i jego współpraca z polską lewicą społeczną w Galicji 1876–1895.* Wrocław, 1968.

Horowitz, Donald L. *The Deadly Ethnic Riot.* Berkeley, 2001.

Hrycak, Jarosław. "Między filosemityzmem i antysemityzmem. Iwan Franko i kwestia żydowska." In *Świat NIEpożegnany: Żydzi na dawnych ziemiach wschodnich Rzeczypospolitej w XVIII–XX wieku/A World We Bade No Farewell: Jews in the Eastern Territories of the Polish Republic from 18th to 20th Century,* edited by Krzysztof Jasiewicz, 451–480. Warsaw and London, 2004.

Hryniuk, Stella. "The Peasant and Alcohol in East Galicia in the Late Nineteenth Century: A Note." *Journal of Ukrainian Studies* 11 (1986): 75–85.

———. *Peasants with Promise: Ukrainians in South-Eastern Galicia 1880–1900.* Edmonton, 1991.

———. "Polish Lords and Ukrainian Peasants: Conflict, Deference, and Accommodation in Eastern Galicia in the Late Nineteenth Century." *Austrian History Yearbook* 24 (1993): 119–132.

Hüchtker, Dietlind. "Der 'Mythos Galizien': Versuch einer Historisierung." In *Die Nationalisierung von Grenzen: Zur Konstruktion nationaler Identität in sprachlich gemischten Grenzregionen,* edited by Michael G. Müller and Rolf Petri, 81–108. Marburg, 2002.

Hundert, Gershon David, ed. "Jews in Early Modern Poland" *Polin: Studies in Polish Jewry* 10 (1997).

———. *Jews in Poland-Lithuania in the Eighteenth Century: A Genealogy of Modernity.* Berkeley, 2004.

Hye, Hans Peter. *Das politische System der Habsburgermonarchie.* Prague, 1998.

Inglot, Stefan. *Historia społeczno-gospodarcza chłopów polskich.* Warsaw, 1970.

Jakubowska, Urszula. "Galicja na progu XX wieku." In *Galicyjskie spotkania,* edited by Urszula Jakubowska. Kalisz, 2004.

Janowski, Maciej. *Inteligencja wobec wyzwań nowoczesności: Dylematy ideowe polskiej demokracji liberalnej w Galicji 1889–1914.* Warsaw, 1996.

———. *Polish Liberal Thought before 1918.* Budapest, 2004.

Jarowiecki, Jerzy. *Prasa Lwowska w latach 1864–1918: Bibliografia.* Krakow, 2002.

Jeż, Mateusz. *Tajemnice żydowskie.* Krakow, 1898.

Jobst, Kerstin S. *Der Mythos des Miteinander: Galizien in Literatur und Geschichte.* Hamburg, 1998.

———. "Die antisemitischen Bauernunruhen im westlichen Galizien 1898: Stojałowski und die polnischen Sozialdemokraten." In *Zwischen Abgrenzung und Assimilation: Deutsche, Polen und Juden; Schauplätze ihres Zusammenlebens von der Zeit der Aufklärung bis zum Beginn des Zweiten Weltkrieges,* edited by Robert Maier, 139–150. Hannover, 1996.

———. "Ein politischer Mord in der Habsburgermonarchie: Das Potocki-Attentat von 1908; Ein Kulminationspunkt der galizischen Krise?" *Österreichische Osthefte* 41 (1999): 25–45.

———. *Zwischen Nationalismus und Internationalismus: Die polnische und ukrainische Sozialdemokratie in Galizien von 1890 bis 1914.* Hamburg, 1996.

Judson, Pieter. *Exclusive Revolutionaries: Liberal Politics, Social Experience, and National Identity in the Austrian Empire 1848–1914*. Ann Arbor, 1996.

———. *Guardians of the Nation: Activists on the Language Frontiers of Imperial Austria*. Cambridge, 2007.

Judson, Pieter M., and Marsha Rozenblit, eds. *Constructing Nationalities in East Central Europe*. New York, 2005.

Kampe, Norbert. *Studenten und "Judenfrage" im Deutschen Kaiserreich*. Göttingen, 1988.

Kaps, Klemens. "Peripherisierung der Ökonomie, Ethnisierung der Gesellschaft: Galizien zwischen äußerem und innerem Konkurrenzdruck (1856–1914)." In *Galizien: Fragmente eines diskursiven Raums*, edited by Doktoratskolleg Galizien, 37–62. Innsbruck, 2009.

Karady, Victor. *Gewalterfahrung und Utopie: Juden in der europäischen Moderne*. Frankfurt a. M., 1999.

Karch, Brendan J. "Nationalism on the Margins: Silesians between Germany and Poland 1848–1945." PhD dissertation, Harvard University, 2010.

Kargol, Tomasz. *Izba Przemysłowo-Handlowa w Krakowie w latach 1850–1939*. Krakow, 2003.

———. "Wirtschaftliche Beziehungen zwischen Galizien und den Ländern der österreichsich-ungarischen Monarchie in der ersten Hälfte des 19. Jahrhunderts." In *Die galizische Grenze 1772–1867: Kommunikation oder Isolation?*, edited by Christoph Augustynowicz and Andreas Kappeler, 33–50. Vienna, 2006.

Karniel, Joseph. *Die Toleranzpolitik Kaiser Josephs II*. Gerlingen, 1985.

Karoshi, Peter. "Ein Versuch, Konzepte der Hybridität auf Quellen zum österreichisch-ungarischen Vielvölkerstaat anzuwenden: das Kronprinzenwerk." In *eForum zeitGeschichte* 2 (2001). Retrieved 30 November 2019 from www.eforum-zeitgeschichte.at/set2_01a4.htm.

———. "Patriotismus und Staatserhalt: Konstruktionen 'österreichischer Gesamtstaatsideen.'" *Newsletter Moderne: Zeitschrift des SFB Moderne*, special issue 2 (March 2003): 12–16.

Katz, Jacob. *From Prejudice to Destruction: Anti-Semitism 1700–1933*. Cambridge, 1980.

———. *Vom Vorurteil bis zur Vernichtung: Der Antisemitismus 1700–1933*. Munich, 1989.

Kertzer, David I. *Die Päpste gegen die Juden: Der Vatikan und die Entstehung des modernen Antisemitismus*. Berlin, 2004.

———. *Prisoner of the Vatican: The Pope's Secret Plot to Capture Rome from the New Italian State*. Boston, 2004.

Kieniewicz, Stefan. *Pomiędzy Stadionem a Goslarem: Sprawa włościańska w Galicji w 1848r*. Warsaw, 1980.

———. *Ruch chłopski w Galicji w 1846 roku*. Wrocław, 1955.

Kieval, Hillel J. "Blood Libels and Host Desecration Accusations." In *The Yivo Encyclopedia of Jews in Eastern Europe*. Retrieved 30 November 2019 from https://yivoencyclopedia.org/article.aspx/Blood_Libels_and_Host_Desecration_Accusations.

King, Jeremy. *Budweisers into Czechs and Germans: A Local History of Bohemian Politics 1848–1948*. Princeton, 2005.

Kirchmann, Kay. "Das Gerücht und die Medien: Medientheoretische Annäherungen an einen Sondertypus der informellen Kommunikation." *In Medium Gerücht: Studien zu Theorie und Praxis einer kollektiven Kommunikationsform*, edited by Manfred Bruhn and Werner Wunderlich, 67–85. Bern, 2004.

Klier, John D. *Russians, Jews, and the Pogroms of 1881–1882*. Cambridge, 2011.

Klier, John D., and Shlomo Lambroza, eds. *Pogroms: Anti-Jewish Violence in Russian History*. Cambridge, 1992.

Komar, Edward. *Kardinał Puzyna*. Krakow, 1912.
Konstantynów, Dariusz. "'Mistrz Nasz Matejko' i antysemici." *Kwartalnik Historii Żydów* 222, no. 2 (2007): 164–198.
Kool, Leslie. *Economic Development on the Periphery: A Case Study of East Galicia*. Ann Arbor, 1994.
Kopp, Josef. *Zur Judenfrage nach den Akten des Prozesses Rohling-Bloch*. Leipzig, 1886.
Kořalka, Jiří. *František Palacký (1798–1876): Der Historiker der Tschechen im österreichischen Vielvölkerstaat*. Vienna, 2007.
Korczyński, J. S. (J. S. Pelczar). *Masoneria: Jej początki, organizacja, ceremoniał, zasady i działanie*. Krzeszowice, 2006.
Kosyk, Ihor. "To Marry the Other: Zur Geschichte der gemischten Ehen in Galizien und Lemberg in der zweiten Hälfte des 19. Jahrhunderts." In *Galizien: Fragmente eines diskursiven Raums*, edited by Doktoratskolleg Galizien, 99–112. Innsbruck, 2009.
Kotula, Franciszek. *Losy Żydów rzeszowskich 1939–44: Kronika tamtych dni*. Rzeszów, 1999.
Kowalczyk, Stanisław. "Ruch ludowy wobec wyborow do Sejmu w Galicji w 1895 r." *Rocznik Dzieje Ruchu Ludowego* 7 (1965).
Kowalska-Lewicka, Anna. "'Cysorz' w folklorze galicjskim." In *Przed 100 laty i dzisiaj: Ludoznawstwo i etnografia między Wiedniem, Lwowem, Krakowem a Pragą*, edited by Ewa Fryś-Pietraszkowa and Anna Spiss, 141–153. Krakow, 1999.
Kowalski, Grzegorz Maria. *Przestępstwa emigracyjne w Galicji 1897–1918: Z badań nad dziejami polskiego wychodźstwa*. Krakow, 2003.
Kozik, Jan. *Między reakcyją a rewolucją: Studia z dziejów ukraińskiego ruchu narodowego w Galicji w latach 1848–1849*. Krakow, 1975.
———. *The Ukrainian National Movement in Galicia 1815–1849*. Edmonton, 1986.
Kozińska–Witt, Hanna. *Die Krakauer Jüdische Reformgemeinde 1864–1874*. Frankfurt a. M., 1999.
Kracik, Jan. *W Galicji trzeźwiejącej, krwawej, pobożnej*. Krakow, 2008.
Kraft, Claudia. "Das galizische Bürgertum in der autonomen Ära (1867–1914): Ein Literaturüberblick." In *Polen und die böhmischen Länder im 19. und 20. Jahrhundert*, edited by Peter Heumos, 81–110. Munich, 1997.
———. "Die jüdische Frage im Spiegel der Presseorgane und Parteiprogramme der galizischen Bauernbewegung im letzten Viertel des 19. Jahrhunderts." *Zeitschrift für Ostmitteleuropa-Forschung* 45 (1996): 381–409.
Kramarz, Henryka. "Tadeusz Rutkowski jako poseł i propagator reform gospodarczych w Galicji pod koniec XIX wieku." In *Celem nauki jest człowiek . . . Studia z historii społecznej i gospodarczej ofiarowanie Helene Madurowicz-Urbańskiej*, edited by Piotr Franaszek, 143–151. Krakow, 2000.
Krawczyk, Karol. *Matejko i historia*. Warsaw, 1990.
Kriechbaumer, Robert. "Das Trauma der unmystischen Wirklichkeit: Die Sehnsucht nach der imaginierten deutschen Heimat." In *Die großen Erzählungen der Politik: Politische Kultur und Parteien in Österreich von der Jahrhundertwende bis 1945*, edited by Robert Kriechbaumer, 160–165. Cologne, 2001.
———. *Die großen Erzählungen der Politik: Politische Kultur und Parteien in Österreich von der Jahrhundertwende bis 1945*. Vienna, 2001.
Krzywiec, Grzegorz. "Między kryzysem a odrodzeniem: O odgłosach afery Dreyfusa w polskich środowiskach radykalnej inteligencji." In *Kwestia żydowska w XIX wieku: Spory o*

tożsamość Polaków, edited by Grażyna Borkowska and Magdalena Rudkowska, 423–438. Warsaw, 2004.

———. *Szowinism po polsku: Przypadek Romana Dmowskiego 1886–1905*. Warsaw, 2009.

Kuberski, Leszek. *Stanisław Szczepanowski 1846–1900: Przemysłowiec, polityk, publicysta*. Opole, 1997.

Kudłaszyk, Andrzej. *Katolicka myśl społeczno-polityczna w Galicji na przełomie XIX i XX wieku*. Wrocław, 1980.

Kuzmany, Börries. "Die Stadt Brody im langen 19. Jahrhundert: Eine Misserfolgsgeschichte?" PhD dissertation. University of Vienna, 2008. Retrieved 30 November 2019 from http://othes.univie.ac.at/2604/.

Kwan, Jonathan. "Review Article: Nationalism and All That: Reassessing the Habsburg Monarchy and Its Legacy." *European History Quarterly* 41 (2011): 88–108.

Lachs, Minna. *Warum schaust du zurück? Erinnerungen 1907–1941*. Vienna, 1986.

Lander, Katja. *Josef Samuel Bloch und die Österreichisch-Israelitische Union: Initiativen zur Begründung einer jüdischen Politik im späten 19. Jahrhundert in Wien*. Saarbrücken, 1993.

Landmann, Salcia. *Erinnerungen an Galizien*. Munich, 1975.

Lang, Julius. *Der Antisemitismus vom katholischen Standpunkte als Sünde verurtheilt*. Vienna, 1890.

Lato, Stanisław, and Witold Stankiewicz, eds. *Programy stronnictw ludowych: Zbiór dokumentów*. Warsaw, 1969.

Lawrence, Orton D. "The Formation of Modern Cracow (1866–1914)." *Austrian History Yearbook* 17 (1983/1984): 101–115.

Łazuga, Waldemar. *"Rządy polskie" w Austrii: Gabinet Kazimierza hr. Badeniego 1895–1897*. Poznań, 1991.

Lechicki, Czesław. "Chrześcijańska Demokracja w Krakowie 1897–1937." *Studia historyczne* 17, no. 4 (1974): 585–608.

———. "Pierwsze dwudziestolecie krakowskiego 'Głosu Narodu.'" *Studia historyczne* 12 (1969): 507–532.

Lehmann, Rosa. *Symbiosis and Ambivalence: Poles and Jews in a Small Galician Town*. New York, 2001.

Leidinger, Hannes. "Suizid und Militär: Debatten – Ursachenforschung – Reichsratsinterpellationen 1907–1914." In *Glanz – Gewalt – Gehorsam: Militär und Gesellschaft in der Habsburgermonarchie (1880–1918)*, edited by Laurence Cole, Christa Hämmerle, and Martin Scheutz, 337–358. Essen, 2011.

Leiska, Christoph. "'Das Geschrei des Herrn von Germanenstolz': Dänisch-jüdische Intellektuelle und der moderne Antisemitismus im deutschen Kaiserreich." In *Einspruch und Abwehr: Die Reaktion des europäischen Judentums auf die Entstehung des Antisemitismus (1879–1914)*, edited by Ulrich Wyrwa, 114–130. Frankfurt a. M., 2010.

Lenart, Maria Paschalisa. *Prowincja krakowska Zgromadzenia Sióstr Felicjanek*, vol. 2: *Leksykon domów*. Krakow, 2000.

Leslie, Robert F. *The History of Poland since 1863*. Cambridge, 1980.

Levin, Dov. *The Litvaks: A Short History of the Jews in Lithuania*. Jerusalem, 2000.

Levine, Hillel. *Economic Origins of Antisemitism: Poland and Its Jews in the Early Modern Period*. New Haven, 1993.

———. "Gentry, Jews, and Serfs: The Rise of Polish Vodka." *Review: A Journal of the Fernand Braudel Center for the Study of Economies* 4, no. 2 (1980): 223–250.

Lichtblau, Albert. "'A Hetz muaß sein!' Der Wiener und seine Fremden." In *Wir: Zur Geschichte und Gegenwart der Zuwanderer nach Wien; Sonderausstellung des Historischen Museums der Stadt Wien*, edited by Susanna Fuhrherr, Peter Eppel, Rainer Hubert, and Eva-Maria Orosz, 145–150. Vienna, 1996.

Lichtblau, Albert, and Michael John. "Jewries in Galicia and Bukovina, in Lemberg and Czernowitz: Two Divergent Examples of Jewish Communities in the Far East of the Austro-Hungarian Monarchy." In *Jewries at the Frontier: Accommodation, Identity, Conflict*, edited by Sander Gilman and Milton Shain, 29–66. Urbana, 1999.

Lindemann, Albert. *Esau's Tears: Modern Anti-Semitism and the Rise of the Jews*. Cambridge, 1997.

Lindström, Fredrik. *Empire and Identity: Biographies of the Austrian State Problem in the Late Habsburg Empire*. West Lafayette, 2008.

Łukasiewicz, Juliusz. *Kryzys agrarny na ziemiach polskich w końcu XIX wieku*. Warsaw, 1968.

Lukin, Benyamin, and Olga Shraberman. "Documents on the Emigration of Russian Jews via Galicia, 1881–82, in the Central Archives for the History of the Jewish People in Jerusalem." *Gal-Ed: On the History of the Jews in Poland* 21 (2007): 101–117.

Mader, Hubert. *Duellwesen und altösterreichisches Offizierssethos*. Osnabrück, 1983.

Maderthaner, Wolfgang. "Kirche und Sozialdemokratie: Aspekte des Verhältnisses von politischem Klerikalismus und sozialistischer Arbeiterschaft bis zum Jahre 1938." In *Neuere Studien zur Arbeitergeschichte: Zum Fünfundzwanzigjährigen Bestehen des Vereins für Geschichte der Arbeiterbewegung*, edited by Helmut Konrad, 527–558. Vienna, 1984.

Madurowicz-Urbańska, Helena. "Die Industrie Galiziens im Rahmen der wirtschaftlichen Struktur der Donaumonarchie." *Studia Austro-Polonica* 1 (1978): 157–173.

Magocsi, Paul Robert. "Galicia: A European Land." In *Galicia: A Multicultured Land*, edited by Paul Rober Magocsi and Christopher Hann, 3–21. Toronto, 2005.

———. "The Kachkovs'kyi Society and the National Revival in Nineteenth-Century East Galicia." *Harvard Ukrainian Studies* 15, no. 1/2 (1991): 48–75.

———. *The Roots of Ukrainian Nationalism: Galicia as Ukraine's Piedmont*. Toronto, 2002.

Mahler, R. "Jewish Emigration from Galicia." In *East European Jews in Two Worlds: Studies from the YIVO Annual*, edited by Deborah Dash Moore. Evanston: 1990.

Majchrowski, Jacek Maria. "'Antysemita': Zapomniana karta dziejów ruchu chrześciańsko–społecznego w Krakowie." In *Idee – państwo – prawo*, edited by Jacek Maria Majchrowski, 191–197. Krakow, 1991.

Manekin, Rachel. "Politics, Religion, and National Identity: The Galician Jewish Vote in the 1873 Parliamentary Elections." *Polin: Studies in Polish Jewry* 12 (1999): 100–119.

Manekin, Rachel. "'The Lost Generation': Education and Female Conversion in Fin-de-Siecle Kraków." *Polin: Studies in Polish Jewry* 18 (2005): 189–219.

———. "Tehillas Daughter and Michalina Araten" (Hebrew), *Ha'arets*, literature supplement, 27 June 2003.

Maner, Hans-Christian. *Galizien: Eine Grenzregion im Kalkül der Donaumonarchie im 18. und 19. Jahrhundert*. Munich, 2007.

———. "Zwischen 'Kompensationsobjekt,' 'Musterland' und 'Glacis': Wiener politische und militärische Vorstellungen von Galizien von 1772 bis zur Autonomieära." In *Grenzregionen der Habsburgermonarchie im 18. und 19. Jahrhundert: Ihre Bedeutung und Funktion aus der Perspektive Wiens*, edited by Hans-Christian Maner, 103–122. Münster, 2005.

Marcinkowski, Karol. *Krwawe Nieszpory we Frysztaku w 1898 r./Patriota Ks. Stojałowski*. Philadelphia, 1983.

Mark, Rudolf. *Galizien unter österreichischer Herrschaft: Verwaltung-Kirche-Bevölkerung.* Marburg, 1994.
Markovits, Andrei S. "Introduction: Empire and Province." In *Nationbuilding and the Politics of Nationalism: Essays on Austrian Galicia,* edited by Andrei S. Markovits and Frank E. Sysyn, 1–22. Cambridge, 1982.
Matheus, Michael, and Lutz Klinkhammer, eds. *Eigenbild im Konflikt: Krisensituationen des Papsttums zwischen Gregor VII. und Benedikt XV.* Darmstadt, 2009.
Meissner, Andrzej, ed. *Chłopi-Naród –Kultura,* vol. 4: *Kultura i oświata wsi.* Rzeszów, 1996.
Mendelsohn, Ezra. "From Assimilation to Zionism in Lvov: The Case of Alfred Nossig." *The Slavonic and East European Review* 49 (1971): 521–534.
———. "Jewish Assimilation in L'viv: The Case of Wilhelm Feldman." In *Nationbuilding and the Politics of Nationalism: Essays on Austrian Galicia,* edited by Andrei S. Markovits and Frank E. Sysyn, 94–110. Cambridge, 1982.
———. *Painting a People: Maurycy Gottlieb and Jewish Art.* London, 2002.
Mergel, Thomas. "Überlegungen zu einer Kulturgeschichte der Politik." *Geschichte und Gesellschaft* 28 (2002): 574–606.
Merunowicz, Teofil. *O metodzie i celach badań nad kwestią żydowską.* Lwów, 1879.
———. *Żydzi.* Lwów, 1879.
Michlic, Joanna B. *Poland's Threatening Other: The Image of the Jew from 1880 to the Present.* Lincoln, 2006.
Miller, Alexey. "Do charakterystyki wsi pouwłaszczeniowej w latach siedemdziesiątych XIX wieku: Panika galicyjska 1872 roku." *Przegląd Historyczny* 79 (1988): 103–107.
———. "Galicia after the Ausgleich. Polish-Ruthenian Conflict and the Attempts of Reconciliation." *Central European University History Department Yearbook* (1993): 135–143.
Miller, Saul. *Life in a Galician Shtetl 1890–1907.* New York, 1980.
Mishkinsky, Moshe. "The Attitude of the Southern-Russian Workers' Union toward the Jews (1880–1881)." *Harvard Ukrainian Studies* 6 (1982): 191–216.
———. "The Attitudes of Ukrainian Socialists to Jewish Problems in the 1870s." In *Ukrainian-Jewish Relations in Historical Perspective,* edited by Peter J. Potichnyj and Howard Aster, 57–68. Edmonton, 1988.
Mochnacki, Józef. *Rozprawa w procesie karnym Jana Matejki przeciw Dr. L. E. o przestępstwo obrazi czci, przeprowadzono w c.k. Sądzie Karnym w Krakowie, dnia 2-go Grudnia 1882.* Krakow, 1883.
Molenda, Jan, Chłopi-naród – niepodległość: Kształtowanie się postaw narodowych i obywatelskich chłopów w Galicji i Królestwie Polskim w przedniu odrodzenia Polski. Warsaw, 1999.
Mommsen, Hans. "1897: Die Badeni-Krise als Wendepunkt in den deutsch-tschechischen Beziehungen." In *Wendepunkte in den Beziehungen zwischen Deutschen, Tschechen und Slowaken 1848–1989,* edited by Detlef Brandes, 111–118. Essen, 2007.
Morawski, Marian. *Asemityzm: Kwestia żydowska wobec chrześcijańskiej etyki.* Krakow, 1896.
Moszyński, Maciej. "Die 'Hydra von der Spree': Die Warschauer Zeitschrift *Izraelita* und die Anfänge des modernen Antisemitismus im Deutschen Kaiserreich." In *Einspruch und Abwehr: Die Reaktion des europäischen Judentums auf die Entstehung des Antisemitismus (1879–1914),* edited by Ulrich Wyrwa, 299–312. Frankfurt a. M., 2010.
Müller, Michael G. *Die Teilungen Polens 1772, 1793, 1795.* Munich, 1984.
Müller-Funk, Wolfgang. "Kakanien revisited: Über das Verhältnis von Herrschaft und Kultur." In *Kakanien revisited: Das Eigene und das Fremde (in) der österreichisch-ungarischen*

Monarchie, edited by Wolfgang Müller-Funk, Peter Plener, and Clemens Ruthner, 14–32. Tübingen, 2002.

Musil, Robert. *The Man without Qualities*, translated by Sophie Wilkins. London, 2011.

Myśliński, Jerzy. "Redaktor w sutannie i ludowy tribun: Ks. Stanisław Stojałowski." *Kwartalnik Prasy Polskiej* 30, no. 3-4 (1991): 127–132.

Narkiewicz, Olga. *The Green Flag: Polish Populist Politics, 1867–1970*. London, 1976.

Nathan, Paul. *Der Prozess von Tisza-Eszlar: Ein antisemitisches Culturbild*. Berlin, 1892.

Natkowska, Monika. *Numerus clausus, getto ławkowe, numerus nullus, „paragraf aryjski": Antysemityzm na Uniwersytecie Warszawskim 1931–1939*. Warsaw, 1999.

Nell-Breuning, Oswald von, and Johannes Schasching, eds. *Texte zur katholische Soziallehre: Die sozialen Rundschreiben der Päpste und andere kirchliche Dokumente*. Bornheim, 1992.

Neubauer, Hans-Joachim. *Fama: Eine Geschichte des Gerüchts*. Berlin, 2009.

Nirenberg, David. *Communities of Violence: Persecution of Minorities in the Middle Ages*. Princeton, 1996.

Noack, Hannelore. *Unbelehrbar? Antijüdische Agitation mit entstellten Talmudzitaten; Antisemitische Aufwiegelung durch Verteufelung der Juden*. Paderborn, 2001.

Nonn, Christoph. *Eine Stadt sucht einen Mörder: Gerücht, Gewalt und Antisemitismus im Kaiserreich*. Göttingen, 2002.

Nossig, Alfred. *Próba rozwiązania kwestji żydowskiej*. Lwów, 1887.

Opalski, Magdalena. *The Jewish Tavern Keeper and His Tavern in Nineteenth-Century Polish Literature*. Jerusalem, 1986.

Osterhammel, Jürgen. *Die Verwandlung der Welt: Eine Geschichte des 19. Jahrhunderts*. Munich, 2009.

Pacholkiv, Svjatoslav. *Emanzipation durch Bildung: Entwicklung und gesellschaftliche Rolle der ukrainischen Intelligenz im habsburgischen Galizien 1890–1914*. Vienna, 2002.

Pajakowski, Philip. "Dynamics of Galician Polish Conservativism in the Late Nineteenth Century." *Jahrbücher für Geschichte Osteuropas* 43 (1995): 19–33.

———. "The Polish Club and Austrian Parliamentary Politics 1873–1900." PhD dissertation. Indiana University, 1989.

Pappenheim, Bertha. *Sisyphus: Gegen den Mädchenhandel in Galizien*, edited by Helga Heubach. Freiburg, 1992.

Paulmann, Johannes. *Pomp und Politik: Monarchenbegegnungen in Europa zwischen Ancien Regime und Erstem Weltkrieg*. Paderborn, 2000.

Pawłowski, Ignacy. *Stronnictwa i programy polityczne w Galicji 1864-1918*. Warsaw, 1966.

Pickhan, Gertrud. "Kulturelle Vielfalt und Mehrsprachigkeit: Jüdische Identitätskonstruktionen im Polen der Zwischenkriegszeit." In *"Wie schön sind deine Zelte, Jakob, deine Wohnungen, Israel" (Num 24,5): Beiträge zur Geschichte jüdisch-europäischer Kultur*, edited by Rainer Kampling, 157–170. Frankfurt a. M., 2009.

———. "Levitan-Liebermann-Gottlieb: Drei jüdische Maler in ihrem historischen Kontext." *Osteuropa* 8–10 (2008): 247–264.

Pijaj, Stanisław. *Między polskim patriotyzmem a habsburskim loyalizmem: Polacy wobec przemian ustrojowych monarchii habsburskiej (1866–1871)*. Krakow, 2003.

Pikulski, Gaudenty. *Sąd Żydowski we lwowskim Kościele Archikatedralnym*. Lwów, 1759.

———. *Złość żydowska czyli wykład talmudu i sekt żydowskich*. Lwów, 1760.

Podraza, Antoni. "Kształtowanie się elity wiejskiej na przykładzie Galicji na przełomie XIX i XX w." *Zeszyty Naukowe Uniwersytetu Łódzkiego* 1 (1979): 61–68.

Pohle, Hans-Jürgen. Was ist Populismus? In *Populismus und Aufklärung*, edited by Helmut Dubiel, 12–32. Frankfurt a. M., 1986.
Pollack, Martin. *Der Kaiser von Amerika: Die große Flucht aus Galizien*. Vienna, 2010.
———. *Galizien: Eine Reise durch die verschwundene Welt Ostgaliziens und der Bukowina*. Frankfurt a. M., 2001.
Polonsky, Antony. *The Jews in Poland and Russia*, vol 2: *1881–1914*. Oxford, 2010.
Poltermann, Andreas, ed. *Literaturkanon-Medienereignis-Kultureller Text: Formen interkultureller Kommunikation und Übersetzung*. Berlin, 1995.
Pompe, Hedwig. "Nachrichten über Gerüchte: Einleitung." In *Die Kommunikation der Gerüchte*, edited by Hedwig Pompe, Jürgen Brokoff, and Jürgen Fohrmann, 131–143. Göttingen, 2008.
Porter, Brian. "Antisemitism and the Search for a Catholic Identity." In *Antisemitism and Its Opponents in Modern Poland*, edited by Robert E. Blobaum, 103–123. Ithaca, 2006.
———. *When Nationalism began to Hate: Imagining Modern Politics in Nineteenth-Century Poland*. Oxford, 2000.
Potkański, Waldemar. *Ruch narodowo-niepodległościowy w Galicji przed 1914 rokiem*. Warsaw, 2002.
Potocki, Andrzej. *Żydzi w Podkarpackiem*. Rzeszów, 2004.
Potoczny, Jerzy. "Oświata dorosłych i popularizacja wiedzy w plebejskich środowiskach Galicji doby konstytucyjnej (1867–1918)." In *Galicja i jej dziedzictwo*, vol. 10. Rzeszów, 1998.
Prokopovych, Markian. *Habsburg Lemberg: Architecture, Public Space, and Politics in the Galician Capital 1772–1914*. West Lafayette, IN, 2009.
Prusin, Alexander Marc. *Nationalizing a Borderland: War, Ethnicicty, and Anti-Jewish Violence in East Galicia 1914–1920*. Tuscaloosa, 2005.
Pulzer, Peter. "Die Wiederkehr des alten Hasses." In *Deutsch-Jüdische Geschichte in der Neuzeit*, vol. 3: *Umstrittene Integration 1871–1918*, edited by Peter Pulzer, Steven M. Lowenstein, Paul Mendes-Flohr, and Monika Richarz, 193–242. Munich, 1997.
Puttkamer, Joachim von. "Ungarn." In *Studienhandbuch Östliches Europa*, vol. 1: *Geschichte Ostmittel- und Südosteuropas*, edited by Harald Roth, 411–430. Cologne, 1999.
Raphael, Lutz. "Habitus und sozialer Sinn: Der Ansatz der Praxistheorie Pierre Bourdieus." In *Handbuch der Kulturwissenschaften: Paradigmen und Disziplinen*, edited by Friedrich Jaeger and Jürgen Straub, 266–276. Stuttgart, 2004.
Rauchensteiner, Manfried. *Der Tod des Doppeladlers: Österreich-Ungarn und der Erste Weltkrieg*. Graz, 1993.
Reichardt, Sven. "Praxeologische Geschichtswissenschaft: Eine Diskussionsanregung." *Sozial. Geschichte* 22, no. 3 (2007): 43–65.
Reifowitz, Ian. *Imagining an Austrian Nation: Joseph Samuel Bloch and the Search for a Multiethnic Austrian Identity 1846–1919*. New York, 2003.
Rosa, Hartmut. "Ideengeschichte und Gesellschaftstheorie: Der Beitrag der 'Cambridge School' zur Metatheorie." *Politische Vierteljahresschrift* 35 (1994): 197–223.
Rosdolsky, Roman. *Untertan und Staat in Galizien: Die Reformen unter Maria Theresia und Joseph II.*, edited by Ralph Melville. Mainz, 1992.
Rosman, Murray J. *The Lord's Jews: Magnate-Jewish Relations in the Polish-Lithuanian Commonwealth during the Eighteenth Century*. Harvard, 1992.
Rozenblit, Marsha. *Reconstructing a National Identity: The Jews of Habsburg Austria during World War I*. Oxford, 2001.

Rudnytsky, Ivan L. "Mykhailo Drahomanov and the Problem of Ukrainian-Jewish Relations." In *Essays in Modern Ukrainian History*, edited by Ivan L. Rudnytsky, 283–297. Edmonton, 1987.

———. "The Ukrainians in Galicia under Austrian Rule." In *Nationbuilding and the Politics of Nationalism: Essays on Austrian Galicia*, edited by Andrei S. Markovits and Frank E. Sysyn, 23–67. Cambridge, 1982.

Rudolph, Richard L. "The East European Peasant Household and the Beginnings of Industry: East Galicia 1786–1914." In *Ukrainian Economic History: Interpretative Essays*, edited by Ivan S. Korporeckyi, 339–382. Cambridge, 1991.

Rumpler, Helmut, and Peter Urbanitsch, eds. *Die Habsburgermonarchie 1848–1918*, vol. 8: *Die politische Öffentlichkeit*. Vienna, 2006.

Rürup, Reinhard. *Emanzipation und Antisemitismus: Studien zur "Judenfrage" der bürgerlichen Gesellschaft*. Göttingen, 1975.

Sahlins, Marshal. *Inseln der Geschichte*. Hamburg, 1992.

Salmonowicz, Stanisław, Stanisław Waltoś, and Janusz Szwaja. *Pitaval krakowski*. Krakow, 2010.

Scheicher, Joseph. *Aus dem Jahre 1920: Ein Traum*. St. Pölten, 1900.

Schiper, Ignacy. *Dzieje handlu żydowskiego na ziemieach polskich*. Warsaw, 1937.

———. *Żydzi w rolnictwie na terenie Małopolski*, vol. 2. Warsaw, 1933.

Schmid, Julia. *Kampf um das Deutschtum: Radikaler Nationalismus in Österreich und dem Deutschen Reich 1890–1914*. Frankfurt a. M., 2009.

Schmidt, Siegfried J., and Peter Vorderer. "Kanonisierung in Mediengesellschaften." In *Literaturkanon-Medienereignis-Kultureller Text: Formen interkultureller Kommunikation und Übersetzung*, edited by Andreas Poltermann, 144–159. Berlin, 1995.

Schnitzler, Arthur. *Lieutenant Gustl*. Berlin, 1901.

Schorske, Carl. *Fin-de-siecle Vienna: Politics and Culture*. New York, 1981.

Schreiber, Georg. *Des Kaisers Reiterei: Österreichische Kavallerie in 4 Jahrhunderten*. Vienna, 1967.

Schroer, Markus. "Grenzverschiebungen: Zur Neukonstruktion sozialer Räume im Globalisierungsprozess." In *Welt.Raum.Körper: Transformationen und Entgrenzungen von Körper und Raum*, edited by Carsten Würmann et al., 15–36. Bielefeld, 2007.

Schubert, Kurt. "Der Einfluss des Josephinismus auf das Judentum in Österreich." *Kairos* 14 (1972): 81–97.

Schulze-Wessel, Martin. *Russlands Blick auf Preußen: Die polnische Frage in der Diplomatie und politischen Öffentlichkeit des Zarenreiches und des Sowjetstaates 1697–1947*. Stuttgart, 1995.

Schütz, Alfred. *Aufbau der sozialen Welt: Eine Einleitung in die verstehende Soziologie*. Konstanz, 2004.

Schwemmer, Oswald. "Die Macht der Symbole." *Aus Politik und Zeitgeschichte* 20 (2006): 7–14.

Serczyk, Władysław A. *Na płonącej Ukrainie: Dzieje Kozaczyzny 1648–1651*. Warsaw, 2007.

Sewell, William H. *The Logics of History: Social Theory and Social Transformation*. Chicago, 2005.

Shanes, Joshua. "Neither Germans nor Poles: Jewish Nationalism in Galicia before Herzl 1883–1897." *Austrian History Yearbook* 34 (2003): 191–213.

Shibutani, Tamotsu. *Improvised News: A Sociological Study of Rumor*. Indianapolis, 1966.

Siadkowski, Marcin. *Szlachcicen: Przemian stereotypu polskiej szlachty w Wiedniu na przełomie XIX i II wieku*. Warsaw, 2011.

Siegel, Björn. *Österreichisches Judentum zwischen Ost und West: Die Israelitische Allianz zu Wien 1873–1938*. Frankfurt a. M., 2010.
Simmons, Thomas W. "The Peasant Revolt of 1846 in Galicia." *Slavic Review* (1971): 795–817.
Skinner, Quentin. "Language and Political Change." In *Political Innovation and Conceptual Change*, edited by Terence Ball, James Farr, and Russel L. Hanso, 6–23. Cambridge, 1989.
Śliwa, Michał. *Bolesław Limanowski: Człowiek i historia*. Krakow, 1994.
———. "Nędza Galicyjska: Mit i rzeczywistość." In *Galicja i jej Dziedzictwo*, vol 1: *Historia i Polityka*, edited by Włodzimierz Bonusiak and Józef Buszko, 145–155. Rzeszów, 1994.
———. *Obcy czy swoi: z dziejów poglądów na kwestię żydowską w Polsce w XIX i XX wieku*. Krakow, 1997.
Śliż, Małgorzata. *Galicyjscy Żydzi na drodze do równouprawienia 1848–1914*. Krakow, 2006.
Słoczyński, Henryk M. *Matejko*. Wrocław, 2000.
Słownik geograficzny Królestwa Polskiego i innych krajów słowiańskich, vol. 5. Warsaw, 1884.
Smith, Helmut Walser. *The Continuities of German History: Nation, Religion, and Race across the Long Nineteenth Century*. Cambridge, 2008.
———. *Die Geschichte des Schlachters: Mord und Antisemitismus in einer deutschen Kleinstadt*. Göttingen, 2002.
Snopko, Jan. "Oblicze ideowo-polityczne 'Sokoła' galicyjskiego w latach 1867–1914." *Kwartalnik Historyczny* 99, no. 4 (1992): 35–55.
Soboń, Marcin. "Merunowicz, Teofil." In *Handbuch des Antisemitismus*, vol. 2/2: *Personen*, edited by Wolfgang Benz, 550. Berlin, 2009.
———. "Polacy wobec Żydów w Galicji doby autonomicznej." Dissertation. Kielce, 2008.
Sofsky, Wolfgang. *Traktat über die Gewalt*. Frankfurt a. M., 2005.
Söndermann, Adolf. *Klostergeheimnisse oder Die lebendig begrabene Barbara Ubryk: Eine historische Erzählung nach authentischen Quellen frei bearbeitet*. Dresden, 1869.
Stachel, Peter. "Ein Staat, der an einem Sprachfehler zugrunde ging: Die 'Vielsprachigkeit' des Habsburgerreiches und ihre Auswirkungen." In *Das Gewebe der Kultur: Kulturwissenschaftliche Analysen zur Geschichte und Identität Österreichs in der Moderne*, edited by Johannes Feichtinger and Peter Stachel, 11–45. Innsbruck, 2001.
Stanislawski, Michael. *A Murder in Lemberg: Politics, Religion, and Violence in Modern Jewish History*. Princeton, 2007.
Statut chrześć-socyaln. Związku w Białej. Biała, 1896.
Staudacher, Anna. "Der Bauernagitator Stanisław Stojałowski: Priester, Journalist und Abgeordneter zum Österreichischen Reichsrat; Ein biographischer Versuch." *Römische Historiographische Mitteilungen* 25 (1983): 165–202.
———. "Die Aktion 'Girondo': Zur Geschichte des internationalen Mädchenhandels in Österreich-Ungarn um 1885." In *"Das Weib existiert nicht für sich": Geschlechterbeziehungen in der bürgerlichen Gesellschaft*, edited by Heide Dienst and Editha Saurer, 97–138.Vienna, 1990.
Stauter-Halsted, Keely. "'A Generation of Monsters': Jews, Prostitution, and Racial Purity in the 1892 L'viv White Slavery Trial." *Austrian History Yearbook* 38 (2007): 25–34.
———. "Jews as Middleman Minorities in Rural Poland: Understanding the Galician Pogroms of 1898." In *Antisemitism and Its Opponents in Modern Poland*, edited by Robert Blobaum, 39–59. Ithaca, 2005.
———. *The Nation in the Village: The Genesis of Peasant National Identity in Austrian Poland 1848–1914*. Ithaca, 2002.

Stefczyk, Franz. *Polen und Ruthenen in Galizien im Lichte der Bevölkerungs- und Steuerstatistik.* Lemberg, 1912.
Steidl, Annemarie. "Ein ewiges Hin und Her: Kontinentale, transatlantische und lokale Migrationsrouten in der Spätphase der Habsburgmonarchie." *Österreichische Zeitschrift für Geschichtswissenschaften* 19, no. 1 (2008): 15–42.
Steinmetz, Willibald. *Das Sagbare und das Machbare: Zum Wandel politischer Handlungsspielräume; England 1780–1867.* Stuttgart, 1993.
Steinweis, Alan E. "Review of Albert S. Lindemann, *Esau's Tears: Modern Anti-Semitism and the Rise of the Jews.*" *H-Antisemitism, H-Net Reviews,* October 1997. Retrieved 30 November 2019 from http://www.h-net.org/reviews/showrev.php?id=1399.
Streubel, Christiane. *Radikale Nationalistinnen: Agitation und Programmatik rechter Frauen in der Weimarer Republik.* Frankfurt a. M., 2010.
Struve, Kai. *Bauern und Nation in Galizien: Über Zugehörigkeit und soziale Emanzipation im 19. Jahrhundert.* Göttingen, 2005.
———. "'Chłopi z chłopami' albo 'Ziemia polska dla Polaków': Das Verhältnis des *ruch ludowy* zu Weißrussen und Ukrainern bis 1939." In *Oblicza wschodu w kulturze polskiej,* edited by Grzegorz Kotlarski and Marek Figura, 99–122. Poznań, 1999.
———. "Die Juden in der Sicht der polnischen Bauernparteien vom Ende des 19. Jahrhunderts bis 1939." *Zeitschrift für Ostmitteleuropa-Forschung* 48, no. 2 (1999): 184–224.
———. "Die Kapitalisierung der Landwirtschaft und die Durchsetzung der Industrialisierung als strukturbildende Faktoren in den Teilungsländern." In *Polen in der europäischen Geschichte: Ein Handbuch,* vol. 3, edited by Michael G. Müller. Stuttgart, 2019.
———. "Galizische Verflechtungen: Die 'Judenfrage' in der Lemberger Zeitschrift 'Przegląd Społeczny' (1886–1887)." In *Die "Judenfrage": Ein europäisches Phänomen?*, edited by Manfred Hettling, Michael G. Müller, and Guido Hausmann, 95–126. Berlin, 2013.
———. "Gentry, Jews and Peasants: Jews as the 'Others' in the Formation of the Modern Polish Nation in Rural Galicia during the Second Half of the 19th Century." In *Creating the Other: Ethnic Conflict and Nationalism in Habsburg Central Europe,* edited by Nancy M. Wingfield, 103–126. New York, 2003.
———. "Peasant Emancipation and National Integration: Agrarian Circles, Village Reading Rooms, and Cooperatives in Galicia:" In *Cooperatives in Ethnic Conflicts: Eastern Europe in the 19th and Early 20th Century,* edited by Torsten Lorenz, 229–249. Berlin, 2006.
Szaflik, Józef Ryszard. "Ks. St. Stojalowski: prekursor ruchu ludowego." In *Chłopi, naród, kultura,* edited by Stanisław Dąbrowski, 13–26. Rzeszów, 1996.
———. "Nieznana inicjatywa polityczna księdza Stanisława Stojałowskiego: Próby do powałania do życia towarzystwa chrześciańsko-ludowego." *Studia historyczne* (1995): 117–132.
———. *O rząd chłopskich dusz.* Warsaw, 1976.
Szanya, Anton. *Der Traum des Josef Scheicher: Staatsmodelle in Österreich 1880–1900.* Innsbruck, 2009.
Szczepańczyk, Czesław. "Problematyka gospodarcza w działalności ks. Stanisława Stojałowskiego." *Studia Historyczne* (1995): 132–150.
Talmud abo nauka o zidovskoi vere. L'viv, n.d.
Thaler, Peter. "Fluid Identities in Central European Borderlands." *European History Quarterly* 31, no. 4 (2001): 519–548.
Ther, Philipp. "War versus Peace: Interethnic Relations in Lviv during the First Half of the Twentieth Century." In *Lviv: A City in the Crossroads of Culture,* edited by John Czaplicka, 251–284. Cambridge, 2000.

Thompson, Edward Palmer. *Plebejsche Kultur und moralische Ökonomie: Aufsätze zur englischen Sozialgeschichte des 18. und 19. Jahrhunderts.* Frankfurt a. M., 1980.

Thon, Jakob. *Die Juden in Oesterreich.* Berlin, 1908.

Thum, Gregor, ed. *Traumland Osten: Deutsche Bilder vom östlichen Europa im 20. Jahrhundert.* Göttingen, 2006.

Tokarska-Bakir, Joanna. *Legendy o krwi: Antropologia Przesądu.* Warsaw, 2008.

Tokarski, Sławomir. *Ethnic Conflict and Economic Development: Jews in Galician Agriculture 1868–1914.* Warsaw, 2003.

Toury, Jacob. "Josef Samuel Bloch und die Jüdische Identität im österreichischen Kaiserreich." In *Jüdische Integration und Identität in Deutschland und Österreich, 1848–1918*, edited by Walter Grab. Tel Aviv, 1984.

———. "Troubled Beginnings: The Emergence of the Österreichisch-Israelitische Union." *Leo Baeck Institute Year Book* 30 (1985): 457–475.

Towarzystwo Przyjaciół Lutczy, ed. *Lutcza w czasach okupacji.* Stalowa Wola, 1995.

Turczynski, Emanuel. *Geschichte der Bukowina in der Neuzeit: Zur Sozial- und Kulturgeschichte einer mitteleuropäisch geprägten Landschaft.* Wiesbaden, 1993.

Tyler, Stephen. "Zum 'Be-/Abschreiben' als 'Sprechen für': Ein Kommentar." In *Kultur, soziale Praxis, Text: Die Krise der ethnographischen Repräsentation*, edited by Eberhard Berg and Martin Fuchs, 288–296. Frankfurt a. M., 1999.

Ucakar, Karl. *Demokratie und Wahlrecht in Österreich.* Vienna, 1998.

Unowsky, Daniel L. "Peasant Political Mobilization and the 1898 Anti-Jewish Riots in Western Galicia." *European History Quarterly* 40, no. 3 (2010): 412–435.

———. *The Plunder: The 1898 Anti-Jewish Riots in Habsburg Galicia.* Stanford, 2018.

———. *The Pomp and Politics of Patriotism: Imperial Celebrations in Habsburg Austria 1848–1916.* West Lafayette, IN, 2005.

———. "Staging Habsburg Patriotism: Dynastic Loyalty and the 1898 Imperial Jubilee." In *Constructing Nationalities in East Central Europe*, edited by Pieter M. Judson and Marsha Rozenblit, 141–156. New York, 2005.

Unowsky, Daniel L., and Laurence Cole, eds. *Limits of Loyalty: Imperial Symbolism, Popular Allegiances, and State Patriotism in the Late Habsburg Monarchy.* New York, 2007.

Van Rahden, Till. "Intermarriages, the 'New Woman,' and the Situational Ethnicity of Breslau Jews from the 1870s to the 1920s." *Leo Baeck Institute Year Book* 46, no. 1 (2001): 125–150.

———. *Juden und andere Breslauer: Die Beziehungen zwischen Juden, Protestanten und Katholiken in einer deutschen Großstadt von 1860 bis 1925.* Göttingen, 2000.

———. "Treason, Fate, or Blessing? Concepts of Assimilation in the Historiography of German-Speaking Jewry since the 1950s." In *Preserving the Legacy of German Jewry: A History of the Leo Baeck Institute, 1955–2005*, edited by Christhard Hoffmann, 349–373. Tübingen, 2005.

Volkov, Shulamit. *Germans, Jews, and Antisemites.* Cambridge, 2006.

Vyleta, Daniel. *Crime, Jews and News: Vienna 1895–1914.* New York, 2007.

Wandruszka, Adam. "Die Krisen des Parlamentarismus 1897 und 1933: Gedanken zum Demokratieverständnis in Österreich." In *Beiträge zur Zeitgeschichte. Festschrift Ludwig Jedlicka zum 60. Geburtstag*, edited by Adam Wandruszka and Rudolf Neck. St. Pölten, 1976.

———. "Ein vorbildlicher Rechtsstaat?" In *Die Habsburgermonarchie 1848–1918*, vol. 2: *Verwaltung und Rechtswesen*, edited by Adam Wandruszka and Peter Urbanitsch. Vienna, 1975.

Wandruszka, Adam, and Peter Urbanitsch, eds. *Die Habsburgermonarchie 1848–1918*, vol. 1: *Die wirtschaftliche Entwicklung*. Vienna, 1973.

———. *Die Habsburgermonarchie 1848–1918*, vol. 4: *Die Konfessionen*. Vienna, 1985.

Weber, Eugene. *Peasants into Frenchmen: The Modernization of Rural France 1880–1914*. Stanford, 1976.

Weeks, Theodore R. "Assimilation, Nationalism, Modernization, Antisemitism: Notes on Polish-Jewish Relations 1855–1905." In *Antisemitism and Its Opponents in Modern Poland*, edited by Robert Blobaum, 20–38. Ithaca, 2005.

———. *From Assimilation to Antisemitism: The "Jewish Question" in Poland 1859–1914*. DeKalb, 2006.

———. *Nation and State in Late Imperial Russia: Nationalism and Russification on the Western Frontier 1863–1914*. DeKalb, 1996.

———. "Poles, Jews, and Russians 1864–1914: The Death of the Ideal of Assimilation in the Kingdom of Poland." *Polin: Studies in Polish Jewry* 12 (1999): 242–256.

Węgrzynek, Hanna. "Pogrom w Kiszynowie (1903): Reakcje na ziemiach polskich i wpływ na postawy Polaków." In *Kwestia żydowska w XIX wieku: Spory o tożsamość Polaków*, edited by Grażyna Borkowska and Magdalena Rudkowska, 453–462. Warsaw, 2004.

Weinberg, Sonja. *Pogroms and Riots: German Press Responses to Anti-Jewish Violence in Germany and Russia (1881–1882)*. Frankfurt a. M., 2010.

Weingart, Brigitte. "Kommunikation, Kontamination und epidemische Ausbreitung: Einleitung." In *Die Kommunikation der Gerüchte*, edited by Brigitte Weingart, Jürgen Brokoff, Jürgen Fohrmann, and Hedwig Pompe, 241–251. Göttingen, 2008.

Weinstein, James. *The Corporate Ideal in the Liberal State: 1900–1918*. Boston, 1968.

Wendland, Anna Veronika. "Die Rückkehr der Russophilen in die ukrainische Geschichte: Neue Aspekte der ukrainischen Nationsbildung in Galizien 1848–1914." *Jahrbuch für die Geschichte Osteuropas* 49, no. 2 (2001): 178–199.

———. *Die Russophilen in Galizien: Ukrainische Konservative zwischen Österreich und Russland 1848–1915*. Vienna, 2001.

———. "Imperiale, koloniale und postkoloniale Blicke auf die Peripherien des Habsburgerreiches." In *Kolonialgeschichten: Regionale Perspektiven auf ein globales Phänomen*, edited by Claudia Kraft and Alf Lüdtke, 215–235. Frankfurt a. M., 2010.

Wernichowska, Bogna. *Tak kochali Galicjanie*. Krakow, 2005.

Whiteside, Andrew G. *Georg Ritter von Schönerer: Alldeutschland und sein Prophet*. Graz, 1981.

Wilson, Stephen. *Ideology and Experience: Antisemitism in France at the Time of the Dreyfus Affair*. Rutherford, 1982.

Wladika, Michael. *Hitlers Vätergeneration: Die Ursprünge des Nationalsozialismus in der k. u. k. Monarchie*. Vienna, 2005.

Wolff, Larry. *Ansichtskarten vom Weltuntergang: Kindesmisshandlung in Freuds Wien*. Salzburg, 1992.

———. "Dynastic Conservatism and Poetic Violence in Fin-de-siècle Cracow: The Habsburg Matrix of Polish Modernism." *American Historical Review* 106, no. 3 (2001): 735–764.

———. *The Idea of Galicia: History and Fantasy in Habsburg Political Culture*. Stanford, 2010.

Wood, Nathaniel. *Becoming MetropolitaIn Urban Selfhood and the Making of Modern Cracow*. De Kalb, 2010.

———. "Sex Scandals, Sexual Violence, and the Word on the Street: The Kolasówna Lustmord in Cracow's Popular Press 1905–06." *Journal of the History of Sexuality* 20, no. 2 (2011): 243–269.

Wortman, Richard. *Scenarios of Power: Myth and Ceremony in Russian Monarchy*. Princeton, 2000.
Wróbel, Piotr. "The Jews of Galicia under Austrian-Polish Rule 1869–1918." *Austrian History Yearbook* 25 (1994): 97–138.
Würgler, Andreas. "Fama und Rumor: Gerücht, Aufruhr und Presse im Ancien Régime." *Werkstatt Geschichte* 15 (1996): 20–32.
Wynn, Chartes. *Workers, Strikes, and Pogromes: The Donbass-Dnepr Bend in Late Imperial Russia 1870–1905*. Princeton, 1992.
Wyrwa, Ulrich. *Branntewein und "echtes" Bier: Die Trinkkultur der Hamburger Arbeiter im 19. Jahrhundert*. Hamburg, 1990.
———. "Die Internationalen Antijüdischen Kongresse von 1882 und 1883 in Dresden und Chemnitz: Zum Antisemitismus als europäischer Bewegung." *Themenportal Europäische Geschichte* (2009). Retrieved 30 November 2019 from www.europa.clio-online.de/site/lang__de/ItemID__362/mid__11428/40208214/default.aspx#_ftn1.
———. "Genese und Entfaltung antisemitischer Motive in Heinrich von Treitschkes 'Deutscher Geschichte im 19. Jahrhundert.'" In *Antisemitische Geschichtsbilder*, edited by Werner Bergmann and Ulrich Sieg, 83–101. Essen, 2009.
Zahra, Tara. *Kidnapped Souls: National Indifference and the Battle for Children in the Bohemian Lands 1900–1948*. Ithaca, 2008.
Zamorski, Krzysztof. *Ludność Galicji w latach 1857–1910*. Krakow, 1989.
Żbikowski, Andrzej. *Żydzi krakowscy i ich gmina 1868–1918*. Warsaw, 1994.
Zellenberg, Ulrich E. "Ein Konservativer über den Parteien: Der 'Kaiserminister' Eduard Graf Taaffe." In *Konservative Profile: Ideen und Praxis in der Politik zwischen FM Radetzky, Karl Kraus und Alois Mock*, edited by Ulrich E. Zellenberg, 225–243. Graz, 2003.
Zgubne zasady talmudyzmu do serdecznej rozwagi Żydom i chrześcijanom wszelkiego stanu podał Profesor Dr. August Rohling, spolszczył J. B. Lwów, 1874.
Ziejka, Franciszek. *Złota legenda chłopów*. Krakow, 1983.
Zielecki, Alojzy. "Zarys dziejów wiejskiego ruchu paramilitarnego w Galicji w latach 1908–1918." In *Chłopi, naród, kultura*, vol. 2: *Działalność polityczna ruchu ludowego*, edited by Stanisław Dąbrowski, 167–183. Rzeszów, 1996.
Żukowski, Edward. *Judztwo*. Krakow, 1885.
Zyblikiewicz, Lidia. *Kobieta w Krakowie w 1880r: Studium demograficzne*. Krakow, 1999.

INDEX OF PERSONS

Adorno, Theodor W., 116
Alexander II, 171n49
Alexander III, 171n49
Araten, Israel Jakob, 234–36, 240–41, 255n189, 255n191, 255n200
Araten, Michalina (Mechtsche), 234–36, 254n181, 255n189, 255n191, 255n195, 255n200

Babiński, Ignacy, 61
Badeni, Kasimir, 17, 18, 39n109, 153, 180–81, 203, 243n6, 257n219
Badeni, Stanisław, 241, 257n219
Bałaban, Majer, 59
Balik, Michał, 126
Bara (family), 137, 139
Bart (family), 224–28, 251n151
Báthory, Stephen, 53
Biliński, Leon, 17, 241
Birnbaum, Elias, 206
Blasbalg, Chaim (alias Blasberg), 205–10, 212, 221
Bloch, Joseph Samuel, 58, 63, 98n65, 232–33, 237, 252n170, 253n173–74
Bober, Piotr, 140
Bojko, Jakub, 203–4
Brafman, Jakob, 52, 57, 89
Byk, Emil, 162–63, 179n197, 191–93, 253n174

Caro, Jecheskiel, 58
Cena, Robert, 110n213
Chciuk, Mikołaj, 137–140, 143, 145, 150–51, 175n125

Chrząszcz, Süßel, 210, 212–13
Ciemięga, Wojciech, 204–5
Constance of Austria, 50
Czołowski, Aleksander, 58

Daens, Adolf, 103n134
Danielak, Michał, 93, 110n213, 110n217, 201, 215, 217, 228, 247n60, 247n67, 251n133
Daszyński, Ignacy, 91, 188–90, 193, 199, 245n40, 246n44, 263
Deckert, Josef, 87, 89
Diamand (family), 137, 139, 141, 145, 149–50
Dreyfus, Alfred, 24, 120, 190, 246n48
Druga, Martin, 210, 213
Drzewiecki, Jan and Jakub, 5, 27, 74
Dutko, Lesio, 135
Dzieduszycki, Tadeusz, 241

Ehrenberg, Kazimierz, 82, 90, 92, 110n211
Eibenschütz, Leon, 55–56, 97n50
Eisner, Jakob, 145
Elisabeth, Empress of Austria, 119, 142, 171n54

Färber, Chaim and Salomon, 217–19
Fedyschym, Lesio, 135
Feiner, Samuel, 132, 145
Felber (family), 1–3, 138, 140, 175n137
Filako, Heinrich, 126
Franko, Ivan, 67, 69–70, 79, 102n120, 106n160, 106n165, 171n59

Franz Joseph I, 11, 119–20, 196, 234, 247n68, 273

Gawłowicz, Feliks, 90
Gliński (mayor of Stary Sącz), 158
Głuc, Józef, 61
Gniewosz, Eduard, 49, 96n20
Gniewosz, Włodzimierz Ritter von, 181
Gołuchowski, Agenor, 17, 48, 96n15
Gorzkowski, Marian, 55–56, 62, 219
Gottlieb, Moses/Moritz/Maurycy, 55, 97n47
Grün, Israel, 208, 210–13, 221
Grzelak, Justin, 214

Hagel, Jacob, 164, 273
Heitlinger, Emanuel, 129
Herzberg-Fränkel, Leo, 34n68, 237
Hilsner, Leopold, 24, 227, 252n168
Hlond, August, 278
Hompesch, Ferdinand, 110n215
Honig, Berl, 214, 251n126
Honig, Pfachie, 214, 221
Hoschyluk, Lesio, 135
Hrůbesova, Agnězka, 227

Jarusiewicz, Tomas, 135
Jeleński, Jan, 56
Jeż, Mateusz, 90, 109n197
Joseph II, 8, 50

Kakol, Leo, 122, 173n82
Kenner, Aron, 3, 26
Klein (clerk in the Ministry of Justice), 206
Kleinmann, Abraham (alias Klainmann), 204
Klier, John Doyle, 152
Klimczykowa, Maria, 206
Kluska, Felix, 126
Koerber, Ernest von, 239
Körbel, Samuel, 131, 174n96
Korn, Salomon, 207
Korna, Michael, 203
Kosmala (family), 205–8, 250n106, 250n108
Koszarski, Antoni, 137–38, 144
Koszarski, Tomasz, 137
Kramer, Naftali, 146–47, 149

Krempa, Franciszek, 193–94, 204–5, 207–16, 247n62–63
Krupski (family), 137–39, 145
Kubik, Jan, 110n213, 201–2

Lachmann, Josel, 214
Landau, Abraham, 216
Leo XII, 71
Lewicki, Jan, 32n43
Lichtig, Issak, 216
Limanowski, Bolesław, 67, 102n119
Lion, Arnold, 50–51
Łobos, Ignacy, 105n151, 190
Lueger, Karl, 84–86, 88, 90–91, 92, 109n207, 180, 192, 243n6, 247n60
Łukaszek, Jędrzej, 140

Mahler, Arthur, 272
Maria Theresa, 8
Matejko, Jan, 54–56, 97n42, 258, 260
Mendelsohn, Moses, 57
Merunowicz, Teofil, 3, 5, 26–27, 42n145, 51–54, 56–58, 62, 69, 96n34, 184, 192, 219, 258, 271
Mickiewicz, Adam, 122, 124–25, 127, 172n70, 172n72, 261
Mnich, Franciszka (Franka), 1, 3–5, 26, 54, 58, 80, 184, 186, 197, 273, 278
Mochnacki, Józef, 55–56, 219
Morawski, Marian, 89–90
Moskal (family), 146–47, 151
Motyka, Antoni, 206
Mousseaux, Gougenot des, 89
Mützer, Hinda, 141

Namer, Franz, 124
Neuwirt, Israel, 214
Nossig, Alfred, 69
Noster, Jędrzej, 4, 74

Ofner, Julius, 234, 238, 254n183
Ordon, Jan, 206
Ordon, Martin, 214

Parnes, Szyja, 216
Pattai, Georg, 192, 209
Pavlyk, Michajlo, 70

Pawlusiak, Wojciech, 205
Piekarz, Jakub, 156
Pikulski, Gaudenty, 57, 58
Piniński, Leon (governor of Galicia), 154–55, 159, 245n40
Potocki, Andrzej, 16, 271
Potocki, Jan, 224, 227–28
Potoczek, Jan, 75, 110n213, 110n218, 188, 191–93, 264
Potoczek, Stanisław, 75
Pszczenicy, Jan, 205
Puzyna, Jan, 82, 104n137, 189, 246n43

Raś, Anton, 214
Rieder, Salomon, 145
Ritter (family), 1–6, 10, 24, 27, 43n153, 52, 54, 56–57, 74, 80, 138, 145, 149–50, 175n137, 218, 273, 278
Rittner, Eduard, 17
Rogosz, Józef, 82
Rohling, August, 3–4, 26–27, 52, 57, 58, 89, 95n6, 98n65, 233
Rokita, Władysław, 146
Rudolf, Archduke of Austria, 120, 135, 151, 171n59
Rusenko, Jan, 278
Rytwiński, Jan, 206

Scheicher, Josef, 246n50, 250n115
Schmerling, Anton von, 245n29
Schönerer, Georg Ritter von, 53, 180
Schöngut, Moses, 132
Schulheim, von (major general), 160, 165
Sęk, Michał, 127
Selinger (executioner), 160, 178n191
Sender (family), 229, 232
Siedlaska, Karolina, 224–25
Siedlaska, Katarzyna, 224–25
Skoroś, Josef, 214
Smolka, Franciszek, 48
Solymosi, Eszter, 3, 58
Spirno, Israel, 207
Stadion, Franz Count von Warthausen, 11
Stand, Adolf, 272
Stapiński, Jan, 75, 106n160, 147, 151, 170n35, 190, 247n62
Steinhardt, Rafał, 207–8, 212

Steinmetz, Izaak, 138, 145
Stochlińska, Salomea, 1
Stochliński, Marcel, 1–5, 26, 80
Stojałowski, Stanisław, 71–77, 79, 81, 84–86, 89, 90, 92, 93, 104n137, 105n148, 105n151, 106n156, 106n162, 107n167, 110n211, 110n217, 117, 121, 134, 137, 147, 148, 151, 172n66, 187, 189, 191–92, 215–17, 228, 247n66, 249n99, 251n133, 264, 274
Straucher, Benno, 234, 237, 254n183, 255n198, 256n207, 272
Südwärts (scribe), 217, 219
Sulima, Ivan, 135
Sułkowski (imperial-and-royal prosecutor), 124, 131–32, 173n77, 173n87
Świnicki, Franciszek, 137–39, 144
Szajer, Tomasz, 110n213, 110n216, 121, 172n66, 183, 184, 196, 198, 228, 247n60, 247n68
Szajnowski (trainee in the district governor's office in Kalwarya Zebrzydowska), 124, 152
Szponder, Andrzej, 93, 110n213, 110n217, 117–19, 121, 127, 173n82, 200–202, 215, 217, 228, 235, 240–41, 246n50, 247n67, 251n133, 261
Szurlej, Jędrzej, 142, 176n147

Taafe, Eduard Count von, 16, 37n92, 238
Tabaka, Katarzyna, 228–32, 273
Taniackevyć, Danylo, 246n50
Tarnowski, Stanisław, 84, 241
Thun, Franz von, 191, 245n40
Torosiewicz, Franciszek, 48–49
Trella, Józef, 205
Trzeciak, Stanisław, 278
Twain, Mark, 244n19

Ubryk, Barbara (alias Anna), 240, 256n215–16
Urban, Mateusz, 139–40, 142, 143, 146

Vignati, Wilhelm, 51
Vyleta, Daniel, 218

Wagner, Richard, 54–55

Wallach, Abraham, 278
Wallach, Chaskel, 139–40, 145
Wątkowski, Piotr, 229, 231–32
Wątroba (family), 210–13, 221
Wiatr (judge from Dukla), 216–17
Wichner, Israel (Śrul), 139
Wiesenfeld, David, 207
Wilk, Jan, 126, 173n82
William II, 181
Wilmer, Schlomo, 278
Winiarski, Jan, 136, 175n117, 201, 249n94, 274, 276n36

Wojas, Johann, 122
Wolff, Karl Hermann, 192
Wysłouch, Bolesław, 67, 69–70, 75, 100n96, 101n105, 101n110, 102n119
Wysocki, Stanisław, 117, 170n36

Zabuda, Jan, 110n213
Zawadzki (apprentice shoemaker from Wieliczka), 118
Żukowski, Edward, 57–58

Index of Places

Andrychów, 125

Bełzec, 255n189, 278
Berlin, 5, 6, 14, 15, 24, 26, 42n147, 51, 218, 258
Biała, 51, 107n167, 110n213
Biecz, 151
Binczice, 235
Borszczów, 134, 177n171
Borysław, 133
Brody, 33n55, 47, 59–60, 62, 63, 69, 99n73, 99n76, 99n78, 99n80
Brzesko, 156
Brzeżany, 48
Brzostek, 164
Buczacz, 253nn173, 254n181
Budapest, 14, 42n147
Buenos Aires, 83
Bursztyn, 134

Cairo, 83
Chmielów, 205
Cyganowice, 203
Czaca, 76
Czarna, 135, 173n88
Czortków, 134, 175n135
Czudec, 176n145

Dobczyce, 118
Domaradz, 137, 139, 140, 142, 175n135
Drohobycz, 55, 133
Dukla, 217, 266, 267
Dulcza mała, 208

Elisavetgrad, 59

Godowa, 146–49
Golcowa, 137
Gorlice, 151, 158, 178n179
Gwoźnica górna, 175n135

Halych, 7

Jaślany, 204
Jasło, 128, 135, 143, 151–52, 154, 160, 173n90, 175n138, 216, 229, 231, 232
Jawornik, 129
Jeleśnia, 132, 174n103

Kalwarya Zebrzydowska, 118, 122–27, 130, 134, 136, 147, 148, 150–53, 164, 172n61, 172n72–73, 173n81–82, 201, 216
Kamienica, 176n145
Kenty, 235
Kiev, 61
Kolomea, 135, 253n173
Königgrätz/Hradec Králové, 14
Koszarowa, 131
Krakow, 3–7, 10, 12, 16, 20, 29n11, 33n55, 35n82, 36n86, 47, 50, 53–56, 58, 59, 64, 65, 70, 76, 77, 81–87, 89–92, 94, 97n42, 97n49, 98n53, 99n85, 104n137, 107n177, 108n182. 109n207, 110n211, 110n213–14, 117, 127, 151, 154, 170n39, 171n51, 172n70, 173n85, 177n170, 189, 196,

200, 206, 211, 217, 219, 222–23, 226,
  229, 231, 232, 234–36, 240, 241,
  246n43, 247n67, 252n160, 253n177,
  254n181, 256n216, 265, 278
Krosno, 132, 230, 266

Łagiewniki, 235
Łańcut, 93, 155, 166
Łęki, 137
Lemberg, 3, 5–6, 12, 16, 33n55, 39n119,
  47, 52–53, 55, 57, 58, 60, 63, 65–67,
  73–75, 82, 83, 91, 92, 94, 97n39,
  98n57, 102n116, 104n135, 108n183,
  125, 151, 152, 177n170, 191, 196,
  248n75, 253n177, 254n181, 256n213,
  266, 267, 277
Leżajsk, 175n138
Limanowa, 142, 156–59, 177n171,
  265–66
London, 87
Łopatyn, 253n177
Lostówka, 222
Lutcza, 1–6, 26, 57, 59, 74, 86, 136, 137,
  140–43, 146, 172n63

Mielec, 204, 208, 211, 214, 247n62,
  251n126
Moszczenica, 202
Mszana dolna, 222, 223
Mszana górna, 222, 223–24
Myślenice, 128, 172n73, 173n87, 216

New York, 60
Niebylec, 144, 176n145, 266
Niewodna, 176n145
Nowosielec, 224
Nowotanice, 225, 227–28, 251n151
Nowy Sącz, 75, 108n180, 110n213, 128,
  131, 151, 157–59, 177n165, 217, 222,
  223–24, 225, 226–27, 252n158, 265,
  275n20
Nowy Targ, 156, 218
Olmütz/Olomouc, 166
Osielec, 129

Pałecznica, 227

Paleśnica, 156
Paris, 10, 60, 87, 172n70
Pielgrzymka, 119
Pilzno, 61, 99n83, 100n90
Podgórze, 61, 128, 216, 254n179
Polna, 98n56, 188, 227–28, 252n168
Polomya, 266
Prague, 3, 6, 26, 243n4, 247n61
Przemyśl, 100n98, 166
Pstrągowa, 267

Racz-Kozar, 238
Radzivilov, 59
Rome, 55, 65, 70, 256n215
Ropczyce, 157, 247n62, 267
Rozdziele, 178n186
Ruślówka, 172n63
Rzeszów, 1, 3, 5, 46, 52–53, 58, 110n213,
  136, 139, 150, 176n141, 177n165,
  178n179–80, 206, 214, 250n105,
  250n108, 266, 267, 275n9, 278

Sambor, 96n20, 120, 135, 178n178
Sanok, 134, 174n111
Schodnica, 133
Siedliska, 266
Sieklówka, 147
Śniatyn, 253n173, 276n27
Sokołów, 232
Solferino, 14
Stanislau, 88, 235
Stary Sącz, 157–58, 263, 274
St. Petersburg, 16
Strusów, 165
Strzyżów, 2–3, 110n213, 126, 128, 136–37,
  142, 146–47, 150, 151, 156–57, 164,
  201, 266, 278
Sułkowice, 124, 173n87, 174n103
Szaflary, 218
Szufnarowa, 176n145

Targanice, 132
Tarnobrzeg, 194–95, 205, 206, 213–14,
  247n62
Tarnów, 32n40, 32n42, 65, 85, 86,
  105n151, 160, 170n45, 190, 204

Taszyce, 170n42
Teschen, 76
Tiszaeszlar, 56, 59, 233
Tłuste, 134, 163, 251n130
Trzciana, 214
Trzinica, 173n90

Ujanowice, 173n90
Ustrobna, 176n145

Vatican, 70, 103n128, 249n99
Vienna, 3–6, 14, 16, 18, 19, 35n71, 35n79, 35n82, 42n147, 47, 50, 55, 60, 63, 65, 73, 76, 81, 85, 87, 88, 90, 91, 92, 93, 97n42, 109n194, 109n202, 121, 125, 153, 160, 164, 166, 170n36, 171n47, 172n66, 180–83, 188, 189, 190, 192–96, 198, 201, 203, 206, 208, 209, 215, 218, 219, 226–28, 231, 233, 236–39, 243n6, 244n29, 247n66, 263–65, 267, 273

Wadowice, 99n85, 107n170, 110n213, 124, 125, 131, 152–53, 163, 172n72, 173n82, 173n87, 201

Warsaw, 3, 38n102, 40n121, 55, 56, 67, 97n49
Warwarzynce, 165
Wieliczka, 109n207, 117–18, 127, 147, 171n48, 176n144, 222, 236, 242, 246n45, 261
Wielopole, 156–57, 163
Wielowieś, 235
Wiśniówca, 157
Wojaszówka, 176n145
Wola Justowska, 235

Zabawa, 170n42
Zabłocie, 50
Zagórza, 134–35, 174n111
Zakliczyn, 40n121, 178n183
Zaleszczyki, 134
Żarnowa, 176n145
Zbyszyce, 178n183
Zebrzydowice, 126
Żmigród, 119, 229–32, 273, 274
Żywiec, 50–51, 61, 82, 87, 96n24, 110n213, 131, 151, 158, 252n158, 258
Żyznów, 146

INDEX OF SUBJECTS

abduction (Jewish girls), 57, 83–84, 95n6, 223–24, 226, 229–43, 253n171–72, 253n177, 254n183, 255n203, 256n207
Alliance Israelite Universelle (AIU), 59–60, 68, 79, 93, 99n76–77, 105n146, 136, 231
antisemitic disturbances. *See* antisemitic riots
antisemitic riots, 20–21, 27–28, 40n121, 50–51, 61–62, 81, 99n83, 111, 114, 120, 122, 124–29, 131–36, 140–45, 147–53, 155–56, 158, 160–67, 167n3, 170n45, 172n63, 172n65, 173n80, 174n95, 176n154, 177n171, 183, 188–90, 191–94, 199–204, 215–16, 221–23, 228, 235, 237, 241, 247n66, 248n75, 249n99, 251n130, 261–65, 267–70, 272–74, 276n27
asemitism, 89–90, 93, 260
assimiliation (Jewish), 12–13, 34n61, 48–49, 51, 54, 63, 68–69, 80, 89, 94, 106n165, 190–92, 233, 243, 253n174, 258–59, 265
Austria, 1, 5, 7–8, 11–17, 34n69, 35n73, 44, 50, 57, 59–60, 70, 91–92, 103n129, 109n203, 181, 188, 190, 192, 219–20, 238–39, 241
Austro-Hungarian Compromise, 14–16

blood libel accusation. *See* ritual murder
boycott, 74, 78–79, 81, 94, 104n145, 110n209, 121, 220, 259–60, 264–72, 278

Catholics Day, 65, 82, 84
Christian Socials, 20, 27, 46, 65–66, 70–71, 76, 81–94, 106n160, 107n167, 108n189, 109n202, 121, 180–81, 187–88, 190–91, 215, 219, 246n43, 250n115, 251n133, 260, 263
Cisleithania. *See* Austria
civil marriage, 34n62, 70, 84, 254n179
conservatives, 15–16, 18, 20, 50, 54–56, 59, 65, 69–70, 73, 75–76, 81, 84–87, 90, 92–93, 110n215, 117, 153, 157–58, 161, 181, 187–190, 192–93, 203–4, 219, 228, 233, 238–39, 241–42, 247n62, 251n129, 263–64
constitution, 12, 14, 16–17, 19–20, 22, 34n65, 47, 53, 55, 70, 130, 132, 159, 169n21, 189, 192, 198, 235, 245n29, 258, 277
cooperation, 8, 10, 18–19, 76, 92, 102n113, 110n211, 128, 131, 155, 158, 181, 186, 188, 193, 198, 211–12, 259, 268, 271
Corpus Christi, 125, 135, 144, 274
court trial, 3–6, 24, 26–27, 46, 52, 55–58, 82, 86, 98n56, 98n65, 129, 139, 140, 150, 159, 162, 165, 175n137, 179n204, 184–85, 188, 206–8, 211–14, 218, 221, 227–29, 232, 233, 239, 255n191, 258, 269

discrimination, 22, 24–25, 28, 49, 52, 55, 113, 170n34, 221, 232, 242–43

Easter, 19–20, 39n120, 57, 95n6, 117–18, 136, 171n48, 201, 222–24, 229–30, 237, 261
Eastern European Jews, 14, 229, 233, 237
economy, 7–12, 17, 20–21, 23, 29n19, 38n108, 49, 52, 63, 66, 68–69, 73–74, 78, 81, 84, 89–90, 92–94, 101n99, 104n142, 109n199, 111–12, 130–31, 140, 150, 152–53, 159, 192, 215, 219–20, 245n35, 249n89, 258–60, 263–65, 269–70
election campaigns, 17, 20–21, 66, 75, 77, 81, 93–94, 111, 117, 130, 189, 261, 271
emancipation (Jewish), 31n27, 47–51, 53–54, 58, 63, 74, 89, 96n22, 229
emergency law. *See* state of emergency
encyclica (papal), 71, 82, 103n126

fraud, 16, 36n88, 56, 73, 79, 153, 199, 205–9, 211, 213–16, 218–22, 245n39, 250n111, 260, 264

Galician autonomy, 16–17, 37n96, 68, 160, 185
Galician slaughter. *See* Rabacja
gendarmes, 2, 5, 9, 51, 117, 126–27, 135–36, 144, 148, 154, 158–60, 162–63, 166, 173n82–83, 175n118, 176n138, 178n171, 178n183, 195, 200–204, 229, 242, 255n200, 256n208, 261–62, 266, 274, 276n36
German Empire. *See* Germany
Germany, 5, 15, 68, 70, 40n127, 54, 68, 70, 97n47, 59n98, 163, 191, 200, 252n167
governor (Galician), 11, 16, 18–19, 39n109, 48, 53, 60, 77, 118, 124–25, 135, 153–54, 156, 159–60, 162–64, 180, 187, 198, 204, 226, 234, 239, 245n40, 256n213, 257n219, 262–63, 267, 271, 276n27
Greek Catholic, 9, 12, 51, 170n35, 174n111, 177n171, 246n50, 271

Hassidic Jews, 48, 52

interpellation, 28, 121, 136, 185–88, 193–222, 224, 227–28, 232, 234–37, 240–42, 245n40, 248n76, 248n81, 248n83, 254n183, 256n211, 264, 269, 274

Jewish conspiracy, 52, 79, 89–90, 92, 117–18, 120, 122, 158, 215–16, 219, 227–28, 246n50, 260
Jewish issue. *See* Jewish question
Jewish question, 21, 23–24, 26, 46–47, 49, 51–52, 54, 56, 62–63, 66, 68–69, 80, 117–18, 186–88, 190, 196–97, 233, 246n43, 259, 271–72

Katzenmusik (cat music), 131, 174n103, 221
Kidnapping (Jewish girls). *See* abduction

Landtag (Galician Diet), 3, 17, 47–48, 50–53, 94, 96n15, 192, 258
  elections, 18, 65, 70, 75, 82, 104n140, 170n45
  deputy, 48–49, 96n34, 100n94, 163
liberal, 18, 46, 48–49, 51, 54, 56, 63, 71, 73, 107n166, 192, 219, 240, 242
  constitution, 22
  intelligentsia, 258
  order, 200
  parties, 85
  politicians, 182, 245n29
  politics, 85
  state, 89, 265
liberalism, 15, 18, 38n108, 47–48, 53, 70–71, 73, 81, 89, 192
liberals, 15–16, 18, 49, 52, 56, 71, 75, 85, 88, 240, 253n174, 258
lud, 18, 67, 73–75, 78, 80, 104n137, 105n117, 122, 196, 201, 220, 270

migrants (Jewish). *See* refugees (Jewish)
military, 10, 14, 37n93, 40n121, 49, 50, 52, 60, 99n83, 127, 130–31, 133, 134, 136, 139, 142, 147–48, 150–52, 155–159, 161–167, 175n117, 176n151, 188, 199–200, 202–3,

Index of Subjects | 313

248n81, 249n89, 261, 263–65, 268–70, 274
militia, 154–56, 177n171, 262–63

narod, 70, 74, 220
National Democrats, 20, 51, 107n166, 209, 271, 274

obstruction (parliamentary), 32n49, 165, 182–83, 203

partitions (Poland-Lithuania), 7–8, 17, 29n11, 67
Passover, 57, 223, 252n153
People's Party (SL), 67, 69, 75–79, 81, 93–94, 105n148, 105n153, 105n156, 106n160, 106n165, 110n220, 147, 158, 170n35, 182–83, 190, 192–94, 197, 203, 246n50, 247n62, 251n133, 271
pilgrimages, 2, 73, 122–23
pogroms (Russia), 24, 59–60, 62, 69, 100n91, 119, 152, 161, 163, 171n49, 171n58, 172n65, 173n84, 177n157, 177n160, 259, 275n20
Poland, 5, 7, 32n36, 38n103, 41n138, 51–52, 55–56, 67–68, 88, 101n109, 191, 193, 227, 240, 250n115, 253n177, 260, 274, 278
Polish Club, 75, 110n218, 181, 187–88, 189, 191–93, 197, 228, 233, 243, 245n39–40, 248n75, 251n129
political Catholicism, 35n82, 45–46, 65–66, 70–71, 76–77, 81–83, 85–89, 94, 103n131, 106n165, 189, 213
populists, 68–70, 74, 78, 85, 100n95, 102n122, 151, 184, 187, 190–91, 203–4, 219, 233, 259–60, 263–64, 270
Prussia, 7, 15, 40n129, 43n154, 67, 163

Rabacja, 10–11, 32n40, 32n43, 61–62, 173n80
railway. *See* train
refugees (Jewish), 59–62, 99n76, 99n78, 101n109, 134, 259

Reichsrat (Imperial Diet), 15–17, 136, 182–91, 193–96, 198, 201–3, 205, 208–9, 211, 213–16, 220, 233, 247n68, 248n83, 256n211, 256n213
  deputy, 51, 65, 75, 110n215, 110n218, 117, 180–81, 187, 190, 210, 224, 228, 232–33, 235, 250n115, 253n173, 263–64, 272
  elections, 18, 20–21, 28, 64–66, 76, 81–82, 84, 87, 91–93, 110n219, 182, 190, 195, 248n75
revolution, 11–12, 17, 29n11, 32n36, 43n148, 88, 89, 91, 104n137, 126, 169n22, 173n80, 237, 271, 275n27
ritual murder, 4, 26, 43n154, 53, 56–58, 95n6, 98n56, 98n63, 172n73, 186, 189, 192, 197, 203–4, 222–30, 233, 236–38, 252n153, 253n172, 256n207, 258, 264, 273
Roman Catholic, 9, 12, 33n60, 57, 66, 75, 134, 174n111, 233
royal-and-imperial
  army, 166, 249n87, 277
  gendarmerie. *See* gendarmes
  governor. *See* governor (Galician)
  judiciary, 26, 226
  prosecutor, 125–26, 172n72, 214, 223, 229
rumor, 2–4, 11, 19–20, 40n121, 50, 54, 59, 61, 63, 114–22, 124–29, 132–36, 139–45, 148–49, 151–52, 155–57, 161–65, 169n20, 169n22, 169n25, 169n27, 170n31–32, 170n34, 170n36, 170n41, 170n45, 171n49, 171n59, 177n169, 186–87, 190, 196–98, 201, 203, 205, 215–17, 220–23, 225, 227, 229–32, 240, 242, 247n66, 251n134, 255n189, 261–62, 265–70, 274, 275n25, 277
Russia, 7, 14, 16, 19, 24, 38n102, 59–62, 65, 67–68, 102n116, 102n122, 119–20, 152, 161, 163, 171n49, 172n65, 174n107, 177n157, 177n160, 259, 271
Russian empire. *See* Russia

serfdom, 9–11, 19, 39n120, 74, 103n135, 117, 169n21
Servituten, 11, 19, 117, 121, 130
Social Democrats, 20, 69–71, 81–83, 85, 87–88, 90–93, 110n218, 132, 161, 187–90, 246n43, 248n75
Stańczyks, 79, 204, 215, 218, 238, 264
state of emergency, 110n221, 154, 159–61, 164, 167, 188, 190–93, 199–200, 202, 239, 246n42, 247n61, 263
Stronnictwo Chrześciańsko-Ludowe (Christian People's Party), 76, 81, 93–94, 103n134, 107n167, 117, 170n35, 191–92, 200, 209, 247n62
synagogue, 50, 55, 117, 166, 241
szlachta, 8, 67, 73, 78, 105n151, 181, 245n41

Talmud, 3, 5, 26, 52–54, 57–58, 87, 89, 98n57, 98n65, 236, 242
train, 7, 19, 50, 74, 117, 134, 142, 156, 222–23, 278

Tsarist empire. *See* Russia

Ukraine, 39, 59, 69
ultramontanism, 66, 70, 73, 89
university, 43n151
   Lemberg, 16, 248n75
   Krakow, 16, 84, 254n179
usury, 56, 79, 98n59, 140, 204–5, 209, 211–12, 214–16, 218, 220, 222, 264

Whitsun, 61, 109n207, 118, 122, 124–25, 136
Wiener Allianz, 63
World War I, 7, 10, 39n115, 273–74
World War II, 272–74

Zionism, 79, 106n165, 179n197
Związek Chłopski (Peasant Union), 75–76, 78–79, 105n156, 158

www.ingramcontent.com/pod-product-compliance
Lightning Source LLC
Chambersburg PA
CBHW071333080526
44587CB00017B/2820